SIENA

JANE
STEVENSON

SIENA

*The Life & Afterlife
of a Medieval
City*

An Apollo Book

First published in the UK in 2022 by Head of Zeus Ltd,
part of Bloomsbury Publishing Plc

9 7 5 3 1 2 4 6 8

A catalogue record for this book is available from the British Library.

ISBN (HB)   9781801101141
ISBN (E):   9781801101165

Designed and typeset by Isambard Thomas at Corvo
Maps by Isambard Thomas
Colour separation by DawkinsColour
Printed and bound in Wales by Gomer

Head of Zeus Ltd
First Floor East
5–8 Hardwick Street
London ECIR 4RG
WWW.HEADOFZEUS.COM

previous page The rooftops of Siena
overleaf The ceiling of the Piccolomini Library in the Duomo

For Mark and Shamsu,
with much love

9

TUSCANY AND SIENA

TUSCANY

Lucca

Arno
Florence

Pisa

Elsa

Via Francigena

Livorno

San Gimignano
Poggibonsi
Colle di Val d'Elsa

Arno

Arezzo

Volterra
Monteriggioni

Arbia

VAL DI CHIANA

Casole d'Elsa
Montaperti

SIENA

Abbey of Monte Oliveto Maggiore

Ligurian Sea

Abbey of San Galgano
Buonconvento

San Giovanni d'Asso

Lago Trasimeno

Massa Marittima

Pienza
Montepulciano

Perugia

Montalcino
San Quirico

Piombino

Abbey of Sant'Antimo

MAREMMA

Gulf of Follonica

Monte Amiata

Elba

Ombrone

Grossetto

Tyrrhenian Sea

Bolsena

Pianosa

Talamone

Lago di Bolsena

Viterbo

Montecristo

Giglio

N

to Rome

Mediterranean Sea

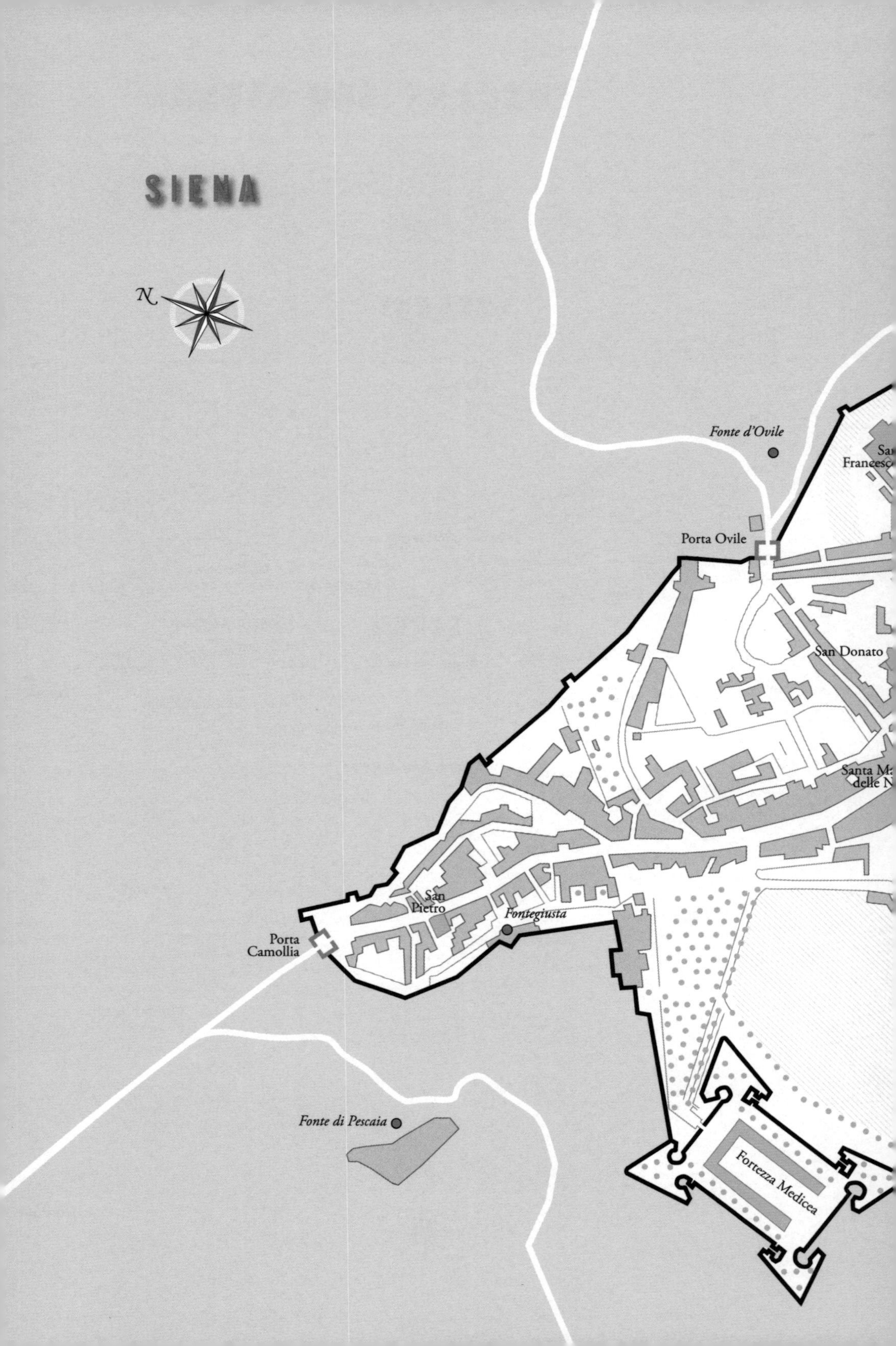

SIENA

N

Fonte d'Ovile

San
Francesco

Porta Ovile

San Donato

Santa M:
delle N

San
Pietro

Fontegiusta

Porta
Camollia

Fonte di Pescaia

Fortezza Medicea

Porta Pispini

Santa Chiara

San Galgano

Fonte di
Follonica

Santo
Spirito

Santa
Maria
dei Servi

Porta
Romana

San Giorgio

San Girolamo

Oratorio di
San Bernadino

San Giovanni
della Staffa

Santa Maria di
Provenzano

Università

Synagogue

San
Cristoforo

Palazzo
Piccolomini

IL CAMPO

Palazzo
Pubblico

San Giuseppe

Sant'Agostino

Porta
Tufi

Fonte
Gaia

Loggia di
Mercanzia

Palazzo
Tolomei

Biblioteca
Comunale

Palazzo del
Magnifico

Opera
del Duomo

Pinacoteca

Accademia
dei Fisiocritici

ntuario di
a Caterina

Palazzo
Reale

Duomo

Palazzo
Chigi

Orto Botanico

an Domenico

Fontebranda

Palazzo
Capitano

S. Maria
della Scala

Porta
Fontebranda

San Sebastiano

S. Maria
del Carmine

Ospizio deglie
Orfani

Porta
Laterina

Porta
San Marco

PREFACE

S iena is one of the best loved cities in Italy, in Europe, in the world. It offers a vision of medieval civic perfection: narrow, enfolding brick streets curving along airy hillsides, all leading in the end to the ample brick-paved slope of the Piazza del Campo, the great town square with its soaring bell tower, and the bright water of Fonte Gaia rippling sunlight up on the carved marble of its walls. This feeling of having entered a place sustained by a benign past is nour-ished by the absence of cars, largely kept out of the city centre, which in itself gives one the feeling of returning to a quieter, simpler world. It is a city to be explored at a walking pace; the narrow streets lined with tall brick hous-es provoke surprise and discovery; emerging into a sunlit square, with a neighbourhood restaurant adorned with pots of gerani-ums and basil, and a decorative ceramic panel with the symbol of one of the seventeen *contrade* (districts or wards) on the wall at the corner. Or you come upon a church you never remember seeing before, like the breathtaking glimpse of Santa Maria in Provenzano seen down the nar-row slope of the Via Lucherini, baroque stone and sunlight at the end of the shadowy street. Siena is a wonderful place to get slightly lost in.

overleaf The Miracle at the Pool of Bethesda by Sebastiano Conca (1731), behind Vecchietta's Risen Christ (1476) in Santissima Annunziata.

Although the overwhelming impression which any visitor receives is of an astonishing concentration of art and architecture from the late Middle Ages, there are also subtle survivors from the Renaissance, Baroque and Romantic eras. Few who have come upon them will forget the sense of personal discovery which accompanied, for example, the realization that the four statues on the Renaissance triumphal arch which frames the altar of the Piccolomini Chapel in the cathedral are little-known early works of Michelangelo. Or that one of Pinturicchio's scenes in the Piccolomini Library attached to the cathedral shows an enchantingly Italianized and idealized imagining of the king of Scotland

enthroned in a loggia on the shores of the Firth of Forth. Or that one of the most complete baroque theatres in Europe is concealed within the venerable structure of the Palazzo Pubblico; or that the church of the Santissima Annunciata in the great Hospital of Santa Maria della Scala has an east wall frescoed with Christ at the pool of Bethesda, the entire fresco a virtuoso exercise in perspective and illusion, a towering vision of great colonnades and sunny hillside temples. And as the Via Enea Silvio Piccolomini approaches the Porta Romana, there are the sphinx-topped gate piers of a shadowy villa garden, and an exquisite neoclassical gazebo or summer house is perched on the boundary wall.

In Siena none of the streets are straight because their gently unpredictable curves reflect the topography of the hills on which they are built. Secure between high walls of warm, pale brick, you lose sight of where you have come from without quite being able to see where you are going. But Siena is small, and you can be fairly sure that after another few steps, a slice of the Campo will appear, or the black and white flank of the cathedral, or the great, gaunt bulk of San Domenico will show up on the horizon, so that, once again, you are oriented. As

Hisham Matar observes, Siena is 'as intimate as a locket you could wear around your neck, and yet as complex as a maze'.[1]

The historic centre predominantly consists of brick and stone, a place of warm earth tones. The houses open straight onto the street: Siena is not a place for private gardens, though there is plenty of green space and trees inside the walls. This is one of the most haunting and lovely aspects of Siena's townscape: the intense urbanity of the Campo is barely ten minutes' walk from the Valle di Follonica, one of the peninsulas of country which extends almost into the heart of the city. Climb almost any street away from the Campo, and it will curve up to one of the city's three hills and offer sudden vistas of undulating countryside lying open under the sky. Looking out from the piazza in front of San Francesco, or coming to any of the brick-built city gates with their fragments of precious fresco under the arch, a fruitful and lovely countryside stretches away to the distant blue ridges of the hills. It is decorated with rows of cypresses and dotted with olive trees, neat rows of vines and patches of woodland, a vision of nature which, like the city itself, represents a vision from the past successfully brought forward into the present. This fruitful serenity, eloquent of olive oil, wine and country bread, enfolds the walls and towers of the city. Since the fourteenth century, Siena's prosperity has depended on its countryside and it is fitting that the two are so intimately related visually. There are only a handful of cities in Europe where the intertwining of town and country is so simply beautiful, and so mutually sustaining.

Monteriggioni: built by the Sienese as a defence against Florence, encircled by its thirteenth-century walls and towers.

As many have said, entering through one of Siena's gates means leaving behind the world of railway stations and undistinguished sub-urbs and entering a secret, labyrinthine, medieval world. Many of the handsome *palazzi* are Renaissance buildings, and Renaissance in design, as is Pius II's conspicuous white marble loggia, with its clothes shop tucked into the side of its plinth, but they blend harmoniously in size and proportion with older buildings. Others are more 'medieval' now than they were when they were built, as the result of Siena's continuous reworking of its own past. This interchange between the contemporary city and its medieval self is everywhere: in the archaic and delicious *panforte* in its bright wrappers, the lettering of which evokes thirteenth-century manuscripts. In the ancient dishes still forming a living part of Sienese food, such as the *pasta all'antica Senese* – sausage, leeks, sheep's cheese, abundant black pepper – whose origins could plausibly stretch back to the time of the Romans. A glance at Lorenzetti's frescoes of the well-governed city suggests that, in fact, we would find medieval Siena quite hard to recognize, a city of loggias and balconies, not the noble flat-fronted buildings we know now. Some of the façades we know were once adorned with colourful frescoes, and the dozens of towers must have made it feel like a medieval version of downtown Manhattan. Only Monteriggioni and San Gimignano today offer some visual hint of that vertical Siena which has vanished. We might also have some difficulty in recognizing the people. Siena today is one of the safest cities in Europe, but its history is one of violence; not just the attacks of the Florentines and other enemies, but internecine strife between noble families, and the ritualized violence which regularly pitted the men of the city's three divisions against one another in mock battles and lethal games. All that seems now to have been successfully canalized into the ninety seconds of madness which is the heart of the famous Palio.

Although so much of the city of today is the result of a sequence of proud local recreations of a remembered golden age, few visitors today fail to sense in some degree that Siena offers a glimpse of that ideal city which has been a constant human dream since antiquity. It is as though the benign influence of Lorenzetti's *Good Government* fresco, that admonishment to just rule on the wall of the council chamber in the Palazzo Pubblico, is powerful still, over the city on its hills and the fruitful land which laps about it.

One of the most beguiling aspects of Siena today is the constancy of its dialogue with its past. In the restaurants around the Via Pantaneto, one of the pasta courses offered is *Pici all'Etrusca*. *Pici* are rough, hand-made spaghetti, the sauce is made of a chopped hard-boiled egg, a fair quantity of olive oil and chopped parsley, mint and basil. Grated pecorino is added at the end. The sauce is plausibly Etruscan, made from ingredients readily available in the countryside round Siena since remote antiquity. Even if the name, like so much in Siena, is a proud reinvention, the egg (which vanishes into the texture of the sauce) certainly calls to mind the symbolic value the Etruscans seem to have given to eggs, which are held and handed on by the blandly smiling, slightly unnerving banqueters who populate Etruscan tomb paintings.

Siena began its long history as a fortified hilltop on the high ground which separates the basin of the River Arbia from that of the Elsa, on the site which is now the Duomo. Siena is divided into three regions, or *terzi*, and the foundational status of this hill is emphasized by the name of the *terzo*, which is Città. By the fourteenth century, two other hills had been enfolded within the new city walls, the *terzi* of San Martino and Camollia. The Campo, with the Palazzo Pubblico, is in the valley between these three heights. The *terzi* are deeply embedded in the structure of Siena. The city's experiments with republican government were extensive and varied through the Middle Ages, but however many people formed the government of the day, that number was always divisible by three.

1

GEOGRAPHY
AND
PREHISTORY

The three ridges on which the city rests are part of a vast Pliocene sea bottom, composed of various layers of sedimentary materials eroded from the Apennines and deposited about 3 million years ago. Since then, glacial melt and subsequent erosion have carved the river valleys which lead from the mountains to the sea. The uppermost layer is a calcium-rich sediment, which has been transformed into a softish rock called tufa, porous, fine-grained and often strong enough to build on, or to use as a building stone. A looser aggregate of coarse and fine materials intrudes between layers of tufa. Beneath all this is an impermeable barrier of clay. When rainwater percolates through the tufa and reaches clay, it is forced to change its course and flow sideways, along the surface of the clay, until it emerges on the hillside as a spring. It is this which made it possible to supply hilltop sites with water.

overleaf
Etruscan tomb frescoes reveal a people profoundly appreciative of life's pleasures, but they were also brilliant engineers and skilled metalworkers.

The Etruscans, who dominated Italy through the thousand years before the birth of Christ, prized the security of hilltop sites, not least because the lowlands harboured malaria, and many of their settlements, such as Murlo and Volterra, began on a defensible hill. The Etruscans were the original founders of Siena. There is some evidence that they were incomers rather than aborigines: an investigation published in the *American Journal of Human Genetics* in 2007 revealed that the genetic heritage of the people of several old Etruscan settlements suggested that they originally came to Etruria from Turkey.[1]

There are traces of Etruscan presence in Siena datable to the third and second centuries BC, but they are not extensive. Siena's fine collection of Etruscan sculpture, now shown in the Spedale della Scala, is drawn from the surrounding region and not from Siena itself.[2] However, the city's name is an Etruscan legacy, since it appears to derive from that of a

powerful Etruscan family, the Saina, who presumably had something to do with the settlement, which was later Latinized as Saena.

The Etruscans were skilled miners, engineers and metallurgists. Their trading economy depended upon the ability to mine ore and transform it into metal objects such as bronze weapon-points and fibulae, which they sold throughout Italy, and even beyond. They also built extensive underground tombs for their rulers, decorated with wall paintings which reveal that they delighted in banquets and dancing. A fine aesthetic sense is also suggested by the art they collected from their trading partners. Much about Etruscan life remains mysterious, since from the fourth century BC onwards their aggressively expansionist neighbours to the south, the Romans, began nibbling away at Etruscan territory, town by town. By the beginning of the first century BC, the last Etruscan settlement had fallen, and there is no surviving Etruscan literature.

We were once holidaying just west of Buonconvento in the guest cottage of an estate, and the owner of the villa sometimes liked to drift over for a few minutes of conversation in the early evening. We were established on a terrace, chatting and enjoying the long view out over the countryside under a darkening sky with the stars coming out, when we heard dance music, played on an accordion. Our host pointed out the fact, which seemed to mildly amuse him, that a *ballo lirico* was being held in a tiny hamlet of four houses or so on a little hill, almost indistinguishable in the dusk, and said, 'it is Porsenna, an ancient Etruscan town', a sentence which instantly brought to mind a verse out of damp England at its Victorian dampest, 'Lars Porsena of Clusium, by the nine gods he swore…', one of Macaulay's thumpity-bump versifications of Roman history, in strange contrast with the warm night, the crickets and the sweet, old-fashioned waltz music.

In many ways Siena's story is directly influenced by its position. A city perched a thousand feet above the nearest river is always going to have problems with one of the basic necessities of life, and the Etruscans were the first to face the problem. But they were excellent excavators, and, in addition to building underground tombs, they also built underground reservoirs, not only in Siena, but also in some of their other hilltop settlements, notably Orvieto.[3] They acquired advanced skills in water management as an aspect of their mining activities, and at Siena they must have taken careful note of a place where an impervious layer of clay caused trapped rainwater to flow from the hillside as a natural spring, near the oldest fountain of Siena, Fontebranda.

Most of the largest and most important of Siena's public fountains date from before 1250. Each of them is built into a hillside and connected to the water-bearing aquifer by a relatively short tunnel, and all of them are downhill from the ridge along which the city is built. Their location and form therefore suggest that they evolved from springs, and that the tunnels follow the source of the water deeper into the aquifer. Thus, over time, as the settlement developed, the Etruscans excavated tunnels following the natural contours of the clay, to collect water from the sand above and direct it to a cistern, the original Fontebranda. As the city grew, later generations elaborated and extended the work. This was the origin of Siena's remarkable system of underground aqueducts which collected and distributed the city's water supply till 1914.

Siena's legendary history has forgotten the Etruscans completely. There is almost no trace of the original Etruscan settlement surviving, since the whole of Città, the first nucleus of the settlement, was overlaid with medieval buildings. From at least as early as the fourteenth century, Siena thought of itself as a Roman town. While there are several Sienese origin legends, discussed later in the text since they were written up in the fifteenth century, at a point where origin legends had become highly political documents, for the most part Siena positioned its foundation immediately after that of Rome itself, as the creation of Aschius and Senius, the sons of Remus, who fled from the wrath of their uncle Romulus after his murder of their father. She-wolves and twins abound in the city, and, tellingly, appear in Ambrogio Lorenzetti's iconic parable of Sienese political life in the Palazzo Pubblico, coiled at the feet of the majestic black and white-clad giant who represents the Good Commune.[4] Dante derided the Sienese as dreamers, and it is true that the city's sense of civic identity rests, to a great extent, on myths of one kind or another.

The first evidence of Siena's ancient history relates to the Roman period. Excavation of a room beneath the Duomo which had been infilled with building rubble revealed that a Roman house had stood on or near the site; fragments of Roman pottery and glass, scraps of worked marble and painted plaster, suggest that around the first century BC a

following pages
Ambrogio Lorenzetti's panorama of a well-governed city, an orderly bustle of buying, selling, building, teaching and dancing.

Roman landowner had built a country villa in order to enjoy the view out over the hills. During the reign of Augustus, a military colony, Saena Julia, was established. Another excavation in the north-west of Città revealed its presence. A Roman well was found, and also three dogs, two of which had been hacked in three. These animals were sacrificed during the ceremony of founding the walls and the city gates.[5] The Roman settlement boasted an aqueduct, at least four gates, and early writers claim up to six temples, four of them inside the medieval city walls. There was a temple of Minerva at the site of the cathedral, and others dedicated to Jove, Saturn, Diana and Quirinus. The temple of Jove was near the modern Campo, and the temple of Diana (possibly a personal shrine) was sited within it.[6] The Roman settlement also had baths, located along the modern Via delle Terme, and possibly a forum. A statue of Venus supported by a dolphin was unearthed in 1325 in the course of digging foundations for a building called *castellare dei Malavolti*, and subsequently placed on the first Fonte Gaia, as we know from a description of it by the Florentine artist Lorenzo Ghiberti in his *Commentaries* (1447), but this fragment of Roman Siena has long since vanished.[7] There are a few Roman inscriptions, the most complete of which is on the Porta Romana. It was put up by a man called Vitricius in honour of the deity Silvanus.

By the year 90, Siena was significant enough for its people to receive Roman citizenship, and the settlement starts to be mentioned by Roman writers such as Pliny, Ptolemy and Tacitus. It is Tacitus who tells the only story about Roman Siena which suggests anything of its character: it suggests that stubborn independence was an early development, and that the Sienese resented any attempt by the Romans to exert their authority. An unfortunate Roman senator paid a visit to the city in the time of Vespasian, expecting to be greeted with honour; instead, he was beaten up on the orders of the local magistrates; following which 'the mob had surrounded him and before his face had wailed, lamented, and conducted a mock funeral, accompanying it with insults and outrageous expressions'.[8] The contumacious citizens were reproved by the Roman senate for their lack of respect. The Sienese may have felt it was mutual. The Romans drove the Via Cassia through the middle of Tuscany, passing through Chiusi, Bolsena, Arezzo and Florence and looping round to Lucca before reaching the sea at Pisa. This was their main highway in Tuscany, and Siena was not on it; the future city was merely a small town on a hill thirty miles to the west. Siena's journey out of complete insignificance has nothing to do with the rise of Rome, and occurred after the collapse of the Roman empire.

In the fourth century, the Emperor Constantine made two momentous decisions. One was to become a Christian, though as late as the reign of his immediate predecessor, Diocletian, Christians had been a hated and persecuted minority. The other was to move the capital of the empire to the other end of the Mediterranean, to Constantinople. Rome therefore ceased to be the seat of imperial power. As a result of these two decisions, the Rome of the Caesars disappeared and the city was reborn as the capital of Christendom. Before leaving Rome for the last time in 326, Constantine had showered the Bishop of Rome with wealth. He had already given him the Lateran Palace as the papal residence, and ordered huge, ostentatious new churches to be built – St Peter's, built over the once humble, but never forgotten, grave of the apostle who had walked by the side of Jesus himself, San Giovanni in Laterano, adjacent to the new papal palace, Santa Croce, San Lorenzo and many others, enormous buildings glittering with marble and mosaic, splendidly furnished and richly endowed. Constantine's gifts of estates and income for the maintenance of the church in Rome amounted to about 300,000 gold soldi, with 25,000 soldi of annual income, at a time when a man could live for a year on three or four soldi.[9] A community of the poor, or at least furtive, was suddenly out in the open, indeed rendered highly visible. Constantine's vast donations ensured that the popes of his reign and after could hold up their heads as social equals in the company of haughty Roman senators from families with roots trailing back to the early days of the Republic. He was prepared to sacrifice a good deal of his personal wealth to achieve this. The early medieval *Book of the Popes* devotes page after page to his incredible gifts: gold and silver chandeliers and sanctuary lamps, silver statues of Jesus five feet high, chalices of precious stones, a font made of precious porphyry, and, above all, a fair-sized chunk of the imperial patrimony to support these ostentatious symbols of a new religious order.[10]

The centuries that followed saw the end of the Roman empire in the West. After Constantine, the emperors turned their backs on Italy, with a single exception, and the collapse of Roman authority in the course of the fifth century was accompanied by the invasion of Germanic tribes, the Goths and Lombards. In the mid-sixth century, the Emperor Justinian (though he never personally left Constantinople) fought a protracted war in Italy to recover the erstwhile heart of the empire, before eventually giving up and withdrawing his troops. These must have been chaotic and terrifying times, as Roman and Germanic armies pursued one another across a devastated countryside, probably the lowest point in Italian urban life since towns first began to appear.

By the end of the sixth century, things were looking a little brighter. The Lombards were in control of Tuscany, including Siena, by 568, and a measure of civil order was being restored throughout Italy. In Siena, the evidence, such as it is, is for a very modest settlement. The excavations beneath the cathedral which gave some indication of a Roman villa also revealed the remains of jars from the sixth or seventh century, suggesting a small community, which would by then have been Christian, further witnessed by four burials in earth graves, and a sixth-century hut. The Lombard kings ruled Tuscia (as they called Tuscany) from Pisa, and put representatives called gastalds into the cities they controlled. In 650, the first known bishop of Siena, Maurus, was appointed by the Lombard king, and was himself a Lombard aristocrat.

The ancient Abbazia di San Salvatore on Monte Amiata, founded by the Lombard king Ratchis.

It was at this point that Siena started to acquire significance. Rome was the only great Christian city in Western Europe in the seventh century, and the Bishops of Rome were using their wealth, political clout and possession of the holy relics of the saints to assert their authority over Christendom, a process accelerated by the extraordinarily able pope Gregory the Great at the end of the sixth century. The popes came up with the idea that a narrow scarf called a pallium was the token of an archbishop's true legitimacy. These slender bands were woven by the nuns of the convent of St Agnes, a much-venerated Roman martyr, from the fleece of pet lambs, and considerable mystique attached to them. For this and other reasons, senior churchmen had to visit Rome.

The old Via Aurelia, which ran along the Mediterranean coast, had been abandoned when Roman life collapsed because it was impossible to defend it against pirates. And the old Via Cassia, running through the Val di Chiana, developed problems with flooding, since there were no longer the resources, skills or personnel to keep it drained, so a new road came into being, on higher ground, which served the needs of visitors to Rome coming from the north. It would come to be known as the Via Francigena, and through the early Middle Ages and beyond it was the principal route to Rome from Western Europe, where the Franks had been Christian since the sixth century, and the conversion of the Anglo-Saxons had begun with a mission to Kent in 597 instigated by Gregory the Great. It ran through San Gimignano to the south of Siena, Siena itself, and San Quirico, a quite different route from the old Via Cassia. Siena thus acquired a new strategic importance and value: it was in a position to monitor and control traffic to and from Rome.

In the mid-seventh century, the new Bishop of Siena, Maurus, controlled only the city of Siena and its immediate environs. Since the gastald of Siena controlled a great deal more, by the early eighth century it seemed obvious to the bishop of the city that his domain should match that of the secular authority. This seemed considerably less obvious to the Bishop of Arezzo, the spiritual authority in the lands in question. As a result, the two cities went to war in 711, and the Bishop of

Arezzo was forced to give way. The story is told by Gerardus, head of the cathedral chapter of Arezzo, writing around 1056, though he claims that his account, which gives us a rare glimpse of the political organization of eighth-century Siena, was based on ancient records.[11]

> At that time the city of Siena was ruled by Aripert, king of the Lombards, and in it dwelt a royal judge, Godipert by name. He, coming with Taipert, the gastald, to the church where Lupertianus, bishop of Arezzo, was, without showing the bishop the least respect, began to hurl injuries at the bishop's men, and to insult them, and to vex them with legal proceedings. This the Aretines attending the bishop tolerated for some time, until, flaring up, they fell upon and killed Godipert, the Sienese judge. Wherefore the whole people of Siena became enraged against Bishop Lupertianus and put him to flight; and they obliged Adeodatus, bishop of Siena, who was the cousin of the aforesaid Godipert, the judge whom the Aretines had slain, to hold that parish whether, he would or no for one year; and there outrageously and against the canons of our church he consecrated three altars and two priests.

In this account, the people of Siena act collectively and put pressure on their own bishop to capitalize on the situation, suggesting that they viewed their bishop as a legitimate ruler, and that they perceived his aggrandizement as a victory for Siena as a whole. This is supported by the fact that aggression against the Bishop of Arezzo was instigated by the secular leader together with another Lombard official, who used his legal knowledge to harass the Bishop of Arezzo, and got himself killed in consequence. Additionally, everyone mentioned has a Lombard name except Adeodatus (which is Latin), and the fact that the bishop and the judge were cousins suggests that the Lombard nobility had come to be thoroughly embedded in the aristocracy of the city.

One result of this coup was that the Sienese acquired a saint, Ansano, whose shrine lay squarely in the middle of the disputed territory. According to legend, Ansano had come to Siena to preach Christianity during the reign of Diocletian, when the Christian religion was proscribed. He was hunted down during the Great Persecution of 303–13 when Diocletian tried to eradicate Christianity from the empire, and martyred at Dofana, in the Sienese countryside, in 304 (it was when Bishop Lupertianus was at Dofana that Taipert and Godibert went to challenge him). This is the first of Siena's many myths about its origins that we know of, since the triumphant Sienese started to claim that

Ansano had been their first bishop. Eventually, in 1108, they removed his relics to the cathedral.

The increasingly Christian character of eighth-century Siena is also witnessed by the foundation of two great monasteries, San Salvatore on Monte Amiata, and Sant'Eugenio at Costafabbri, very near the city. The American historian Ferdinand Schevill writes, 'Leaning from the rampart outside the gate of San Marco, a large red mass rises into view. It is the monastery of Sant'Eugenio, called by the Sienese with a pleasant familiarity Il Monistero, as if it were the only one of its kind.' It is of Lombard origin, founded by the gastald Warnefrid in 730.[12]

One far-distant event which had a direct effect on Siena's fortunes was the birth of the Prophet Muhammad and the rise of Islam, in the mid-seventh century. Only a generation after Constantine had declared Christianity to be the religion of the Roman empire, Christians had started to visit the Holy Land in order to tread in the steps of Christ, worship at the tomb and visit the room where the Last Supper took place, and other holy sites. As St Jerome wrote in 386, full of enthusiasm, 'can we suppose a Christian's education complete who has not visited the Christian Athens?'. One fourth-century pilgrim we know of started from distant Bordeaux. It is quite possible to imagine that, if Islam had not arisen, the Christian church might have developed a tradition analogous to the Muslim Hajj, a once-in-a-lifetime affirmation of religious faith by journeying to the sacred city.

The Muslims, however, conquered Jerusalem in 637, and made Christian access to the sacred sites extremely difficult. But in the wake of this disaster, the habit of Christian pilgrimage, three centuries old by then, did not so much disappear as reconfigure. The idea of the Holy City was enshrined in Christian thought, notably in the Book of Revelation 21: 2: 'I saw the Holy City, the new Jerusalem, coming down out of heaven from God, prepared as a bride beautifully dressed for her husband.' To St John, this meant an otherworldly city, which could only be reached after death. I remember being disconcerted by the discovery that Sion is an actual district in old Jerusalem, because a memory crowded with hymns tells me so insistently that Sion is 'the city of God', and not part of this world. But, in the thinking of the seventh century, could there be such a thing as a new, Christian, Jerusalem?

Constantine decreed that Constantinople was a New Rome; the

imperial centre. And there was only one city in the Christian West which could be repurposed as a New Jerusalem. The Eternal City held the shrines of St Peter and St Paul, both of whom were martyred there, a piece of the True Cross, countless relics of the martyrs. Tacitus described Christians used as human torches under Nero, and less distinguished writers told the stories of many later sufferers under successive pagan emperors from Decius to Diocletian. The cult of the saints developed as it did because early Christians believed that the saints, as Prudentius observed in the fourth century, 'listen to our prayer and straightaway carry it to the ear of the everlasting King'.[13] They also believed that the saints listened harder if you were physically in proximity to their holy remains, and that took them to visit shrines, above all, that of St Peter.

Prudentius tells us that vast throngs of pilgrims were already thronging Rome in his day, visiting the martyrs, and above all praying

at the tomb of the apostle. Since he had been given the power to bind and loose by Christ himself, Peter could give a penitent sinner access to heaven. King Canute, who probably had a fair amount on his conscience, went on pilgrimage to Rome for hard-headed, Viking reasons: 'wise men have told me that the Apostle Peter has received from God the power of binding and loosing and carries the keys of paradise. I therefore deemed it useful in no ordinary way to seek his patronage before God.'[14] Thus people tended not to speak of going 'to Rome'; more often, they thought in terms of going 'to the threshold of St Peter'. As well as asking St Peter to pray one into heaven, pilgrims sought healing, fulfilled vows they had made when they were ill, or prayed for other things. A deaf and dumb Englishman went to Rome around 787, hoping for a miracle; and a charter of 1063 in Rouen records that a wealthy couple called Germund and Bersenta were preparing to go to Rome on pilgrimage because they were childless.[15] Also, Rome had plenty for Christian visitors to see. Thanks to Constantine, there was a splendid variety of opulent basilicas. So the pilgrims started to arrive, and kept on coming; floods of travellers venturing down the Via Francigena to pray at St Peter's tomb and the shrines of the martyrs. To these visitors, Rome was above all the city of the apostle, and not that of Augustus.

The abbey church of Sant'Antimo: its origins are obscure but it was refounded as a Benedictine community by Charlemagne in the eighth century.

Even women dared the long journey, despite the risks. An English abbess, Eangyth, wrote to the Anglo-Saxon missionary St Boniface around 720: 'we [she and her daughter] have long wished to go to Rome, once mistress of the world, as many of our friends have done. We would there seek pardon for our sins.' They seem to have made it back home, but some twenty-five years later, Boniface wrote to the Archbishop of Canterbury, 'it would be well and favourable for your church if your synod and your princes would forbid matrons and veiled women [nuns] to make these frequent journeys back and forth to Rome. A great part of them perish and few keep their virtue. There are few towns in Lombardy or Frankland where there is not a prostitute of English stock.'[16] But there was safety in numbers: the more travellers there were on the Via Francigena, the fewer bandits would dare to prey on them. And for these burgeoning numbers of pilgrims, Siena was an essential stop. We tend to think of pilgrims as poor, solitary figures, travelling on foot, with nothing but a scrip and a staff, and there must have been many who fitted this description. But if a king went on pilgrimage to Rome, as Offa did in the eighth century, or Canute in the eleventh, he would go with a sizeable entourage, all on horseback. When they stopped for the night, these richer and worldlier pilgrims would want stables for their horses, decent food and wine and comfortable beds. All that translated into economic opportunity for the fortunate towns along the way.

The next development to have an impact on Siena came in the second half of the eighth century, when the king of the Franks, Pepin, entered into an alliance with the papacy which had long-term historical consequences, including the rise of the Papal States. He was the founder of the dynasty which would come to be known as the Carolingians, after his son Charlemagne, who was crowned as the first Holy Roman Emperor by the pope in the year 800. The swathe of central Italian territory thus gifted to the popes had previously been held by the Lombards. The Lombards also lost their grip on Tuscany, and Siena became subject to the Franks. This meant that Lombard gastalds were replaced by Frankish counts. Franks married into the existing Sienese nobility and left a legacy that can be seen in the abbeys they founded throughout Sienese territory. Founding abbeys, as the Berardenga family did, for instance, in the ninth century (now Castello Badia Berardenga), allowed these warlords to tap into the increasing power and wealth of the church.

Under the Carolingians, the region which included Siena was known as the March of Tuscany. It came into existence after Charlemagne finally conquered the Lombard kingdom in 773/4, and succeeded the Lombard duchy of Tuscia. This regime change did not greatly affect Siena, because the city continued to be an essential stop on the Via Francigena, and, with the newly-minted entente between the papacy and the Frankish kings, the road from northern Europe to Rome was busier than ever. The abbey of Sant'Antimo was constructed on the site of an ancient Roman settlement during the Frankish era, and grew to become a rich and powerful community. In 833, a Frankish adventurer called Adelrat attempted to carve out a kingdom for himself, centred on Siena, which would comprise the territories of Siena, Florence, Volterra, Chiusi and Arezzo. He was unsuccessful, but the venture serves to emphasize the increasing importance and desirability of Siena in this new, Christian world. The city was even visited by a Frankish emperor, Charles the Fat, in 881.

Adelrat was a symptom of changing times, the arrival of an era of warlords. The ninth century saw aggressive Muslim raids from Spain and North Africa, and new pagan threats to Christendom, Vikings from the north and Magyars from the east, while the Carolingians lost their grip on their sprawling empire. The Europe-wide political crisis gave opportunities to local magnates in Tuscany, who built themselves hilltop castles, called themselves counts and subdued as much territory as they could hold. The powerful families of the countryside around Siena, rather than identifying their interests with their city, concentrated on castle-building and establishing their domination over rural territories, extracting tribute from the peasants who lived there.

The great beneficiaries of this new situation were the bishops. Bishops always retained a strong attachment to their cities, because their cathedrals were located within city walls. As Siena's aristocratic families turned their attention to building and fortifying their *castelli*, the power of the bishop expanded to fill the vacuum in the city. Additionally, as the world approached the end of the first millennium, record-keeping was increasingly important, and knowledge was power. The bishop stood at the head of a literate clerisy, the essential personnel for creating a civil service. Armed with their records of the local people and their property, the bishop could not only claim the right to tithe the population, he could exercise it effectively, with excommunication, the threat of losing access to the sacraments which were deemed essential to salvation, as his weapon.

The bishop was also a highly useful individual. He was the only person with the moral and spiritual authority to settle differences between noble clans. Again, the trust generated by his office made him the natural overseer of public works, and allowed him to administer justice. In 911, the Bishop of Siena consecrated a new church on Terzo di Città: the first mention of what would become the great Duomo of the Middle Ages.

2

EARLY
CHRISTIAN
SIENA

In theory, tenth-century Siena was part of the March of Tuscany, which had its capital at Lucca at this time. Its ruler, the margrave, owed allegiance to the Holy Roman Emperor. Through the ninth and tenth centuries, the margrave was essentially a great lay dignitary, whose support for the ruler of Italy was very far from being automatic. The first Tuscan margrave was appointed under the Carolingians: Adalbert I was granted that title in 846. His family held the region until 931, when Hugh of Arles, who had made himself king of Italy, dispossessed them, and granted Tuscany to his brother Boso. In 1027, the last of Boso's heirs was deposed from the march by the Holy Roman Emperor Conrad II for opposing his claim to be king of Italy as well as emperor. Conrad then bestowed the margravate on the count of Canossa, Boniface III, who was already colossally wealthy, with extensive lands in Emilia. His heir was a daughter, the formidable Matilda, one of the great figures of early medieval Italy, who wielded her power and influence to the benefit of the papacy and brought Conrad's successor, Henry III, to abject surrender at Canossa.

The emperors' principal power lay north of the Alps, so to exert any control in Italy they were forced to delegate. The political history of the March of Tuscany illustrates a general tendency of imperial government, which was to try and hold onto authority by granting local power to trusted magnates and hoping that they would remain loyal. Of course, what tended to happen is that the magnates developed strong local ties, and passed from thinking of themselves as imperial servants to thinking of themselves as local lords. The sources for the history of Siena are poor during the whole eleventh century both for the city and the countryside, partly because early medieval Siena was not subject to the Dukes of Tuscany but, instead, formed part of the royal patrimony, and continued to be administered by counts.

The extreme scarcity of judicial documents drawn up in Sienese territory in the eleventh century suggests that the Sienese were solving their own problems without recourse to the external authority of the margraves, hence nothing came to the imperial archives. Matilda spent time in Pisa, Florence, Lucca and Mantua, and visited Arezzo, but is not known to have set foot in Siena, perhaps because it was not directly under her authority. However, with her death in 1115 the era of the feudal princes had passed in northern Italy, to be replaced by the dominance of city-states, maritime republics and communes.

In the early Middle Ages, the relationship between political and secular authority was complicated. By 900, the church was a pervasive fact of life, defining the shape of the year, controlling who one could marry and even what one could eat (fasting was enjoined during Lent and Advent, and on Wednesdays and Fridays). The disciplines of Christian life were generally accepted, and the power of the church over the individual was considerable. Since salvation depended on staying within the church, and bishops had the power to cast an individual out, temporarily or permanently, they had a mighty weapon at their disposal. Under the Carolingians, secular and religious authorities were envisaged as acting in partnership. Charlemagne created *missi dominici* (investigators) who travelled in pairs – one lay, one cleric – throughout his empire, to evaluate local rulers and report back. He both established counts to govern secular affairs and gave bishops considerable executive power.

Matilda of Tuscany: a formidable politician, and one of the great personalities of the eleventh century.

The bishops of Siena were less powerful than many. Bishops had become important urban leaders in the great cities of the empire by the end of the fourth century, but Siena was not a great city at that time, and, indeed, it is far from clear that there was a bishop in Siena before 650. When one was created, his diocese was small, as we have seen.[1] But in the tenth century, when the March of Tuscany was ruled by margrave Ugo, Siena seems to have been a sort of 'grey area'. The military aristocracy was apparently detached from the city, living in their castles in the countryside and immersed in local politics and rivalry, instead of maintaining significant relationships with the city. The Bishop of Siena thus became a civic leader owing to the absence of alternatives. The ecclesiastical centre, including the bishop's residence and the cathedral, was built on the highest hill in the area, Castelvecchio,

MATHILDIS LUCENS·PRECOR HOC CAPE CARA VOLUMEN:·

a long-inhabited site on account of its defensive location. Siena's first defensive walls were constructed around this nucleus, dividing the city, which was administered by the bishop, from its surrounding territories, which were a patchwork of aristocratic landholdings. By 1055, Emperor Henry III gave the city's religious leader, then known as the Bishop of Castelvecchio, authority over lands in the Sienese rural hinterland of the city, the *contado*. By adding the land bestowed by the emperor to the power invested in him by the pope, Siena's bishop became both a sacred and secular lord.

Another aspect of the bishops' power was that an important aspect of early medieval thinking, as we have seen, was belief in the power of the saints, and the importance of personal contact with their holy remains. In the accounts of the lives and posthumous miracles of the saints, their holy bones could turn back fire, or prevent plague. In the face of mundane domestic tragedies, such as a child falling out of a window or a chimney catching fire, early medieval people fell to their knees and prayed to whichever saints they considered efficacious. Since very few illnesses or injuries were actually curable, people also took their physical problems to the saints. Thus it is understandable that the Sienese were prepared to fight the Bishop of Arezzo for the mortal remains of St Ansano; his bones were a valuable asset because they would both protect the city and attract visitors.

Siena was not very well off for saints: by the thirteenth century, Ansano and three other rather shadowy early Christian martyrs were recognized as protectors of the city, since they are shown kneeling at the front of Duccio's *Maestà*, but their reputation was purely local. Savinus had been venerated by the Benedictines since the eighth century, and the Sienese came to think of him as the first bishop of the city. Crescentius was prayed to simply because, in 1058, the bishop acquired his mortal remains. Victor was equally shadowy, while Ansano was believed to have been the evangelist of Siena. However, by 1300 the canon was established, and the four were collectively made the object of a cult, as the 'patrons and defenders' of the city. By the early fifteenth century, the reliquary busts of the four city patrons were brought to the high altar on the annual feast of the Four Crowned Martyrs on 8 November, which looks like a somewhat cynical attempt to link Siena's four male patrons with this prestigious group of universal saints, and may in itself be an indication of the rather modest status of the local cults.[2] It may also help to explain why the city put itself under the special protection of the Virgin.

Some important new developments show the way that Siena was developing as a Christian city. The hospital of Santa Maria della Scala, dedicated to the Madonna 'of the ladder', was perhaps founded as early as the ninth century to shelter pilgrims and care for the sick. According to later legend, an expectant mother had a miraculous dream in the year 832, in which she saw her future son climbing a ladder to heaven. Once the boy was born, she named him Sorore and he grew up to found Santa Maria as a hospital for pilgrims. The first documented record of Santa Maria as a 'xenodochium et hospitalis' is of 29 March 1090, but legend suggests it could have been in existence for a century by then. It was one of more than a dozen hospitals in Siena, but became one of the largest, growing rapidly from the donations of pilgrims who fell sick or died en route and were nursed in its hospitable halls. It constitutes important evidence for the tie between the pilgrim route of the Via Francigena and the development of Siena.

Although it was probably founded by the canons of the cathedral, it was run by friars and lay brothers and sisters who may well have fabricated the legend of its foundation by a layman, not a priest.[3] The hospital predates the earliest civic documents by at least a generation, but its history is inextricably tied to civic ideals, and the commune clearly desired to claim it as a civic institution from a very early date. A papal bull issued by Celestine III in 1193 removed it from the control of the cathedral and made it into a free-standing lay institution. One reason why it became as wealthy as it did is that it was headed by a rector who was usually a rich merchant or banker who had decided to retire and give some attention to his prospects in the next world: on appointment, he bequeathed all his possessions to the hospital. Other individuals, similarly, retired to the hospital and received lodgings plus a modest annual stipend in exchange for leaving the institution all their property; an arrangement with obvious benefits for a childless, ageing couple, but with such bargains being struck it is no wonder that the hospital grew wealthier and wealthier.[4]

The statutes of 1305, written by an Augustinian canon, the Blessed Agostino Novello, describe a powerful autonomous organization within the city and state of Siena owning much land, granaries and other smaller hospitals. Judith Hook notes that by the fourteenth century,

MATER·S̄COEI · SIS·CAVSA·SEN̄IS·REOVIEI·SIS·OBCIO·VITA·TEODIA · PIN̄XIT·ITA·

'after the commune itself, the hospital was the most important corporate body in Siena'. The wealth it acquired was invested in land, and by the fourteenth century it owned enormous amounts of the Sienese countryside and was a major supplier of wheat to the city. Over the course of the 1200s a grange system was developed whereby the mother hospital set up satellite hospitals and farms throughout the countryside, each of which was a complex with a tower, living accommodation for the manager and the workers, granaries, mills and cattle byres. The scale of its operations by the late fourteenth century is suggested by the fact that the hospital was buying 100 to 150 oxen a year to work its estates. Oxen have a working life of only two or three years, so they must have owned four to five hundred of them at any one time.[5] Some estimates suggest that by the end of the thirteenth century Santa Maria della Scala owned a third of the arable land under Sienese control.[6]

Some of these granges are still present in the countryside, gaunt, impressive structures built of pale brick, standing amid farmland. The biggest still standing is at Cuna, and there is another at Spedaletto. The attractive hilltop village of Serre di Rapolano has grown up around another of these complexes, and now has a Museo dell'Antica Grancia e dell'Olio in the processing areas of the original grange, where the olive oil mill and other tools can still be seen.

Duccio's *Maestà*: a milestone in the development of Western art, painted for Siena's cathedral. On either side of the Madonna, the four patrons of the city lead a crowd of saints in prayer.

The people who did the work in these granges, and throughout the countryside, have left very little record. However, there is some archaeological evidence for life in the countryside around Siena, which emerged from investigation of two cemeteries at Poggibonsi, one from around the eighth to tenth centuries, the other medieval. None of the people buried in the early medieval cemetery were older than forty-five. Their struggle for survival was suggested by the state of the enamel on their teeth, which indicates that they experienced periods of stress in infancy and childhood. Their diet consisted mostly of bread, which was ground in a quern, and thus contained particles of grit which wore down their teeth. Many of their teeth were also decayed, perhaps suggesting that they ate sugary fruit such as dried figs, and also that they lacked vitamins A and D, meaning that they did not eat much meat, fish, or milk.[7] Elisabeth Romer, in her splendid book about life and food on a Tuscan farm, mentions an impoverished family in the 1940s who fed their children on bread and dried figs – 'this was regarded as the food of the really poor'.[8] The people buried in the medieval cemetery were shorter, and less robust than their early medieval predecessors, who were perhaps of Germanic stock, but their teeth were less worn, suggesting that, while their diet was similarly based on bread, their flour was less gritty, and that, even though they were smaller, they were probably better fed.

Bread apart, the diet of the early medieval peasants probably leaned heavily on the onion family, since that remained true for centuries. An old Tuscan dish, *Pappa di olio*, consists of bread moistened with olive oil and water and flavoured with garlic and salt. A tenth-century monk named Giovanni passed an elderly pilgrim returning from Rome and was sickened by the smell of the garlic, onions and leeks the old man carried along with his loaf of bread.[9] Apart from bread, soupy and porridgy mixtures of all kinds were consumed; for instance, a document issued in Lucca in 765 directed that a food dole should be distributed to the poor three times a week, a polenta made of foxtail millet and broad beans – unappetizing sounding, but certainly nourishing.[10] Other indications of the food of poor Italians in the early Middle Ages suggests that life was fairly marginal even in years where no actual famine is recorded. An etymological index of this might be the Italian word for soup, *minestra*. It derives from Latin 'ministrare', meaning 'to administer, dole out', suggesting that it was rationed, served out from a central pot by the figure of authority in the household.

Italian peasants were inventive in their search for food, especially in hard times. An archaeological investigation of the people of Colonna, in Lazio, in the eighth to tenth centuries, found that, like their contemporaries at Poggibonsi, they were poorly nourished, with bad teeth. The grain which went to make the bread they ate was bulked out with ilex acorns, sorghum and millet.[11] Italians have long been resourceful in exploiting the wealth of the countryside.

3

NEW
BEGINNINGS

After the effective collapse of imperial government in Italy during the eleventh century, local forces were able to take advantage of the power vacuum. The attractiveness of a pro-imperial policy, known as Ghibellinism, in Italy was precisely that imperial allegiance no longer meant much, since the emperors were occupied north of the Alps, while for those who followed a Guelf, or pro-pope, policy, the Holy Father was all too present. In the north, successive Holy Roman Emperors were quite unable to regain control, though in the south a new, powerful Norman kingdom emerged, centred on Sicily.

The twelfth century was a time of revolutionary change in Siena, as it was in other northern Italian cities. Europe was finally regaining a stability which it had not enjoyed since the fall of the Roman empire. The pagan Vikings had turned into the Christian Normans, and become a force for order. The pagan Hungarians had been successfully seen off by the emperors of the tenth century, and by 1000 they had also accepted Catholicism and were living under a king, St Stephen of Hungary, who was subsequently canonized. Muslim expansion into Christendom had been contained. In this more peaceful world, population and production were increasing everywhere. Economically, Siena and the other Tuscan towns were benefiting from an agricultural boom. Plentiful crops in the *contado* not only created an agricultural surplus for trade, but led to increased birth rates and, in turn, to immigration to the cities in search of economic opportunity as well as prosperity in the countryside. The growing cities needed more food, and the countryfolk were able to provide it. More land was brought under cultivation, and new rural settlements developed.

At the same time, the rise in urban population encouraged developments in technologies and trade, which created a virtuous spiral of growth. The cities of northern Italy all expanded enormously in the twelfth century. The emerging culture of trade and consumption might have benefited from stability, but unfortunately the northern Italian cities were anything but stable politically. However, the papal–imperial power struggle which was expressed in terms of Guelfs versus Ghibellines took the attention of both the pope and the emperor away from cities such as Siena, allowing them to develop ambitions towards self-government. Increasing trade throughout Europe, which depended on manufacturing, banking, and travel through northern Italian cities, brought wealth to almost every level of urban dweller in Siena.

The first crusade was called in 1095, and through the twelfth century the crusades increased traffic down the Via Francigena, as well as increasing the number of Christian vessels going to and fro in the Mediterranean. The Normans had completed their conquest of Sicily and southern Italy in the 1070s, and with their formidable assistance the Christians regained control of the Mediterranean, which had been dominated by Muslim powers for three hundred years. A Sicilian Muslim poet wrote apologetically to the ruler of Seville, who had invited him to his court, that 'the sea belongs to the Romans, and our ships circulate there only by exposing themselves to great risks; only the mainland belongs to the Arabs'.[1] However questionable in other respects, the crusades were a major spur to economic development in Italy. It was Italian vessels which took would-be crusaders and pilgrims to Italy, and every port in the Levant which fell to the crusaders was taken with the help of an Italian fleet. As well as acquiring immense amounts of booty, the Italians were rewarded with entire quarters of the captured ports where they built trading stations and warehouses. It was obviously the coastal and maritime powers of Pisa, Genoa and Venice that benefited directly from the Christian reconquest of the Mediterranean, but Siena doubtless benefited as well, since much of its wealth came from supplying the needs of travellers, and knights and merchants, as well as poor pilgrims, were on the road in large numbers, while some of the survivors were trailing back across the Alps, laden with wealth.

Like other such towns, Siena was motivated to seize control of its own affairs by the quickening tempo of commercial life, and the incentive this gave to establish fairs and permanent trading relations with like-minded merchant communities in Italy and beyond.[2] Over

The Emperor Frederick Barbarossa, flanked by two of his sons: Henry VI, his successor, is on the left. From a manuscript of the *Chronicle of the Welfs*.

the course of the next decade, the Sienese entered into league with neighbouring cities to gain independence from the Holy Roman Emperor, then Frederick Barbarossa. Barbarossa's official recognition of northern Italian communes, including Siena, was precipitated by a series of battles between the newly formed leagues of northern Italian cities and German forces, culminating in the Peace of Constance (1183), a treaty that became the formal foundation of communal autonomy.[3] Barbarossa's concessions were formalized in a charter issued by his son, Henry VI:

> In the name of the Holy and Indivisible Trinity, We, Henry VI, by divine favour, king of the Romans... make known to all the faithful of the empire, present as well as future, that in view of the merits of our trusty subjects, the citizens of Siena, we grant them all the free election of their consuls. However, the consuls shall receive the investiture annually from our hand or that of our most glorious father, Frederick, emperor of the Romans, or that of our successors, without any charge or exaction... In addition we grant them full jurisdiction in the city of Siena, and outside the city, in the contado, over the men belonging to the bishop of Siena or to any Sienese resident at the time this document is drawn up, saving the right of appeal in cases amounting to more than twenty pounds... All nobles outside the city and all other men throughout the Sienese comitatus, except those noted above, with all jurisdiction over them, their fodrum [a tax on the nobility] and services in general, we retain in our power. Also, we concede to the Sienese the privilege of coining money in the city of Siena. ... In witness whereof... [a long list of witnesses follows, the seal of King Henry, and the date, October 1186].[4]

There are significant limitations to Siena's power. The emperor is happy to sign away the bishop's temporal land holdings. However, he reserves the right to appeal directly to the nobles for feudal service and money (a provision which the Sienese promptly began undermining). One very important concession is that the Sienese were allowed to set up a mint.

The form of government which developed in twelfth-century Siena was a supreme magistracy headed by consuls, who were drawn from the urban nobility: the new opportunities for wealth creation in the city had drawn some of the magnates out of their rural strongholds and into urban palaces. This suggests that the model for governance was fundamentally the Roman Republic. The newly independent communes developed rapidly. At the core of their identity was an oath which the members swore to each other, and the elected officials such as the consuls swore to the whole executive body. Medieval society took oaths extremely seriously. Since terms of office were short, these oaths were regularly repeated, considered to be a good thing in itself, since it consolidated the new commune's sense of identity, and reminded it of its aims and intentions.[5]

By 1167, Siena had established its own office of finance and, by 1176, it not only had a system of legislature in place, documented by a constitution, but also a college to train judges and notaries to uphold its laws. Early Italian cities preferred their lawyers to be locally trained. Moreover, after the Emperor Frederick Barbarossa's official recognition of Siena's right to self-rule, the city expanded its power in the region by absorbing smaller communities into its thriving organization. Thus, Siena was eventually more than a commune or city. It became a city-state, extending its system of laws and governance to smaller, nearby communities and, in turn, collecting taxes and requiring allegiance from these dependencies.

Unlike many bishops in twelfth-century northern Italy, the Bishop of Siena played no direct part in government, and ecclesiastics do not appear to have been key actors in the early commune. The charter of 1186 gives the city sovereignty over the territories belonging to the bishop. He thus ceased to be a territorial magnate in his own right, as he had been in the previous century, and his temporal affairs were subject to the jurisdiction of the city.[6] By 1259, the bishop had also given up the right to collect money for building the cathedral to the commune, and similarly, the Spedale (hospital) of Santa Maria della Scala was detached from the control of the cathedral clergy and taken over by the city.[7] Thus Siena developed an unusual degree of separation between church and state for medieval Italy from quite an early period. The type of episcopal power that developed in Siena did not rest on secular rulership, but, rather, on pastoral prerogatives, sacrality and the centrality of the city's bishop to ritualized representations of urban identity such as coming together in the Duomo on the Feast of the Assumption of the Virgin. The bishop's presence at assemblies and his function as a mediator between various social groups defined a role for the see in the city's political life which allowed bishops power and influence, while at the same time keeping them above day-to-day politics. However, since it rested on consensus, this type of episcopal lordship faced enormous challenges when relations between the pope and the city were strained. As early as 1167, the commune of Siena declared its independence from episcopal control. In 1168–9, Bishop Ranieri, a Guelf, excommunicated the city under interdict, but the Sienese, rather than toeing the line, forced him into exile in 1170.

By 1145, Siena was already big enough for an Arabic geographer, al-Idrisi, writing for Roger II, the Norman ruler of Sicily, to describe it as 'a populous centre, endowed with markets, artisans, and riches'.[8] Like all Italian communes, the city of Siena was ambitious to expand its territory: more ground meant more tax revenue, and, at least as importantly, more security with respect to food production. Their biggest problem was Florence. It was only thirty-three miles to the north, while the actual frontier with Florentine territory was a mere nine miles from Siena. Other potential rivals were Volterra and Pisa to the north-west, Arezzo to the north-east and Perugia to the south-east. Siena's best chance of territorial gain was therefore to expand south and south-west towards Monte Amiata and into the Maremma. The former was mountainous, the latter swampy, and both were hard to control, and dominated by major feudal families such as the Aldobrandeschi, but they offered mineral deposits of various kinds and extensive pasture. The Sienese therefore made it their business to secure control over them. Another highly significant development of the 1170s is that silver was discovered in the mineral-rich hills known as *le colline mettalifere*, near Massa Marittima in southern Tuscany. The first notice of Siena's gaining an interest in the silver mines to the west appears in 1137 when the bishop, on behalf of the commune, received the citadel (*castello*) and silver mines of Montieri, twenty-two miles south-west of the city. In 1147 Siena continued its seaward expansion with the acquisition of Montepescali, twelve miles further than Montieri. Sometime before 1180 Siena had lost its rights to Montieri, but by 1180 it regained a quarter of the citadel and mines. The silver thus mined was put to good use when Frederick Barbarossa granted Siena the right to mint its own coinage in 1186. A supply of silver gave a welcome boost to the Sienese economy.

Possession of a mining region provided immediate wealth, but in the long run the most important contribution it made to the economy may have been expertise and technical knowledge. Two skills which went hand in hand in the early Middle Ages were mining and hydraulics, since mines frequently had to be drained, and before the age of steam, water power was used to drive all kinds of machinery. Drawing on their technological expertise in mining, the citizens of Massa Marittima had managed to channel water to the heart of their city at a time when most other towns still relied on water drawn from low-lying areas well outside the city walls, as was the case with Siena's Fontebranda. Siena's own problems with water meant that attracting people with this knowledge was hugely significant for the development of the city. Engineers were vital to the construction and maintenance of Siena's water system, which therefore became an important training ground for them. Throughout its golden age, Siena's capacity to draw on a supply of highly skilled workers, and the specialized technical knowledge of hydraulics which miners guarded closely, was essential to the development of the city, and also created a school of experts whose specialist technical knowledge brought them wealth and fame.

Twelfth-century Sienese history is filled with small local wars under-taken to subdue the feudal aristocracy. About the same time that we first hear of consuls, we hear also of the first 'submissions' made to the city. In 1137 the Soarzi family surrendered a fourth part of Montecastelli and other dominions to Siena. In July 1151, Count Paltonerius of the Forte-guerra family gave up San Giovanni d'Asso, a fortified place to the east; in 1157 the Ardengheschi sold the hill of Orgia, just beyond the southern gate of the city, after the Sienese had taken and burned the castle there. Step by careful step, the Sienese state nibbled away at the power of the independent noble lords who had made a political patchwork of the countryside since the tenth century.

One of the frescoes in the Palazzo Pubblico seems to show the process of incorporation, though it is very damaged. It depicts a little town on a hill, with a sizeable stone castle which has a watchtower. The town is surrounded by a palisade, and another, inner palisade, guards the approach to the castle. The castle door and both palisade gates are standing open, signifying that the city has surrendered. Two figures stand out in the countryside. One wears a long green robe, and his belt was once gilded. He also wears a sword belt, and his left hand rests on the hilt of a long sword: all these details suggest that although he is in civilian dress and not clad for fighting, he is a noble and a warrior, and that the town is his citadel. His right hand is raised in a gesture suggesting that he is in dialogue with a second figure, who is more plainly dressed in grey-brown and has no military accoutrements, but who is looking the green-clad lord in the eye, and carrying a pair of expensive gloves.[9] Thomas De Wesselow observes that he seems a little too deferential to represent the power of Siena, but if, as De Wesselow suggests, the fresco originally covered the entire width of the wall (the first third is now covered by Sodoma's much later Sant'Ansano), he could have been one of nine, perhaps flanking the Podestà.[10] In any case, all this suggests that the fresco represents either the moment when one of the rural lords surrendered his castle to the commune of Siena, or a statement of the harmony of city and countryside.

The terms of submission, recorded in the city archive, varied, since some arose from military victory, others from intimidation, and perhaps others simply from the city buying the feudal rights of a noble family over a particular area. But all the treaties affirm the same basic purpose, that of drawing the nobility within the radius of the city's influence, and limiting their power. The terms of submission generally involved swearing an oath which specified a variety of commitments: a promise to help Siena whether in peace or war, to supply a specified number of cavalry and infantry, to accept officials who were either Sienese or chosen by the city and to accept a Sienese garrison. In return, the nobles were generally offered Sienese citizenship, though this had a price tag: the new citizens had to undertake to build or buy a house in Siena and to live there for at least part of the year.[11] Thus the nobles were enticed out of their fortresses in the countryside as the benefits of city life began to dawn on them: it offered protection, participation in government, the capacity to hold influential and perhaps lucrative offices, and free medical treatment for war wounds, among other advantages.

A combination of greed and reckless personal courage was a necessary attribute for medieval magnates, who spent their lives defending their castles and feuding with their neighbours. As city-dwellers, they may frequently have been a headache for the nascent commune, but this aristocratic combination of characteristics and values also offered enormous potential benefits for the city. The great merchant families of Siena's golden age did not descend from the rural aristocracy, but arose independently: 'it was not the aristocracy which made the communal city, but the communal city which created an aristocratic class', as Paolo Cammarosano comments.[12] But the new money, as so often, married into the old aristocracy, and absorbed its values. And it was entrepreneurship which allowed the city to step into a whole new world: international banking. In the early days of banking, entrepreneurs combined their own funds and funds from outsiders to provide credit for economic growth, gambling with their family patrimony. The commune of Siena produced companies which were among the most successful and innovative of the time. Much of the animating force behind Sienese growth in the field of international banking came from companies (called *societates* in Sienese documents) built round the new magnate families, notably the Bonsignori and Tolomei.[13]

In these companies, a number of investors agreed to act together for a defined period of years, just as local lords might ally with one another for military purposes. Their agreements defined the objectives of the alliance, the amount which was to be invested and the division of the resulting profits and losses. What made twelfth-century banking such a gamble was that the consortium accepted joint and unlimited responsibility. This, of course, encouraged investors to trust them, but it meant that it was only too possible to lose disastrously as well as to gain spectacularly.

The first evidence for Sienese long-distance trade comes in 1193, when a group of Piccolomini in Rome collectively sold a consignment of cloth to the abbey of Passignano. In 1209, we find the first recorded evidence for a commercial *societas*, founded by Buonsignore di Bernardo. It was a consortium of eight merchants who did a deal with the Aldobrandeschi counts of Grosseto and the commune of Siena to supply the city with salt, an important commodity. The counts, the consortium and the commune each got a third of the selling price. The Tolomei were not far behind: the first evidence for a Tolomei combining with non-family members for commercial purposes comes in 1223.

Another important development of the twelfth century was that other schools, such as medicine, grammar and rhetoric, added themselves to the existing college of professional canon lawyers. As we shall see, in the thirteenth century, these various teachers began to coalesce into a *studium*, or university.

4

SIENA,
CITY OF THE VIRGIN

I t was the evening of 3 September 1260 and the citizens of Siena were
in despair. Their city was surrounded by the superior forces of her
enemy, Florence. Despite the backing of Emperor Manfred and his
troops, defeat for Siena (and, thus, for the Ghibelline cause in Tuscany)
seemed unavoidable. A prominent Sienese, Buonaguida Lucari, led his
fellow citizens in procession to the cathedral, where he was met by the
bishop. Buonaguida laid the keys of the city on the main altar before an
image of the Virgin Mary, and addressed her thus, according to the early
fifteenth-century chronicler Paolo di Tommaso Montauri:

> Glorious Virgin, Queen of Heaven, I give and dedicate to you this city of
> Siena and all of its territory; and as a sign of this I place the keys to the city
> gates on your altar… I pray… that you guard this city, its surrounding lands,
> and its citizens from the hands of the arrant curs of Florence, and from all
> those who would occupy, oppress, and destroy her.[1]

Having officially donated the city of Siena to the Virgin, Buonaguida
led the bishop, priests and the citizenry in procession with the sacred
relics of the cathedral, including the painting before which the donation
ritual had been performed, and they wound their way through the
narrow streets of the entire city. That night, a white mist concealed the
Sienese camp, like the mantle of the Virgin – the 'Madonna of Mercy', in
which the Virgin is depicted sheltering a crowd of worshippers beneath
her cloak, is a familiar medieval image. The following day, the Sienese
met the Florentines at Montaperti, east of Siena. After a gruelling battle,
the Sienese defeated their enemy in an unexpected victory which was
attributed to the direct intervention of the Virgin.

This is how the story was told by the Sienese chroniclers of the
fifteenth century and later, though it may have a basis in fact. In
Constantinople, the icon of the Virgin Hodegetria (a representation of

ao ·τ ela cãpana si reggra
pbia del popolo uecchio ·τ
ni nellosi. Lasceremo di q
amo adire come ifiozeti
te sopza ifanesi dxe presono
co ·τ a quello di meccano ·τ a
desanesi ·τ puosonsi atoste
almonistero disanta petoz
o allantipozto delacittade
ui presso isu uno poggetto
si uedea alquanto delacitta

danno ·τ molti popolari ·τ ec
alloza feciono cattiua uista
ptema dxenõ fossero maggio
oza alafine rauegendosi pze
me · aladifensa contra itedes
quanti tedeschi usaro di si
rimasero mozti nel cãpo desi
mozti ·τ cetti tedeschi lansegn
oz anfredi auea lozo data di
ifiozetini lastrasenaro ptutt
poi lancrecaro afirenze facce

the Virgin which was highly influential on Sienese art) was processed around the streets of the city when it was threatened by the invasion of the Avars in AD 626, and in the thirteenth century the degree of contact between Siena and the Byzantine world could have made this a point of reference.[2] Gerald Parsons and Diana Webb are among the scholars who have argued for the substantive truth of the story, noting that the terms of submission for both Montalcino and Montepulciano after the victory at Montaperti describe the Virgin as *defensatrix* and *gubernatrix* (defender and governor) of Siena.[3] But whether or not it actually happened, the legend is still significant, because its developed form illustrates several central facts of Sienese civic life: the fusion of civic and religious ideals, fierce anti-Florentine sentiment and the central role of art in the definition and expression of Sienese civic identity. Another important feature of the myth of Montaperti is that it depicts a citizenry who, for much of their history, were notoriously riven by faction, as united and working together for the common good.[4]

Florence and Siena were on a collision course during the first half of the thirteenth century for reasons which went beyond economic and territorial rivalry: the run-up to the battle was a long one which involved international politics. Rome, naturally, was a Guelf city, since the Guelfs owed primary allegiance to the pope. Florence was also Guelf, and Siena lay between them. Consequently, the Holy Roman Emperors from Frederick II to Manfred perceived Siena, which was traditionally Ghibelline, as an essential support of their project of restoring the rights of the Holy Roman Empire in Italy. The Sienese were wary of opposing the pope, because of the immense profits to be turned from acting as papal bankers, but since they were committed to challenging Florentine ambitions in Tuscany, they considered the emperor more of a friend than not, and understood their value to him. Part of the Sienese strategy in the mid-thirteenth century for dealing with its larger and more powerful neighbour was to ally with one of the factions vying for control over Florence, on the principle of divide and rule, usually the Florentine Ghibellines. When the latter were exiled in 1258, Siena sheltered them.

On their side, Rome and Florence could also see the strategic significance of Siena, and understood that decisively defeating Siena would be the most effective way of weakening their enemies in Tuscany,

The Battle of Montaperti, from the chronicle of Giovanni Villani, illustrated by the workshop of Pacino da Bonaguida. Their shields show that the attackers are Sienese allies from Terni.

while, for Florence in particular, also offering considerable practical benefits. Throughout the spring and summer of 1260, both sides canvassed support from allies, raised funds and made preparations. The Sienese army included soldiers sent by every Ghibelline town in Italy, plus at least four hundred German knights sent by the Emperor Manfred. The total size of the army was between 15,000 and 20,000 men, which must have put an immense strain on the city's resources. The Guelfs, meanwhile, put together an army of perhaps double the size. They left Florence in August 1260, and made for Montalcino, which was under siege by the Sienese. Having liberated the town, they headed towards Siena, where they sat outside the walls and sent heralds to demand the city's surrender. After a couple of weeks of intense negotiation, during which the Salimbeni banking family shelled out for more German mercenaries, the city's metalworkers frantically made additional weaponry, and anyone not directly involved knelt in the churches praying, the Sienese decided to give battle, after dedicating the city to the Virgin.[5]

Siena puts itself under the protection of the Virgin (again), in a *biccherna* cover of 1483: Duccio's *Maestà* is visible in the background, covered by a curtain.

Leaving supernatural interventions to one side, the Sienese probably owed their victory to superior planning. Manfred's professional soldiers ambushed the Florentines, and, according to Dante, Florentine Ghibellines sabotaged their own army. The Ghibelline Bocca degli Abbati chopped off the hand of the Florentine standard-bearer, an act of treachery which earned him a spot in the lowest circle of Hell with the great traitors of history, according to the poet. Without a standard to follow, the Florentines fought without direction and the result was a bloodbath. Thousands and thousands of prisoners were taken to Siena, so many that the city, already crowded with borrowed warriors, had to pay for 472 guards and rent buildings around the city to house them.

The victorious Sienese then advanced on Florence, which was only saved because a Florentine Ghibelline called Farinata degli Uberti convinced his party not to destroy it: despite this heroic patriotism, Dante consigns him to Hell as well, since he was posthumously convicted of atheism. Montalcino also suffered for its resistance to Siena. However, the pope, Alexander IV, had his own weapon against Siena, in the form of excommunication. This is why the Sienese had been so wary of offending him, not least because excommunication had economic as well as spiritual implications. Alexander's successor, Urban IV, who

APREXENATIONE DELECHIAVI QVANDO TV I
QVATRO EMONTI SADVSSENO ADVNOM

QVESTE LENTRATE E LVSCITA DELLA GENERALE CABELLA DEL MANGNII
COMVNO DISIENA P'TEMPO DVNO AÑO INCOMICIATO ADI P DI DIGENAIO M
CCC LXXXII & FINITO ADI VLTIMO DI DICEBRE M.CCCC LXXXIII ALTE 3P
ELI SPECTRBILI HOMINI PAVOLO DILANDO ESBERGHIERI K E MIS ANGNI
ORBANO DEL TESTA GIOVANI DANTNI DINERI MARTINI ANTONIO DIMARI
PACINELLI GIOVANI DI IACOPO GHABRIELLI EXECVTORI
P LPMI SEI MESI & MISS SAVINO DIMEO DANT DIGHVIDO AN
TONI DIBARTA SPINELI BART CRISTOFANO BERTI BART DANTI
DIGHVELF EXECVTORI P LSECODI SEI MESI ANGNIOLO DIM
DIIOREZO SCRTORE & ANGNIOLO DIMEO DANGNIOLO DIGHI

COLLE DI VALDELSA

recognized the importance of Siena's banking companies, confirmed and even strengthened his predecessor's actions in 1261 by releasing their debtors from their obligations and threatening to confiscate their property in Rome. However, the Bonsignori were exempted from these sanctions because the papacy found them so useful. It is very clear, therefore, that the great victory of Montaperti, which delivered the whole of Tuscany apart from Lucca into the hands of the Emperor Manfred, did not, contrary to the legend, unite the citizens of Siena. It was papal patronage which allowed Sienese merchants to adventure as far as distant England, and the popes expected their bankers to further the current policy of the Holy See. This meant that the financiers who were making Siena rich were Guelfs in a Ghibelline city, and, from their point of view, the tremendous victory was an enormous embarrassment. Many of them went into exile.

One reason why the victory of Montaperti had no lasting effect is that economic warfare was effective, and the financial muscle of Siena was on the side of the pope. Therefore, when Urban IV decided to curb Manfred's power by assigning the kingdom of Sicily to the French king's younger brother, Charles of Anjou, the Tuscan banking houses united behind him and raised loans on the surety of church property. Both Urban and the financiers thus staked everything on Charles's victory, and won their bet, since he defeated and killed Manfred at Benevento in 1266.[6] With the Ghibelline cause thus left in disarray, Siena's mercantile community persuaded the rest of the citizens to make peace with the papacy, and there was a formal reconciliation with Florence and the Guelfs. But in 1269, the Sienese were persuaded to rejoin the Ghibelline cause, and went to war with Florence at the Battle of Colle di Val d'Elsa, where they were humiliatingly defeated. The following year, 1270, Siena was forced to join the majority of cities in the region and identify itself as Guelf. This Guelf alliance put Siena in touch with Naples and France for the first time.

The Ghibellines were led by Provenzano Salvani, who had led Siena's forces to victory at Montaperti, but a mere nine years later the city could not afford to remember this. Not only were the Sienese Ghibellines forced out of power, the Salvani family palace was destroyed, and left as a prominent heap of rubble for a good seventy years – though the spoil heap was raided by the Tolomei, who salvaged limestone blocks

The Siege of Colle di Val d'Elsa: a defeat for the Ghibellines, cancelling the victory of Montaperti, and the end of Ghibelline hopes in Tuscany.

for their own new palace.[7] The extinction of the old imperial family of the Hohenstaufen, and the ascension of the Habsburgs to the imperial throne in 1274, made Guelf/Ghibelline partisanship increasingly irrelevant, since the Habsburgs were papal allies. In a sense, the two positions became something like political parties. Ghibellinism, with its links to the emperor, represented the interests of the nobility, while Guelfism promoted the aims of the increasingly powerful mercantile elite, who were becoming more powerful than ever, since the new king of Sicily was followed to his domain by a goodly selection of the Tuscan merchants and bankers who had been his creditors, and benefited mightily from access to one of the wealthiest and best-organized states in thirteenth-century Europe.

At this time, Siena was still governed by 'consuls' who were local aristocrats, a form of rule which had developed in the twelfth century. It was problematic, because it was hard for consuls to resist using political office holding to settle scores with other noble families. Magnate families were also perfectly capable of allying with families from enemy cities for family advantage, and it was not unknown for those who sat on civic councils to sabotage city projects if such plans might benefit rivals, since fundamentally, for aristocrats, family interests came first. In an attempt to halt the scheming and violence that marked the early consulships, Siena followed the lead of neighbouring communes and looked for an outside party who could administrate the city's affairs without possessing allegiance to any one family or group within the city. This outsider was called the Podestà (a word which simply means 'power'). He was normally a non-Sienese, the hope being that he would have had no stake in local feuds and intrigues. Government by Podestà commended itself to early Italian communes, because it reconciled two opposing needs: a strong authority, who was at the same time impartial and detached from factional concerns, but responsive to the desires and opinions of leading citizens. Outsiders of good reputation and known ability were approached and asked to serve, usually for a year, with powers and duties carefully defined beforehand. He would be head of the commune, guardian of the law and the highest judge, master of the bureaucracy, and chairman of the various councils, defender of the internal peace of the city and commander-in-chief should war break out. He brought with him a staff which included professional soldiers and a number of judges, thereby ensuring that both policing and judging were carried out by people who answered to the Podestà and not to one of the city's factions.

Siena's first Podestà was Orlando Malapresa, who came from Lucca, and served in 1206. By the turn of the thirteenth century, power within Siena was balanced between this hired foreign official and an oligarchy made up of elected citizen representatives from the city's wealthiest, mostly noble families. Although the employment of a Podestà addressed one inherent civic problem, other imbalances of power in civic administration soon became evident. While nobles enjoyed exclusive privilege in the earliest councils, there were non-nobles who were amassing substantial wealth through banking and trading, and they were not content to be excluded. Conflicts between the nobles and the *popolani*, or non-noble party, marked the first half of the thirteenth century and this civic strife seemed certain to undermine any kind of communal identity. Several steps were therefore taken to accommodate non-nobles, including the creation of new offices and separate councils, but the *popolani* were not satisfied until an entirely new government was defined. This new compromise government of twelve nobles and twelve *popolani*, which was established in 1233 and lasted until 1270, was called the Twenty-Four.

In political and economic terms, the 'Golden Age' of the Sienese Republic began with the magistracy of the Twenty-Four, which marked both the entrance of the *popolani* into the city government and the establishment of republican political institutions in Siena. The era of the Twenty-Four also saw Siena, which had become one of the most important commercial and banking centres in Europe and the centre of imperial influence in Tuscany, challenge Florence for economic and political pre-eminence in the region.

The new government continued to worry about the power of the aristocracy. While their wealth and control over their followers ensured that the magnates remained a major force in the city, the Twenty-Four were determined to drive them out of political power. A constitution of 1274 states that only 'good merchants of the Guelf party' could sit on city councils. In 1277, the government re-formed as a committee of Thirty-Six. A new social conflict became central to civic administration, as this new oligarchy of merchants abruptly turned its back on Siena's traditional Ghibelline allegiances, instead aligning itself with Florence and the other Guelf cities. The Thirty-Six had to figure out what to do with the city's once powerful, and still power-hungry, noble families. Their solution was to legislate them out of power in a series of measures documented in statutes from 1277 onwards. These laws were explicit attempts to limit the power of fifty-three Sienese families known as the *casati*. Siena was far from unique in enacting anti-magnate laws, since many other cities had similar problems. In fact, Sienese laws against the noble *casati* were less punitive than those in other cities. As the medievalist Daniel Waley observes, 'Members of these families were now banned from membership of the Thirty-Six, but they were not to suffer the other legal disadvantages which characterized the "anti-magnate" legislation of many of the Italian communes.'[8] The *casati* still provided Siena with war captains, ambassadors, castellans and judges, and they intermarried with the wealthiest of the new mercantile elite, so they had a big enough role in the city for them to be content, most of the time, with this limitation on their civic participation.[9]

Banning an entire class from power shows that despite attempts to balance power between nobles and non-nobles, there remained a sharp and often violent division within Sienese society. Though civic administration may have been officially in the hands of wealthy merchants, they still felt threatened by the power of the nobles, and probably with reason, since the Thirty-Six lasted only ten years. After the demise of their regime, the city was ruled from 1280 until 1286 by another explicitly compromise government, the Fifteen. The city was looking for a magic formula, and in 1287 they came very close to finding one. A new merchant-class oligarchy was instituted, the Nine, which would be the city's most stable and effective regime, lasting from 1287 to 1355. Perhaps the biggest difference between the Nine and its predecessors is that, instead of trying to erase the presence of nobility in the city, the Nine embraced the traditions and symbols of wealth and aristocracy in their own way. The Nine promoted themselves as proud representatives of a *mezze gente*, or middle class, neither noble nor *popolani*. Although the members of the Nine were not descendants of Siena's early aristocracy, they invested in the symbols and trappings of nobility. They also cooperated with the aristocracy, and allowed certain nobles to hold office and participate in civic administration so long as these individuals swore to uphold civic values above their own familial alliances.

Despite the inability of its government to contain interclass strife and faction, it was during the thirteenth century that little Siena became a major economic power. Sienese merchants travelled north to what was then the hub of international trade, the great fairs of Champagne. The Tolomei were particularly associated with the fairs, where they combined banking with commerce, exchanging money and making loans, but also buying fine cloth, spices and other commodities to take back to Siena. They also took Sienese goods for export: wax, pepper and spices, the pepper and spices presumably acquired by trade with the Mediterranean. Since Sienese goldsmiths were beginning to make a name for themselves, and small, valuable items were eminently suited to long-distance trade, they perhaps also took some of their work.

The Sienese travelled far: Sienese merchants appear in records from England as early as 1227, and they also had a strong presence in southern France.[10] Though Mediterranean commerce was dominated by Venice, Genoa and Pisa, all coastal cities, the Sienese made attempts to break into the lucrative Eastern trade. Sienese merchants had warehouses and sizeable businesses in Venice, Genoa and Pisa, and in July 1268, Conrad II, king of Jerusalem, conceded exemptions from taxes and privileges of commerce in Acre to the Sienese. This regularized an existing situation, since Sienese had traded in Acre earlier in the century, but stealthily, by representing themselves as citizens of Pisa, which had trade privileges.[11] This was not a major contribution to Sienese prosperity, but is important in another way: as Anne Derbes has shown, by the mid-thirteenth century not only was Byzantine art influencing Sienese painters, Sienese painters were influencing artists in the Middle East.

overleaf
The ruined Abbey of Monte Galgano, home to a Cistercian community which exercised a huge influence on both the life and the architecture of medieval Siena.

It is hard to make a firm distinction between commerce and banking in the thirteenth century, as the activities of the Tolomei in Champagne make clear. But Siena was one of the first Italian cities to move into banking as such, a burgeoning industry that they came to dominate over the course of the century, as the personal bankers of both popes and emperors. The city's increasing wealth was actually earned by individual Sienese banking families, such as the Tolomei, Salimbeni and Piccolomini, who were appointed by the church to collect and transfer tithes and other papal taxes from Europe to Rome. For almost the whole of the century, Sienese were the mercantile and banking aristocracy of

Europe.[12] Papal taxation expanded considerably in the course of the thirteenth century, in ways that offered new opportunities to bankers. For example, bishops had to pay a tax to the pope before taking full possession of their sees: they might well need to borrow money in order to do so. Initially, the popes had employed the order of Templars when they needed to deposit, transfer, loan or exchange money, but in the thirteenth century they realized that Italian bankers were more reliable and efficient, which brought huge profits to the Bonsignori and Tolomei in particular. As Robert L. Reynolds observed of these early entrepreneurs, 'a house could grow big on ordinary business, but only on princely business could it grow mighty'.[13] One special advantage the Bonsignori and Tolomei had, besides their experience and organization, was that Siena produced silver, then the currency of exchange. Much of the movement of money was in the form of promissory notes rather than coinage, but sooner or later the actual bullion had to be produced. The Bonsignoris' association, founded in 1209, was the foremost banking institution in Europe, and took the name of the Gran Tavola. Through the thirteenth century, the society established agents in all parts of Europe, engaging in banking on an unprecedented scale. In 1289, details of a reorganization revealed that it controlled a capital of 35,000 gold florins that year, while popes, emperors, kings, barons, merchants and cities were among its clients.

Though twelfth-century Siena had been tiny, as the city became more prosperous in the thirteenth century it began to assume its present form. One religious institution outside the city itself was nonetheless of great importance to it. This was the Cistercian abbey of San Galgano, founded on the site of the hermitage of a penitent knight, Galgano, in the valley of the Merse around 1200. The Cistercians brought with them a French Gothic tradition of architecture which was influential on both the secular and ecclesiastical buildings of Siena. Another Cistercian tradition was the sophisticated management of water, and the monks brought another strand of expertise in hydraulic engineering which was enormously useful to the city. They seem to have helped the Sienese with the refurbishment and construction of the *bottini*, the underground channels which brought water to Siena, and the city fountains. By the beginning of the fourteenth century, several Cistercians had served as *Operaio*, or chief administrator, at the cathedral, and many more had taken charge of the city's finances as *Camerlingo*, or treasurer, of the Biccherna and the Gabella, the two major financial offices of the medieval city. These roles needed men with a clear head and a mathematical training, and Cistercians were chosen because of their honesty, impartiality and competence.[14]

The first wave of building in Siena itself was down to the church: the medieval church always set store by building to the glory of God. In addition to the Duomo, the Dominicans, Franciscans and others began to build churches in the city. The rise of these mendicant orders is a major feature of the thirteenth century. They practised a new form of religious life. In principle, they lived by begging for charity, and they concentrated their activities in towns, whereas monks, such as the Cistercians, lived in rural communities and supported themselves by agriculture. They were known as friars (from Latin 'frater', brother). The followers of St Dominic (d.1221) came to be called the Dominicans, and had a principal focus on preaching against heresy. In time they did come to accumulate wealth, but this was often in the form of income from donated lands, rather than direct ownership of property. While St Dominic (Domingo de Guzman) was a Spaniard, the other great mendicant order was native to Umbria. St Francis of Assisi (1182–1226) was the son of a rich merchant. After a self-indulgent youth, he turned his back on the world and made a vow of poverty. Like Dominic, he was an immensely successful preacher, but he was not so much concerned with heresy as with the imitation of Christ. The Franciscan order was founded in 1210, and in 1212 St Francis of Assisi paid a visit to Siena: we are told that 'there was great enmity between the People and the nobles, and he caused peace and unity to be made among them'. Both orders were enormously popular. In 1233, the Dominican John of Vicenza and the Franciscan Anthony of Padua were so successful as preachers that they created a wave of religious fervour through northern Italy, and many cities (briefly) committed themselves to a policy of peace.

In Siena, as soon as the news of the death of St Francis came to the city, two years before his canonization, the commune decreed that a church should be built in his honour. This was completed in 1255, though the present San Francesco, which superseded it, was begun in 1326 and only completed in 1475. Like St Francis, St Dominic also visited Siena, where he impressed a member of the Malavolti family who gave him part of his land on the ridge called Camporegio to build the first Dominican church in Tuscany.[15] This is now the crypt of San

Domenico, and was under construction by 1220, before St Dominic's death. It was replaced in the thirteenth century by a more impressive building which took two centuries to complete: the campanile was in place by 1340, but the whole building was not finished till the end of the fifteenth century.[16] These churches played a major role in the life of the city. Many of the leading confraternities were directly attached to one or the other, and family altars in both churches indicate the close attachment between leading Sienese families and the friars.

The other great builders were the aristocracy, who were not called *casati* (house-holders) for nothing: the possession of castles, or fortified palaces, was central to their self-perception and status, and their adventures in banking gave them the necessary wealth. The first recorded tower in Siena is that of the Gallerani, which they were given permission to construct in 1186. The historian Lauro Martines has observed that 1160–1260 was the great age of tower-building in Italy, peaking around 1200.[17] The first of the noble families to create a 'great palace' in the city were the Tolomei, who built a fortress for themselves in 1208.

The Tolomei and Gallerani were rapidly followed by other nobles, since a tower was a testament to rank and privilege: only noblemen were legally permitted to build them. The purpose of the towers was mostly defensive – until the development of effective cannon fire, they were militarily useful – but they were also status symbols, and expressions of family pride, so once one noble family had started to build, the rest followed, unwilling to be left behind.[18] The urban strongholds of the nobility were each constructed around a small courtyard, with a defensive exterior wall with few doors or windows (hence the courtyards, which were needed as lightwells). Increasingly, these aristocratic townhouses sprouted towers, which loomed above the tiny timber or wattle-and-daub houses of ordinary citizens, rising to a height of fifty or sixty metres. The houses of the nobility clustered in the centre of the city, along the main thoroughfares, along the ridges of Siena's three hills. Thirteenth-century Siena must have looked like San Gimignano: an eighteenth-century Sienese antiquary called Giovanni Antonio Pecci found references to fifty-six different towers.[19] As late as 1526, a contemporary painting of the Battle of Porta Camollia depicts a city still bristling with them.

Each tower was owned by a *consorteria* of anywhere between ten and forty sworn associates, all men of the same family and descended from a common male ancestor, who swore a group oath to support one another. When the sons of the founding members came of age, at fifteen, they were inducted into the society by swearing the oath. The agreement might well include swearing not to marry into certain specified enemy families, a sanction which sheds light on the plot of *Romeo and Juliet*. The earliest version of the Romeo and Juliet story, *Mariotto and Ganozza*, was set in Siena, not Verona: it is a novella by Masuccio Salernitano written in 1476.[20]

The members of the *consorteria* would live in the immediate vicinity of their tower, so Siena had a 'Tolomei neighbourhood', a 'Piccolomini neighbourhood', and so on. The towers symbolized a family's control over their particular region of the city, and were used to dominate the locality. For example, the commune saw the need for a second street in the Terzo di Camollia besides the Via Francigena, essentially because of the noblemen's houses on the main road: 'The men from the other Terzi who have to go to Camollia neither can, nor wish, to pass in front of the houses of certain nobles.' This suggests that within each fortress an eye was kept trained on the street, and if an enemy or his followers put in an appearance, retainers would rush out and beat him up.[21] Because palaces and towers were of great practical and symbolic value to the aristocracy, if the commune needed to discipline rebellious nobles they destroyed their houses. In 1270, all the houses of the Incontri were either burned or pulled down. It also became customary to add insult to injury by using the rubble and building stone of demolished houses for municipal purposes.[22]

In this phase of the city's history, the municipality had not yet begun building imposing structures on its own account. Council meetings were held in churches, usually San Pellegrino or San Cristoforo, which were conveniently central, and sometimes in the cathedral. Secular palaces, such as that of the Tolomei, were rented for municipal use, and officials such as the Podestà were found lodgings in others.[23] Max Grossman has argued that the enormous Tolomei palace, built by one of the leading Guelf families, was designed from the start as dual-function, a private residence on the upper floors and a government building at ground level. The Tolomei began building just after Guelfs took over the city in 1270: they had owned an earlier palace, which had been destroyed under the Ghibelline regime of the Twenty-Four. The General Council of the

Nine occupied the ground floor of the Tolomei palace from 1275 to 1284, when they finally acquired their own premises.[24]

The towers gradually vanished from Siena's skyline, though it took four centuries for the last but one of them to come down. In the thirteenth century, some were destroyed on the orders of the city as a political punishment, while others were lost due to the policy of destroying houses to contain an outbreak of fire. In 1300, the tower of the Incontrati family collapsed onto neighbouring buildings: nine of the Incontrati themselves died, and the total death toll was over seventy.[25] Unlike the municipal buildings of the fourteenth century, which were of brick, the palaces of the nobility were built of stone, so in the mid-sixteenth century the Spanish garrison used some of them as quarries for building stone for the fortress they constructed, while an earthquake in 1798 brought down others. But the tower of the Ballati still looms from behind the Piazza dell'Indipendenza, and the footings of the tower of the Forteguerri stand on the corner of Piazza Postierla and the Via di Città. Even if the other towers no longer reach for the skies, a good few thirteenth-century tower bases and palaces still survive in modified form: the mid-thirteenth-century Palazzo Rinuccini is in Via Cecco Angiolieri, and the bases of the medieval Accarigi and Piccolomini towers are in the Costarella dei Barbieri and at the corner of Via Pantaneto and Via Follonica respectively. As this suggests, the commune, which had already successfully reduced the bishop to a purely religious leader, was nibbling away at the power of the urban magnates.

However, another trick the urban aristocracy had up their sleeve was the church itself. Apart from a single decade, the bishopric of Siena was held by a member of the Malavolti for most of a century, from 1282 to 1371. Because of the Malavoltis' own interests in the city's stability, they helped the Nine to retain power and legitimacy.[26] An instance of this is the attempted coup incited by the Tolomei. Men of the three *terzi* met for an organized fist fight in the Campo on the Sunday before Carnival in 1325: these ritual battles were a regular part of civic life, which both expressed the factional tensions of the medieval city and sought to give them a safe outlet.[27] The two other *terzi* turned on Città, and the combatants began arming themselves: before long, there was a pitched battle which continued even after mounted soldiers waded in to try and restore peace, while more and more came to join the fight, wielding crossbows and other weapons. Since the people were defying civic authority, the regime itself was in danger. According to a contemporary chronicler, Bishop Donosdeo Malavolti 'summoned the priests and friars of the city and, with a cross borne before them, they entered the Campo and passed through the middle of the fighting... At the bishop's entreaties, and those of the priests and friars, the fighters began to let themselves be separated so that the fighting ceased.'[28] Similarly five years earlier, when an earthquake struck Siena in 1320, it was the bishop who calmed the city, holding special masses and leading civic processions until the tremors subsided and order was restored.[29] The cathedral canonry was dominated by members of old families, so the Duomo was pretty much a *casati* enclave. This had a definitely positive aspect for the city, since it meant that the bishops were local men, not outsiders appointed by the pope, but also goes some way to explaining why most medieval Sienese seem to have been more attached to one or other of the friars' churches than to the Duomo, even though all civic ritual took place there.

Another institution which was clearly flourishing in the thirteenth century was the university, though it was not yet called a *studium generale*, since in February 1348 the commune granted its representatives authority to spend whatever sums proved necessary for obtaining papal recognition for the Sienese university.[30] Nearly a hundred years earlier, on 26 December 1240, Ildebrandino Cacciaconti, then the Podestà of Siena, signed a decree imposing a tax on citizens who rented rooms to students. This tax was used to pay the salaries of the teachers. It was further supported when, in 1252, Pope Innocent IV declared both its teachers and students completely immune from taxes and forced labour levied on their persons or property by the city of Siena. Moreover, the commune exempted teachers of law and Latin from military service and teachers of Latin were also excused from citizen duties as night watchmen. By the early fourteenth century, there were five teachers of Latin, logic and law, and two doctors of medicine. A Portuguese doctor named Pietro Juliani who taught medicine in Siena from 1245 to 1250 later rose to become Pope Giovanni XXI. Maestro Tebaldo, a Sienese, was teaching grammar in Siena from the 1240s. He was described as 'the living source of the grammar faculty', and early in the 1260s made a strategic withdrawal to Arezzo, since the commune had to coax him back by offering him a salary (it was normal at this time for teachers to take money directly from their students). A Maestro Fantino joined him in teaching grammar in the 1270s, and by 1278 Maestro Guidotto da Bologna was teaching rhetoric. Increasingly, these teachers were supported on public funds.[31]

As Siena prospered, we begin to get glimpses of its people. The first faces we can see are from the thirteenth century. The most important office in thirteenth-century Siena was the Biccherna, the principal department of finance and administration. The monks of San Galgano were frequently asked to serve as treasurers, presumably because they were considered to be skilled, disinterested and incorruptible. Don Ugo, a monk of San Galgano, chose to inaugurate what would become a distinctive Sienese tradition: the large folio pages on which the Biccherna officials entered their accounts were bound and cased in wooden covers at the end of the financial year, the well-known *tavolette di Biccherna*. Don Ugo took it into his head to ask Gilio di Pietro to paint his portrait on the front in 1258, wearing his white Cistercian habit and sitting looking through the accounts at an elegant red desk. Decorating the year's *tavoletta* became a custom: they sometimes feature a portrait, but more often they show a group of men at work, or a notable event of that year, such as the inauguration of Pius II as pope.

The life of the Blessed Andrea Gallerani, painted on the door of a cupboard which contained his relics.

The second Sienese we can put a face to is the Blessed Andrea Gallerani, who died in 1251, the founder of the Misericordia hospital. A nobleman by birth, he murdered a man in a fit of rage, but subsequently dedicated himself to a life of penance. Guido da Siena painted the shutters of his reliquary cupboard in the church of Santa Maria della Scala a decade or so later, between 1260 and 1290, in which he depicted the saint several times (reliquary cupboards were large, wall-mounted structures built into the sacristy of a church where powerful relics in their often extremely valuable containers could be stored securely: many of them displayed elaborate painted programmes on their doors). In one painting, the Blessed Andrea extends a hand to welcome a group of barefoot pilgrims to the Hospital of Santa Maria della Scala, where he had founded a confraternity, and, in another, he kneels in front of a crucifix with his rosary beads in his hand. An odd macabre detail is that he has a noose round his neck, so if he falls asleep, he would choke himself and wake up; a curious aid to devotion.

Despite the religious zeal which is evident in much of the city's life, the names thirteenth-century Sienese gave their children are unexpectedly

secular. In 'the City of the Virgin', few baby girls were named Maria. 'Gemma' was the most popular name for a daughter, followed by 'Benvenuta'. 'Fiore' was common, as were 'Divizia', 'Diamante' and 'Riccha': Jewel, Welcome, Flower, Wealth, Diamond, Riches.[32] Siena was prospering, and the girls' names reflect this. Most boys were named after the apostles, 'Giovanni' and 'Giacomo' in particular, or bore names chosen with the hope of conferring a blessing on their owner, such as 'Buonaventura', 'Benvenuto', 'Benincasa'. The parents of Siena's future merchants and bankers evidently considered that their boys needed all the luck they could get.

The poets of the late thirteenth century give us some glimpses of Siena's *jeunesse dorée*. One bizarre manifestation of Siena's increasing wealth is the 'Brigata Spendereccia', the Company of Spendthrifts, who eventually spent their way to Hell, according to Dante (*Inferno*, XXIX). Foreshadowing today's *Rich Kids of Instagram*, they were led, and perhaps instigated, by one Niccolò Bonsignori. Because they are mentioned by Dante, they are discussed by his commentators, some of whom say that there were twelve of them. They were the children of the rich and privileged, in a society where the Franciscans were preaching holy poverty; another rich young Sienese, a near contemporary of the Company, Giovanni Colombani, heeded the message, abandoned his wealth, 'espoused Most High Poverty' and wandered through the city and country, preaching a gospel of love. His followers formed an order called the Gesuati. But the young people who formed the Company reacted in the opposite direction to the double messages offered them by their society: they rejected penitent asceticism, but they also revolted against the values of their parents, and scorned the hard work and discipline of their merchant banker fathers. Instead, they embraced unabashed hedonism. They clubbed together and bought a villa in Siena, the 'Consuma', on Via Garibaldi (the site is now occupied by an estate agent), where they lived together and were reputed to enjoy every luxury they were capable of imagining, with the avowed intention of spending all their money in an orgy of conspicuous consumption. A Dante commentator, Benvenuto da Imola, claims that in twenty months of sustained extravagance they wasted 216,000 florins. Wild stories were told about them; that they had their horses shod with silver and threw gold plates out of the window. Eventually, they succeeded in reducing themselves to poverty, and had to trail back to the real world and survive as best they could.

Another unsatisfactory son of privilege was one of the city's poets, Cecco Angiolieri. It is hard to know how autobiographical his writing is, and how much of his splenetic versification is a pose, but, like the stories of the Brigade, his oeuvre is suggestive of intergenerational conflict in late thirteenth-century Siena. He was born in a house which still stands in what is now the Via Cecco Angiolieri, opposite the Palazzo Rinuccini. He seems to have been the ne'er-do-well son of a wealthy banking family, and by his way of it, his father, who intensely disapproved of a love affair he was pursuing with a leatherworker's daughter called Becchina, attempted to pressure him into marrying a highly suitable young lady who talked all the time. He responded with a furious poem. 'S'i' fosse foco, arderéi 'l mondo; s'i' fosse vento, lo tempesterei':

> If I were fire, I'd torch the whole world;
> if I were wind, I'd whirl it all to hell;
> if water, why not drown it? Might as well.
> If I were God, I'd drop it down the void.
> If I were pope, I'd be a happy boy
> When every Christian plundered and rebelled...
> If I were Death, I'd soon track down my dad;
> if Life, be gone! I'd run like mad from him...
> If I were Cecco (so I am, have been)
> I'd choose young ladies who could gladden me,
> and leave the older ones for other men [Brett Foster's translation].[33]

This reads like a young man's tantrum in verse, and only the gleam of humour in the last three lines redeems the ugliness of Cecco's call for his parents' death. Even if there is an element of pose here, his father's meanness is one of his principal topics as a poet. At the least, he was clearly indifferent to embarrassing or distressing his parents. They were not, to be fair, very lovely people: his father was a member of a minor mendicant order which had essentially been set up as a tax dodge, the sort of thing which in Dante's view would have sent you straight down to the Circle of Hypocrites in Hell.

Others of his verses are about his relationship with his girlfriend Becchina, who is very far from being a refined and otherworldly damsel like Petrarch's Laura or Dante's Beatrice, and perhaps gives us a tiny glimpse into the world of Siena's artisans. She's a tough girl, by his account, since he shows her giving at least as good as she gets:

> Cecco: 'You're hiding your real feelings.'
>   Becchina: 'Go to hell!'
> Cecco: 'You don't really mean that!'
>   Becchina: 'Why wouldn't I?'
> Cecco: 'Because you're sweet.'
>   Becchina: 'But not to you. Nice try...'

Another of his poems is a direct challenge to the friars' call for holy poverty, and most contemporaries, in that world of tight-knit families, would have found it shocking:

> Preach what you will
> Florins are the best of kin
> Blood brothers and cousins true,
> Father, mother, sons, and daughters too;
> Kinfolk of that sort no one regrets,
> Also horses, mules, and beautiful dress...
> Florins clear your eyes and give you fires,
> Turn to facts all your desires
> And into all the world's vast possibilities...[34]

Cecco appears in several legal documents, not as a model citizen. He is fined for being absent without leave while on military service, several times, for failing to respect Siena's curfew, and on one occasion cited for wounding a man called Dino di Bernardino. And though his much-maligned father predeceased him, he died in debt. All the same, he was a friend of Dante, whom he teased, and his coarse, comic talent was recognized by posterity. And there is something else to note about this poem. In 1252, Florence was the first city to mint a gold coin, the florin. Very soon after that, Italy was on the gold standard, which meant a poor lookout for Siena, with its silver currency.

Other young contemporaries lived elegant lives without being as self-defeating as the Company of Spendthrifts. The poet Folgóre di San Gimignano left poems on the amusements proper to each month, and the occupations for each day of the week, dedicated to what he refers to as 'a noble and courteous brigade' of friends in Siena: it sounds as if the Sienese tendency to form associations, still evident in the city's *contrade*, was already well established by 1300. His sonnet for January is a splendid evocation of comfort and aristocratic ease.

> In January I give you
> a hall with fires of dry grass burning,
> bedrooms and beds with the most beautiful furnishings,
> sheets of silk and blankets of fur,
>
> confitures, sweets and sparkling wine,
> clothes of silk from Douai and of wool from Arras;
> and in this way may you remain sheltered,
> whether sirocco or libeccio or tramontane may blow.
>
> May you go outside sometimes during the day,
> to throw balls of beautiful white snow
> at the damsels around you;
>
> and when the company is tired,
> all may return to the hall
> and may the noble brigade rest.[35]

His sonnets paint a word-picture reminiscent of a verdure tapestry; of well-dressed and handsome young men setting out to hunt, mounted on fine horses, with hawks on their wrists, and hounds gambolling at the horses' heels, or seated by a fountain with their girlfriends, singing and listening to music.

5

THE
DEVELOPMENT
OF THE
COUNTRYSIDE

The territory controlled by Siena was extremely diverse. It included much good farmland, but also the malarial swamps of the Maremma, the mountainous region round Monte Amiata and the badlands of the Crete Senesi, thus eloquently described by Iris Origo: 'long ridges of low, bare clay hills – the crete senesi – ran down towards the valley, dividing the landscape in to a number of steep, dried-up little water-sheds. Treeless and shrubless but for some tufts of broom, these corrugated ridges formed a lunar landscape, pale and inhuman.'[1] We shall return to the Crete Senesi in a moment.

overleaf
Monte Amiata: the most significant mountain in Sienese territory, home to a distinctive community which exploited the resources of its wooded slopes.

The area round Siena itself, the Masse, has long been intensively farmed, with fields of wheat interspersed with vineyards, olive trees and patches of oak woods for pasturing pigs, gathering firewood and making lime. While earlier in the Middle Ages the emphasis was on wheat production wherever possible, by the fifteenth century peasants were required to plant four fruit trees and four olive trees each year if their holdings were large enough, reflecting the increasing diversity of food production after the Black Death.[2] Every inch of ground was used. Other crops were grown around the olive trees, because working the ground around olives conserved water as well as producing food. Sheep might also be grazed, and oxen, since the latter were essential as draft animals, though little land could be spared for their pasture. Instead, they might get coarse grains such as sorghum, tree leaves, vine shoots and other pruning refuse, and the grass growing along drainage ditches.[3] The Italophile writer and sportsman Peter Beckford observed in the 1780s that 'pasture in Tuscany is so scarce that not a blade of grass is left uncropt, nor a bank on the ditches that is not fed by cattle led in a string, by a horse tied by the leg, or by sheep as tame as dogs, and ragged as colts'.[4] This

would have been just as true three hundred years earlier, since the land encircling the city was both fertile, and particularly valuable because of the easy access to the urban market.

We get a glimpse of fifteenth-century life in the Masse from two little account books kept by a peasant named Benedetto del Massarizia from 1450 to 1502. He was one of the wealthiest men in his small community of Montalbuccio, and probably one of the most enterprising. He owned a real bed, with a good mattress bought from a wool merchant, and a chest decorated with inlay (though it took him nine years to pay off his debt for this furniture), and he had some smart clothes, including a pair of red stockings and a belt with silver and gold buckles.[5] He married Mariana di Chele in 1438, and when she died twenty-one years later, he married Giovanna, who ended up leaving him. He had a family of five boys and two girls by these two wives, and his affairs were extremely complicated, since he both owned land and worked for others as a sharecropper. For a man such as Benedetto, working a sharecropped farm provided him with income insurance. It was often preferable to renting, since if his crops failed or were looted by soldiers, he still only owed the landlord half of what was left rather than a fixed amount, an interesting sidelight on the debate as to whether sharecropping was exploitative. However, in 1477 he chose to rent a farm belonging to a Sienese church, the Margione, which brought him up against one of Siena's most notable personalities, Alberto Aringhieri, the *Operaio* of Siena Cathedral, when he failed to pay all of what he owed. Duccio Balestracci, who discovered these documents, writes, 'at the conclusion of his labyrinth of debts and engagements, Benedetto managed to pull out and not lose his lands... Contrary to every expectation, when Benedetto bet against urban capital, he won.'[6]

Benedetto was generous as well as wily. He helped out other members of his family, looking after his widowed mother, and his brother's widow and children. He was also lucky, because he had only two daughters, and daughters could be calamitous. His cousin Giovanni started from a similar position, but was much less well off, because, as well as three sons, he and his wife had eleven girls. Eleven dowries on top of all the other problems of life pushed him into debt, and he died in financial difficulties, leaving his three sons a pittance.

In the late Middle Ages, Monte Amiata was quite densely populated, far more so than it is now. Its vegetation was divided into distinct zones: there were orchards, vineyards and fields planted with cereals at the bottom, chestnuts halfway up, which were not natural forest, but carefully managed and maintained woods, and beech trees at the top. All of this was useful, and was exploited. The population was concentrated in *castelli* which circled the mountain at altitudes of 600–800 metres. The people could not produce enough cereals, or wine, to meet their own needs. Because the soil was poor, the cereals they grew were primitive wheats, emmer and einkorn, which have grains surrounded by tough hulls. They need to be pounded to remove these before the grain can be ground.[7] Though labour-intensive to prepare, they are considerably hardier than wheat as such, and so worth the effort. Additionally, chestnuts were a major resource for the people of the mountain. The trees produce enormous numbers of nuts. These were harvested and dried over a low, cool fire for two or three weeks, after which both the outer husk and inner skin could be easily removed: 'what remained after a slight winnowing was a hard, butter-coloured, extremely durable nut that weighed only two-thirds what it did when fresh, could keep over two years, but still contained the excellent nutrition it had originally.'[8] Most of the people lived off the forest: shepherds and swineherds pastured their animals, typically grazing sheep in chestnut woods, since the nuts were needed for human consumption, and pigs in oak or beech woods, where they were not competing with the peasants (people did sometimes eat acorns, but only as a last resort). Woodcutters and charcoal burners availed themselves directly of the trees, as did woodworkers. There were also many blacksmiths: Monte Amiata was rich in minerals, and iron ore was being smelted there in blast furnaces by the mid-fourteenth century. Mountain rivers provided hydraulic power which was used to operate hammers and bellows. By the fifteenth century, these metalworkers included gunsmiths.[9]

Also on Monte Amiata was the great abbey of San Salvatore, founded in 743, and by the Middle Ages one of the richest and most powerful religious communities in Tuscany. Since it was surrounded by woodland, the monks raised a lot of pigs, and produced cured pork products for the market. They also created one of most important monastic libraries in Italy from before the year 1100.[10] For a time, it housed the famous Codex Amiatinus, the earliest surviving complete manuscript of the Latin Bible, created in Northumbria around 700 and carried to Rome as a gift from Abbot Ceolfrid of Wearmouth-Jarrow to

Pope Gregory II in 716. It was listed among the abbey's relics in 1036, but there is no way of knowing how it got there. The volumes the monks produced themselves were decorated de luxe products, with magnificent painting and elaborate initials in various styles, which feature 'portraits' of Moses, Ezra, Gregory, Bede, Paul the Deacon, Alcuin and other authors.[11] This was made easier for them since minium, the mercuric oxide which medieval scribes used to make red ink, was to be found on Monte Amiata itself.[12]

Between Monte Amiata and the coastal town of Talamone, which the Sienese were hoping to develop into a port, lay the Maremma, a vast alluvial plain threaded by many waterways which in some areas merged into marshes and stagnant pools. In the distant past, the Etruscans had drained the region and settled it quite intensively, but in the centuries after the fall of the Roman empire, much of it had reverted to swamp. In Etruscan times there had been a marine saltwater lake, Lake Prile, at the mouth of the Ombrone, which was a useful fishing ground for their settlements at Vetulonia and Roselle. It progressively silted up, and by the Middle Ages had become stagnant marshland. Dante used the woods of the Maremma as a model for the forest where the souls of the Suicides were gathered, in the seventh circle of Hell. Other areas of the Maremma were good pastureland, or scrub dominated by Spanish broom, juniper and blackthorn, and woodlands, principally chestnuts and oaks of various kinds, as we have seen, excellent pasture for pigs. Despite its fertility, the Maremma was much less densely populated than Monte Amiata, because its stagnant marshes were a breeding ground for malaria, and it was extremely unhealthy. For centuries, the people suffered severely from the ravages of the disease, and life expectancy was very low. Malaria was still common in the Maremma at the beginning of the Second World War.[13] The only communities of any size in the Middle Ages were Massa Marittima, the principal mining centre of southern Tuscany, which had more than a thousand inhabitants between 1200 and 1400, and Grosseto. Conquered by the Sienese in the thirteenth century, Grosseto prospered in the first half of the fourteenth century and the population rose to 1,200 men, so presumably, to more than twice that many people.[14] After the Black Death in 1348 and the famine of 1370, it collapsed completely to a community of 100. This was partly due to

An illuminated page from the Codex Amiatinus depicting Christ in majesty, created in Northumberland and kept as a treasure in San Salvatore for much of the Middle Ages.

mortality, but also because survivors abandoned the city in the hope of finding better conditions elsewhere.[15]

Under the Nine, considerable efforts were made to reclaim and maintain swamplands, including the Maremma, but to no great effect.[16] It was not until Ferdinand, Grand Duke of Tuscany, undertook the task around 1600 that the Maremma was reclaimed, and the area was only finally brought under control in the time of Mussolini. Malaria was eliminated in the early 1950s, since when the region has seen a considerable revival. As Gabriella Piccini observes, 'Siena's attempts to colonise the area without undertaking basic reclamation projects resulted in demographically fragile communities whose inhabitants were soon overtaken by malaria and poverty.'[17] In the days of the Sienese Republic, therefore, the Maremma was an untamed landscape, with too many mosquitoes and too much cover for bandits, and this made life at the harbour town of Talomone an unattractive proposition. It also made

Gathering and cooking chestnuts: chestnuts were a staple for many peasants, particularly people living in mountainous regions.

it hard for the Sienese to police and protect the route from Talamone, which they were trying to develop in the hope of rivalling Pisa as a maritime power, to the city. With hindsight, it would have been better for the city to invest more in the Maremma and less in grand urban projects.

In the era of the Nine, despite its small population, the Maremma was the granary of southern Tuscany. But this was not sustainable after the arrival of the Black Death halved the population. Without enough people to till the fields, the economy shifted to livestock farming, and the area was crossed in spring and autumn by stock moving between winter and summer pastures. Though the cause of malaria was not known, it was perfectly obvious that people became sick in the summer. Life in the Maremma was therefore long characterized by movement: up until 1897, the *estatura* was a Maremma custom. Every summer people migrated from villages in the plain to villages in the hills and on Monte Amiata, to escape the mosquitoes, taking their cattle and sheep with them. By the end of the Middle Ages, the Maremma was one of the most important interregional resources for the livestock supply of the entire peninsula. Charcoal makers also came down from the Apennines for the winter to make use of the region's extensive woodlands. *Aquacotta*, the well-known Tuscan soup, was first made by these itinerants, forming part of their basic diet. They would carry an earthenware pot, which when they prepared their meal was filled with water, plus a slice of stale bread and whatever they could find: wild onions and garlic, dandelions and other herbs, perhaps mushrooms. In today's *aquacotta* you will find tomatoes, onions, olive oil, grated cheese and a poached egg. The primitive version would have had none of these things, except perhaps the onion.[18]

The Maremma had, and still has, its own distinctive animals. The native fauna includes wild boar, foxes and porcupines and in earlier centuries there were also wolves. The domestic animals indigenous to the region include Maremmano horses, hardy working beasts capable of dealing with hard weather and rough terrain, and noted for their endurance. They are descended from an ancient local population going at least as far back as the Etruscans.[19] From the fourteenth century if not before, they were ridden by *butteri*, a tough breed of cowboys who shepherded the stock on their migrations. Maremma sheepdogs, also

called Maremmanos, accompanied them to guard the stock from wolves and other predators. These powerful white dogs are also of ancient ancestry. Descriptions of white guardian dogs are found in ancient Roman literature, in works by Columella, Varro and Palladius, and depicted in Roman art. Their training probably also goes back to ancient times. Future sheepdogs are placed among the sheep as puppies no more than six weeks old, so that they bond with the flock, while human contact is kept to the absolute minimum. If there are already guardian dogs in the flock, the puppy imitates them and learns directly from their behaviour. The Maremma dogs are therefore not handled like English sheepdogs, but regard the flock as their family, and protect them for that reason. They are extremely effective guardians, and in recent years their success as working sheepdogs in Australia has led to their redeployment as protectors of indigenous creatures such as penguins from non-indigenous predators.

A white Chianina ox, sketched by John Singer Sargent. This breed is of ancient ancestry, and was the principal source of power in Tuscany before farming was mechanized.

There are also Maremmana cattle, a native longhorn breed with grey coats, which can manage without pasture for much of the year, foraging for leaves, and can survive in difficult environments. They lead a more or less feral existence, tended by the *butteri* who follow and guide them throughout the year. Maremma sheep, like the cattle, lead a semi-wild life, and so, for centuries, did

the pigs: Maremma pigs were small, primitive black animals, whose principal virtue was that they could look after themselves. They were called Macchiaiola, because their natural habitat was the *macchia*: Mediterranean light woodland, where they could find grass, chestnuts and acorns. Their meat yield per animal is very low compared with that of modern breeds, so they almost became extinct in the twentieth century, until a few were discovered on Monte Amiata. Since it was then discovered that while yield is low, the quality of their meat is superb, the breed has experienced a revival.

Other distinctive breeds are native to different regions of the Siena *contado*. White Chianina cattle are well known, and provide the beef of choice for *bistecca alla Fiorentina*. They are native to Val di Chiana (hence their name), and the middle Tiber Valley. Chianina cattle have been raised in central Italy for at least two thousand years: Columella, describing types of oxen in about AD 55, says that 'Umbria breeds huge white oxen'.[20] Until the mechanization of Italian farming after the Second World War, they were the principal source of power in the Sienese countryside. There is also a specifically Sienese pig: in Lorenzetti's The Effects of Good Government, a peasant approaches the city driving a black porker with a white band round its middle. This animal is a Cinta Senese, a breed once widely found throughout Tuscany. Like the Macchiaiola, it produces excellent and distinctive meat, and consequently this breed has similarly seen a revival in recent years, reared for the gourmet market.

Other special local products include saffron, particularly around San Gimignano. The town's wealth in the early Middle Ages is demonstrated by its towers: fifteen of an original seventy-two still stand. This wealth came from the saffron trade, which peaked at the end of the thirteenth century.[21] The area offered ideal growing conditions for the saffron crocus, and at the end of October each year the town was surrounded by shimmering lilac-coloured fields, alternating with vineyards planted with the white Vernaccia grape, another local speciality. Saffron was a highly valuable, and valued, spice in the Middle Ages, but, as has so often been the case with Italian manufactures, the town's very high-quality product was outcompeted by cheaper alternatives, and production almost ceased in the course of the seventeenth century. Like rare-breed pork, it has seen a modest revival in recent years as a niche product.

Another distinctive part of the Sienese *contado* is the Crete Senesi, situated between Siena and Monte Oliveto. Despite high sodium levels, a legacy from the Pliocene sea which once covered the area, the *crete* is fertile if it is watered, and in the fifteenth and early sixteenth centuries, the valley of the Orcia was covered in wheatfields and the slopes were wooded. But the area was depopulated during the wars of the mid-fifteenth century and never recovered. The *crete* has formed since that time, due to soil erosion, though since the 1950s much of it has been reclaimed.[22] Iris Origo saw it for the first time in the 1930s, when it struck her as utterly inhospitable. Nonetheless, she and her husband bought an estate in the Val d'Orcia, and worked hard to reclaim the *crete*, with considerable success. More recently, it has been described as 'a vanishing landscape', since the use of bulldozers and other heavy earthmoving machinery has transformed the eerie, arid hills into smoothly rounded, productive slopes. It produces one highly valued product, white truffles. Truffles have thus far resisted cultivation, and have to be hunted out by trained dogs in areas where they are known to grow. San Giovanni d'Asso markets itself as the centre of Tuscany's white truffle production and has an annual truffle fair and even a truffle museum.

One group of travellers in Tuscany, unlike the pilgrims on the Via Francigena, were bent on pleasure. The undulating Sienese countryside was richly endowed with mineral springs and spas, which attracted both invalids and pleasure-lovers, as they still do. Their hot, mineralized water was thought to cure skin trouble and aching bones – they are also, of course, very pleasant to wallow in for the sheer fun of it. In his 'Sonnets of the Months', Folgóre da San Gimignano recommended his readers to go, in November, 'to Petriolo to the bath, with thirty mules laden with coins. Its roads are all covered with silk, cups of silver, leaden with wine caskets.'[23] The hot springs of Petriolo are near Siena, and the remains of a Roman thermal bath still stand there, dating from AD 404. The water emerges from the ground at 43°C, smelling pungently of hydrogen sulphide, and gushes down into a series of small baths, ending in a large pool.

Saturnia in the Maremma was developed by the Etruscans, though it fell out of use in the Middle Ages, only to be restored in the late nineteenth century when spas were greatly in vogue. Another set of hot springs, also first developed as a resort by the Romans, is Bagno Vignoni. It is only just off the Via Francigena and therefore highly accessible. Lorenzo the Magnificent was a regular visitor, and another famous patron was Catherine of Siena. Its unique piazza was developed in the Renaissance around the spring itself, and is consequently full of hot water. The water exits the piazza and heads down towards the River Orcia, powering several medieval mills, which are now preserved as an attraction in themselves. After that, the water is free to enjoy; little canals meander down the hillside, and it is very pleasant to sit for a while bathing one's feet in the hot, invigorating turquoise water.

Siena brought a number of towns and their territories under its dominion. Everyone has their favourites among the hill towns. I have occasionally cherished a fantasy of living in the utterly charming Murlo, a miniature city of Etruscan origin, consisting of a set of walls crowning a steep hill, with houses built directly onto the walls, two streets, a church, wonderful views out over undulating blue hills and a very small bishop's palace which is now an Etruscan museum.

San Gimignano, with its splendid towers, is far bigger and better known. As already mentioned, saffron was its most profitable product, but it also boasted glass and cloth industries. Life in medieval San Gimignano was enlivened by a particularly vehement and localized feud between Guelfs and Ghibellines, since one of the two leading families, the Salvucci, were Ghibellines, and the other, the Ardinghelli, were Guelfs. In the thirteenth century, the Piazza del Duomo, between their respective towers, was a no-go area.[24] The town's divided allegiance did it no favours, since the Guelfs were in the ascendancy at the time of Montaperti and so shared the fate of the Florentines, while by the time of the Battle of Colle di Val d'Elsa, they were fighting with the Ghibellines and shared their defeat. San Gimignano submitted to the Florentines after the Black Death, but culturally it belongs to Siena. The Collegiata Santa Maria Assunta is San Gimignano's main church. It is decorated with frescoes by Sienese painters, which began in the 1340s and continued through three phases in the fourteenth and early fifteenth centuries. The New Testament scenes in the north aisle are by Lippo Memmi (c.1340), and the Old Testament scenes in the south aisle by Bartolo di Fredi (1367), and a depiction of the Last Judgement on the east wall and in the first bay of the nave are by Taddeo di Bartolo (c.1413). Lippo's frescoes are remarkable for the expressiveness of the faces. Judas being rewarded by the high priest looks at once evil, hangdog and utterly unreliable. His *Maestà* in the Palazzo Communale is closely modelled on that of Simone Martini (his brother-in-law) in the Palazzo Pubblico, with the difference that while Simone's Virgin is entreated by Siena's four patron saints, in San Gimignano it is the Podestà who kneels in supplication, wearing a striking black, white and pink robe. In the fifteenth century, after the town's submission to Florence, the Florentine Benozzo Gozzoli frescoed scenes from the life of St Augustine in Sant'Agostino, at the other end of the town.

Montalcino, twenty-five miles south of Siena in the Val d'Orcia, is particularly close to it politically. It came under Sienese rule in 1260, and when a defiant Sienese government refused to accept that Charles V had conquered them, it was to Montalcino that they retreated. The town, perched on a steep hill, may take its name from the holm oak (*Mons Ilcinus*), especially since, in the Middle Ages, it was known for leather production and oak bark was used by tanners to process hides. It used to be known for a sweet wine, Moscadello, which was obliterated by phylloxera, but in the twentieth century it developed the now-famous Brunello di Montalcino. As its reputation spread, the oak woods have been replaced by vineyards producing some of Tuscany's best wines.

Judas rewarded by the High Priest; a detail from Lippo Memmi's frescoes in the Collegiata di Santa Maria Assunta in San Gimignano.

6

THE MAKING
OF THE
CITY

E ven by the standards of the cities and towns of medieval Italy, the city-state of Siena had an unenviable reputation for political instability. It was a faction-ridden city, but one exceptional period has always been recognized; the rule of the 'Nine Governors and Defenders of the Commune and People of Siena' who took power in 1287 and kept it until the descent of the Emperor-Elect, Charles IV of Luxembourg, into Italy in 1355. Almost three generations of Sienese citizens enjoyed the benefits of the stable, prosperous and peaceful rule the Nine brought to their city – or suffered under what was by any standards a highly authoritarian regime. The creation of a sixty-eight-year period of uninterrupted rule was, within the context of Sienese politics, a remarkable achievement.

Under the Nine, power was distributed though quite a large section of the city's upper middle class, since an individual only served for two months: fifty-four men therefore served the city in any one year. The Nine all had to be Guelfs, over thirty, and 'merchants'. They were an oligarchy, members of a prosperous upper middle class, about ninety families of Guelf merchants and bankers, which did business with the nobility and married into noble families. Their wealth and status varied considerably: their ranks included wool processors, spice-merchants, rentiers and craftsmen. Some of them must have been strong personalities and men of great ability, but we are quite unable to detect who these were: the Nine's decisions were collective, and a mask of uniformity was successfully maintained. The nobility were excluded from power (though of course wealth and status gave them plenty of influence), as were the poor.

The Nine responded harshly to any kind of public protest, whether it was from the lower ranks of society, or the magnate families. They were nervous of guilds, which gave the lower classes a form of collective political expression, and at one point tried to suppress all of them except the wool guild, which was by far the most important. Their political instincts were sound, since in 1297, an alliance of guilds and magnates attempted to overthrow them, and again in 1318, an alliance of butchers and animal dealers with some of the Tolomei and other aristocrats attacked the Palazzo Pubblico. Following this rebellion, the houses and towers of the rebel magnates were pulled down, thus weakening their power.[1]

If the rule of the Nine was oppressive, this has to be seen in light of the fact that the Sienese were an unruly populace. Apart from making occasional efforts to unseat the Nine, several of the noble clans, such as the Piccolomini and Salimbeni, maintained traditional enmities and fought one another in the streets. The Nine passed laws forbidding those entitled to bear arms from doing so outside their houses at night, in an attempt to curtail magnate violence, and established curfews. If a quarrel escalated into mounted combat, the commune owned heavy chains which could be stretched across the narrow streets attached to the iron horse-tethers which decorated the façades of the magnates' towers, effectively preventing a cavalry charge.[2] At a lower social level, the men of the city's *terzi* engaged in ritual combats with one another which could easily escalate into major civil unrest, and sometimes did. Though the Nine did their best to ban violent games in the Campo, they were not, in practice, easy to prevent. In the game of *elmora*, teams of young men from the three *terzi*, dressed in light armour and armed with wooden swords and stones, attempted to drive their rivals out of the Campo: after eleven gentlemen and an unknown number of 'the baser sort' were killed in 1291, *elmora* was banned, and *pugna*, a fist fight, substituted in its place. All this goes to explain why fourteenth-century Siena had the startlingly high ratio of one policeman for every 145 inhabitants. These men were hired foreigners, so this was a substantial investment for the city.[3]

Two main reasons suggest themselves for the longevity of the Nine. The first was the broad basis of their power, the second the care the Nine devoted to their own protection and the reinforcement of their authority. Although an oligarchy, the Nine were representative of a large body of Sienese citizens. The domestic policy of the Nine, in which every aspect of civic life was subject to governmental control, was carefully calculated to preserve order within the city. Institutions which were expressions of nobility lost importance, as did those too closely associated with artisans, such as the guilds. Both nobles and guildsmen were excluded from membership of the nine. The Podestà, once the principal authority in the city, was demoted to being a simple magistrate, while the societies of arms were rendered harmless and became the Nine's communal guard. The Nine also made inroads into ecclesiastical power, taking over responsibility for charities, festivals and rituals which had previously been the business of the church or the confraternities, and assuming financial responsibility for the cathedral and the Hospital of Santa Maria della Scala. Above all, the magistracy of the Nine set in train the beautification of the city through civic patronage of art, architecture and grand projects as a primary role of government.

The glorious era of the Nine was actually one of incipient economic decline for the city for reasons beyond its control: the fairs of Champagne, which had long been serviced by Sienese bankers, were losing their importance. Following overt discrimination by Philip IV of Burgundy against Italian and Flemish merchants, the volume of trade handled by the Champagne fairs decreased. Even without Philip's protectionist activity, as Bruce Campbell observes, 'from the 1290s Europe found itself in the grip of a worsening commercial recession from which there was little immediate prospect of relief'.[4] The Via Francigena was less significant as a commercial artery than it had been in the thirteenth century. The tax which the city levied on goods entering the city yielded only a modest revenue by 1300, suggesting that Siena was no longer commercially significant. Like their Florentine rivals, the great Sienese banking companies were struggling to survive, and some of them, notably the once-mighty Bonsignori, did not. The Bonsignori bank, known as the Gran Tavola, failed in 1298, and its collapse heralded the end of Siena's real importance as a banking centre.[5]

To contemporaries, things looked very different. It was the government of the Nine which made Siena what it is today. They sculpted the civic landscape, widening major roads, regularizing building façades and connecting new territories to the original civic nucleus. It is not that the Nine's civic goals were all that different from those of their predecessors, just that they were better at achieving them. As William Bowsky, a distinguished historian of medieval Siena, explains, conscious originality and innovation did not distinguish their government and were not their aims. Changes occurred through pragmatic experimentation. Their style was, if anything, a pragmatic one that emphasized the institutionalization, formalization, and regularization of practices and offices that worked.[6]

Over and over again, the legislation of the Nine emphasizes that the citizenry should work together to make Siena somewhere to be proud of; driving home the message that the beauty and amenity of the city was a collective responsibility.

Given the tensions between the nobility and the civic government, and the commune's desire to emphasize a separation of powers between church and state, it began to seem less and less appropriate for the governing body to meet either in a church or in a rented noble palace – perhaps especially that of the Tolomei, who had proved to be unruly subjects on more than one occasion. Work on civic buildings began in the mid-thirteenth century on a then little-used field, the *campo fori*, at a distance from the city's commercial and religious centre, this being the Duomo, the Piazza del Duomo (a focus of bustling mercantile activity) and the Hospital of Santa Maria della Scala directly opposite the cathedral. The first structures to be built on the Campo were a Dogana, or customs house, and a mint: it is easy to see why the commune would prioritize keeping customs and coinage under their own control. The site was chosen because it was located at the point where the territories of the three *terzi* converged, and was a sort of no man's land. In 1259, there is a reference in town records to 'the mint, or commune palace by the campo fori', and thereafter the mint building is sometimes referred to as 'the palace'.[7] It was, by virtue of its function, a high-security structure, but to be called a 'palace' it must also have been equipped with a meeting room at the very least. However, the city officials were still being lodged in the homes of the magnates at public expense, and once the Nine arose as a merchant oligarchy committed to keeping the nobility out of power, this began to seem less and less appropriate.[8]

After the Nine came to power, the *campo fori* was developed far more ambitiously. A new city hall, the Palazzo Pubblico, was built around 1300 in a surprisingly short space of time: begun in 1298, it was finished in 1310. It did not move beyond planning and discussion until the year after the Nine took power, so the speed of its construction is an index of their commitment to civic architecture. As they explained to the people of Siena, 'it seems delightful to the eyes and heart and a joy to each of the human senses, and even a great honour to each and every citizen, that their magistrates live beautifully and honourably.'[9] In 1298, the mint/palace had a group of adjacent noblemen's *palazzi* with their towers frowning down on it, reminders of the military and political power of the aristocracy. As the Nine tightened their grip on power, this became less and less acceptable to them. They had decided that their site should become the centre for communal power. As well as a place for the consistory to meet, they also wanted to construct a residence for the Podestà – an office which was under their control. By 1293, they were buying up houses in the vicinity of the mint to make space for their new palace, a large-scale capital investment. The style of the Palazzo Pubblico they built, with its distinctive pointed arches, represents a grafting of native building tradition onto a Burgundian template, which was derived from the Cistercian abbey of San Galgano.[10] The early development of Sienese public buildings owes much to the Cistercians.

overleaf The heart of Siena, as the Nine conceived it: the Palazzo Pubblico (on the right), the Campo, and the soaring Torre del Mangia, a celebration of civic pride 102 metres tall.

The new Palazzo Pubblico was set off by a new Campo; Siena's unique town square, with nine lines of stone radiating fanlike from immediately in front of the Palazzo Pubblico, which was paved in 1300, a particularly prosperous year for the city, because Boniface VIII had proclaimed it a holy year, bringing tens of thousands of pilgrims down the Via Francigena. The space is more or less shell-shaped, but may be intended to evoke the Virgin Mary's protecting cloak, which had been cast over the Sienese at the Battle of Montaperti. The Campo is an essential aspect of the experience of being in Siena. Inside the city walls, one walks along narrow medieval streets, with flat-fronted, four- and five-storey buildings towering on either side and blocking the sun from reaching the grey basalt paving blocks for most of the day. Thus all vistas collapse into narrowly constrained views of 200 metres at most, since, though some of the streets are long, none is perfectly straight. After about ten minutes of walking from the Porta Romana, one begins to notice shafts of brightness, before suddenly emerging into the sunlight in the vast open area of the Piazza del Campo, the physical and cultural heart of the city. The writer Hisham Matar observes a curious feature of the square: 'no matter where we were in the square, we were able to see the entire

place. Not one person was hidden. This strange effect was made possible by Il Campo's unusual fanning shape and by the way the ground dips dramatically… it was a space of mutual exposure.'[11]

The site of the Campo was achieved by pulling down towers which had belonged to families of the previous Ghibelline ruling elite, and the lines of stone divide it into nine sections. Thus both actually and symbolically, the Campo and the palace proclaim the power of the Nine. In late medieval Siena, architecture is a concrete expression of political ideas. In 1310, the Nine also dictated the design of the palaces which now ring the open space. Any new house constructed with a façade onto the Campo had to have fenestration of the same type as the municipal palace. Balconies were forbidden, as were banners and window coverings which might interrupt the harmony of the Campo.[12] The dimensions of walls were regulated with equal care, and the result was, as we can see for ourselves, astonishingly harmonious, but it must not be forgotten that in its original context it represents the imposition of a civic style which reinforced the authority of the regime, and quite consciously repressed aristocratic individualism in the interests of the common good. Siena, in fact, developed the most complex and far-reaching building code to be developed in any medieval city.[13]

Finances for building the town hall were approved in 1297. The new *palazzo* was designed in three units, and deliberately executed in brick rather than the stone of the demolished magnate towers. The roofline is decorated with nine huge merlons. Since each of the *terzi* had begun on a hilly ridge, it lay in the declivity, with the cathedral, at the highest point of the city, and the nobles' towers looking down on it. It was therefore necessary to counteract the impression of insignificance created by being, literally, looked down on, and this was achieved by building the tallest bell tower of any Italian city, the Torre del Mangia, which was much taller than any of the private towers, and was visible even outside Siena.[14] As Judith B. Steinhoff observes, 'from its completion, the Torre became both a point of visual focus for the entire city, and a powerful symbol of communal authority'. It rose to the same absolute height as the bell tower of the cathedral, and was, in effect, in dialogue with it. It was a collaborative work: two brothers Rinaldi from Perugia began constructing it in 1325, and it was completed by Agostino di Giovanni in 1344. The stone bellchamber at the top of the brick tower was designed by Lippo Memmi, and the name is derived from the nickname of the first bellringer, Mangiaguadagni, or 'spendthrift'.

In 1342, Siena's hydraulic engineers managed the remarkable feat of bringing water to a new fountain, the Fonte Gaia, in the Campo, after eight years of work: the first running water to be available in the city centre. This was of great practical and symbolic importance, since all of the pre-existing fountains were outside the first circuit of city walls, and hence fortified as defensive outposts. Because the Sienese could not take water for granted, they attached an almost mystical significance to it, and creating a water source right at the heart of the civic centre was as important symbolically as it was practically. The water was brought to the Campo through some twenty-five kilometres of aqueducts and *bottini*. It was a hugely expensive enterprise: in the final stages, the committee responsible were assigned the entire income from the then flourishing community of Grosseto to spend on the fountain.[15]

The Fonte Gaia was given an elaborate makeover by the sculptor Jacopo della Quercia between 1409 and 1420, in another burst of civic pride after Siena regained its independence from the Visconti (his work is now represented by an incomplete nineteenth-century copy by Tito Sarocchi). The original basin must have been somewhat plainer, though it is probable that the first Fonte Gaia was also a rectangle, walled on three sides, like its replacement, in response to the sloping surface of the Campo. It was made of marble and carved with plants in relief. It was also adorned for a time with a statue of Venus supported by a dolphin, a Greco-Roman antique discovered in 1325 while foundations were being dug for some new houses, and, maybe because of the dolphin, was mounted on the basin perhaps in the 1340s, where it was much admired by the city's artists, according to Lorenzo Ghiberti.[16] He concludes his anecdote by saying that the City of the Virgin then began to worry about having a pagan statue on their fountain, and decided that the Venus was bringing them bad luck (as well they might, since plague hit the city in 1348), so they took her down and buried her secretly in Florentine territory. There is documentary proof that a statue was taken down in 1357.[17]

During their two months of office, the Nine were expected to sleep in the Palazzo. They took steps to ensure that the atmosphere

overleaf The present Fonte Gaia is a nineteenth-century copy of the badly-eroded original by Jacopo del Quercia (1419), reconstructed by Tito Sarocchi.

was business-like and serious: according to the Constitution of 1310, houses fronting onto the Campo were not allowed to put tables outside, prostitutes were not to come within 200 *braccia* of the building, violent games were banned in the Campo, and women were expressly forbidden from entering the Palazzo itself.[18] A grimmer expression of civic power was the decision to use the Campo as a site for the public execution of sodomites and other offenders classed as heinous criminals, such as heretics.

In addition to the many capital projects undertaken by the Nine, they tried to improve their city as a whole, building new roads that were larger, straighter and more unified, and widening and straightening existing streets wherever possible. They laid down that major streets should be about twenty-four feet wide, and side streets twelve, and the constitution of 1310 decreed that houses built of loam should replace their front façades with brick 'to lend beauty to the city'.[19]

Just as the thirteenth-century aristocracy had vied with each other to build towers, the state-sponsored building of the fourteenth century embodied a strong spirit of competition. The argument for building a public park in 1309, the Prato di Camollia, just outside the Camollia Gate, was essentially that, since other Tuscan cities had one, Siena should have one, too:

> Among the cares and responsibilities that pertain to those who undertake the government of the city is especially that which regards the beauty of the city, and in any noble city one of its principal beauties is that it should have a meadow or place for the recreation and delight of citizens and strangers, and the cities of Tuscany and also certain other towns and cities are provided and adorned with such meadows and pleasant grounds.[20]

Alongside the public building programmes, private and ecclesiastical building continued apace. New *palazzi* arose, following the stylistic lead of the Palazzo Pubblico. One of the key aesthetic principles of building under the Nine was uniformity. Money was lavished on the cathedral – the subject of a separate chapter. Other city churches were embellished: in 1286, Sienese Franciscans asked the commune for help in building the façade of their new church, because 'when cardinals and bishops visit our convent, or prelates or ambassadors from other cities in Tuscany, they see that the façade of our church is incomplete, and this does not redound to the honour of the city of Siena'.[21]

One ornament the Nine very much wanted for their city was a prestigious university. San Bernardino voiced a widely held belief when he said young nobleman should 'learn to live like men, so that if their country needs it, they can serve as ambassadors for the Republic… a man who has studied will always cut a fine figure in the world, but of what use is one who cannot even speak correctly?'[22] They were prepared to offer scholars lavish privileges and favours in order to build up the small *studium* of the thirteenth century, such as tax exemptions and freedom from military service. Unlike the universities in many other medieval towns, this *studium* was not formally affiliated with the church, but was a civic project, motivated in part by competition with Florence.[23] An Englishman who joined the faculty in 1279 seems to have been regarded as a prize, since he was awarded twice the basic rate of pay.[24] In 1321 the entire University of Bologna, the most famous *studium* in Italy, left that city after a dispute with the authorities and was looking for a home. The Nine were prepared to offer an inducement of 6,000 florins to persuade them to make that home in Siena, with another 500 for the rector.[25] By 1324, most of the Bolognese had trickled back home, but the Sienese continued to offer lavish incentives to notable scholars from other cities in Tuscany, and even from as far afield as Germany. The Sienese were hampered by the fact that their *studium* did not yet have the privileges of a *studium generale*, which were normally conferred by the pope, though the Holy Roman Emperor could also issue an imperial charter granting much the same privileges. In 1339, they were prepared to bribe the curia with a gift of 1,000 florins and engage in major diplomatic manoeuvres in order to gain papal approval, which was not forthcoming. This was one of the few ventures of the Nine which was frustrated. The university's privilege was not granted until 1357, after the fall of the Nine, when, ironically, it was granted by their enemy, the emperor.

A more rewarding site for civic patronage was the Hospital of Santa Maria della Scala. It was already old, wealthy and famous throughout Tuscany when the Nine came to power, and was co-opted by them into their civic programme. The earliest documents relating to the administration of the hospital, which date to 1090, are clear that it was then controlled by the canons of the cathedral via a rector, whom they elected. The Nine subtly subverted the old regulations of the hospital, gradually transferring much of the responsibility for its administration from the rector to themselves. They used their control over it to finance their own civic policies, and to add an overtone of charitable munificence to their projects. In the revised constitution which the Nine issued in 1310, they go so far as to declare that the hospital is a civic amenity owned by the commune. This was vehemently challenged by the bishop, to no effect.[26] In effect, medieval 'charity' was transmuted into social welfare, since Santa Maria della Scala was feeding the poor, tending the sick and bringing up foundlings on behalf of the state. The plaques bearing the commune's coat of arms which are affixed to either side of the main door are a testimony to this victory.

The wealth of the hospital made it a prize worth fighting for, especially since so much of its wealth was farmland, because one of its most important charitable duties was to provide bread to the poor. Partly, it was rich because it was old, and had had a long time to accumulate bequests, but additionally, for no very clear reason, increasing numbers of Sienese started remembering the hospital in their wills shortly after the Nine came to power in 1287, so its wealth increased considerably. Stephan Epstein estimates that by 1316 the hospital controlled almost 5,000 hectares of land on which it produced more than 37,000 *staia* of wheat (a *staia* is about seventy-five pounds).[27] Having secured control over the hospital, with its vast resources, and virtual control over grain production in the Sienese *contado*, the Nine used it to secure and guarantee loans to fund their ambitious building projects, an ideal arrangement from their point of view. Borrowing money from Santa Maria della Scala at artificially low rates of interest was infinitely preferable to dealing with private lenders, cheaper, and far more secure, and helps to explain how the Nine were able to spend so much on the city so quickly, as well as making huge investments such as buying the city port of Talamone and trying to create a great university. Having control over the hospital's resources meant the Nine also controlled the grain supply to the city, a major issue in any medieval economy. The hospital was rewarded for its services to the commune with an expanded church, and a grand hall for receiving pilgrims, which was frescoed in the 1440s.

The Nine also paid attention to the *contado*. Making, maintaining and policing roads was as important to the good governance of the city as what went on within the walls; roads facilitated pilgrim traffic and trade, and, as the population got bigger and bigger, it was vitally important to link Siena efficiently with the sources of its grain supply and other foodstuffs. They appointed an official to take care of roads, and found that he needed a deputy. The Via Francigena, besides being a pilgrim route, was the main road for goods and services, and several of Santa Maria della Scala's granges were located along it. Another reason for the Nine to pay attention to roads was that the power of the magnates rested on their extensive landholdings in the countryside, and so if the commune could move troops quickly and efficiently it stood a better chance of controlling contumacious nobles.[28] A third road official was created, with far-reaching powers, whose task was to police the roads and deal with malefactors, paying particular attention to security on the Via Francigena.

One area in which the Nine were less successful was public hygiene. Householders and shopkeepers were responsible for sweeping the street immediately outside their own premises, but because clean water was brought in by underground pipes, it was very difficult to construct sewers in Siena without compromising the safety of clean water coming in: wastewater was therefore carried off in open gutters. Cesspits had to be emptied, and the waste from butchers' shops, stables and other sources of organic filth disposed of: it was all supposed to be taken out of the city, though busy households and commercial premises certainly cut corners if they could get away with it. The Nine legislated repeatedly and probably to little effect; as Daniel Waley observes, 'from these clauses one could compile a list of Siena's unofficial public privies and litter dumps'.[29] The sheer quantity of legislation relating to filth is an indication of its ineffectiveness. Provisions were made for regular sweeping and cleaning of the Campo's fine new pavement, but day-to-day cleaning of the Campo was achieved by a small, privileged herd of pigs; they consumed organic refuse, to be sure, but they also, inevitably, converted it into strong-smelling excrement.[30] Sumptuary legislation directed at women forbade them to wear dresses with trains, but given the state of the streets it is amazing that any of them would want to. The humanist writer Leon Battista Alberti commented, 'Not only does the whole town stink, at the beginning and end of the night watch, when refuse receptacles are emptied out of the windows, but during the day as well, it is filthy and offensively vaporous.'[31]

A vision of a clean and orderly city is enjoined by the city statutes, and corroborated by Ambrogio Lorenzetti's 1340s fresco, The Effects of Good Government, but there was a substantial gap between aspirations and actuality. In Lorenzetti's well-governed city, the streets are level, wide, and, above all, clean. Although they are being used by men and women, horses, donkeys, sheep, and dogs, they are level, dry and free of dung, refuse, or even puddles. A group of elegantly dressed dancers protect their feet with colourful, thin-soled shoes, not mud-caked boots. However, the complete absence of any system of sewerage in the actual city must have meant that civic cleanliness was, however desirable, effectively out of reach. In 1295, the urgency of Siena's quest for water is suggested by the seventy-five lira the *Operaio del Duomo* was given to search for a mythical underground river, the Diana, the alleged existence of which was purely down to collective wishful thinking. A commission composed of the painter Duccio and four stonemasons was instructed to sink wells wherever they thought appropriate to try and find it.[32]

Siena's rise to wealth was based on banking and trade, and arose from its position on the Via Francigena. But by the beginning of the fourteenth century it was clear that the city's geography had its downsides, and that generating further wealth through industrial production presented major difficulties. Despite Siena's commitment to science and technology, the nature of its site prevented it from catching the next wave of economic development, which was the application of water power to manufacturing processes. Florence, on the other hand, could take full advantage of this, because it had the Arno running through it. When Siena's wool production was at its peak in the 1330s and 1340s, Florence's production in the same period was at least ten times greater, 100,000 cloths compared with Siena's 9,000 or 10,000.[33] The limitations imposed by Siena's hilly site prevented the industry from further expansion, because wool production needs water, particularly for dyeing and fulling (fulling being the process of shrinking woollen cloth and making it denser after it has been woven). 'Fulling was a process that demanded not only skill and a certain amount of equipment but also a considerable space of open ground for drying and a plentiful supply of clear, fresh water.'[34] Consequently, fullers had to move out of the city entirely and establish mills along watercourses in the countryside. The best mill sites in Sienese territory were several kilometres beyond the walls of the city, and therefore could not be protected in times of emergency.

In the fourteenth century, towns built along rivers that could be dammed and channelled to power waterwheels were at a massive advantage. A settlement located along the fall line of a river could take full advantage of the increasingly elaborate water-powered technologies of the Middle Ages which served many industries, not only dyeing and fulling, but linen manufacture, papermaking and milling, none of which could be carried on without copious water supplies. People also needed water to drink, and for their animals to drink, for washing clothes and for many kinds of food preparation, such as cleaning animal intestines to make sausage casings. Many of them also needed water in their working lives, for other industrial processes, as well as water for firefighting. Butchering had to take place in the city, because the meat was sold there, so tanning also had to take place there because processing a hide needs to start immediately after its removal from the animal. Both industries generated enormous quantities of organic filth, and, of course, the absence of sewers meant that the excrement of humans, horses and other denizens of the city had somehow to be disposed of.

The sheer complexity of Siena's water management is suggested by the Sienese historian Giugurta Tommasi, writing in 1625:

> Branda is the most copious of all the fountains. After the big horse
> trough, the water flows into the laundry basin to whiten the linens, and
> then making a pool that serves first to bathe the horses and then to wash
> the intestines of the carcasses – which are carefully butchered for the use
> of the whole city. The water then descends outside the walls of the city,
> where it powers a mill. Afterwards it forms pools for cleaning wool and
> cloth, and for curing the hides in a lime bath. Finally, before it joins
> the [River] Tressa, it powers nine other mills with much benefit to
> the city.[35]

Siena never really had enough waterpower for industrial use, except on a very modest scale, and intricate regulations governed the industrial use of such water as it had, all designed to ensure that only human consumption and the most delicate operations used water direct from the spring: as Tommasi reveals, the outflow was directed from basin to basin and used for dirtier and dirtier tasks. Preventing water polluted with poisonous dyes, tanners' effluent and animal waste from contaminating drinking water was, of course, a whole other set of problems. Once the great days of the international bankers had come to an end, Siena's prosperity was primarily derived from its function as a regional market and banking centre, since its capacity for increasing collective wealth through industrial development was circumscribed by the water supply. This is a pattern repeated in numerous hill towns throughout northern

Italy, and a key reason why so many of them are well preserved: they were simply unable to develop during the heyday of waterpower, and Italy's economic recession of the seventeenth century and after left them stranded in time.

The great enterprise of medieval Siena with respect to the countryside was loosening the grip of the noble families on their rural territories and laying claim to the land. Since Siena was gradually ceasing to be an international financial power, especially after the failure of the Tolomei bank in 1319, the Nine could see that it was increasingly important to develop as a regional centre, and to control as much territory as possible. The government of the Nine avoided major wars, but deployed its military forces to enlarge Sienese territory. At the apogee of its power, Siena claimed general rule and supervision over a radius of roughly thirty miles from the city. The Sienese were only too conscious of the limitations imposed on the city by its mountainous and landlocked site. They keenly felt the absence of a river, and devoted the utmost ingenuity to the question of improving the water supply, but the other great advantage of possessing a river would have been a link with the sea. Therefore one of their more ambitious ventures was buying themselves a port in 1303.

One of the ingenious devices of Taccola, the 'Sienese Archimedes', using horsepower to turn a crankshaft. Crankshafts had many practical applications.

The natural direction for territorial expansion was westwards towards the Tyrrhenian Sea, since other directions were blocked by Florence, Arezzo and Pisa. In the course of the thirteenth century, the Sienese crept towards the coast, making inroads into the territory of the Aldobrandeschi, a sprawling magnate family with castles all across the Maremma. In 1224, the Sienese defeated Grosseto, which had been an Aldobrandeschi dependency, with an army of 3,100 men. As a contemporary chronicler noted, this was 'to the increase of her strength and power, which henceforth extended as far as the sea'.[36] The crucial factor for the Sienese was that they now possessed a moderately secure line of communication from the coast to the city, a distance of about fifty-five miles, so they could reach out for Talamone, also originally a possession of the Aldobrandeschi, sited on a promontory where the Uccellina Mountains fall down towards the Tyrrhenian Sea. It had passed into the hands of the abbot of San Salvatore of Monte Amiata by 1303, and he was prepared to sell it to the city.

Talamone, it was hoped, would alleviate the commune's almost total dependence on the Via Francigena for trade, since the fact that Pisa could easily block and cut off trade to the north was an ever-present threat.[37] Another important reason for developing a port was to bring in precious salt and grain. Tuscany was subject to frequent famines in the first half of the fourteenth century, owing to its dense population, and the resources of Santa Maria della Scala were not always sufficient. The city often had to import grain. Both 1303 and 1306 were years of acute food shortages in Tuscany, and the commune was well aware that nothing led to civil discontent and regime change more quickly than hunger. Additionally, there were definite disadvantages to using a port which belonged to another city. While the thirteenth-century Sienese had engaged in some trade with the Mediterranean and the East, their warehouses in Venice or Genoa or Pisa had to pay local customs duties. They were also made vulnerable by the principle of reprisals: if a Sienese merchant in Pisa defaulted on a payment to a Pisan, the courts gave the native the right to seize the goods of any other Sienese with property in the town.[38] This was another good reason for the Sienese to want a port of their own.

In Lorenzetti's *Good Government*, only one site is labelled with a name: 'Talam', an indication of the hopes that it represented. It may also be the 'City by the Sea' in an atmospheric little landscape panel attributed to Sassetta, *c.*1425, which shows a heavily fortified coastal city bristling with defensive towers, and may have been part of something like a sacristy reliquary cupboard. Dante ridiculed Siena's hopes for Talamone in *The Divine Comedy*, writing of 'those vain people who place their hope in Talamone', but Florence took the venture seriously enough, and regularly negotiated with Siena for access to the port up to the early fifteenth century. The Sienese gave much thought to their new prize; a plan was drawn up in 1306 which details the building plots granted to the new inhabitants.[39] There was provision for churches, an adequate supply of fresh water, and each settler was to have a homesite, orchard, vineyard and several plots of farmland.

Talamone, unfortunately, was not well suited to its intended role. After the 1224 conquest of Grosseto, the smaller city regained its independence, but was definitively reconquered in 1338. Since the Sienese were determined to keep Grosseto and its wheatfields under their control, a major highway linked the two cities. However, after Grosseto, the way led through marshy and difficult country, which up to 1336 was controlled in part by the Aldobrandeschi. The Nine built a new road linking Talamone with Paganico, but did not extend this as far as Grosseto.[40] While the Nine were eventually successful in bringing the Aldobrandeschi counts under control, winning a number of towns in the southern Maremma in consequence, their battle with the family extended from 1313 to 1336, exactly the period when they were trying to develop Talamone.[41] Because the way to Talamone was both long and insecure, it was impossible for the Sienese to protect their nascent port, and it was repeatedly seized by hostile forces of one kind or another: Ghibelline exiles in 1312, Genoese exiles in 1320, and by other enemies in 1326, 1327 and 1328. As early as 8 December 1304 there is an entry in the records of the deliberations of the General Council for the reinforcement of the port. The vulnerability of Talamone must have deterred Sienese who considered settling there, and there were serious problems with the harbour itself. Despite considerable expenditure on construction and dredging, it kept silting up.

The Sienese preoccupation with achieving a usable port continued for another century, and is reflected in the drawings of the 'Sienese Archimedes', Mariano di Jacopo, better known as Taccola, in 1433. His book of designs for useful engines includes a variety of designs for ferries, ship-loading cranes and devices to trap enemy ships. He describes the ideal harbour of his day:

> Good harbours must be narrow at the entrance and large inside. They must
> be deep. At the entrance always provide fortresses or guard towers. At this
> place, let an iron chain be provided which can be drawn in at night by a
> wheel or a drum. Make it long enough that it can go down into the
> water…[42]

The idea was that, during the day, the chain rested on the seabed so that legitimate ships could go in and out. At night, it was stretched tight across the entrance, so that no enemy could sneak in. The port of Pisa had chains of this kind. Another of his devices was a bucket chain, particularly useful for dredging up silt, and he devised ingenious methods of building firm foundations for a tower in the sea.

THE DUOMO

The first cathedral of Siena seems to have been in Città, on top of the hill also called Castelvecchio, and it was dedicated to St Boniface. Which St Boniface this was is revealed by the fact that the victory of Montaperti occurred on 4 September, also identified as 'the feast of St Boniface'. The dedication must therefore be to the pope of that name, Boniface I (418–422), who was venerated on 4 September, rather than the eighth-century Anglo-Saxon missionary to Germany, whose day is 5 June. Boniface continued to be honoured in Siena after the re-dedication of the cathedral to the Virgin, since the altar in what is now the Capella del Voto was originally dedicated to him, and Guido da Siena's *Madonna of the Graces* (1270s) was placed there.[1] The site of the first cathedral subsequently became that of the Convent of Santa Margherita, and, in the eighteenth century, that of the Istituto Pendola, founded in the 1820s, an enlightened and innovative institution for educating the congenitally deaf. The church and the bishop's palace moved to their present site, near Fontebranda, in the twelfth century. According to fifteenth-century tradition, the new cathedral was consecrated by the Sienese pope, Alexander III, in 1179, though this is unlikely to be the case.

overleaf Siena's Duomo, with its distinctive stripes and a splendid façade designed by the sculptor Giovanni Pisano. The belltower was one of the city's major landmarks.

As Siena became more and more prosperous, the twelfth-century cathedral was supplanted by a new building constructed over the course of the following two centuries. Work on the new cathedral began around 1220. The choir and altar were completed around 1260 and aside from decoration and work on the façade, the structure was probably more or less complete by 1280. The three-aisled nave was the same size as in the present cathedral, but the transepts and choir were shorter. There was

a crypt, where the four city saints were worshipped, which must also
have contained a sacristy. In order to make room for it, the choir was
at a higher level than the nave. When the building was redesigned, the
cathedral authorities took the decision to sacrifice the crypt in order to
put the choir on the same level as the nave, with the result that only a
small section of the crypt survives, though it is of considerable interest
since it was decorated with frescoes in the thirteenth century. These
wall paintings, only rediscovered in 1999, are by a variety of hands, and
depict scenes from the Old and New Testaments.[2] A new sacristy was
built, leading off the choir, which was probably rather more convenient.

Another masterpiece which survives from the first phase of the
cathedral is the pulpit by Nicola Pisano, created between 1265 and
1268, which has a complex iconographic scheme.[3] Eight of the columns
on which it is supported stand on lions devouring other animals or
feeding their cubs, which fascinated the art critic John Ruskin, who
made several detailed drawings of them. He commented, 'it goes far
beyond my Lombard griffin in naturalistic power, but it is still fearfully
cruel – no Greek could have borne to carve the jaws crashing into the
horse's skull, exactly through its eye, as the Italian does.'[4] They perhaps
represent fallen nature. The middle column has the seven liberal arts
and philosophy sitting round the base, which seem to stand for human
intellect, by means of which mankind can raise itself from mindless
survival and engage with the divine. At the top of the columns are the
Christian virtues, and the sides of the actual pulpit are exquisitely worked
scenes from the life of Christ in a classicizing style which suggests that
the artist has carefully studied Roman sarcophagi.[5]

From 1196, there was a special committee to oversee work on the
cathedral, the Opera di Santa Maria, though most of the funding came
from the commune. In 1259, the Bishop of Siena formally renounced
his ecclesiastical prerogative to collect funds for work on the cathedral,
and ceded these rights to the city.[6] The administration of the *Opera
del Duomo* was headed by the *Operaio* who was accountable to the
communal authorities. He was elected annually to his post, though the
position could be, and often was, renewed. In 1258, the direction of
the Opera was handed over to the monks of the Cistercian abbey of
San Galgano, which had been founded in 1244, since they were trusted
by the commune as men of probity and competence. The *Operaio* was
chosen from among the monks until 1314, though for the rest of the

fourteenth century and beyond all the people elected to the post were laymen. The monastery of San Galgano is in a French Gothic style, which had considerable influence on the building style of Siena in general.

The monks seem to have had some input into the design of the cathedral; it is probably down to their influence that the choir was, as it still is, straight-ended, without an apse, probably looking much like the choir of San Galgano, which still stands, albeit without a roof.[7]

The original front of the cathedral was plain masonry, apparently decorated with mosaic,[8] but towards the end of the thirteenth century the commune decided to replace it with a splendid façade, entrusted to the sculptor Giovanni Pisano, who was *Operaio* from 1284 to 1296. The lower level, with its three broad doors, was probably designed by him. He carved the statues of prophets and philosophers that inhabited the niches until they were replaced by copies in 1869. The upper façade was built in 1376, inspired by the cathedral of Orvieto, though the three large gold-ground mosaics which now adorn it are a nineteenth-century addition, made in Venice in 1878. The bronze central door is also recent, replacing a wooden original: called the Porta della Riconoscenza, or 'Door of Recognition', it was commissioned in 1946 as a thank offering to the Virgin for saving the city from bombardment during the German retreat from Tuscany.[9]

The thirteenth-century cathedral probably had a barrel-vaulted roof, with a masonry cupola.[10] The original dome was topped off with a bronze ball, which was paid for in 1264.[11] Cupolas were considerable feats of engineering, and consequently prestigious: they seem to have come to Tuscany around the end of the eleventh century, since the elliptical dome of Pisa cathedral and the dome of the baptistry of Florence were complete by 1100. The word *duomo* derives from Latin 'domus', the house of the Lord, and is equivalent to 'cathedral': it does not mean 'a church with a dome'. However, possessing a *duomo* with a dome was evidently a source of considerable local pride – perhaps especially so for the Sienese because Florence's Duomo did not acquire its dome until 1436.[12] The Siena dome was remodelled in the 1320s, against the advice of a panel of experts; made bigger and more imposing by building another skin around the pre-existing structure. The lantern which now crowns it is a seventeenth-century addition by Bernini, part of the interventions in the fabric sponsored by Pope Alexander VII.

The structure of the Duomo is actually brick, with a decorative skin of white and very dark green marble, now almost black from oxidation. This was also a feature of the thirteenth-century cathedral, since the accounts for 1226 show large amounts of money being spent on black and white marble.[13] Decorative banding is used as a design element in a number of medieval Italian cathedrals, notably the Duomos of Florence and Orvieto, and more locally, the Duomo of Grosseto, but is particularly dramatic at Siena; perhaps because black and white are the colours of the city shield. Siena is frequently represented by fourteenth- and fifteenth-century painters, and their shorthand for the city is a set of walls, some unspecific towers and three of the city's most iconic structures, the striped bell tower and dome of the cathedral, and the Torre del Mangia.

As early as 1309, the Nine were considering enlarging the Piazza del Duomo and upgrading the clerics' houses. In 1317, the choir was extended to accommodate a new baptistery, dedicated to John the Baptist and completed in 1325. Also in 1317, the cathedral acquired a new sacristy and four side altars flanking the high altar (by then adorned by Duccio's *Maestà*), in honour of the four civic saints, who had previously been venerated in the crypt. The Nine were by this time in charge of cathedral finances, and the work on the baptistery reflects this. As with the development of the Campo area, they purchased and demolished houses in the vicinity of the old baptistery to make more space, and appointed an architect, Giovanni Pisano. By making the south side of the cathedral more accessible and more prominent, the new baptistry changed its relationship to the Palazzo Pubblico, to the south. The enlarged door made it possible for sizeable groups of people to move directly from the baptistery to the Campo, or vice versa, allowing for processions which would integrate civil and religious authorities. An additional stimulus to the efforts of the Nine was that the Dominicans and Franciscans had started building large, impressive churches: it is probably no accident that a programme of expanding San Domenico began in 1309, and the Nine started discussing expanding the Duomo in 1311.

In 1339, the commune decided that this modest enlargement was not nearly sufficient. Plans were drawn up for a vast and hubristic extension,

opposite
A view up into the starry interior of the cathedral dome with its playful angels, lit by Bernini's lantern.

overleaf
The terracotta busts of the popes are another notable feature of the interior, often commented on by travellers.

...IVS I INNOCENTIVS I ZOSIMVS

a new three-aisle nave, considerably longer than the original, which would reorient the church through ninety degrees, violating the east–west orientation which is traditional for a cathedral. The foundation stone was laid in 1335, and the project was directed by the goldsmith Lando di Pietro, who was recalled from Naples, where he had been working for Robert of Anjou. Work initially proceeded quite quickly, and the new façade was erected, but it came to a halt when the plague came to Siena in 1348, halving the population. When the Sienese had recovered sufficiently to return to the project in the 1350s, they realized that there were insurmountable problems with the design. The foundations were too shallow for the colossal weight they would need to support, and not all the building materials used had been of adequate quality. A competent Florentine architect, Benci di Cione, paused his work on the cathedral of Florence, and came to Siena to assess the situation. His judgement was that work should cease, since if building continued the whole thing would probably fall down. The right-hand aisle was spared, and the pillars bricked in to create a space for cathedral offices (it is now the Museo dell'Opera del Duomo), while the new façade, now called the Facciatone, was left standing, a monument to unrealized ambition.

In the nineteenth century, many of the works of art created for the cathedral were moved into this museum, such as Duccio's stained-glass window for the choir, and replaced by copies at the original site. Between 1830 and 1850, the sculpture workshop of Antonio Manetti copied Giovanni Pisano's originals, Donatello's *Madonna del Perdono*, and other masterpieces. The cathedral museum thus houses a substantial collection of medieval art which can now be appreciated at close quarters.

Having decided to content themselves with the cathedral at its current size, the Sienese continued to ornament it. Apart from the long project of the cathedral floor, which was noticed and admired by almost every visitor, an additional feature which Protestant visitors almost always commented on is the gallery of 172 terracotta busts of popes which look down from a cornice along both sides of the nave: in the 1590s, the Lincolnshire traveller Fynes Moryson was intrigued to observe that the portraits included the mythical 'Pope Joan'. He must have been one of the last visitors to notice this image, since, on the orders of Clement VIII, the statue was removed around 1600 and replaced by a portrait of Pope Zacharias.[14] Why she was included in the first place remains a mystery, since by the time the popes were added to the cathedral interior in the fifteenth century no educated person believed that Pope Joan had ever existed.

The Duomo played an important role in the lives of the citizens, but not necessarily on a daily basis. The population of the city gathered in the Duomo for special occasions, such as the high feasts of Christmas, Easter and Pentecost. The cathedral was also the starting point for processions on the three days of litanies before Ascension Day. On 15 August, the Feast of the Assumption, Siena offered special veneration to the Virgin. Everyone capable of doing so went to the cathedral to offer a wax candle. The citizens were as splendid as possible, since it was on that day that the servants of the commune were issued with new clothes each year, and it was only on the three days of celebration that women were allowed to wear their finest clothes in public.[15] The cathedral was therefore part of collective religious experience, and an important aspect of what it meant to be Sienese. However, for most people it was not the place where their personal piety was focused. People rich enough to commission personal, family altars tended to site them in the city's Dominican and Franciscan churches rather than the cathedral, suggesting that for many Sienese, their primary religious attachment was to the mendicant orders, which were highly respected for their lively preaching, the personal austerity of the friars' lives and their growing reputation for erudition.[16] Parish churches were also of great importance to individuals, and were similarly sites for family commemoration, though less so in Siena than in other Tuscan cities. The first altar founded in the Duomo by someone other than the cathedral authorities was the altar of the Four Crowned Saints, founded in 1368 by the guild of stonemasons at the completion of the cathedral: since it was their hands that had done the work, they had a special attachment to the building as their greatest and grandest project. The first private altar was as late as 1430 and its donor also had a special relationship with the cathedral, because she was the widow of an *Operaio*. She commissioned an altarpiece with the *Madonna della Neve* from Sassetta to furnish their family chapel.[17]

THE MARBLE PAVEMENT

The cathedral floor is unique in the history of art. It consists of more than fifty intarsia marble panels, mostly black and white, but with some use of red and yellow. It now occupies the entire floor and represents the work of countless craftsmen over six hundred years. It gradually replaced earlier floors, the first of which may have been brick. The first hint of decoration of the cathedral floor comes in 1310, when the Nine released funds for mosaic decorations to the floor by the high altar, despite 'the intolerable expense'.[18] A painting from c.1435–40 by the Master of the Osservanza shows St Anthony Abbot attending mass at what is recognizably a side altar behind the high altar – a side view of Duccio's great *Maestà* is visible. This suggests that in the fifteenth century the floor round the high altar was laid with a geometric pattern of tiles in black, white and pink. The earliest inlaid marble designs to survive are the image of the she-wolf of Siena surrounded by the symbols of the allied cities, originally created in 1373, the 'Wheel of Fortune' from 1406, and another circular design with an imperial eagle in the centre and twenty-four radiating columns. These became illegible through wear, and were replaced in the nineteenth century by Leopoldo Maccari. Between 1833 and 1844, Maccari and another sculptor, Antonio Manetti, were repeatedly paid for repairing areas of the floor.

A celebration of the Mass behind the high altar of the Duomo: a glimpse of Duccio's *Maestà* is depicted on the right. In the late fifteenth century, the floor is clearly still a relatively simple pattern of tiles.

Thus, before the major campaign undertaken in the fifteenth century, there were several pavement panels of secular subjects in the nave, the three which survive, and perhaps others. Two of these seem to be a statement about current politics. A central symbol of Siena, surrounded by the animals which represent the twelve cities with whom she was allied, is clearly a civic subject, and the eagle, a symbol of the emperor, may be a nod to Siena's Ghibelline heritage. The Wheel of Fortune is a standard medieval admonition that prosperity may meet with sudden reversal, or vice versa, and thus potentially a prompt towards civic virtue and meeting sudden calamity with fortitude. There may have been other roundels which expanded on the themes of political identity and good government, since the Sienese seem to have been strongly committed to expressing political ideas in pictorial form, but the documentation of the cathedral, though extensive, does not go into details about iconography. The choice of decoration for the floor was constrained by the fact that the Middle Ages were sensitive about blasphemy, and treading images of Christ, his mother and the saints underfoot was not acceptable. This explains why the first group of images are secular, and

why the subsequent evolution of the floor drew on pre-Christian and Old Testament themes.

The fifteenth century saw a renewal of interest in increasing the area of pictorial paving. Between 1423 and 1426, the Old Testament cycle in the upper transept was created, including a 'story of Joshua' designed by Sassetta. This may have something to do with the fact that Pope Martin V convened a church council in Siena in 1423, which met in the cathedral. The centrepiece of the cycle was a tondo at the foot of the high altar depicting King David playing the harp and singing psalms with his musicians, a place of honour, since David was the royal ancestor of Christ, though also a site which saw a great deal of traffic, which is why the image as it is now was reworked by a Florentine, Matteo Pini, in 1777, on the basis of drawings.[19]

Many of the panels of the floor date to between 1480 and 1505, and were the special project of the then *Operaio*, Alberto Aringhieri, who seems to have taken the existing panels as a starting point for the construction of a more or less orderly narrative, a more humanist approach to decoration which aimed to create a coherent iconography. His pavement commissions created thematic links and correspondences between panels, and sequences of panels. Aringhieri probably exercised more influence over the decoration of the cathedral than any other single man, and it is therefore fitting that he is represented in it. He is depicted by Pinturicchio in the chapel of St John the Baptist, in the habit of a knight of the order of St John of Jerusalem, and again in the Piccolomini Library, as one of the grandees witnessing the betrothal of the emperor and his bride.

A brief examination of Alberto Aringhieri's commissions for the pavement of the cathedral will give the reader an idea of his iconographical interests. In chronological order the pavement panels are as follows:

1. Massacre of the Innocents, left transept, 1480–81
2. Five Sibyls, right side aisle, 1482
3. Story of Jepthah, right transept, 1482–3
4. Five Sibyls, left side aisle, 1483
5. Expulsion of Herod, left transept, 1483–5
6. Baptistry floor repaved with decorative opus sectile, 1486
7. Hermes Trismegistus. first panel of the nave, 1487–9
8. Allegory of Fortune, fourth panel of the nave, 1504–5
9. Two vases inscribed FEL and MEL, outside the church, in front of the two side doors, 1480–1505?

This is a mix of Old Testament and humanist subjects: the Sibyls were pre-Christian women who prophesied the birth of Christ, and Hermes Trismegistus was believed to be the ultimate source of pre-Christian knowledge. The texts associated with him were taken extremely seriously in the fifteenth century because they were believed to be very ancient: it was only in the seventeenth that they were correctly dated to the second or third century BC. In the Allegory, designed by Pinturicchio, Fortune has led a group of men to the island of wisdom. Ascending with difficulty up a rocky path, they find Knowledge sitting on the summit. She is flanked by two philosophers, Socrates, to whom she offers the palm to show he is wisest of all, and Crates, who is emptying a basket of jewels into the sea, illustrating the vanity of riches. From which we see that true virtue is attainable, but only with great effort.

The current scheme for the nave thus mixes fourteenth- and fifteenth-century designs. The worshipper of Aringhieri's time, about to enter the cathedral, would note that vases labelled 'Fel' and 'Mel' are depicted in front of the left-hand and right-hand doors; 'Gall' and 'Honey', perhaps representing the bitterness of human suffering, and the sweetness of heavenly reward (these have since been remodelled and now say 'Mel' and 'Lac', 'Milk' and 'Honey'). As they proceeded down the nave, they would be aware that, to

This roundel depicting the Sienese she-wolf surrounded by emblems of allied cities is the earliest of the cathedral floor decorations we know of, designed in 1373.

CRATES

either side, the Sibyls, each with a careful explanatory label, prophecy the coming of Christ. They might also have observed that two of the Sibyls in the left aisle mention bitter gall in their prophecies. They passed over Hermes Trismegistus, another figure of pre-Christian wisdom, Siena with her allies, the eagle which may represent the emperor, and the Allegory of Fortune. Here they contemplated the virtue of Wisdom, and the capriciousness of Fortune, emphasized by the last scene, that of Fortune's wheel. Perhaps they might recollect the contrast of honey and gall. Finally, the worshipper reached the transept where the massacre of the innocents, the story of Jepthah and the expulsion of Herod reflect themes of martyrdom and sacrifice: the babies murdered on Herod's orders are a type of Christ because they suffer though innocent, as is Jephthah's daughter, equally innocent and sacrificed for the good of her people. The expulsion of Herod, conversely, counterbalances the massacre of the innocents and shows crime appropriately punished, another theme dear to the commune of Siena.

Many of Siena's greatest painters produced designs for the floor: Sassetta contributed a Samson, and Francesco di Giorgio Martini, the story of Judith. Domenico di Bartolo, artist of the frescoes in the Pellegrinaio of Santa Maria della Scala, created a scene with the Emperor Sigismund, the only contemporary to be honoured with a portrait on the floor. Work continued in the sixteenth century, when Domenico Beccafumi was commissioned to create nine Old Testament scenes of startling complexity. Most of them are taken from the Book of Kings. They are complemented by a second Book of Kings cycle, designed by Alessandro Franchi in 1878, which is a remarkable exercise of historical imagination, since his panels are barely distinguishable from those of Beccafumi created more than 360 years earlier.

Pinturicchio depicts the philosopher Crates throwing a basketful of jewels into the sea, though most contemporary Sienese would have found it hard to eschew ostentatious display.

Though the Sienese remained committed to developing and extending this pictorial decoration for centuries, they could see for themselves that it was not entirely practical, and needed incessant repair. By 1600, the images were protected for much of the time and uncovered on special occasions, such as the Feast of the Assumption. The English Catholic priest and travel writer Richard Lassels observed in 1670, 'The Pavement is the best in the world; and indeed too good to be trode on; hence they cover a great part of it with bords hansomely layd together, yet easy to be taken up, to show strangers the beauty of it.'[20]

The pavement was not the only part of Siena Cathedral embellished under Aringhieri's authority. Many important projects initiated under him are still in evidence in the church today, notably the chapel built to house St John the Baptist's arm, and the Piccolomini Library. While the Piccolomini Chapel was commissioned by Cardinal Francesco Todeschini Piccolomini, the cardinal and the *Operaio* were political allies, and the two chapels were designed to harmonize. Both structures, together with the Piccolomini Library, bring a classical Renaissance element to the cathedral, which was a major stylistic departure from earlier work. The frescoes of Old Testament prophets by Guidoccio Cozzarelli and Bastiano di Francesco lining the drum of the dome, and the elaborate carvings on the interior side of the church portals, are also Aringhieri commissions.

One of the earliest of Siena's she-wolves stands outside the Duomo, suckling the city's legendary twin founders, Aschius and Senius.

Aringhieri was forced to abandon work on the cathedral on which he had spent much of his life when Pandolfo Petrucci rose to power in 1500. Later interventions in the cathedral fabric will be discussed in subsequent chapters.

8

EARLY
SIENESE ART

Siena developed a highly distinctive art tradition in the mid-thirteenth century. One of the few pictures from before 1250 which was cherished, for external reasons, was a rather primitive looking image known as 'The Madonna with Big Eyes', which was kept because 'this madonna was the one which harkened to the people of Siena when the Florentines were routed at Montaperti'. That is, this was the painting which stood on the high altar of the cathedral and was presented with the keys of the city before the Battle of Montaperti. From the fifteenth century onwards, the tradition takes a very different direction from the contemporary art of Florence, both formally and in terms of what painting was for. Much Florentine art is portraiture, which reflects the fact that most art was commissioned by private individuals. Sienese art is mostly public, in the service of church or state, and portraiture is very rare.

The Sienese school which developed after 1250 shows a debt to the Byzantine tradition of icon painting, which was much admired in thirteenth-century Italy. This Eastern influence on Sienese painting may stem from the city's trading connections with Venice and the East, but Byzantine painters visited Italy in the thirteenth century, according to Vasari.[1] Anne Derbes has shown that this was a two-way street, and that thirteenth-century painters in the Middle East were influenced by Sienese painters.[2] Sienese art achieved a sophisticated expressiveness as early as 1285, when Duccio's *Rucellai Madonna* successfully reinterpreted the monumentality and profound religious feeling of Byzantine icons in the light of the more realistic gothic art of Western Europe. This work was, incidentally, commissioned by Florentines and widely recognized as a ground-breaking masterpiece, not merely in Siena.

The origin of the Sienese painting tradition in Byzantine icons suggests that the mainspring of Sienese art is religious, and in particular

stems from Siena's devotion to the Virgin. Byzantine icons of the Madonna can be sorted into a number of types. One form which became particularly important to Sienese painters is the Virgin as 'Seat of Wisdom', in which she is seated on a throne, often with a long cylindrical cushion behind her, flanked by angels and/or saints, with a Child on her knee, who has a precociously adult pose and expression. The Virgin herself tends to have a long nose, a grave face and narrow eyes with deep sockets, and to wear a dark blue cloak which covers her head. Icons apart, this way of representing the Virgin also appears in mosaics, such as those in the fifth-century Roman church of Santa Maria Maggiore. Another Byzantine type which struck a chord in Siena is that of the Annunciation, with the winged angel Gabriel approaching with some suggestion of swiftness, and a Mary who shrinks away from him in alarm. One of the first major Sienese painters, who flourished in the second half of the thirteenth century, is known as Guido da Siena. A number of pictures are attributed to him, including a very Byzantine-looking Annunciation.

opposite
The so-called 'Madonna with Big Eyes', one of the earliest known Sienese paintings. It gives little indication of the direction which Sienese art would take in the next generation.

Another Byzantine format which was adopted in Siena is that of the 'vita icon': a full-scale saint in a central panel, with little scenes from his or her life on either side. Another painter, Guido di Graziano, active in Siena in the last quarter of the thirteenth century, painted *St Francis* and *St Peter Enthroned* following this format; both are now in the Siena Pinacoteca.[3] As the type developed in Italy, the relation between the series of small scenes and the main image was rearranged so that they ran beneath it, rather than to either side (and came to be called a predella). Some fourteenth-century Sienese altarpieces, such as that of the *Blessed Agostino Novello* (*c.*1328) by Simone Martini, or that of the *Blessed Umiltà* (*c.*1335) attributed to Pietro Lorenzetti, continue to use the Byzantine format, with scenes from the life on either side of the principal portrait.

overleaf
Guido da Siena's *Annunciation* follows Byzantine tradition in representing Mary's initial reaction to the angel as surprise and alarm.

Despite these debts to Byzantium, the local style rapidly developed in a direction of its own. Duccio di Buoninsegna (born *c.*1255) was one of the city's most important painters. His first commission was twelve coffers for keeping archives in, fulfilled in 1278. He subsequently went to Florence, where he painted the *Rucellai Madonna* in 1285 for a Dominican confraternity based in Florence's Santa Maria Novella, the

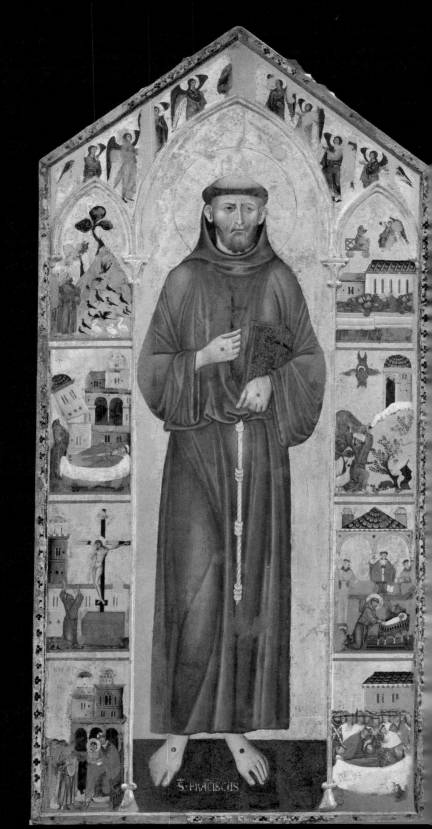

·S·FRACISCUS

Compagnia dei Laudesi. In 1591 it was moved to the adjacent, and much larger, Rucellai family chapel, hence its name. It was long attributed to Cimabue, and thus Vasari, under the impression that it was a Florentine painting, considered it the first step on the road to the art of the Renaissance.[4] Duccio was also influenced by French Gothic art, which was admired in Siena: the monastery of San Galgano, built 1224–88, is one of the most completely French Gothic buildings anywhere in Italy, and Duccio himself, under the name 'Duch de Siène', is recorded as having been in Paris in 1296, in a street where many painters lived.[5] His *Madonna of the Franciscans* is posed against an elaborately patterned background, representing a precious cloth which is held up by angels, an effect which resembles a contemporary French miniature.

'The Madonna with Big Eyes' was honourably retired in 1311, and Duccio's enormous *Maestà* (see page 48) put in her place. On 9 June 1311, the Bishop of Siena, Ruggiero da Casole, led a great procession to celebrate the completion of the new altarpiece. It was a monumental, double-sided work with the enthroned Virgin and Child surrounded by saints on one side and detailed narratives of the passion of Christ on the other. It had been commissioned in 1308 by the *Opera del Duomo*, and was the result of three years' labour and the investment of a great deal of money. A contemporary Sienese chronicler, Agnolo da Tura, describes the festivities:

The composition of Guido da Graziano's *St Francis* is based on that of a Byzantine 'vita icon', with small representations of the saint's deeds on either side of the principal image.

> On the 9th of June at midday, the Sienese led the panel to the Duomo, with grand devotions and processions, with the bishop of Siena, Messer Ruggiero da Casole, with all the clergy of the Duomo and with all the religious of Siena, and the Signori with all the officials of the city, the Podestà and captain and all the citizens in order of worthiness, with candles lit in their hands; and then after the women and children went through Siena with much devotion around the Campo in procession, sounding all the bells in glory; and this entire day the shops stayed shut for devotions, [and] throughout Siena they made many alms to the poor with many prayers and requests to God and to his Mother, Our Lady the Ever Virgin Mary, who helps, preserves, and enhances in peace and in a good state the city of Siena and its jurisdiction, as advocate and protectress of the city, and protects us against every danger and from every evil. And so the panel was placed in the Duomo on the high altar… Everything [is] ornamented with fine gold; and it cost 3,000 gold florins.[6]

The Sienese were obviously enormously proud of their painting, a focal point alike of religious devotion and civic pride, not least in how expensive it had been, but rumour has probably inflated its price by a factor of ten. The art historian Enzo Carli suggests that instead of 3,000 gold florins, the probable cost was 300 florins, which would still have made it more expensive than any other contemporary altarpiece.[7] The monumental figure of the Virgin, cloaked in darkest blue, a very costly pigment, is flanked by more than thirty saints wearing richly decorated robes in subtle variations of gold, red and white, with Siena's four patrons kneeling at the front. For all its formality, the painting is beginning to move away from the Byzantine tradition. The child has a distinctly more babylike face and proportions, and his little hands clutch at his pink wrapping. On the reverse of the *Maestà* were twenty-five small scenes representing the Passion of Christ, with the Crucifixion at the centre. These were not seen by the public, but by the cathedral clergy, who sang their offices in the choir, behind the main altar. On ordinary days, the painting was kept covered so that its impact would not be dulled by exposure: an inventory of 1423 speaks of 'a vermillion hanging to cover the said altar; and a hanging to cover the predella, with a silk fringe, painted in the middle with many colours'.[8] The picture is shown covered in the background of a *biccherna* panel depicting the offering of the city keys to the Virgin (see page 67).

The cathedral continued to be a major patron of the arts throughout the fourteenth century, commissioning works such as painted altarpieces and sculptures, including a set of paintings intended for altars at the east end of the cathedral dedicated to the city's four patron saints, illustrating episodes from the life of the Virgin; her birth, the Annunciation, the Nativity and the Purification, each scene flanked with representations of the city's patrons.[9] The other principal religious patron was the Hospital of Santa Maria della Scala. A fourteenth-century series of mural paintings illustrating the life of the Virgin, executed by Simone Martini and the Lorenzetti brothers, decorated the façade of the hospital for centuries until they were removed in 1720.[10]

Siena is now a city of brick and stone, but the murals on Santa Maria della Scala are a reminder that, in its heyday, the streets blazed with colour. Many of its buildings were plastered in order to take frescoes.

The Blessed Ambrogio Sansedoni swoops to the rescue of a child plummeting from a broken balcony, adroitly catching the loose plank, in this painitng by Simone Martini. The child is shown again on the right, none the worse.

Both the Porta Romana and the Porta Camollia bore frescoes of the Virgin. The exterior of the Palazzo Pubblico was frescoed with scenes from Roman history by Ambrogio Lorenzetti, the first manifestation of a Sienese tradition of civic decoration with Roman themes,[11] notably the city's many she-wolves and twins, Taddeo di Bartolo's frescoes in the Palazzo Pubblico (1414), and Beccafumi's a century later.[12] There were also frescoes of a different kind, *pittura infamante*: as elsewhere in Tuscany, after the execution of a particularly heinous criminal, he was painted on the exterior of the Palazzo Pubblico, often hanging upside down, with an identifying label.[13] The palace of the notaries' guild, which faced onto the Campo, was decorated with a polyptych of the Virgin by Gentile da Fabriano in 1425.

While the origins of the Sienese tradition seem to be in creating images for veneration, principally Madonnas, fourteenth-century Sienese painters also developed a remarkably early interest in landscape which seems to derive from government patronage: Lorenzetti's *Good and Bad Government* frescoes in the Palazzo Pubblico feature panoramic views of the Sienese countryside: the later portrait of the *condottiere* Guidoriccio da Fogliano in the Sala del Mappamondo similarly includes an extensive landscape featuring the castle of Montemassi and the surrounding country. A series of paintings of subject territories, commissioned in 1330, also once decorated the Sala del Mappamondo. Between 1314 and 1331 at least seven castles were painted. A document in the Archivio delle Riformagioni dated 2 August 1328 notes that Simone Martini was paid for painting Montemassi and Sassaforte in the Palazzo.[14] He added Arcidosso and Castel Del Piano in 1331. Around 1345, many of these frescoes had to make way for the Mappamondo, the World Map, by Ambrogio Lorenzetti which is now lost. In the seventeenth or eighteenth centuries, major restoration work was carried out to restore images that had been lost during the construction of the Mappamondo, suggesting that landscapes were commissioned for the specific purpose of asserting control over the area depicted. The magical small paintings known as *The City by the Sea* and *The Castle by a Lake* may be cut-down fragments, but if they are not then they are the first purely landscape paintings in Western art.

It is important to recognize that in the first half of the fourteenth century Sienese painters were widely perceived as practising a new and original art. Simone Martini stood out among the Sienese painters of this period, since he was the quasi-official painter to the commune: it was not until he moved to Avignon around 1335 that major commissions went to other artists. The poet Petrarch, who became acquainted with Martini in Avignon, hailed him as one of the two greatest contemporary painters (the other being Giotto, a Florentine).[15] Martini's masterpiece was a second *Maestà*, painted for the Palazzo Pubblico, which shares the formal qualities of Duccio's painting, but to rather different effect. The enthroned Virgin is seated under a huge ceremonial canopy supported on poles, wearing an intricately patterned pale blue gown, with the four civic saints kneeling in intercession, and ranks of saints on either side, as in Duccio's painting. Her features and colouring continue the trend towards a more naturalistic representation of divine figures. The Christ Child holds a scroll which reads, 'Love Justice, you who judge the earth', for this image is not aimed at the people of Siena, but at the city's rulers. This is the Madonna as a figure of Justice: poems in Italian terza rima, inscribed on the steps, use her voice to warn the Nine to fulfil their duties and refrain from oppressing the poor.

overleaf The *City by the Sea*, perhaps by Sassetta: the community is an aristocratic one, since it possesses a citadel and bristles with towers. It is not Talamone, since it has no harbour.

The originality of Sienese art was recognized by one of the first English speakers to discuss it, the mid-nineteenth-century art historian Anna Jameson: 'the painters of Siena alone retained a particular stamp of nationality, which in the course of two centuries they never wholly lost. While the school of Florence developed into increasing vigour, elegance, and dignity, that of Siena leaned towards pathos and sentiment – qualities remarkable in Duccio and his successors, and which characterized the Siena pictures even when that peculiar pathetic grace was afterwards modified by the grand drawing of the Florentine school.' She particularly admired Simone Martini's painting of St Louis, painted in Naples, where it remains, for Robert of Anjou.[16] When another lady traveller called Mrs Westropp, an educated woman with an eye for paintings, visited Siena in 1854, she was puzzled but moved by early Sienese art: 'All the early paintings were on golden grounds and on Scriptural subjects, and all were so holy, so expressive, notwithstanding their quaintness and stiffness.'[17]

One of the interesting things about early Sienese art is the strength of the emotional response it engenders. It leaves some completely cold, but provokes intense reactions from others. John Pope-Hennessey, who started working on Sienese art at a time when it was completely

out of fashion, is clear about this. 'The virus I caught at Oxford was emotional, and I have never recovered from it. Sienese pictures spoke to me (as they must have done to so many other people) in accents so seductive and so intimate that to look at them was like a conversation on a scrambler telephone.'[18] The British-Libyan journalist Hisham Matar voices a similar sense of intimate connection. He lives in London, and visits two of Duccio's panels from the reverse of the *Maestà*, now in the National Gallery, again and again. He writes: 'the precision and particular generosity of Duccio's work opened up a door through which others could pass. This unveiling of new territory must be one of the most remarkable achievements that an artist can attain.'[19] He has a sense above all of emotional closeness. Gazing at Duccio's *Madonna of the Franciscans* in Siena itself, 'I felt that the painting was painted specifically for me and as though by a brother, not only because Duccio, like all men and women, is a fellow human being, but because it was obvious to me that he did not intend his picture to be approached from a place of affiliation or allegiance, but rather from the simple position of being human.'[20]

previous pages
Simone Martini's *Maestà* warns the Nine to carry out their duties with scrupulous justice.

opposite
Duccio's *Madonna of the Franciscans* is on a smaller scale than his *Maestà*, but still formidably majestic. The green-patterned cloth behind her suggests French influence on his development.

One of the best known of all the frescoes in the Palazzo Pubblico is the image of a single armed knight on a caparisoned horse riding between two hilltop towns, with the date 1328 in Roman numerals. This identifies the subject as Guidoriccio da Fogliano, who secured the castle of Montemassi for Siena in that year. The fresco has long been recognized as an early triumph of landscape painting. Additionally, the Polish poet Zbigniew Herbert responded strongly to the sheer power of the image of the *condottiere* commander, and the sense of mastery it exudes: 'both rider and beast constitute a single body emanating tremendous energy and strength, though they ride at walking pace. Had the chronicles been silent about the cruelties of the *condottieri*, this portrait would furnish sufficient indictment.'[21] Beneath Guidoriccio was Ambrogio Lorenzetti's World Map, rotating on a central spindle, which has scratched great concentric rings into the wall on which it hung. From surviving descriptions, it seems to have put Siena at the centre of the inhabited world. This was mounted over an earlier fresco depicting the surrender of a fortified town to Sienese authority.[22]

· ÂNO · DÑI MCCCXXVII ·

·TCCC·XⅩ·VIII·

The Sala della Pace – the council chamber of the Nine in the Palazzo – contains a suite of three frescoes, also by Ambrogio Lorenzetti, which form one of the greatest and most original painted compositions of the Middle Ages: they were known to contemporaries as 'Peace and War', though they are now usually called *Allegory of Good and Bad Government*.[23] These constitute a complex allegorical statement on behalf of the regime of the Nine, created by a painter who is known to have been an educated man.[24] They were apparently made for the edification of the whole community, not just of those who served as members of the Nine, since a fourteenth-century Sienese chronicle states that they are 'in the communal palace, at the top of the staircase, the first door on the left, and if you go there, you can see it'.[25] 'Everybody', however, must mean 'all men', since women were not permitted to enter the Palazzo Pubblico.[26]

previous pages
Guidoriccio da Fogliano pacing through a pacified countryside: the black and white flag of Siena flutters from the citadel on the right. The low green structures are soldiers' bivouacs covered with leafy branches.

The fresco on the shorter wall depicts the qualities necessary for a well-governed city. Justice is the central quality, informed by Wisdom: with one hand, she punishes vice and rewards virtue, and with the other guarantees weights and measures. Beside her, six female Virtues sit, three on either side of a monumental figure wearing the black and white of Siena's shield, the *balzana*: he is the Good Commune, and they are Peace, Fortitude, Prudence, Magnanimity, Temperance, with a second figure of Justice, balancing the severed head of an executed man on her knee. The longer east wall represents the effects of good government in city and countryside: the orderly hum of civic life, with a building under construction, pupils learning in a school, buying and selling; a group of beautifully dressed dancers (nine of them, perhaps a reference to the Nine), flocks of sheep, donkeys with their burdens and pots of flowers perched on windowsills. Outside the city, peasants are at work and aristocrats enjoy the pleasures of the countryside. This is one of the first major landscape paintings in the history of Western art. On the opposite wall, and unfortunately in poor condition, is a fresco showing the effect of bad government; a building is being torn down, the bricks allowed to fall carelessly into the streets, which are the haunts of rapists, murderers and sodomites: Dennis Romano has observed that one of two young men depicted is seducing his companion.[27] Similarly, the country is a ravaged wilderness where ghostly armies trample untended fields and villages lie in burning ruins. Economic and moral breakdown go hand in hand; there are no animals in either city or countryside, and nobody is engaged in productive work of any kind. Repeatedly, the *Good Government* panels remind the viewer that crime should be punished, as San Bernardino noted in a sermon. The figure of 'security' flies over the peaceful *contado*, holding a gibbet with a hanged man: 'I see a man being hanged in order to maintain holy justice. And for this [reason] everyone lives in holy peace and concord.'[28]

The political message of the Lorenzetti frescoes was underlined by other artwork in the Palazzo Pubblico which celebrated the Roman republican tradition. In the *Allegory of Good Government*, a she-wolf suckles twins at the feet of the personified Good Commune, an indication that the Sienese had grafted themselves onto the Roman origin legend by 1338. But Lorenzetti also painted scenes from Roman history (no longer extant) on the façade of the Palazzo, which are very likely to have been illustrations of the defence of republican virtue taken out of Livy. Certainly, Simone Martini painted Marcus Regulus in 1338 in the Sala del Concistoro (this no longer survives): Regulus was a sort of republican saint, since rather than break his word he returned to Carthage to face certain death by torture.

Sienese artists were not unaware of other traditions, but adopted them in their own way. Duccio was not the only artist to show some influence from International Gothic style. Many of the distinctive features of fourteenth-century Sienese art emerge from the fact that art patronage appears to have been almost entirely either religious or civic and communal. Majestic altarpieces were commissioned for the city's churches, and splendid decorations in the Palazzo Pubblico. This art was demotic; apart from Guidoriccio, who is celebrated as a successful military leader, not a ruler, the principal subject is the city itself, its saints and the Virgin. Sienese artists represent their city over and over again, and they represent civicness, especially in Lorenzetti's great *Allegory of Good Government*. In paintings illustrating miracles, homely saints swoop to the rescue of little children falling from recognizably Sienese balconies, and the *biccherna* panels often represent the city in the form of a graphic shorthand; the Torre del Mangia and the striped bell tower of the Duomo, supported by the towers of the magnates. Alternatively, they depict a group of citizens engaged in serving the state.

Another aspect of the Sienese art tradition is that painters seem to have been perceived more as craftsmen than artists. The Sienese painting tradition demands exceptional levels of skill: painters and patrons alike were aware of the technical ability required to lay on gold leaf, transform it to shimmering mystery with delicate little punches, glaze transparent colours over gold and perhaps scratch it away again to create the effect of brocade. Despite their expertise, they did not make much money: Sano di Pietro stood at the head of a flourishing workshop, but his tax returns suggest that he was not a wealthy man. Sassetta was the most highly regarded painter in Siena in his day, but the doctor's fees for his care during his final illness (pneumonia) used up all his capital and his funeral had to be paid for by mortgaging his last remaining property.[29]

Gold was not the only valuable and technically problematic material used by late medieval and Renaissance painters. Paints and glazes were difficult to prepare and often required expensive ingredients: ultramarine blue was made by grinding lapis lazuli, from Afghanistan, and was as expensive as gold, if not more so. If for some reason a painting was no longer required by its owners, sometimes the gold ground, or even the more expensive pigments as well, were scraped off the panel. The fifteenth-century Sassetta's *God the Father, Blessing* lost its gold in this way, as did the panels of an altarpiece he made for the Piccolomini.[30] Simone Martini's *Madonna and Child* from the village of Lucignano d'Arbia (c.1320–25) was discovered in 1957 by Enzo Carli under a sixteenth-century painting of the Madonna and Child, now in the Siena Pinacoteca. The gold background and the Virgin's cloak of ultramarine blue have been completely removed, leaving only the swaddled Child, and the Virgin's head, neck and a triangle of her dress.[31]

Other important pigments include cinnabar red, which is mercury sulphide, and usually came from Almadén in Spain (though it was to be found on Monte Amiata), and orpiment yellow, which is arsenic sulphide. Both are extremely toxic. Additionally, orpiment, though it gave a bright and long-lasting yellow, was hard to use because it was incompatible with lead-based pigments (also toxic); if other lead-based paints were being used, then lead-tin yellow had to be deployed instead. A successful painter was therefore a man who had mastered a wide variety of technical skills and had a considerable understanding of practical chemistry. Painters did not work in isolation: Simone Martini headed up a workshop of considerable size, and on many occasions painters of similar standing collaborated on major works. The paintings attributed to the Master of the Osservanza were probably produced by a collaborative workshop.[32] The complicated carpenter's work involved in creating an altarpiece, with its many panels, was also part of the workshop's tasks.[33] Apprentices needed to acquire technical knowledge, and many hands were needed for tasks such as making paint, gilding, preparing surfaces for painting and laying down large areas of lesser interest such as the sky. Painting ran in families, and, additionally, painters often married other painters' daughters.

Despite the collaborative nature of artistic production, patrons did not hold all painters as producing work of equal value. It is clear that Duccio, Martini and Ambrogio Lorenzetti were each in their turn considered the best painter in Siena. Contracts drawn up between patrons and painters often stipulate that all the painting should be from the master's hand – or, at the very least, that only he should do the faces.[34] They also specify that particular, expensive pigments are to be used, with no skimping on quality, and fine gold should be used for the gilding. Since the painter's fee covered his materials as well as his work, there was a considerable temptation to use cheaper colours. In Duccio's *Maestà*, the huge, dark mass of the Virgin's cloak is very striking; but we do not think, as his first admirers would have thought, that it represents an enormous outlay on ultramarine blue, any more than we think about the quantity of gold leaf used in the painting as a whole in terms of its bullion value.

In 1348, plague hit Siena for the first time, and Ambrogio Lorenzetti was one of the victims. The only master painter to survive into the second half of the century was Lippo Memmi, Simone Martini's brother-in-law and imitator, who lived till 1356. It seems that younger painters trained by the Lorenzetti brothers must also have died, since they left no followers. Bartolo di Fredi was probably the most important new painter of the second half of the fourteenth century. Samuel Cohn has noted that demand for art increased after the Black Death, but this did not necessarily produce a new crop of maestros and masterpieces. Because of the shortage of painters, as of other artisans, workshops economized and rationalized. Paintings themselves became smaller, cheaper and less sophisticated. Cohn calculated that individual paintings realized one-fifth of the price they fetched before the plague, basically because they were mostly small-scale.[35] Between 1348 and 1363, Siena's painters formed a flexible cooperative, working together and absorbing aspects of one another's techniques.[36] Much Sienese patronage was still collective rather than personal, with the mendicant orders well to the fore: Bartolo di Fredi's fellow painter Andrea Vanni was commissioned to create a large number of Virgins of Humility in 1394, one for each nun's cell in a new Dominican convent in Venice, as near to mass production as the fourteenth century was capable of.[37]

The hospital of Santa Maria della Scala's coffers were bursting after 1348, owing to the number of people who had died having left their property to the hospital, and they splashed out on a collection of important relics. A go-between, the Florentine Pietro di Giunta Torrigiani, acquired a collection of relics from the imperial chapel at Constantinople in 1359, in exchange for 3,000 florins and a house in Siena.[38] This was one of the largest and most prestigious groups of relics in Italy, and included one of the nails from the Cross, and relics of Mary, including her girdle.[39] The hospital was already extensively decorated with exterior frescoes by Simone Martini and the Lorenzettis (now lost), but they commissioned a great Assumption of the Virgin from Bartolomeo Bulgarini in the mid-1360s to celebrate their acquisition of the girdle: he was a painter who worked for them quite regularly.[40] Confraternities also sponsored artworks: Bartolo di Fredi's fine *Adoration of the Magi* was one such. Many of Bartolo's commissions came from religious organizations to which he belonged.[41]

As Siena began to recover from the difficulties of the fourteenth century, a new major artist appeared. This was Sassetta (c.1392–1450), a delicate, visionary artist whose work unites the Sienese tradition of gold grounds and refined and elaborate patterning with a new interest in perspective. He was much favoured by the Sienese government for public commissions, but also worked for other organizations and for private clients. Art patronage, like other aspects of Sienese society, was beginning to change in the fifteenth century. The wealthy were increasingly interested in leaving money for private chapels as family memorials, though in Siena their altarpieces were less likely to include donor portraits than elsewhere in Italy. Sassetta's *Madonna della Neve* is an indication of changing times: though it was painted for the Duomo, it was a private commission, by Donna Ludovica, widow of Turino di Matteo, the *Operaio* of the Cathedral Works.[42]

One of the predella panels, the small images beneath the main picture, for the altarpiece Sassetta made for the Sienese wool guild (*Arte della Lana*), which celebrated the miracle of the Eucharist, shows his grasp of new Florentine ideas about perspective. It depicts St Thomas Aquinas in prayer: in the distance is a view through to a garden with a well, and, on the right, a monastic library with books laid out on desks, all treated strictly according to the rules of perspective. The main panel, which is lost, is known to have shown a monstrance, a vessel for displaying the Eucharistic wafer, carried by angels and floating above a landscape with towns and castles, suggesting that Sassetta had made a study of Lorenzetti's *Allegory of Good Government*. Others of his paintings which survive also show great interest in the Tuscan landscape. The *Arte della Lana* adopted the Carmelite feast of Corpus Domini (later called Corpus Christi), a new, conspicuous and very popular devotion, in 1367, and the altarpiece was created solely for this major public festival. It was kept in in a cupboard in the *Arte della Lana* headquarters, and brought out once a year to decorate a temporary altar which was the final resting place of an elaborate monstrance containing the Host which had been paraded through the city under a baldachin in the course of the day.[43] Sassetta died suddenly in his fifties of pneumonia, which he contracted while working out of doors painting a fresco of the Coronation of the Virgin on the Porta

overleaf Sassetta shows more interest in perspective than earlier Sienese painters. The views through to a courtyard with a fountain, and a library with books laid on desks are carefully worked out.

Romana, a reminder of the physical hazards faced by painters, who ran a daily risk of poisoning from the pigments they used and frequently had to paint from a scaffold, or outdoors. Several of the paintings he left unfinished were taken over by Sano di Pietro, five years younger and trained in his style, including the Porta Romana fresco.[44] Sano di Pietro was the head of an extremely productive and prolific workshop, which continued to produce somewhat generic 'Sienese' paintings of otherworldly Madonnas and favoured saints until his death in 1480, by which time his art was something like a century out of date. It is therefore revealing about Sienese taste that his work was not only marketable, but popular. In 1448, Sano was asked to paint a predella for the Cappella dei Signori in the Palazzo Pubblico, which was to represent 'five stories of Our Lady like those that are above the door of the Scala Hospital' – thus, to base his work on paintings a hundred years old.[45]

He was not the only Sienese to be able to paint in an anachronistic style. Lippo Vanni painted *The Battle of Val di Chiana* in 1363, in the Sala del Mappomondo. The commune decided to commemorate the Battle of Poggio Imperiale, fought in 1479, and commissioned a painting from Giovanni di Cristofano Ghini and Francesco d'Andrea which looks as if it was contemporary with Vanni rather than a work of a hundred years later. Similarly, Giovanni di Pietro's *Annunciation*, painted in the mid-1450s, is a reworking of Simone Martini's *Annunciation* of 1333. An important aspect of the Sienese approach to art is the maintenance of dialogue with earlier, venerated works, so that the public art of the city gradually became an unfolding conversation.

The Florentine perspective imposed on art history by Vasari has been slow to dissolve, and it has taken centuries for the Sienese painting tradition to be appreciated. The lens through which the first of its admirers, nineteenth-century critics such as Anna Jameson and John Ruskin, were able to understand early Sienese painting was religion. Later, by 1900, the American art historian Bernard Berenson and others were beginning to appreciate its formal qualities, but Sienese painting was not compatible with modernist distrust of representation and illustration, and if it was admired at all in the mid-twentieth century it was for its use of colour. Postmodernism, however, took a more relaxed view of representation, and the British painter and curator Timothy Hyman, visiting Siena as an art student in the 1960s, found the work of Sassetta and his contemporaries relevant to his own for completely other reasons: 'the concerns of Sienese painters – intensity of flat colour, spatial experimentation, narrative, the representation of the city – seemed to converge astonishingly with those of my contemporaries.'[46] Modern painters who have consciously referenced early Sienese work in their own art include R. B. Kitaj, Ken Kiff, Anne Redpath and Bhupen Kakhar.[47]

OTHER ARTS

There was a good deal of crossover between painting and applied arts. In addition to being a painter, Simone Martini was a skilful miniaturist, goldsmith, enamellist and expert in ivory work. By the fourteenth century, working with metal was something of a Sienese speciality. One particular area of expertise was goldsmith's work, in which Siena achieved a European pre-eminence. In particular, the Sienese makers' development of new, translucent enamels played an essential role in the development of the goldsmith's art in medieval Europe. The area to be enamelled was worked in very fine bas-relief, and when the coloured glass paste was put in and baked, the translucent colour showed deeper where it was thicker, lighter where it was thin. Siena in the fourteenth century was a trading city and its merchant bankers went all over Europe. Small, high-value items were easy to carry, and thus Sienese goldwork circulated very widely, and was highly prized.

One type of object for which there was always a ready market was a chalice for the mass. Since they were used for a sacred purpose, chalices were made of precious materials. A typical fourteenth-century chalice had a broad foot and a knop halfway up the stem, below the actual cup. Both foot and knop could be, and often were, heavily decorated, and offered an excellent field for decorative enamelwork. The earliest known Sienese silver-gilt and enamel chalice was made by a goldsmith called Guccio di Mannaia between 1288 and 1292 for Pope Nicholas IV, which he presented to the basilica of St Francis in Assisi, where it remains. It is decorated with ninety-six translucent enamels which include depictions of the Crucifixion, the Virgin and Child, Franciscan saints and Pope Nicholas himself. The colours used include azure, violet, yellow-gold, green, brown and blue. These are exquisite miniature works of art which indicate that the new technique was already fully developed by the late thirteenth century. Another goldsmith who served the papacy was Toro da Siena, who flourished c.1320, the first goldsmith admitted to the papal court in Avignon by Celestine V and John XXII, where he worked from 1299 to 1323: a pastoral mitre made from precious materials survives from his hand.[48]

We know the names of dozens of Sienese goldsmiths, since they frequently signed their work, and we also know that there was a major dynasty, the 'dei Tondi', which includes Tondino di Guerrino, the maker of a remarkable chalice now in the British Museum. Another chalice which is in the Victoria and Albert is the work of Giacomo di Tondo. It is engraved with the arms of the Rocchi family of Siena, suggesting that it was made for a church within the city and presented to it as a gift. It was common to bequeath a chalice to a specific church important to the giver, usually linked to a request for commemorative masses to benefit the souls of the giver and his or her family.

Some commissions were extremely ambitious. The late thirteenth-century reliquary of the head of St Galgano, in the Museo dell'Opera del Duomo in Siena, is in the form of a turret, just over a metre tall, made of copper and gilded silver. It represents the adoption of a Northern Gothic idea of making reliquaries in the form of miniature architectural structures, and shows that Sienese craftsmen both influenced those of other countries and were influenced by them. Panels tell the history of St Galgano as well as depicting other saints. Another early and very important Sienese reliquary contains the Holy Corporal of Bolsena, believed to be stained with Christ's blood during a mass which was said in 1263, when the host began to bleed and stained the corporal, the cloth on which the chalice was resting. It was made in 1337–8 by Ugolino di Vieri, and is the first representation of the miracle. The design, like that of the Galgano reliquary, is architectural, and based on the façade of Orvieto Cathedral, where it is preserved.[49]

A slightly later reliquary from 1376 is that of St Agatha, the patron saint of Sicily, and extends the goldsmith's art in a different direction; it is a half-length figure of the saint, her face exquisitely enamelled in flesh tints, and clad in a sumptuous cloak. It is attributed to Giovanni di Bartolo and was made for the cathedral of Catania, where it still is. The bust is an indication of the close relations that the Anjou dynasty, which then controlled the kingdom of Naples, had with Siena: there were several visits by Anjou rulers to Siena, and many Sienese craftsmen spent part of their career in Naples, including Simone Martini and Lando di Pietro. The Hungarian connections of the house of Anjou took some Sienese even further afield. Charles, grandson of Charles II of Naples and Mary of Hungary, was invited to Hungary in 1301, and was accompanied there by a Neapolitan knight, Philip Druget. With Druget's assistance, Charles overcame his enemies and was elected king in 1308, after which Druget was rewarded with extensive lands in north-east Hungary. His servants included two Sienese goldsmith brothers, Pietro and Niccolo Simoni, who were so favoured that they rose from being artisans to minor aristocracy, and received the estate of Jamnik as a royal grant.[50]

The reliquary bust of St Agatha in the cathedral of Catania is a triumph of the Sienese goldsmith's art. Its elaborate baroque setting bears witness to the continued importance of the saint's cult.

Siena continued to produce extremely skilled metalworkers and goldsmiths in the sixteenth century. One such was Simone di Giovanni Ghini, who created the reliquary bust of St Andrew commissioned by Pius II for his new cathedral in Pienza. Another was Pastorino Pastorini, a master glassmaker who made several stained-glass windows for Siena Cathedral under the direction of Baldassare Peruzzi before realizing that he had an exceptional talent for portraiture, and switching to making portrait medals in the second half of his career.

9

THE
BLACK DEATH
AND AFTER

Europe had a rough fourteenth century. A run of exceptionally cold winters from 1303 to 1328 caused the Baltic Sea to freeze over completely in 1303, 1306 and 1307, something never previously recorded. Famine and disease were widespread: Tuscany suffered famines in 1318 and 1323, and food was short enough to provoke rioting in Siena between 1328 and 1330. Another famine struck the region in 1347. Part of the reason for this is that the population had risen dramatically. By 1318, the population of Siena was already 52,000, enormous in medieval terms.[1] In fact, Siena was bursting at the seams, and attracting settlers from the smaller towns in the *contado*. The Sienese chronicler Agnolo di Tura reports that in 1323 it was necessary to build new walls and gates in the district of Valdimontone to accommodate new city dwellers, and in 1345 the walls were extended in all three of Siena's *terzi*, still to be seen on the ground.[2]

Siena's position on one of Italy's most significant roads had been one of its greatest assets. In 1348, it became a spectacular liability, when a new and terrifyingly transmissible disease came to Europe from the East. The natural home of the plague bacterium, *Yersinia pestis*, is now understood to be the Tian Shan Mountains, on the border between western China and eastern Kyrgyzstan, where it is an endemic disease of various desert rodents, and mostly transmitted by their fleas, though it can linger in the soil under certain conditions, and can also be transmitted by eating infected animals.[3]

It has now become possible to sequence the genome of *Yersinia pestis*, and to compare modern strains with ancient ones, because the DNA of the bacterium can be extracted from the tooth pulp of fourteenth-century victims. By the time of death, the blood in the tooth is full of bacteria, and the outer enamel layer protects it through the centuries. For most of its history, *Y. pestis* had very limited genetic diversity, but this changed suddenly at some point in the thirteenth century, when four still-surviving variants arose within a short time period.[4] The Black Death can now be traced to a single one of these new strains of *Y. pestis*.[5] Its original home lay deep in the Mongol empire created by Genghis Khan late in the twelfth century. The Mongols' superb horsemen created a communication network which ran from Russia to Persia, and from the Punjab to Manchuria. It is commonly thought that Mongols came into contact with infected insects or rodent hosts as early as the thirteenth century, and carried the disease with fatal swiftness across Asia, because they hunted one of the principal natural hosts for the plague, marmots, large rodents up to about ten kilos in weight, whose meat the Mongols considered a delicacy. They also made 'nomad leather' from their skins, which was both waterproof and very warm.[6] The Mongols seem to have brought the new and virulent strain of *Y. pestis* with them when they advanced into China, since several sieges they undertook between 1218 and 1232 were accompanied by outbreaks of epidemic disease, in which as many as a thousand defenders died each day.[7] However, as Monica Green observes, 'the fact remains that Mongol sources record nothing *systematically* catastrophic for the thirteenth century in the way that western Eurasian sources will do at the onset of the Black Death'.[8] Bruce Campbell has suggested that an underlying reason why it was the fourteenth century that saw a pandemic rather than merely outbreaks of epidemic disease is that the climate was changing. The climate disturbances of the mid-fourteenth century brought rain to the dry deserts of Central Asia. This will have increased the numbers of wild rodents, and also the amount of interaction with them, since humans would have taken advantage of pasture for their horses.[9]

Much of what we think we know about the plague comes from studying the second outbreak which occurred in the late nineteenth century. But the disease then identified as *Yersinia pestis* proved not as infectious as all that. It had a complex means of transmission, which was only discovered in the early twentieth century: fleas which had sucked infected blood from their rodent hosts could pass on the bacterium when they bit humans.[10] So an outbreak of plague was signalled by a very obvious outbreak of disease among rats. A witness observed in 1894, 'the rats... would come out of their holes in broad daylight even, and tumble about in a dazed condition and die'.[11] Their fleas sought human victims only when they had run out of rats.

However, there are significant differences between the fourteenth-
and nineteenth-century diseases. The bacterium which caused the
fourteenth-century variety was not biologically identical to current
variants, and its effects were different. Though some modern plague
victims develop a bubo (usually only one), they do not go on to develop
the dark boils or pustules all over the body which are mentioned, and
illustrated, in medieval chronicles.[12] Moreover, not a single medieval
witness observed rats dying in large numbers. The nightmarish scenes
described by chroniclers indicate that the disease was violently infectious.
Transmission by rat fleas alone is not compatible with the speed at which
the disease travelled, especially since it reached areas of Europe where
black rats were not found. Transmission via human fleas and perhaps
lice has been suggested.[13] But many witnesses report that victims were
spitting blood, so airborne transmission from one human to another
was certainly possible, and there was possibly additional danger from
animal bites, contact with infected blood, handling infected clothing
or objects, or eating diseased meat. From the point of view of terrified
medieval people, the arrival of the plague meant watching loved ones
falling victim to an agonizing and disfiguring illness, spitting blood and
burning with fever, while dark spots developed all over their bodies.

What all this suggests is that the disease which exploded out of western
China took a very different form from the plague of the nineteenth
century. Scientists working on ancient plague pits have confirmed that
the pathogen was indeed a variant of *Yersinia pestis*, but it was one which
was different from the modern variety. One group discovered 'a *Y. pestis*
variant that has not previously been reported', and confirmed that 'no
extant *Y. pestis* strain possesses the same genetic profile as our ancient
organism'.[14]

By the fourteenth century East–West trade was quite extensive.
Sienese paintings depict members of the heavenly court wearing Eastern
silks, and the food of the wealthy was flavoured with Eastern spices. There
was a caravan route from northern China to the Black Sea, protected by
the Mongol Peace, which was enforced by the Mongol khans to ensure
that trade would prosper. There were also two important sea routes: one
across the Indian Ocean to the Persian Gulf, the other going from South
Asia around Arabia to the Red Sea, whence merchandise was taken
overland to the Mediterranean. Genoese merchants were waiting at the

Black Sea, and Venetians and Pisans in the southern Mediterranean, to load these desirable goods into their own vessels and carry them to Italy.

In 1347, these traders returned home carrying the seeds of the greatest human pandemic yet experienced. Plague came to Constantinople in 1347 and ripped through the Byzantine empire. Simultaneously, homebound Genoese ships brought it to Italy. In *The Decameron*, Giovanni Boccaccio mentions that in 1347 the Florentines had heard of a plague raging in the East, but it had evidently not occurred to anybody that it might spread: the dangers of an interconnected world had yet to be understood. In fact, the plague grimly demonstrated the disadvantages of a world linked by commercial, diplomatic and religious ties. After only a year, in 1348, it had reached London, which implies that it was travelling across Europe at a rate of more than two miles a day. It hit the rest of England the year after, and was in Scotland by 1350. Marchionne di Coppo Stefani's *Florentine Chronicle* reveals something of the human impact:

there seemed to be no cure. There was such a fear that no one seemed to know what to do... The symptoms were the following: a bubo in the groin, where the thigh meets the trunk; or a small swelling under the armpit; sudden fever; spitting blood and saliva (and no one who spit blood survived it). It was such a frightful thing that when it got into a house, as was said, no one remained. Frightened people abandoned the house and fled to another. Those in town fled to villages... And many died with no one looking after them. And many died of hunger because when someone took to bed sick, another in the house, terrified, said to him: 'I'm going for the doctor'. Calmly walking out the door, the other left and did not return again.

A particularly dramatic representation of a plague-struck city by Josse Lieferinxe; people collapse in the street while victims wrapped in sheets are hastily buried. A tiny St Sebastian kneels on a cloud, praying for mercy.

Another classic account of the plague came from the Sienese Agnolo da Tura, a shoemaker who also held a number of minor civic offices. His wife Nicoluccia was rather given to telling him that she had married beneath her. They had five children. This unexceptional family was devastated in 1348. He writes,[15]

The mortality began in Siena in May [1348]. It was a cruel and horrible thing; and I do not know where to begin to tell of the cruelty and the pitiless ways... And the victims died almost immediately. They would swell beneath their armpits and in their groins, and fall over dead while talking. Father abandoned child, wife husband, one brother another; for this illness seemed to strike through the breath and sight. And so they died. And none could be found to bury the dead for money or friendship. Members of a household brought their dead to a ditch as best they could, without priest, without divine offices. Nor did the death bell sound. And in many places in Siena great pits were dug and piled deep with the multitude of dead. And they died by the hundreds both day and night, and all were thrown in those ditches and covered over with earth. And as soon as those ditches were filled more were dug. And I, Agnolo di Tura, called 'the Fat', buried my five children with my own hands. And there were also those who were so sparsely covered with earth that the dogs dragged them forth and devoured many bodies throughout the city… And it was all so horrible that I, the writer, cannot think of it and so will not continue.

He does not mention her here, but his wife Nicoluccia also died. Agnolo goes on to observe the psychological impact on the survivors: 'those that survived were like persons distraught and almost without feeling.' About half the population of the city died, either of the plague itself, or from being abandoned to die of thirst and starvation. The total breakdown of ordinary human relations under the pressure of selfish terror is attested again and again by chroniclers all over Europe; the helplessness of doctors, the abandonment of the rituals of Christian death, human bodies treated as carrion. Major industry ceased in Siena, and wool production shut down almost completely. For about three months, most governmental activity ground to a halt, as did buying and selling. Almost all work ceased; in the countryside, mills were closed, fields were neglected and animals left untended. In a brave but somewhat pathetic attempt to cope with the crisis, Siena's governors elected a group of citizens, with a budget of a thousand gold florins which they were to distribute to the afflicted and those too poor to bury their dead.[16]

A contemporary Florentine novelist, Franco Sacchetti, illustrates the gallows humour of some survivors with a little story. A man, dying of the plague and abandoned by all his kith and kin, summoned a notary and got him to write 'that his sons and heirs, every year on the feast day of St Jacob in July, must give a basket filled with a *staio* of sliced pears to the flies', because 'in this my present illness, I have received assistance from neither friend nor kin, all have abandoned me, except the flies'.[17]

Samuel Cohn, using the evidence of wills, shows a remarkable shift in Sienese mentality after the plague. The survivors of 1348 showed an amazing emotional resilience and continued to behave like their parents and grandparents. When they died, they left a large proportion of their wealth in the form of dozens of pious little legacies; to their parish church, to the Duomo or the hospital, to the Franciscans, or to a convent, with no strings attached.[18] What really changed the Sienese was not the plague of 1348, but the return of the disease in 1363, for two reasons. Firstly, it showed that the plague was not a single monstrous event, but would keep on coming back. Second, the 1363 bout predominantly killed those born in the fifteen years since the first visitation – thus the city's children, and with them, hope for the future. This tendency grew even stronger in successive visitations. The records of Siena's Dominican cemetery show that the third time the plague came to Siena, in 1374, more than half the dead were children, and the fourth time, in 1383, they comprised 88 per cent of the victims.[19]

What this suggests is that medieval people adapted quite successfully to the plague and developed a degree of immunity. Levels of mortality dropped from outbreak to outbreak, and it seems as if as early as the 1380s it was primarily a disease of children, carrying off those who had not previously been exposed to it. In consequence, doctors were increasingly confident in their ability to deal with the disease; though in fact the declining mortality rate had more to do with increasing levels of natural immunity than with their often curious nostrums. However, a surprising by-product of the plague was more, not less, respect for doctors, and more generally perhaps an increased belief in the capacity of human ingenuity to find answers rather than simply turning to God and the Virgin, since this unheard-of calamity had been effectively surmounted.

However, Cohn finds that after 'the plague of the children' in 1363, Sienese attitudes to their own deaths changed. The value of pious bequests trebled, but the number of legatees decreased sharply. One increasingly popular form of pious bequest was to leave money to dower poor girls and thus enable them to marry – clearly, rebuilding the population was very much on people's minds. But, also, the Sienese show a new anxiety about being *remembered*. Money left to a church increasingly stipulates that a priest should say anniversary masses for the testator. Or the testator wants their gift acknowledged by putting up their family coat of arms – or, at a wealthier level of society, they leave money to build a family chapel.[20] As Cohn observes, on one level, this shows a confidence that there will be a future. While the unfortunate Agnolo di Tura said, 'so many died that all believed that it was the end of the world', that sense evidently wore off surprisingly rapidly. However, the pestilence seems to have left many Sienese wondering if their family would survive, and anxious in a new way to ensure that the family name would be remembered. In other Italian cities, notably Florence and Arezzo, this new focus on memorialization led to a notable increase in portraiture: firstly, in the form of donors kneeling at the feet of a chosen saint, later, of secular portraits. The Sienese were still apparently reluctant to commission portraits, even as donors, though it is clear that the aggrandizement of collective family identity was just as strong there as anywhere else in Tuscany, since they commissioned many coats of arms, family altars and chapels. Andrea di Bartolo's *Assumption of the Virgin* (closely modelled on the slightly earlier version which Bartolomeo Bulgarini painted for the Duomo) contains donor portraits, but his patron, Domenica, was a woman from Urbino, not a Sienese. She commissioned the painting to commemorate her deceased husband, Ser Palamedes, and their son, Matteo, who are shown kneeling beneath the sacred drama.

One notable casualty of the plague in Siena was the rule of the Nine. In 1355, the most durable political regime ever achieved by an Italian city state came to an end, after sixty-eight years. In the aftermath of the plague, the Nine had been forced to raise taxes, rendering them very unpopular. This led to rioting, which gave the nobles, who had been officially excluded from positions of authority under the Nine, an excuse to rise up, together with allies from the artisan class, against the government. They were further encouraged in this by the descent of the emperor elect, Charles IV of Luxembourg, into Italy. He visited Siena en route to Rome, where he was accommodated in the palace of a leading magnate family, the Salimbeni, rather than by the government, and doubtless encouraged their political ambitions. A mob comprising both magnates and artisans arose, yelling, 'Long Life to the Emperor, and death to the Nine', and forced their abdication. Siena was briefly ruled by an unstable coalition of nobles and artisans, but within a few months, for reasons that are not entirely clear, the nobles again found themselves excluded and Siena was firmly in the hands of the artisan class. This new government was the Twelve, or *Dodici*, who hung onto power for thirteen years.

The Siena they ruled was not the city it had once been. The Sienese economy began to shrink in the mid-fourteenth century under the pressure of famine and disease. Merchants who had once traded across Europe now restricted themselves to the local market, and increasingly invested their capital in land and agriculture. By 1422, the commune had to admit that 'the Sienese guilds do nothing and are reduced to a miserable state'.[21]

Since the Sienese were increasingly living off their land, it is important to register that agricultural patterns changed in the second half of the fourteenth century. Previously, the emphasis was on producing grain, in order to feed a large population almost entirely on bread. But cereal farming is labour-intensive. Once the plague had halved the population of Siena and its territories, that level of grain production was neither necessary nor possible. Fields which had been laboriously brought into cultivation began to return to a more natural state.[22] Animal husbandry needs less labour, so in suitable areas, such as the Maremma, which had once been a leading grain producer, the land was turned over to pasturing sheep and cattle. In 1370, the General Council of Siena complained, 'As many Sienese know, the Maremma population has diminished... due to the shortage of manpower, land has not been cultivated. As a result, where 40,000 moggi of wheat used to be harvested, now only 5,000 are harvested: it is for this reason that we have a scarcity of wheat in the city, creating famine and hunger.' A Grosseto *moggia* was equivalent to 553.20 litres of wheat. [23]

Potentially, this change in agricultural patterns should have left the lucky survivors much better off. Land was cheaper, wages higher, as all employers struggled to attract sufficient labour, available food was more varied. This road to recovery was periodically blocked by repeated famines and visitations from the plague, but, as if that were not enough, Siena was also grappling with another extraneous problem in the second half of the century: the Free Companies. These were armies of mercenaries, short of employment after the end of the Hundred Years War in 1453, who had turned to extortion as a means of support. The best remembered of their leaders is the Englishman Sir John Hawkwood, principally because of the memorial painting by Uccello in Florence's Duomo. A Sienese chronicler tells a little story which illustrates the ruthlessness of his mentality: he found two of his men quarrelling over a girl who had been abducted from a convent. His solution was to stab the luckless young woman to death; in so doing, he removed a cause of disunity in his army and preserved her virginity. Since she had devoted herself to God, he was somewhat concerned that the Company might attract divine retribution if she was raped.²⁴ Sometimes the Companies were hired by one city-state to attack another; alternatively, they settled in the *contado* and made a nuisance of themselves until they were paid to go away. But whether they were for the city or against it, they were expensive.

Siena was harassed by the Companies throughout the later fourteenth century. As had been the case with the Black Death, Siena's location on the important Via Francigena was a mixed blessing, since mercenaries knew the road well. Though depleted in population, Siena was a handsome city, with a splendid cathedral, churches and civic buildings. The captains of the Companies deduced, therefore, that there was money in there, and they presented a formidable challenge to the civic authorities. They were large, well-trained, battle-hardened communities, who had acquired extensive experience in the course of the Hundred Years War. Two mercenaries, Hannekin Baumgarten and Albert Sterz, formed the Company of the Star, which rampaged through Sienese territory in 1364. It cost the Twelve 77,679 florins to get rid of them, approximately 56 per cent of all communal expenditure for that semester.

There were four major Companies at large in Italy by 1366, when they were outlawed and excommunicated en masse by the pope, and between them they materially hindered Italy's economic recovery. In 1374, an anonymous Sienese chronicler complained that 'all the roads through the Maremma were insecure, they killed merchants and robbed whoever passed there... I am not able to write of all the things there were, of the raids, the prey and prisoners, of men murdered and robbed... on the streets.'²⁵ The destruction they wrought in the *contado*, destroying homes and fields, and killing or stealing animals, made it extremely hard for the peasants to produce food, which in turn exacerbated famine, while the danger they posed to travellers was a brake on the entire economy of the region. The Companies therefore simultaneously made insatiable demands for money, and deprived the commune of the capacity to generate wealth. While the Florentines increased the demands they made on the countryside in an attempt to deal with this economic crisis, Siena did not. The basic tax levelled on the countryside dropped from 12 per cent of income passing through the Biccherna in the first half of the century to 6 per cent: a humane response to the immense difficulties the people of the *contado* were facing, though for many still more than they were able to pay. Officials could see for themselves that peasants, in despair, were deserting their holdings because of debt, adding to the problem of depopulation.[26] When a community was really desperate, the government waived taxes completely.

However, as Mattia Fochesato has demonstrated, despite the immense difficulties of the decades after 1340 the Sienese state maintained fiscal capacity, and adapted.[27] In 1369, a shortage of wine and wheat in the city was addressed by lifting the gate tax on these commodities until the emergency was over. They developed new and progressive forms of taxation. In a government headed by the rich, there is always a temptation to raise taxes indirectly: if a loaf of bread becomes 10 per cent more expensive, all citizens are affected, but it is only of consequence to the poor. What Siena in fact did, unusually, was to shift the lion's share of indirect taxation from food to imported goods and pasturing animals: many stock rearers who were not themselves Sienese grazed their animals in the Maremma. Thus tax was raised to a significant extent from outsiders.

Despite the considerable ingenuity employed by their rulers, many Sienese must have looked at Lorenzetti's 'Effects of Bad Government', and found it hideously prophetic. Between 1342, when the first of the Companies appeared, and 1399, Siena paid approximately 291,379 florins to mercenary companies, a figure which would have more than met the entire communal expenses for three years.[28] Alternatively, they could have bought Arezzo six times over with that amount of money, or three Luccas: Lucca had been bought by Florence in 1341 for 80,000 florins. Some of this money went in bribes; some of it was paid to one troop of mercenaries to defend the city from another. Either way, it was money poured into the sand.

The desperate need to pay, or pay off, mercenaries, had political consequences. According to the *Balìa* (ad hoc committee) which was established in 1382 to address Siena's financial difficulties, '[The] citizens [were being] taxed beyond their means, and there is nothing so dangerous to the welfare of a state than for this to be so.'[29] While the government was in fact struggling with forces completely beyond its control, it was natural for the citizens to conclude that they were suffering the effects of bad government, and to blame their leaders. The pressure the Companies were putting on the city is suggested by the repeated changes of regime. Four governments were formed and fell in the space of a single year, 1368. This ultimately resulted in the ascendency to power of the so-called 'Reformers' (*Riformatori*) representing a social class still lower than the previous Twelve.

Sir John Hawkwood's most intense period of activity in Sienese territory occurred in the years from 1379 to 1385, during which time he either led or took part in five separate raids. Catherine of Siena wrote to him exhorting him to put his talents to the service of the church by going on crusade, a suggestion which, unsurprisingly, he ignored. From 1382 to 1385, there was a major breakdown of local rule. The *Riformatori* were replaced by a new government composed of four members of the Nine, four members of the Twelve and two members drawn from the *popolo minore*, the lowest element of society, a yet lower social group than the Reformers. They called themselves 'the Lord Priors Governors', though documents of the period referred to them simply as the 'priors'.

In their desperation, the Sienese began to consider relinquishing even their cherished independence. Milan, ruled by Giangaleazzo Visconti, was prosperous and aggressive, with the military might and strength to come to Siena's aid. Further, Visconti was the enemy of Florence. In June 1388, the Concistoro took the bold step of voting to place Siena under the protection of the 'magnificent Count of Virtù' in the hope that he would grant them 'help and defence from every 'Signore' community and company [Free Company] that wished in any manner to oppress our community, contado, land or district'. The slightly unexpected name given here to this ruthless and ambitious tyrant sprang from the fact that his French first wife had brought him the small French fief of Vertus, in Champagne, as her dowry. Visconti was committed to an aggressive and devious policy of expansion, but, being occupied with the conquest of Padua at the time, declined the offer. However, after enduring another terrible decade, on 6 September 1399 the city council solemnly approved a *translatio dominii*, that is the transference of the sovereignty of the city to Giangaleazzo Visconti. In return for its loss of independence, as stipulated in the terms of the agreement, Siena could rely entirely on Visconti to defend it 'from all who wish to make war on the said city, contado, and district, and from all [enemy] peoples and mercenary companies'.

A miniature representation of Giangaleazzo Visconti crowned by King Wenceslaus of Luxembourg, from an initial in a missal in Sant'Ambrogio, Milan.

This was a sad comedown for the city. In 1299, Siena had been one of the richest and most populous communities in Italy. In 1399, it had become a pawn on Visconti's chessboard: its population halved, and suffering from a weak economy and high public debt. Having thus secured Siena (and Pisa), Visconti then turned on two much more powerful cities, Bologna and Florence. Three years late, he seemed to be on the point of fulfilling his ambitions and securing power over the whole of northern Italy. His victory at Casalecchio in June 1402 gave him control of Bologna, leaving Florence isolated and defenceless. But before he could advance on Siena's old enemy and consolidate his victory, he died suddenly on 3 September, probably from plague. Without undue fanfare, the Sienese resumed self-government.

ORIGIN LEGENDS

As we have seen, Siena was a small and insignificant town in the days of the Roman empire, though Tacitus's tale of the unfriendly welcome given to a visiting Roman senator (see page 32) suggests that the Sienese resented any attempt by the Roman senate to assert its authority. However, as Siena became more important, this simple narrative was inadequate to support the Sienese people's sense of their own dignity. Siena was the only major Tuscan town *not* to have a significant Roman history. As the actual domination of Rome faded away into a distant legendary past, the idea of Rome shone more brightly than ever, so a suitable story had to be invented, not least because one of the planks of the Florentines' assertion of primacy over Siena was based on their demonstrable Roman heritage. Giovanni Villani, a Florentine writer of the early fourteenth century, was the first to make this argument, which was repeated in the next century, in Leonardo Bruni's standard Florentine history, *Historiae florenti popoli*. Origin legends had become hotly political by the fourteenth century.

Several different stories were told about Siena's origins within the city itself. The first legend which is attested associates it with a Gaulish tribe called the Senones, who were one of Rome's most inveterate enemies in the early days of the republic, and captured Rome under their great leader Brennus in 390 BC. They were defeated by Furius Camillus, one of the great heroes of the Roman Republic. The Gaulish origin of Siena is mentioned by the twelfth-century English writer John of Salisbury, though he notes that this is tradition and not history.[30] It was also a mistake on his part; the 'Senna Gallia' founded by Brennus was not Siena but Senigallia. However, according to the story as it was told in Siena, Brennus and his troops, moving south after having entered Italy, set up camp near what would become Siena, and built a fountain at Fontebranda. But when the army continued southwards toward Rome, they left their sick and wounded behind so that the functional army could move faster. These outcasts organized themselves, and founded a community.

At the same time, Brennus's nemesis, the Roman general Furius Camillus, was also associated with the foundation of the city, since he was considered to have given his name to the *terzo* of Camollia. According to Agostino Patrizi, who served Pius II and was from 1483 Bishop of Pienza, the majority of Sienese considered that although the Senones had founded Siena, Camillus had established the Terzo di Camollia because he pitched his tent there before defeating the Gauls. Frescoes painted by Taddeo di Bartolo in the antechapel of the Palazzo Pubblico reflect the significance of this legend to the medieval Sienese. They depict a programme of Roman personages and political Virtues accompanied by inscriptions in Latin hexameters. The paintings are sited in the anteroom entrance to the Consistory chamber, located in the centre of the piano nobile between the great hall and the smaller rooms to the front of the palace. The cycle is linked to Ambrogio Lorenzetti's frescoes in the Sala dei Nove, with their lessons in political theory, and continue the message. The inscription located below Furius Camillus acclaims him as the second founder of the city. It reads: 'I refounded the nation, the destruction of the Gauls is my glory; and as I pursued the routed stragglers across the country my name was adopted for Camollia, the third part of your city of Siena.'

A completely different legend has the shape of a folk tale, with a legendary hero. Once upon a time, there was a community ruled over by a giant king, living in marshes in the environs of Lake Trasimene. The king wanted to move his community to a more salubrious home, but left the decision as to where to the gods: he took a great iron club, and solemnly declared, 'wherever this club falls, our new city will be built'. He threw it with all his might, and the people went to look for it, finding it, of course, on the site of Siena. Wherever this story came

from (it looks as if it emerged from Sienese popular culture), it has left no impression on Sienese art.[31]

The version of Siena's origin which prevailed over both that of Brennus and the Gauls, and the marsh-king, was the one which linked it with the origin of Rome itself. Most European origin myths graft peoples onto the history of Troy – Virgil does this for Rome in his *Aeneid*, in which Aeneas is an exiled Trojan prince. In the Rome of the first century BC, claims to Trojan origin were so common that there were two different scholars who wrote a book called *On the Trojan Families* (both of which are now lost). But the Trojan origin of the Romans jostled uneasily with another story the Romans told about themselves, which seems to date to the late fourth century BC: that of Romulus and Remus. The two stories were eventually reconciled by explaining that Aeneas was the twins' ancestor.

The Romulus and Remus legend is told by Livy, among others. Briefly, Romulus and Remus were the sons of the god Mars, fathered on a Vestal Virgin, and suckled by a she-wolf after they had been thrown in the Tiber by their uncle. As adults, they came to the Seven Hills, intending to found a city of their own. They then quarrelled – Romulus began to build a wall round the Palatine Hill, but when it was only a course or two high, Remus jumped over it to show his disdain for his brother's enterprise. The quarrel turned serious, and Romulus, or in some versions, his follower Celer, killed Remus.

In this detail from a 1480 *biccherna* cover by Neroccio di Barolomeo de Landi, the Virgin commends Siena to God: the banderole declares, 'This is my city'.

The principal Sienese foundation legend ignored Troy, but instead, grafted itself neatly onto the Romulus and Remus story. Siena felt connected to the Roman origin legend by the thirteenth century at the latest, and used wolves as a symbol of this. In the written constitution of 1262, a reward is offered for live wolves: 10 soldi for a female, 5 for a male, 3 for a cub. Tame wolves were evidently kept as city mascots: according to the eighteenth-century diarist Girolamo Gigli, actually in the Palazzo Pubblico, where one of them tore the canvas of the Mappamondo.[32] In Ambrogio Lorenzetti's fresco, the *Allegory of Good Government*, the she-wolf appears sprawled at the feet of Justice, with Romulus and Remus/ Aschius and Senius vigorously suckling. She has turned her head tenderly to lick the back of one of the babies, an attractive maternal touch. There are she-wolves all over the city, including another fourteenth-century representation of the twins and the wolf in the amazing pavements of the Duomo. Siena's early sense of connection to Rome is also witnessed by the scenes from Roman history which once adorned the exterior of the Palazzo Pubblico, suggesting that the Nine were using the idea of Rome to bolster a sense of republican civic identity long before the Renaissance.[33] Literary attention to foundation myths in the fifteenth century, and an increasing interest in Roman republican models, inspired a proliferation of she-wolves with suckling twins: the first, of gilded bronze, was by Giovanni di Turino and set up in 1429.

The legend of Aschius and Senius, founders of Siena, was attributed to an ancient Roman with the notably un-ancient-Roman name of Tisbo Colonnese. The earliest known manuscript is from the fifteenth century, though some version of the story must have been circulating earlier.[34] 'Tisbo' relates that Remus, himself a twin, became the father of twin sons, called Aschius and Senius. After the murder of their father, the sons feared for their own lives and escaped from Rome. Worrying that they might be captured by their uncle's men, the twins attempted to invoke divine assistance, and vowed to build a temple to Apollo if they successfully escaped from the clutches of Romulus. Apollo sent them two horses, one black and the other white, on which they managed to escape. Despite the hastiness of their departure from Rome, Aschius and Senius took a marble statue of the she-wolf from the Capitol with them. When they reached the site of Siena, they built a shrine to house the statue, and founded a city which they consecrated as a 'new Rome'. They ordained great sacrifices to Apollo and Diana in gratitude for having overcome their enemies. When they built altars and offered sacrifice to Apollo and Diana, their protectors, thick black smoke rose from the altar of Apollo, pure white from that of Diana. They concluded that black and white were the colours of Siena, and ever after the city's symbol was the *balzana*, the black and white shield of the city, which appears in so many public places. One important difference between the Romulus and Remus narrative and that of Aschius and Senius is that the brothers did not quarrel. The city of Siena was perennially faction-ridden, but its myths of itself – Brennus's rejects bravely establishing themselves as a community, Montaperti, with the whole city united in an appeal to the Virgin, and Aschius and Senius collaborating as founders – are all about unity.

Somehow it didn't bother the Sienese that Aschius and Senius managed all this strenuous activity while they were babes in arms, who still needed to be suckled by a she-wolf during their travels, a duplicate of the she-wolf who had saved Romulus and Remus, just as Aschius and Senius are duplicates of their father and uncle. The Sienese were very clear that they had a she-wolf of their own. This legend gave Siena an ancient and prestigious origin, linked it with the foundation of Rome itself and neatly elided the absence of any substantial evidence for the city in the Roman era.

10

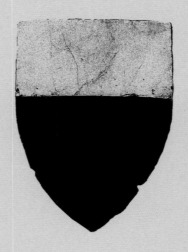

SIENESE SAINTS
AND
HERETICS

S iena venerated four early Christian saints, Ansano, Crescenzio, Savino and Victor. In Simone Martini's *Maestà* they kneel prominently at the front of the host of saints, imploring the Virgin's protection for her, and their, city of Siena. In the course of the fourteenth century, they were joined by a whole gallery of Sienese 'citizen saints'. A unique feature of fifteenth-century Siena is the way it centres civic religious celebration on images of modern, local saints, above all Catherine and Bernardino. During the years leading up to Catherine's canonization, the placement and function of her images transformed her cult from a small group of personal followers to the entire city. From the 1440s, the painter Vecchietta produced important images of home-grown saints, some of whom were never officially canonized. Among them are Ambrogio Sansedoni, a Dominican preacher and papal diplomat, and Andrea Gallerani, who founded the Misericordia hospital. Gallerani was one of the earliest Sienese to be painted: only about twenty years after his death in 1251, Guido da Siena painted reliquary shutters with scenes from his life. Several paintings from the fifteenth century show Ambrogio Sansedoni tenderly cradling a little Siena in his hands, a shorthand representation of his protective care for the city.

Most of the new local saints were attached to one or other of the preaching orders, which were an enormously important part of Sienese religious life. The Franciscan and Dominican orders, both founded in the thirteenth century, attracted many adherents and admirers. In earlier centuries, monks had secluded themselves in monasteries. The innovation of St Francis and St Dominic was to create a new kind of dedicated life as preachers, dependent on charity but very much part of the structure of daily life in the city, and not removed from it. St Francis of Assisi made a personal visit to Siena in 1212, in which he endeavoured to make peace between the nobles and the people, with only temporary success. Franciscan and Dominican churches were built in Siena from the mid-thirteenth century onwards.

The mendicant orders offered something of a challenge to the spiritual authority of the bishop and secular clergy. Additionally, under the Nine, the commune took funding for the cathedral into their own hands and developed close links between the cathedral chapter and the secular regime. Among the Nine's political goals was the undermining of the power of the nobility, who were excluded from office. Among the magnates' response was exploiting the power of the mendicant orders and encouraging their sons to become friars. The local *beati* Ambrogio Sansedoni and Joachim Piccolomini, and the popular Dominican preacher Dom Petrus Paulus Salimbeni, were all members of the Sienese aristocracy. However, such was the delicacy of the Nine's checks and balances, the commune rather ostentatiously supported the work of the friars. A year after his death, the Blessed Ambrogio Sansedoni was honoured with a civic festival, including a palio race run in his honour, and thus deftly redefined as a Sienese *beatus* rather than a Dominican. Similarly, the city adopted the Blessed Agostino Novello, an Augustinian friar. The hugely popular Franciscan San Bernardino preached from a pulpit set up in front of the Palazzo Pubblico, thus identifying his message as directly related to social ethics and good government and not just to individual consciences.

The Blessed Antonio Sansedoni illumined by the Holy Spirit while conversing with Pope Clement V, painted by the Sienese Francesco Vanni in 1584.

Another Sienese Franciscan, of humble origins, was the Blessed Pietro Pettinaio (d.1289), so called because he made combs for a living (*pettine* being the Italian word for a comb). He became a member of the Third Order of St Francis, which meant that he continued to live in the world rather than joining a religious community. Due to his honesty, the strength of his devotion, his sweet nature and charity to the poor and the sick, a cult sprang up immediately after his death, encouraged by the Franciscans. He features in Dante's *Purgatorio,* in which the author encounters a Sienese noblewoman, Sapia Salvani, suffering among the envious. She explains that she was so vindictively disposed towards her family that she prayed the Sienese would lose the Battle of Colle di Val d'Elsa, which they did; but because Pietro, with a merciful kindness which was the opposite of her own hard-heartedness, had prayed for her, he had won her a place in Purgatory. Another Franciscan who was

celebrated as a local saint is Peter of Siena, who went with a group of other Franciscans on a preaching mission to India, where they were martyred for blaspheming against the Prophet Muhammad in 1321. Their martyrdom was depicted by Ambrogio Lorenzetti in the church of San Francesco in Siena, but was whitewashed over and only rediscovered in the nineteenth century.[1]

A Sienese of the next generation, Giovanni Tolomei (1272–1348) was a professor of law and a member of one of Siena's most important families, but at the age of forty he temporarily lost his sight. He prayed to the Virgin and promised that if she restored his vision he would renounce the world. When his vision returned, he kept his promise, took the name Bernardo and with two companions retreated to Monte Oliveto in the Crete Senesi where the trio lived as hermits. They formed the nucleus of a small community of the like-minded, and after six years Pope John XXII directed them to adopt the Benedictine Rule. In time, the community became the great abbey of Monte Oliveto, but Tolomei died, alongside other members of the order, back in Siena, where they had returned in order to nurse the victims of the first wave of the Black Death in 1348.

Giovanni Colombini was another renunciate who founded his own order. His date of birth is unknown, but he married in 1342 and he seems to have been a member of the Nine. Around 1355, like Tolomei he abandoned the world. It may be relevant to this choice that the Nine were defeated in 1355. He divided his possessions between the Benedictine convent of Santa Bonda (SS Abbondio e Abbondanzio), where he had placed his thirteen-year-old daughter, and the Hospital of Santa Maria della Scala, though with the proviso that an income from his donation to the hospital should be paid to his wife during her lifetime. Having thus taken care of his womenfolk, like St Francis, he committed himself to total poverty and became an itinerant preacher, wandering through the city and countryside, preaching a gospel of love and reconciliation. His followers were known as the Poveri Gesuati, a name given to Colombini and his disciples because of their habit of calling loudly on the name of Jesus at the beginning and end of their ecstatic sermons. The Twelve banished him from Siena for 'imparting foolish ideas to the young men of the city', but he continued to teach in other parts of Tuscany until he was recalled to the city on the second outbreak of the bubonic plague

Sano di Pietro's depiction of San Bernardino preaching in front of the Palazzo Pubblico to a segregated audience: not only are men and women separate, local worthies are on a dais with tapestry hung behind them.

in 1362. He and his followers dedicated themselves to caring for, and burying, its victims. The order was approved by Urban V in 1367, only weeks before Colombini's death.

Siena's greatest saint was born in 1347, the year before the first onslaught of the plague. Catherine was one of the last of more than twenty children born to a dyer, Jacopo Benincasa, and his wife Lapa. Several of Catherine's brothers would grow up to take part in the government of the Twelve in the 1360s, so the family was thus active in Siena's political life, at least until 1371, when the *Riformatori* forced the Benincasa brothers out of Siena, leaving Catherine, her mother and sisters behind. Catherine's own astute political sense may be related to this family background.

A child of rebellious and tenacious character, she grew up at what is now No. 6 Via Costa di Sant'Antonio in Contrada dell'Oca. She dedicated herself to God from a very early age, and though her parents wanted her to marry she eventually got her own way. Though her father was well off, and could have afforded a convent dowry, she did not become a nun, but at eighteen adopted an intermediate way of life under the aegis of the Dominicans, as a 'Mantellata', dressed in a habit, but living at home in a small room by herself; a compromise which gave her a good deal of practical independence. Though she practised scarifying austerities, and barely slept or ate, she was not constrained by an external rule. Another alternative she might have chosen was to live as a recluse in a little cell, a popular option for religious women earlier in the century. There were at least 230 hermits, most of them women, in Siena at the time of her birth. Again, this would have constrained her considerably, since by definition she would have had to stay in one place.[2] After three years in seclusion which culminated in a vision of her mystical marriage to Christ, she emerged to take up an active life of service in the city along with her fellow Mantellate, tending the sick. She associated herself with the Dominican order from the 1360s, and was asked to appear before the Dominican General Chapter in Florence in 1374, after which she was recognized as a prophet and mystic. Thereafter, she spoke and acted with the sanction of the Dominicans. She had Raymond of Capua as her confessor and spiritual director (and biographer), a powerful advocate, since in 1380 he became Master General of the Order.[3]

The abbey of Monte Oliveto in the Crete Senesi: most of the structure dates to the fifteenth century.

In the last years of the so-called Avignon captivity, she went to great lengths to convince the pope, Gregory XI, to return to Rome. Since the return precipitated the disputed papal election of 1378 and a schism which lasted until 1417, in the short term it damaged the cause for her canonization and is one of the reasons why this was delayed by eighty years, though in more recent centuries the return of the papacy to Rome tends to be seen as one of her most significant achievements.[4] Details of her life were preserved by men who were very close to her, notably Raymond of Capua, but they have to be read critically. Her admirers represented her according to the clichés of female sainthood: they thus had to present her as a frail and uneducated woman, who yet, because

of her total devotion to God, becomes a conduit for divine wisdom, sent by God to shame learned and powerful men.[5] In order to be perceived as a saint, she had to be presented as a mystic, ascetic and prophet, not a political activist, spiritual director and politician; a considerable simplification of an exceptionally powerful personality, who was all these things, and also a major female writer.

Far from being an otherworldly mystic, Catherine was an active agent in the politics of her day. Her agendas, as revealed by her letters, were the pacification of Italy, the return of the papacy to Rome and the unification of Christendom by means of a crusade against the Turks, a preoccupation she shared with Gregory XI (and with Pius II, who eventually canonized her). She seems to have exercised diplomatic functions on behalf of both Gregory and his successor, Urban VI.[6] From around 1370 to 1376, she travelled extensively in Tuscany, a fact her biographers cannot entirely gloss over, though normally unmarried girls were heavily criticized if they didn't stay at home. She also wrote many letters of exhortation and instruction to the pope himself and other influential figures of her time, forcefully reminding them of their duties and responsibilities; this, again, was highly unusual for a woman. As with her contemporary St Bridget of Sweden, her believers had to contend with the strain in Christian thought which denied women any sort of role as preacher or teacher.[7]

This painting by Giovanni di Paolo represents St Catherine as directly inspired by Christ, and dictating to a Dominican amanuensis. She did eventually learn to write.

Catherine was by no means universally beloved. A poet of the Gesuati, Bianco dall'Anciolina, sent her a long poem warning her of the dangers of vainglory and spiritual pride. One serious problem for those who had not fallen under her spell was that her accounts of her visions and mystical experiences depended entirely on her say-so, and without there being any evidence; the stigmata she claimed to have experienced were invisible, as was the wedding ring given to her by Christ. Very few of her claims to an exceptional relationship with Jesus, other than that she was anorexic and sometimes went into a trance in church, could be corroborated in any way. Many people were profoundly impressed by her, but there were others who thought her a self-promoting hysteric. The Franciscans, because of the rivalry between the two preaching orders, were particularly suspicious of her, not least because she claimed to have received invisible stigmata, and they were anxious to preserve the uniqueness of St Francis's claim to have received this token of holiness.[8]

Another problem was her political affiliations. She spent several months with the powerful and wealthy Salimbeni family in their holdings at the Rocca near Bagno Vignoni, in the Val d'Orcia. She claimed that her presence there was to enable her to broker a peace between two warring branches of the family, but this raised a few eyebrows because the Salimbeni had engaged in countless plots against the government of Siena and were allied with the Twelve, the party to which Catherine's family belonged. She had recently founded a convent, and stood in need of powerful sponsors, and she persuaded two Salimbeni widows to join her; it is therefore hard to believe that her relationship with the family was entirely disinterested.[9]

Catherine died in Rome in 1380, at the age of thirty-three, according to tradition the age of Christ at his Passion. The Dominicans were promoting her claims to sanctity even during her lifetime, and this intensified after her death. Tommaso di Antonio Caffarini, a Dominican based in Venice, was particularly active in promoting her cult, and commissioned woodcuts to spread her image far and wide, making him one of the first to have grasped the power of the press, sixty years before the invention of printing as such.[10] He also ordered an altarpiece for the Dominican convent in Venice in 1394 from Andrea di Bartolo, depicting Catherine flanked by other Dominican Mantellate with a claim to sanctity. Andrea could easily have encountered St Catherine in person, since he had an aunt, Suor Pia Buonanotte, who was a member of her community. This painting may therefore reflect what she actually looked like, though the face is not strongly individualized. She is, however, identified as a teacher and writer, since she holds a sheaf of letters in one hand and a book in the other.

The Sienese treated Catherine as a saint long before her cult was officially sanctioned. In 1384, Raymond of Capua had her tomb opened and removed her head, which he secretly had transported to San Domenico, where it remains to this day. He then informed the Sienese authorities, who decreed massive civic rejoicing in the form of a procession from the Palazzo Pubblico to San Domenico. On 5 June 1446, the Feast of Catherine was celebrated at San Domenico in Siena in the presence of the city magistrates. An estimated 20,000 people were present.[11] Her house has been preserved as a shrine, and now contains the thirteenth-century crucifix before which she is reputed to have received the stigmata in Pisa, and pictures celebrating her life by a variety of artists. Near the Fontebranda, on Via Santa Caterina, stands the homonymous church converted from her father's warehouse and built during the same period as the sanctuary. She was finally canonized in 1461, by the Sienese pope, Pius II. Part of his motivation for doing so, eighty years after her death, was to promote a Sienese *beata*, but that he chose Catherine was the result of the Dominican order's efforts to promote her cause in the intervening years.

The other great Sienese saint is the fifteenth-century San Bernardino (1380–1444), the first to be naturalistically represented by contemporary artists. His sunken cheeks and pointed chin are immediately recognizable, and appear again and again in Tuscan painting and sculpture. Bernardino emerged from the minor nobility, since his father, Albertollo degli Albizzi, was governor of the Sienese territory of Massa Marittima. He was orphaned at six and looked after by an aunt until he was eleven, when she also died. He was then taken to Siena where he was cared for until adulthood by two other aunts, both of them markedly pious: one was an Augustinian tertiary and the other a Franciscan tertiary. As a young man, Bernardino was educated in the liberal arts, and began a degree in canon law at the university of Siena, which he did not complete. He was deeply religious, and in 1398 he joined the Compagnia della Vergine Maria della Disciplina, the flagellant wing of a confraternity, the Compagnia della Vergine, which met in the hospital. When plague broke out, he devoted himself to serving victims in the Hospital of Santa Maria della Scala, and caught the disease himself. He recovered to find his Augustinian aunt, Bartolommea, had become blind and deaf, so he looked after her until her death.

Later, after he had joined the Franciscan order, Bernardino acquired a tremendous reputation as a preacher. He made use of images from everyday life, which brought his words alive for simple listeners, and which today bring their lives vividly before us. He valued clarity: 'speak plainly and openly. Call a loaf, a loaf.' He had a strong sense of humour, and he both teased and rebuked his audiences, depicting for us the men lounging in the porch of the church talking about their oxen and how the ploughing is going, and then nipping in just in time for the Elevation of the Host (something I have myself seen often enough, though these days they discuss cars, tractors and football); the two women in the congregation in front of him who have dropped off propping one another up; and the overdressed lady with a hat that puts him in mind of a pancake.[12]

Perhaps his central concern as a preacher was with peace. Siena was a city riddled with political factionalism, in which the members of the city's political parties struggled for the supremacy of their own faction. Again and again, Bernardino preached peace between men, mutual tolerance and compassion. Compassion was tempered by his belief in justice and good government, in the terms set out by Ambrogio Lorenzetti in his frescoes: 'as refuse is taken out of the house so as not to infect it, so wicked men should be removed from human commerce by prison or by death.'[13] A firm believer in retribution, his main concern was that the rigour of the law should be applied fairly and even-handedly. Less attractive are his obsessions with witchcraft and sorcery, with Jews and usury, and with sodomy. He was firmly convinced that witchcraft existed, that there were those who desired to harm their neighbours and that the only answer was to find them and execute them. This particular anxiety met with a lukewarm reception, and there were no witch-hunts in fifteenth-century Siena, though in his opinion there clearly should have been. Though he distrusted the Jewish presence in what he thought should be an entirely Christian city, he has little to say about the Jews, except that they are linked in his mind with one of his most urgent concerns: the essential wickedness of lending money and charging interest. He saw this as usury, an offence against charity and fraternity.[14] That it was central to the economic life of the city was of no interest to him.

San Bernardino depicted by Sassetta: toothless and emaciated, his gaze is fixed firmly on the crucifix he holds, and he seems to be possessed by an inward vision.

His attitude to sodomy is connected with his particular location in time, as Tuscany struggled to recover from the disasters of the late fourteenth century. Whereas Catherine had dissuaded her followers from marriage, and advocated chastity as a means towards total union with God,[15] Bernardino was a strong advocate of marriage. He was determined above all that every act of copulation should be for procreation, a preoccupation which made him the determined enemy of 'sodomites': 'Oh my lads,' he exhorted, 'if you want to exterminate your city and motherland, I tell you, keep on being sodomites; I tell you, if you want her to be exterminated, then don't give up your sodomizing.'[16]

Religious feeling in Siena also found heterodox forms of expression. One eccentric and fanatical figure of the sixteenth century was Brandano,

born 1486. Having been a dissolute young man, fear of damnation brought about his conversion, and thereafter he wandered around Italy, France and Spain, preaching penance and prophesying divine retribution for the general sinfulness of mankind. His most notable appearance was in Rome on 18 April 1527, Holy Thursday, at the moment when Pope Clement VII had just raised his hand to pronounce his blessing on the city and to the world. Brandano, half-naked, with long, tangled, red hair falling wildly round his shoulders, scrambled up onto the statue of St Peter with a halter round his neck, a crucifix in one hand and a skull in the other, shouting at the pope: 'You bastard of Sodom, Rome will be destroyed for your sins! Confess and convert, because in fourteen days God's wrath will fall upon you and the city!' He made another appearance on Easter Saturday, after which Clement had him thrown in prison. A mere eighteen days later, Rome was captured and sacked by the mutinous troops of Charles V: for probably the only time in his life, Brandano's prophecy was fulfilled.[17] He survived the pillaging of the Eternal City by German, Spanish and Italian mercenaries and returned to Siena where he died in 1554. His body was exposed for three days to the veneration of the people in the church of San Martino.

Siena produced religious thinkers even less orthodox than Brandano. In 1321, while the scholars of the University of Bologna were in the city, a major heresy was openly discussed in the university (the chronicler does not mention which one). Many were convinced of the validity of this belief, in particular a member of the Nine, Barrocino Barocci. This worried the then serving Nine so much that they arranged a debate between Barocci and several doctors of theology, who explained his error. He refused to recant, even when threatened with burning at the stake, and on 16 November 1361 he was accordingly burned in the Campo.[18]

In the sixteenth century, though the primitive and fanatical Brandano evidently had his admirers, there was a freethinking side to Sienese intellectual life. The radical poverty advocated by St Francis of Assisi and by Siena's Giovanni Colombini was authorized by the Roman Catholic Church, and considered acceptable. However, the followers of Peter Waldo, who had preached voluntary poverty in the late twelfth century, were deemed heretical, and persecuted. Despite this, Waldo attracted Italian followers in his own time, and subsequently. An early sixteenth-century Sienese nobleman, Bartolomeo Carli Piccolomini, seems to have been discreetly Waldensian, and to have had like-minded friends.[19]

The Reformation, which we associate principally with Martin Luther and John Calvin, included a Sienese voice, that of Bernardino Ochino (1487–1564). Ochino was initially a member of a Franciscan sub-group, the Capuchins. He was an admired preacher, and part of a circle of religiously sincere intellectuals, both lay and clerical. Like his friend Pietro Martire, he was attracted to the doctrine of justification by faith, which was deemed heretical. When he was invited to Rome to account for himself, he instead crossed the Alps and joined Calvin in Geneva. He subsequently became minister of the Italian Protestant community in Augsburg and in 1548 went to England, where he was received as a leading Protestant intellectual and made a prebendary of Canterbury Cathedral. Some of his sermons were translated by the scholar-courtier Anne Cooke, while another of his works was translated into Latin and English by the future Queen Elizabeth I. He left England when the Catholic Mary Tudor came to the throne, and died in Moravia. Ochino emerges from a Sienese context of reform-mindedness, which reached artisans as well as intellectuals. In 1544, a working-class youth called Pietro Antonio publicly declared that Christ alone was mediator, and denounced the cult of saints. He attracted a good deal of attention and sympathy before being forced to recant.[20] We know also that Reformation ideas were being discussed behind closed doors, and pro-Protestant literature was in clandestine circulation, a fact which helps to explain Cosimo de' Medici's suspicion of Sienese intellectuals in the late sixteenth century.

The most important Sienese heretics are the Sozzini. The first freethinker in the family seems to have been a professor of law, Mariano Sozzini (1397–1467), whose portrait we have, in the form of a splendid tomb-sculpture by Vecchietta. His descendants include Lelio and Celso Sozzini, and their nephew Fausto, who carried on the family tradition of scepticism. They were deeply dubious about the doctrine of the Trinity: Lelio and Fausto both in fact left Italy for Switzerland in order to avoid investigation by the Inquisition. Subsequently they went to Poland, where the Socinians, as their followers were called, became an important religious movement.

11

PIUS II
AND
THE RENAISSANCE
IN SIENA

After the death of Giangaleazzo Visconti in 1402, Siena was able to escape from Milanese control. The political life of the city stabilized after the disasters of the fourteenth century. Power now rested in the hands of the *monti*, all more or less oligarchic groups, which were in effect more like tribes than political parties, since they were composed of the descendants of groups which had ruled the city at one time or another. The Twelve attempted a coup, but were successfully resisted by three of the other *monti*, the Nine, the Populace and the Reformers, who formed a coalition government which lasted almost eighty years, from 1403 to 1480, excluding the Twelve and the party of the nobles, the Gentlemen (*Gentiluomini*). They even managed to defeat the contumacious Salimbeni. The new government worked by selecting 480 men, 190 from each *terzo*, every eight years. Every two months, nine men from this long list were asked to serve on the Council of the People; the principle, as so often in Sienese history, was to try to prevent one man, or one faction, from becoming overly powerful.

Siena's population had plummeted in the second half of the fourteenth century. The fifteenth saw a degree of recovery, but the population did not return to pre-plague levels in either city or countryside (and would not do so until the twentieth century). Siena's remaining people showed a surprising resilience. A mere two years after the arrival of the Black Death, the papal jubilee year of 1350 brought new prosperity to innkeepers and others doing business along the routes to Rome. A chronicler reported, 'everyone became rich in Siena who ran a hotel or who trafficked in or otherwise used the streets for business'.[1] The government promptly taxed the hospitality industry with a *presta* of 4,000 florins. By 1353 Siena was approaching the rare achievement of a balanced budget, without having to devalue the coinage, despite having had to remit fees granted to tax farmers and renters damaged by the plague.[2]

One result of population decline was a greatly reduced demand for grain, the most important commodity to be carried long distances, and this affected international patterns of trade. Another commodity which was enormously important to medieval economies was woollen cloth, which, more than any other product, guaranteed economic strength in Renaissance Italy. But Siena's lack of a river presented the city with an insurmountable logistical problem, preventing expansion, and in consequence, Siena could no longer maintain the illusion that it rivalled Florence. While fifteenth-century Florence was a major power in the peninsula, Siena had become relatively insignificant. However, tax revenue records suggest that the economy of Siena was healthy through the first half of the fifteenth century, though it was unambitious. The reduction in population had rebalanced the economy, which had come to be based on agriculture and small-scale trade, banking and industry. Essentially, Siena was the central market for southern Tuscany, rather than being the major international power it had been in the thirteenth century.[3] There were occasional exceptions to Siena's economically more modest performance during this era. The banker Ambrogio Spannocchi managed to make a substantial fortune, but he had few peers. The richest men in Siena were simply not as wealthy as the richest Florentines, though they still had money to build grand palaces: the Palazzo Spannocchi was one of the grandest. This, of course, provided work for poorer folk.

The lifestyle of those who survived the plague and the onslaught of the Free Companies improved quite notably at the lower levels of society. The remaining workers could demand higher wages, so more people, instead of living hand to mouth, had some disposable income and thus money to spend to boost the economy. Those who survived inherited property earlier, and more of it. Land was cheaper because of the depopulation of the countryside, and waged workers were in greater demand.[4] Even though the wool industry could not expand for environmental reasons, linen grew well in the *contado* and became a profitable industry. The Hospital of Santa Maria della Scala and the dozen or so other hospitals associated with it were the biggest consumers, providing a steady and regular market. After the plague, the Maremma became grazing land for the most part, rather than arable, not only producing meat for those who could afford it, but also large quantities of hides.[5] Leather production was also profitable.[6]

However, Siena's wealthy were less and less entrepreneurially minded. Though Siena's great families had made their money as merchant bankers, and arose within the city itself, they increasingly embraced aristocratic values, bought land in the *contado* and lived off the profits of landowning rather than the potentially more lucrative, but riskier, profits of trade, banking and investment. Hence, among other things the viciousness of Sienese political life in the post-Visconti period: the profits of office were one of the few ways that upper-class Sienese could make money. All the *monti* were determinedly trying to acquire, and control, access to power, and to limit it, if possible, to themselves and their allies.[7]

The Renaissance was expensive, so where did the money come from? How did Italy achieve this tremendous resurgence after half a century of disaster? A distinguished scholar of the Italian Renaissance has observed a conspicuous investment in art and architecture in the fifteenth century, much of it financed by profits from business.[8] For one thing, Italians' role as international financiers and transmitters of specie remained intact as far as trade with the East was concerned, and increased in the West. Their manufacturing base expanded rapidly, particularly in military supplies (for which there was an endless market), glass, both vessels and mirrors (a speciality of Venice), and luxury goods, particularly textiles. Italian manufacture of all kinds was noted for its extraordinarily high quality. Fifteenth-century Italy was also exporting ideas, and matchlessly skilled engineers and technicians to execute them. Siena was not a major producer, except perhaps of engineers, but benefited from the general increase in prosperity. Additionally, demand was boosted by psychological factors. The chronicler Agnolo di Tura claimed that after the plague survivors devoted themselves to pleasure. It was not the only possible reaction, but some people at least benefited from inheriting property, and, with a sharp sense of the uncertainty of life, seized the day with a vengeance. There was a surge in demand for luxury goods of all kinds, so the economy expanded.[9]

One area where we see a marked change from the fourteenth century is in food production. Before the Black Death, agriculture was over-whelmingly focused on producing grain, with wine and olive production bringing up the rear. Peasant diet focused on bread and porridge, with onions and garlic as the principal flavouring.[10] Some vegetables might be grown, space and time permitting – parsnips, cabbages, leeks, lentils, chickpeas and fava beans. Countryfolk near the city probably grew more vegetables, because many of them held land on the *mezzadria*, or sharecropping, system, in which landowners leased their land to peasants in return for half the produce. Their landlords would want vegetables for their own tables,[11] and also the surplus could be taken to the Campo to be sold. If they had time to forage, peasants could collect salad leaves and mushrooms, but the bulk of their calorific intake came from bread, made of wheat if possible, but often mixed with coarser grains such as millet or sorghum, or even acorns and chestnuts. A fifteenth-century short story about a peasant stealing peaches describes the ordinary peasant diet as 'turnips, garlic, leeks, onions and shallots, along with sorghum bread'. Many peasants were too poor to eat bread at all: a fifteenth-century Tuscan statute declares, 'chestnuts are the bread of the poor' and they remained a staple until the Second World War.[12] During the famine of 1338, 'the poor were eating thistles cooked with salt and wild herbs. They would cut weeds and the roots of milk thistles and cook them with mint.'[13] Grain porridge, or polenta, was another basic foodstuff, made with grains such as millet and sorghum before maize (a New World plant) was introduced. Though we think of pasta as typically Italian, it was developed in the Arab world by the eighth century and came from Andalucía to Italy via Sicily in the fourteenth. It was not used in Renaissance Tuscany, but was widely adopted in the eighteenth century (the English Catholic writer Alban Butler notes in the 1740s that 'vermicelli' has become ubiquitous).[14]

The fifteenth century was a period of inflation, and this gave a boost to the *mezzadria* system, because landowners could both put food on their own tables without paying the sales tax on food bought in the market and benefit from the rising price of food in a time of inflation by compelling their *contadini* to concentrate on cash crops rather than on their own needs.[15] From the peasants' point of view, this had upsides and downsides. Peasants who had become *mezzadri* were registered as possessing no taxable property (unless they also owned separate plots of their own) and thereby were protected from tax burdens imposed by the city. At the same time, however, they suffered losses in individual freedoms. Unlike their parents and grandparents, who owned their smallholdings, large numbers of *mezzadri* were increasingly subjected to rules set by landlords on short-term contracts of two years or less to blunt any attachment to the lands they cultivated.

Mezzadria got a bad name in the eighteenth century, and in most places became highly exploitative. But in the context of the fifteenth century a post-plague wave of urban investment in the land generated agricultural improvements, increase in animal husbandry and diversification of crops. Many scholars, notably David Herlihy, now argue that the system was functional in the fifteenth century and benefited both the land itself and those who lived on it. Because of the massive loss of population, marginal, low-yield lands were abandoned, leaving only prime farmland under cultivation, which needed less labour for a given quantity of food. Because there was less pressure to produce grain, the agricultural landscape was transformed by a new mix of agricultural produce.[16] Vineyards and olive groves were interspersed with wheat and other grains. The agricultural organization of the *contado* began to assume the appearance familiar from Renaissance paintings, and continued into the twentieth century: a mix of fields, olive groves, gardens, orchards and vineyards in place of the near-monoculture of wheat which had characterized earlier medieval agriculture. It is no coincidence that artists showed a new interest in landscape – or that there was an extensive genre of

overleaf 'The labours of the months', illustrated in a fifteenth-century manuscript of Pietro Crescenzi's book on farming: a depiction of peasants' unending toil.

literature satirizing peasants, since city and country were brought into mutual proximity. A Sienese, Gentile Sermini, took refuge from the plague among mountain peasants south of the city and asserts that if he had to make the decision all over again he would rather have died in the city than live among such brutes. He derides their coarse, crude dialect, the filthy clothes they never change and their primitive houses stinking of animal and human excrement. And, like other city dwellers, he shudders at their consumption of garlic.[17]

The Tuscan fondness for vegetables was a byword by the fifteenth century. The humanist Bartolomeo Sacchi, known as Platina, author of the first cookbook to be printed (in 1474), wrote, 'Tuscans, who are particularly fond of fruit and green vegetables, eagerly consume serpentine cucumbers flavoured with nothing more than a dash of salt.'[18] He gives a recipe for a mixed green salad, dressed with oil, salt and vinegar.[19] The expatriate Italian writer Giacomo Castelvetro, pining for decent fruit and vegetables in Jacobean London, wrote a lyrical essay

about them for Lucy, Countess of Bedford, who was a great gardener. He reveals the sheer ingenuity with which Italian peasants wrung every last available calorie out of the fruits of the earth, explaining, for example, that lupin seeds 'are very bitter but can easily be sweetened by putting them in a deep stream of clear running water in a tightly fastened bag… so that the current flows right through them. The lupins are left there for two or three whole days, until they have lost their bitterness and become sweet.' The original bitter flavour probably derived from poisonous alkaloids, but nonetheless peasants had evidently worked out a way of coaxing the little seeds into an edible state.[20]

Castelvetro's nostalgia for Italian vegetables is due partly to the fact that many new species were being grown in Italy from the fifteenth century onwards which were as yet unknown in the London of the early seventeenth century. A whole range of plants originating in Asia, such as rice, carrots, aubergines, spinach, pomegranates and oranges, were brought into Italy during the Renaissance. There were multiple contacts between Italy and the Muslim world, due to trade with the East, but Muslim Spain in particular was vital to the development and spread of new vegetables. Its rulers sponsored botanical gardens, presided over by professional agronomists, from as early as the eighth century, when 'Abd al-Rahman I turned a country estate near Córdoba into a botanical garden. Muslim traders ranged widely over the Old World, and many of them, when they were served appetizing but unfamiliar dishes on their travels, took the trouble to collect seeds and bring them home. Plants from as far afield as India, such as aubergines and spinach, were grown experimentally in the botanical gardens of Andalucía, and new cultivars developed which could tolerate dry summers, whence they filtered out into other countries with a Mediterranean climate, such as Italy.[21] Though artichokes are native to Italy, they were greatly improved by the gardeners of Muslim Spain. The improved variety was brought back to Florence by Filippo Strozzi in 1466, where it was an instant hit.[22] The orange carrots we eat today originated in Afghanistan and are first described by the twelfth-century Andalucían agronomist Ibn al-'Awwam. In a demonstration of how rapidly these new vegetables were transferred to Italy, the Milanese writer Bonvesin da la Riva noted that spinach was much grown in Lombardy as early as the beginning of the fourteenth century.[23] Thus many of the vegetables we think of as typical of Tuscan food, such as spinach and artichokes, probably only came into widespread use in the fifteenth century. Lemons and oranges were also introduced, and though sugarcane was too tender to survive a Tuscan winter it would grow in Sicily, and sugar was eagerly bought by the better off. Refined eating increasingly leaned towards sweet-sour flavours, balancing fashionable sugar with vinegar, verjuice (made from unripe grapes, which lent a fruity flavour to food)[24] and citrus. A recipe which looks very like a survival of Renaissance foodways is still made in Livorno: large prawns are dusted with flour, fried in olive oil and seasoned with salt, pepper and cinnamon. They are set aside while pre-soaked raisins are added to the pan, sautéed briefly in the oil and then cooked with lemon juice until the sauce has thickened. The sweet-sour sauce, the presence of exotic cinnamon and the absence of onions and garlic, which were deemed suitable only for peasants, are all characteristic of Renaissance Italian food.[25]

Another major food development came in the sixteenth century: Tuscans are sometimes described as *mangiafagioli* (bean eaters), but the white beans they typically cook are a New World crop and came into Italy together with other New World plants, tomatoes, peppers, zucchini and potatoes. The sixteenth century is also when bulb, or Florence, fennel, as opposed to the leaves of fennel as a herb, was developed. Another plant which was successfully turned from a herb into a vegetable is celery, but today's celery, with its swollen stalks, was only developed in the seventeenth century. Thus it would seem that the basics of Tuscan cuisine came together during the Renaissance, and it has been evolving ever since: cooking the typical Tuscan *soffritto* of onion, carrot and celery, the basis of so many recipes, has only been possible for the last three hundred years.[26]

We have some information about fourteenth-century Tuscan gastronomy from a cookbook which dates to 1338, ten years before the arrival of the Black Death. It is certainly Tuscan, and probably from Siena. It is addressed to what seems to be something like a dining society, since '*XII gentili homini giotissimi*', twelve gluttonous gentlemen, are often invoked in the text.[27] Recipes include a dish of turnips, which are first boiled then sautéed in oil with the addition of onion and salt, and 'some spices', a classically Tuscan approach to vegetable cookery. A cooked onion salad involves roasting onions whole in the embers of a fire, skinning them, then cutting the soft flesh into strips and dressing it with vinegar, salt, oil and spices.[28] The gluttons also liked cheese toasted on a spit, and served on a thin slice of bread, egg dishes and little faggots, based on pork liver, wrapped in caul and poached in wine with saffron and pepper.[29] Saffron was produced in Italy, particularly around San Gimignano, but pepper was imported.

LUXURY TRADES

One of the after effects of the plague seems to have been an increased demand for luxury goods. Sienese were engaged in luxury trades from at least the thirteenth century, notably goldsmiths' work of one kind or another, and, of course, art. In the great era of Sienese merchant bankers, it made excellent sense for the city to produce small, high-value items which could be easily carried to the great fairs of medieval Europe. In the fifteenth century it was more a question of diversification, since the woollen industry was incapable of further expansion. An alternative route to prosperity was therefore to create new industries which would focus on producing higher-value items, given that Siena was full of versatile and highly skilled craftsmen.

Silk production came to Italy in the twelfth century, to Lucca, where it remained jealously guarded. However, when Lucca was conquered by the *condottiere* Uguccione della Faggiuola in 1314, many Lucchese left the city and sought refuge elsewhere, taking their technical know-how with them. Florence got in ahead of Siena at this point, and offered sizeable inducements to the exiles to settle in their city. By the fifteenth century, Italians were the biggest producers of silk in Europe and their exquisite textiles were hugely in demand, both locally and internationally.[30] The first stirrings of a silk industry in Siena came in 1412. Mino and Checco di Roba Squarcialupi, descendants of a well-known Sienese family, spent several years in Florence, where they learned how to process and weave silk. They offered to bring their four silk-weaving looms to Siena in exchange for 300 florins, to be returned after four years. Silk cloth was very much more valuable than woollens, and silk production needed less water, so it was a suitable industry for Siena to develop. In the early days of the Italian silk industry, floss silk was imported from the Middle East, and dyed and spun in Italy, but by the fifteenth century silk was also produced locally by hatching out and tending silkworms. White mulberry trees were planted in large numbers to feed them.[31]

Through the fifteenth century, the commune was visibly eager to attract people with specialist knowledge and skills. For a silk industry to flourish, dyers were needed as well as weavers, and also gold-beaters, since gold thread was made by working gold into long strips and wrapping these around a fibre core, usually silk, and it was much used in fine textiles. Gold-beaters also made gold leaf, which was needed in quantity by Sienese painters. In 1339, the guild of painters complained to the General Council of the commune that, because there wasn't a gold-beater in the city, they had had to spend 4,000 florins on gold leaf. They suggested that the commune should employ a Genoese, Iacomo di Giovanni, who was known to be extremely skilful. The commune offered him an annual salary of twelve florins for three years. An important part of the deal was that he should take some Sienese apprentices for free. There was such demand in the city for gold thread and gold leaf that his brother joined him, with the same privileges, and again took apprentices, laying the foundations of a new craft and supporting two of the city's major industries.

In 1439, the commune were even more certain that Siena would benefit from a silk industry. They concluded, 'considering how much silk manufacturing is honoured and brings great convenience and utility to the cities where it has developed (this being deduced by experience from how little has so far been done in our own city), it appears an honourable and very useful thing to ensure that the said silk manufacturing grows and increases as much as possible'.[32] The Florentines naturally took the opposite view, and were anxious to prevent the Sienese from establishing a silk industry. After 1435, when the Squarcialupi stopped producing, Siena tried to attract new silk weavers, which put them in direct conflict with the Florentine silk guild, Arte di Por Santa Maria. In 1440, the Florentine guild managed to bribe the only man in Siena who knew how to dye silk crimson – in fact, he may have been the only dyer in the city. Kermes, from which crimson was made, was fabulously expensive, and very high-status: for example, the Palio banner was nearly always red in the Middle Ages.[33] The commune tried to attract a dyer by offering a salary of eighty florins, guaranteed for six years. The offer was taken up in 1451 by a sixty-year-old Florentine, Pietro di Neri, who decided to withdraw from the competitive world of Florence and accept the Sienese offer of a subsidy. It is probably relevant that the offer languished until the foundation of a Sienese silk guild, which was incorporated in

November 1451, since only then could the dyer be certain that he was working in a properly structured industry. Unfortunately, when he died in 1461, he had no successor: the commune had failed to ensure that he trained apprentices. They advertised again that year, offering a salary of ninety-six lire (the lira being at this point a money of account, rather than an actual coin, and worth about a fifth of a florin), guaranteed for three years. Owing to the difficulty of finding an experienced dyer, Siena had problems with producing crimson silk on and off for fifty years, which was unfortunate since it was high-value and much sought after. Despite these setbacks, Siena established a successful silk industry, producing sumptuous brocades and velvets, though it was never very large: David Hicks has observed that rich Sienese were not investing enough money in silk workshops for the industry really to take off.[34] However, the countryside also benefited, since by the fifteenth century silkworm culture had reached Tuscany and the Marche, and the industry no longer relied entirely on imported silk.

Another luxury trade which came to Siena in the fifteenth century was tapestry. Giachetto di Benedetto, a Flemish weaver from Arras, established a tapestry workshop in Siena in 1442. He was commissioned to complete three tapestries copied from the Lorenzetti frescoes *Good and Bad Government* painted in the 1340s. This was a campaign to provide the Palazzo Pubblico with quality tapestries, very expensive creations which had come to be a marker of status and prestige.[35] In Sano di Pietro's 1444 painting *San Bernardino Preaching*, the citizenry kneel in the Campo to listen, men to the right, women to the left. But the city's rulers are kneeling on a dais raised immediately in front of the Palazzo Pubblico, and tapestry has been hung behind them. In preparation for the visit of Emperor Sigismund in 1432, the government borrowed tapestries wholesale from rich citizens to decorate the rooms to be occupied by the court, a measure of how essential they had come to be. The commune liked one set of twelve tapestries so much that they bought them from their owner for the Palazzo Pubblico.[36] This investment in Siena's collective glory suggests both that the city was achieving a measure of economic recovery after the disastrous late fourteenth century, and that its rulers were very deliberately reinforcing the Sienese sense of collective identity. The fifteenth-century Sienese still admired the Lorenzetti frescoes, as we know from St Bernardino's sermons, preached to rapt audiences in 1401–3:

At times when I have been away from Siena and have preached on war and peace, I have thought that you have it painted here, and that this was certainly a wonderful idea. Turning towards peace, I see business activities taking place, I see dances, I see houses being restored, I see the land and vines being farmed, and sowed, and people going to the baths on horseback. I see maidens getting married, I see flocks of sheep etc. And I see a man hanging from a noose, in order that justice be preserved; and because of all these things, everyone lives in holy peace and concord.[37]

The images thus remained an important touchstone of civic identity; and the advantage of tapestry is that it is portable. The Lorenzetti images could be taken out of the Sala dei Nove and relocated as backdrops to civic activity in other contexts. Giachetto worked in Siena for at least ten years, diversifying Siena's luxury market production. As with the silk workers, he received an annual income (fifty florins), tax-exemption privileges and was required to train Sienese apprentices. He enjoyed life in the city, since in 1456 he appears in the records again, petitioning the government to be allowed to stay on in Siena.

PIUS II

Fifteenth-century Sienese history is enlivened by a highly individual character, Aeneas Sylvius Piccolomini, later Pope Pius II, the only pope to write both an autobiography and a novel. He was born in Corsignano, which he made over as the beautiful little Renaissance town of Pienza in 1405. The Piccolomini were one of the leading families in thirteenth-century Siena, but were driven out, with other noble families, in 1385. They lost their property in the city and failed to consolidate their landholdings. For some, expulsion from the city could have a positive outcome: it enabled excluded citizens to forge business and personal contacts abroad, while maintaining contact with Siena with an eye to returning home eventually. In the fifteenth century, Sienese connections to Naples and Rome were strong, thanks above all to the Piccolomini, Spannocchi and Chigi.[38] However, Aeneas's grandfather was not one of the success stories. He retreated to an estate he owned at Corsignano and died there shortly afterwards. His posthumous son was sent to the Visconti court at Milan for a nobleman's education. When he came of age, he found his resources so limited that all he could do was go home and live on his modest estate. He married a noblewoman, Vittoria Fortiguerri, who bore him eighteen children of whom only three, two girls and a boy, survived to adulthood. Aeneas grew up in very straitened circumstances, though he loved his home with its long views out to Monte Amiata, and he developed a deep love for the natural world. It was clear to the family that their surviving son was very bright. He was sent to the parish priest to start his education, and his father taught him the refinements he had learned in Milan in the hope that he might eventually become something more than a struggling small farmer.

Aeneas had a stroke of luck when he was fifteen, because the University of Siena arrived in Corsignano en masse. Often, when there was plague in the city the entire learned community decamped to a hill town for the summer, and that year they chose Corsignano. This brought a much-needed boost to the local economy: rooms could be let out as lodgings and local produce sold to the scholars. The university stayed on into the autumn, and in those weeks and months they gave Aeneas a glimpse of a much wider world: he began to dream of studying at the university himself.

Fifteenth-century student life was not luxurious. One 'Edward the Englishman' came to Siena in 1481, and as was the custom, rented a furnished room. It contained a bed with a straw mattress and a feather bed on top, two feather pillows, a blanket, and a 'shabby yellow coverlet' (no sheets). Otherwise, he had a bench to sit on, two small cupboards, one for bread and one for his books, and a chest for his clothes.[39] Aeneas's parents could just about afford to let him live like this.

When he was eighteen years old, the family arranged for him to stay with his uncle and aunt, Niccolò and Bartolomea Lolli, who were far from well off and consequently had been allowed to stay in the city when other family members were exiled. Aeneas threw himself into his studies, making up for the time he had lost because there had been no humanist books in Corsignano. He worked from before daybreak until bedtime. His family must have scraped together a meagre allowance for him, since he went without supper three evenings a week to save a little money for buying books. What he bought, in fact, were blank books. He borrowed volumes from his richer friends and copied out long passages. He studied grammar, but the first teacher really to inspire him was Mariano Sozzini, despite the fact that Sozzini's subject, law, did not interest Aeneas very much. However, Sozzini himself was charming, erudite and a humanist, and Aeneas admired him greatly: Sozzini became his mentor and model. The famous Florentine humanist Francesco Filelfo taught in Siena from 1429 to 1434, and drew Aeneas into his orbit – Aeneas studied Greek with him – but the other man who seriously impressed him as a student was San Bernardino, who came to Siena the year after Aeneas arrived there, in 1425, and preached in the Campo to vast crowds of townspeople. Aeneas was so inspired that he thought of becoming a Franciscan, though his friends successfully persuaded him he was not cut out for the life of a friar. But his conscience was restless; and a few years later he walked to Rome, where Bernardino then was, to ask if he was justified in remaining in secular life. Bernardino kindly told him he was being unnecessarily scrupulous; he should lead the life best suited to his talents. All his life Aeneas remembered the saint as one of the greatest men he had ever met.

Aeneas's first great opportunity came in the autumn of 1431, when he was twenty-six: Cardinal Domenico Capranica encountered him, and offered him a position as secretary. Aeneas accepted with alacrity and went with his new master to a church council that was being held in Basel. The first of Pinturicchio's frescoes of episodes in his life in the Piccolomini Library in Siena Cathedral shows the cardinal's cavalcade setting off, with the young secretary looking back over his shoulder for a last glimpse of his city. Meanwhile, in Siena the following year, the Emperor Sigismund arrived, en route to his coronation in Rome. Aeneas must have heard plenty about this from his friends, who were much impressed by the splendour of the imperial cavalcade. They also told him that the young ladies of the town had lost all interest in the students and were fully occupied in making eyes at the emperor's beautifully dressed courtiers.[40]

Aeneas's new master was out of favour with the pope, Eugenius IV, and part of his business at the council was to gain recognition for his status as cardinal. While Capranica succeeded on paper, Eugenius withheld his income, so he was forced to dismiss his servants, including Aeneas. The young man found a job with the Bishop of Freising, who took him to Frankfurt, then another with the Bishop of Novara, who took him back across the Alps to Milan. This appointment was similarly short-lived, since this bishop also lost the confidence of the pope, but then Aeneas found a job with Cardinal Niccolò Albergati, who took him back to Basel in 1435. These frequent changes of employment gave the young humanist a considerable variety of experience, and a chance to observe men and manners of many different kinds, making up for the limited horizons of his early life in Corsignano. After some months in Basel, Aeneas and his master went to the Congress of Arras, where nine thousand diplomats of all kinds had converged to bring an end to the Hundred Years War.

While the cardinal was negotiating with the French king and the Duke of Burgundy, he sent his secretary on a secret mission to the king of Scotland. The aim of this clandestine embassy seems to have been to ask James I to raid across the border into England, requiring the English to deploy troops north to guard the border, and therefore making them unavailable for an expedition into France. Henry VI, then only fourteen, had theoretically inherited the French throne from his grandfather Charles VI, but his uncle Charles VII, with the assistance of Joan of Arc, had made good his counter-claim. However, the English might well have sent over troops as a last attempt to restore Henry's notional rights. On this, his first solo mission, Aeneas rather naively went to London and applied for letters of safe conduct to Scotland, which were refused. He hung about London for a time, which he found very impressive, and visited St Paul's, Westminster Abbey and London Bridge; above all, he admired (and coveted) a ninth-century copy of a Latin translation of Thucydides' *History of the Peloponnesian War* in St Paul's sacristy. This was presumably written in the beautiful, clear, Caroline minuscule that was copied by Italian humanists, but Aeneas probably desired it for its contents: his Greek was poor, and there was then no Latin translation to be had (it wasn't until around 1450 that a humanist, Lorenzo Valla, retranslated the text). He also visited the famous shrine of St Thomas à Becket at Canterbury.

Having returned to Belgium, he waited a long time for a ship bound for Scotland and set forth again. After so many delays, it was now winter. The vessel ran into a storm, and was blown so far off course that they were in sight of Norway. Three years previously, the same mishap had befallen a Venetian merchant, who ended up in the Lofoten Islands in 1432, where he encountered Norwegian salt cod, and started a trade of considerable importance to both Norway and Italy. The storm that Aeneas's vessel was caught in blew out before the vessel was crushed against the cliffs of Norway, and the skipper was able to get it back on course for Scotland, but Aeneas was so traumatized that he made a vow to the Virgin that if he came safely to land, he would make a barefoot pilgrimage to her nearest shrine. It perhaps came naturally to a Sienese to put himself under the Virgin's protection. After eleven hellish days, the ship arrived safely at Dunbar, and Aeneas, true to his promise, set off barefoot across the rough, icy ground to Whitekirk, some seven miles away as the crow flies. It was a painful journey. By the time he reached the shrine, he was so weak and stiff he had to be carried to shelter. He subsequently believed that the arthritis which dogged him for the rest of his life was the result of this ordeal. When he was able to do so, he went in search of the Scottish king. James had been captured by the English as a child, and kept a prisoner in England for eighteen years. He was therefore not averse to causing trouble for his erstwhile captors: Aeneas later described him as 'small and fat, hot-tempered, and greedy for vengeance'.[41] The Scots began raiding across the border, and this continued until James was murdered, a year later, so the mission seems to have been a success.

Aeneas found Scotland a very curious place. Unlike his compatriots, the Scots ate a lot of meat and fish, and very little bread, and they had no vineyards. While his description of the country is rather sour, he was hardly in a position to see its best side; it was the middle of winter, he had half crippled himself and he was also tormented by toothache. However, he thought Scottish women very attractive and remarkably friendly; so much so that he left an illegitimate son behind him, who died in infancy. After the trauma of his direct journey to Scotland, he decided to travel south through England and use the short Dover–Calais crossing. He was supposed to need a royal permit to leave the country, but, wiser now than he had been when he first went to England, he left the authorities well alone and simply bribed the port officials. He looked for his employer in Basel, where he was told he was in Italy, then went to Milan and was finally reunited with the cardinal in Basel, having crossed the Alps twice more.

The Council of Basel was disintegrating, having achieved none of its objectives, which had to do with curtailing the powers of the papacy, leaving Aeneas embarrassingly associated with an anti-pope, Felix V, which would make it difficult for him to return to Italy. He was present at the coronation of Frederick III at Aix, and managed to attach himself to the imperial court. In 1442, he was appointed poet laureate by the emperor. One important friend he made in his new life was the imperial chancellor, Kaspar Schlick, his immediate superior. Schlick was half-Italian, and he had accompanied the previous emperor, Sigismund, to Siena in 1432, where by chance he lodged with the Lollis, Aeneas's uncle and aunt. He became so close to them that he was asked to be godfather to their grandson. Naturally, therefore, he and Aeneas talked about Siena, and it would seem Schlick told him about an affair he had had with a beautiful Sienese lady.

The result was Aeneas's bestseller, *The Tale of Two Lovers*, a *roman-à-clef* set in Siena in 1432. There are dozens of manuscript copies and it was in print by 1470, one of the first works of fiction to be printed.[42] Though Aeneas had not set foot in the city for a decade or more, Siena was clearly vivid in his memory. The story opens with the arrival of the emperor and his court, who are greeted by a committee of four cultivated and lovely ladies. This episode was based on a true event, and Kaspar Schlick, who was susceptible to women, doubtless remembered it well. In the novel, one of the four is Aeneas's heroine, Lucretia. As a young married noblewoman, she cannot wander about in public, but she can sit in an upper room of a *palazzo* overlooking a street: aristocrats' houses, as we have seen in earlier chapters, tended to be situated on thoroughfares. So, from her window, she can watch the emperor and his entourage passing to and fro, on horseback, and see her Euryalus, a magnificent figure dressed in Chinese silk.[43] This is a highly realistic detail. In Giovanni Mansueti's painting *The Miracle of the Relic of the Holy Cross* (1494), a funeral procession winds across the scene, almost entirely male, while well-dressed women peer out of upper windows to watch it pass.[44] Another, anonymous, Sienese painting from about 1475 shows the moment when eyes first meet: the girl stands at a first-floor window, the young man is in the street with a group of friends.[45] San Bernardino, who often invented nicknames for the sinners he scolded, pointed his finger at 'Miss Window' (Monna Finestraiola): the girl who is always looking out to observe the life of the city.[46] As Euryalus later discovers, this blonde beauty is twenty years old and married to an old curmudgeon. They fall in love, and find ways to meet and begin an affair. After ten months, this eventually has to come to an end. Euryalus has been living in the present and deluding himself (and Lucretia) that he would abandon his career rather than lose his lover, but as soon as the snows melt Sigismund sets off for Rome and Euryalus inevitably accompanies him. Like Virgil's Aeneas, he follows his duty rather than his inclination. He eventually marries a wife chosen for him by the emperor, but cannot reconcile himself to losing his Sienese beauty. Meanwhile, Lucretia, being a Christian, does not commit suicide like Aeneas's Dido, but she loses interest in life, pines and dies. Ultimately, the message seems to be that illicit sex may offer temporary joy, but results in lasting sorrow.

Fabrizio Nevola has suggested that, as well as being a romance, like Boccaccio's tales, there is a sub-text: Lucretia is a metonym for Siena, losing her (its) heart to the emperor; 'an expression of the spell cast by Siena on foreign visitors, and conversely, of the Sienese pride in winning such exalted guests as visitors at all'.[47] The importance of this imperial visit to Siena is suggested by the fact that Sigismund is the only contemporary to be represented in the famous intarsia floor of the Duomo, executed in 1434 in memory of the visit. Aeneas Sylvius thus adroitly flatters his patron, ten years later, by representing Siena's courtship of its imperial guest as a love affair, perhaps hoping to remind him of how gracefully he had been received.

overleaf
The gendered city: civic ritual is men's business, women observe from every window. 'Dressing' the houses by hanging precious textiles from windows was done on special occasions.

Aeneas spent eight years in Germany with the emperor. He was successful in that his talents were valued, but he did not enjoy the life of a courtier. In 1445, Frederick sent him as the head of an embassy to Eugenius IV, in an attempt to close the rift between pope and emperor. Aeneas was well aware that his association with Felix, and with a council which had tried to curtail papal power, would not endear him to Eugenius, and he made a very full apology, which the pope graciously accepted. The embassy was a success, and he returned to Germany. But he no longer valued the intricate, temporary successes of diplomacy, or found satisfaction in exercising his rhetorical gifts.

In March 1446, Aeneas was ordained deacon in Vienna. He had always been hardworking and led an austere way of life. In his humanist days he had never concealed the fact that he had an enjoyable sex life, which produced two illegitimate children (like the first, the second also died in infancy), but the fact that he never married, not even once he was a well-off senior courtier, suggests that he had long thought that he might one day take holy orders. After his ordination, there were no more girlfriends. Eugenius fell mortally ill early in 1447, while Aeneas was once more in Rome on a mission from the emperor. One of his last acts was to make Aeneas an apostolic subdeacon, an indication that he

was marked for promotion. Eugenius was succeeded by an old friend of Aeneas's, a scholarly humanist who took the name Nicholas V. A few weeks later, the Bishop of Trieste died, and Aeneas was given his see. He was still called on for imperial service from time to time. Towards the end of 1450, Frederick informed him that he had decided to marry Leonora, niece of Alfonso of Aragon and Sicily, and, furthermore, he wanted to receive the imperial crown from the new pope. Aeneas was sent to Naples to negotiate the fine details of marriage with the Portuguese princess.

During his return journey, he called on his first cousin Jacopo Tolomei in Ferrara, where he learned that the Bishop of Siena had died and that Pope Nicholas had translated him from Trieste to his native city. He was overjoyed; he loved Tuscany, and, having left the city aged twenty-six, he had been scampering around Europe for almost twenty years. The Sienese gave him a warm welcome in January 1451, receiving him in a procession of clergy and people, and holding a golden canopy over him as he entered the city. Their enthusiasm for having a bishop known to be exceptionally able and hardworking was, however, tempered by other considerations. He was a Sienese aristocrat, descended from a family of exiles, thus strongly identified with a party the then government was anxious to keep at arm's length. He was also close to the emperor, so after that first rapturous welcome the Sienese became alarmed, and hostile. Aeneas had suggested that Frederick and his bride should meet in Siena. He was probably thinking that, as with the previous imperial visit, it would provide an impetus to spruce up the city and bring in large numbers of strangers with rent to pay and money to spend. But the Sienese were suspicious; they feared that having the emperor in the city would put them in his power, and that Aeneas would talk his erstwhile master into compelling them to reinstate the noble families they had exiled. However, the Sienese government allowed the imperial visit to take place, though the city authorities prudently sent members of the traditionally pro-imperial parties, the Twelve and the Gentlemen, into temporary exile. Having decided to go ahead, the city put on a magnificent show. They borrowed tapestries and other luxury movable goods from leading citizens, to make sure the rooms for the imperial party were as splendid as possible.[48] Aeneas spent two months at the port of Talamone waiting for Leonora, as arranged; on account of adverse winds, her ship ended up putting in at Livorno, and the welcome party had to scurry off to meet her there. In February 1452, Frederick and his bride finally met, just outside the Porta Camollia, after which the emperor slowly processed along the Strada Romana to the Duomo, through streets dressed with expensive textiles, which were hung out of the windows, laurel garlands and other greenery. His bride entered after night had fallen, in a blaze of torches and candles which all the commentators agreed made a very splendid effect.

The next morning, the imperial couple were taken to the Campo in a triumphal chariot, where they found a stage richly decorated with tapestries, and rows of seating, with two thrones in the middle. The civic dignitaries ranked themselves around their guests, and watched an entertainment which included dancing and a Latin speech of welcome by Battista Berti, wife of Achille Petrucci, who made such a good impression that Frederick offered her any reward she might care to claim. She promptly asked for exemption from the sumptuary regulations which prevented women of the elite from showing off their finery in public. While the city's government had reluctantly to cede to this request or risk causing offence, they only suspended the prohibition for one day.[49]

The fall of Constantinople in 1453 came as a tremendous shock to the great powers of Europe. In Aeneas's view, both the pope and the emperor were inappropriately tepid in their response: he considered that they should immediately have gone to the defence of the Christian Greeks, and argued vehemently in defence of this position. He shared this view with the pope who succeeded Nicholas, the elderly Alfonso Borgia, who became Calixtus III, and who made him a cardinal. After Calixtus's death in 1458, it was Aeneas's turn for the papal tiara. He chose the name Pius, in reference, presumably to the epithet associated with his namesake in the *Aeneid*, 'pius Aeneas'.

The news must have been received in Siena with mixed feelings. On the one hand, the home city tended to benefit from producing a pope, and there had not been a Sienese pope since Alexander III's death in 1181. However, the fact remained that he was a nobleman and he made no secret of the fact that he wanted the nobility to be allowed to return from exile. This was less popular with the government than ever, since in 1456 there had been an attempted coup led by Antonio di Cecco Rosso Petrucci, assisted by another Petrucci, Bartolomeo di Giacoppo, who escaped the commune's clutches and took refuge in Pisa. However, when the news of the election came, there were three days of bell-ringing and celebration and on the day of the papal coronation in Rome a parallel ceremony was staged in the Campo. This was magnificently decorated, with triumphal arches all round. A priest acting the part of Pius was enthroned on a stage surrounded by actors representing the heavenly host. This group, and the assembled citizenry, watched the Assumption of the Virgin, a repeat of a show which had been played on the Campo some weeks earlier. That year's *biccherna* cover, by Vecchietta, depicts Pius II being crowned by the Virgin in person. Beneath the main image is a view of the city of Siena, hinting that the Virgin, as protector of Siena, had intervened to put a Sienese on the throne of St Peter.[50]

In fact, Pius's main concern at that time was still the plight of the Christian Greeks, and he convened a congress in Mantua to try and talk the various powers of Europe round to his point of view. It took nearly six months to sort out the details, but in January 1459 Pius was finally able to leave Rome. He indicated his dissatisfaction with the Sienese, who were yet to readmit the nobility, by travelling north via Perugia, Arezzo and Florence, avoiding Siena, a deliberate slight. The Sienese government, observing his route, realized that he was heading towards Florence and hastened to send a fulsome invitation to their city. After leaving them guessing for a while, he turned for Siena, which was *en fête* and beautifully decorated. However, as they feared, he used the occasion to plead for the restoration of the nobility. Intense negotiations followed, and a compromise was achieved which gave the nobility some access to political power.[51] The quid pro quo was that he gave Siena the fortified town of Radicofani, and raised the see to the status of an archbishopric. It is no surprise to find that the first archbishop was a Piccolomini, one of the sons of Pius's sister Laudomia, who had married a Todeschini.

Vecchietta's *biccherna* cover conflates the actual ceremony in Rome, where Pius was crowned by cardinals, and the dramatized version performed in Siena. The imperial eagle is shown on the left; on the right, the Balzana is quartered with the lion of the Sienese people.

Pius returned to Siena after the Congress of Mantua, partly because he hoped that visiting the spas near the city would alleviate his various ailments. He was greeted with enthusiasm: a chronicler reported:

> The entire route was decorated between the Duomo and the Porta Camollia, that is at the painted gate, where a beautiful apparato was prepared which imitated a choir of angels, or of Paradise itself. And when Pius reached that place, an angel descended from that angelic host and sang some verses, and

EVSCITA

QVESTA E LENTRATA DELLVENERABILE AVGNIOLO DIPIET
RO DIBALDO EHMARLEVGO ALTEPO DE SAVI HVOMINI FILIP
O DIPIEROMIDI BANTONIO DABAGNIAIA EPERO DIBARTOLOME
O DICHARLO ETO MASSO DORBANO GIOVANNELI ETOMASS
O DIMISERE GIORGIOTOMASSI EANTONIO DIGIOVANIPINI EL
OTIODICHELO DERONDINA EGIORGIO DIFRANCIO DACHA
RIGI ROMEI E DOMENICO DIVENTVRINO VENTVRINI MCCCC60

then turned from the image of the Virgin Mary to the pope, and commended Her and our city of Siena to him.[52]

We might imagine the actors wearing something like the angel costumes belonging to a fifteenth-century Florentine confraternity, which consisted of a set of shot-silk tunics, wings made of peacock feathers and gold thread, and gilt-paper diadems.[53]

Because Pius was planning to stay in Tuscany in order to visit the spas, as with the visit of Frederick III, the papal court, including fifteen cardinals, had to be accommodated in the city. Pius took over the bishop's palace, while cardinals and various Vatican bureaucrats were billeted in *palazzi* close to the cathedral, or in monasteries. Pius was also planning to leave a permanent impression on the city. His widowed second sister Caterina began building a *palazzo* in 1459, where she would live with her daughter and son-in-law, the Palazzo delle Papesse, financed by repeated and liberal grants from her brother. Additionally, the city granted her a variety of tax breaks, to help 'make the house very honourable, and with great expense, to the greater glory of this magnificent city'.[54] It must have been a source of considerable satisfaction to the pope to see the Piccolomini thus triumphantly returned from exile. His other sister's four sons were also made use of. Francesco had a clerical career, as we have seen, but his brothers were readmitted into the Monte of the Populace, and became active in government offices; at the same time, they also put their stamp on the city.

The elegant Piccolomini loggia, attributed to Sienese architect Antonio Federighi: one of the first Renaissance buildings in antique taste to be erected in Siena.

Siena's Renaissance is less obvious to visitors than its medieval phase, but there are many buildings that show that humanism had come to Siena by the fifteenth century and some of the first of them are associated with the Piccolomini. The city was keen for the Strada Romana to show magnificent façades to visitors, so the Palazzo delle Papesse enhanced both the Piccolomini family and the city itself. With papal patronage, the Piccolomini began to make their presence felt once more. They built a magnificent, three-bay marble loggia, which still stands. The first column was put in place on 18 May 1462, and it was completed by September, at a total cost of 3,811 ducats.[55] It is a structure in the new, classicizing taste, with antique capitals. As Pius explains in his *Commentaries*, owning a loggia denoted noble status. A loggia was used to make public events out of family gatherings such as betrothals,

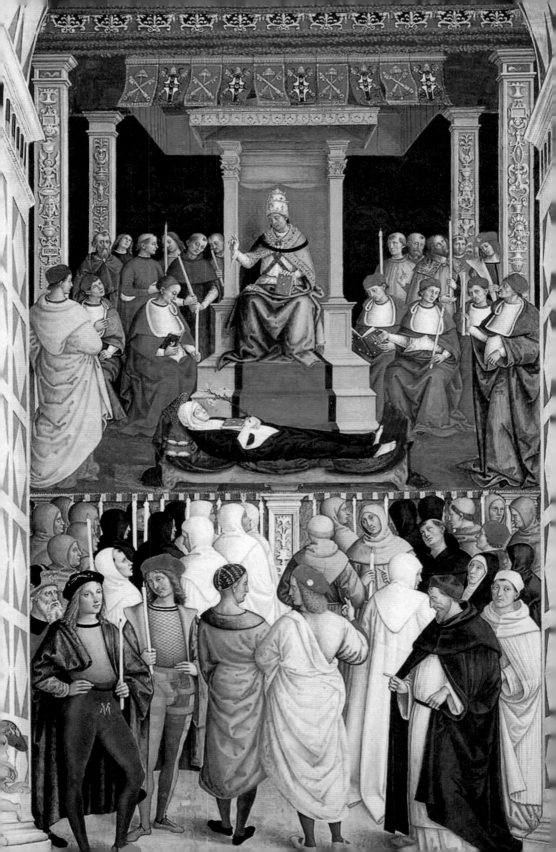

weddings and funerals; and probably also as an informal, day-to-day meeting place. Additionally, the Piccolomini loggia had two little shops and a warehouse tucked beneath it, which were intended to generate income; unfortunately, they were rather damp, so they turned out not to be easy to let.[56]

Also in the 1460s, the massive Palazzo Todeschini Piccolomini was begun, though not completed until after the pope's death. The first Renaissance *palazzo* to be constructed in Siena, it was designed by Bernardo Rossellino and begun by Porrina in 1469. It was jointly owned by two of Pius's nephews, Giacomo and Andrea, sons of his other sister Laudomia Todeschini Piccolomini, and tells two different stories. Giacomo's is stone-faced, and Florentine in style, whereas Andrea's half, the Palazzo Vecchio, was much more traditional, using brick as the building material. This allowed it to blend unobtrusively into the fabric of the city's main square. It may be relevant that Andrea was far more politically significant than his brother.[57]

Another mark of favour which Pius showed to Siena was the canonization of their most recent holy person of note, Catherine Benincasa. The other really famous Sienese saint of the fifteenth century, Bernardino, had been canonized by Martin V only six years after his death. Catherine had to wait eighty years, since she had died in 1380, but throughout that time she had been the focus of a lively, unofficial popular cult. Only nine months later, she was made a patroness of the city, and by the end of the fifteenth century had almost superseded the Virgin.[58] Her canonization raised the status of the city, as did Pius's donation of St John the Baptist's right arm – the arm which had been used to baptize Christ. This had been given to him by Thomas Palaeologue, younger brother of the Byzantine emperor who had fallen in 1453.[59] Since John the Baptist was the patron saint of Florence, the Sienese may have felt they had got one up on their old enemy by acquiring this prize.

Pinturicchio's representation of the canonization of St Catherine of Siena, from the Piccolomini Library in the Duomo, depicted as if Pius II and Catherine were contemporaries. The young men at bottom right are portraits of Pinturicchio himself and his friend Raphael.

In the fifteenth century Siena and its economy were no longer expanding, and their reaction was to turn inwards. They established an Office of Adornment (Ufficio dell'Ornato), to beautify the city and unify and embellish the urban fabric. Property owners were encouraged to maintain their buildings, restore their properties and unify an architectural style. The Office of Adornment also paved the rest of Siena's streets and made both streets and palaces more linear.[60]

Other more cosmopolitan Sienese followed the pope's lead in adopting Renaissance elements in their buildings. Ambrogio Spannocchi, one of the city's wealthiest men, was active outside Siena for much of his career, as papal banker and banker to the royal court of Naples, which was employing sophisticated architects such as Luciano Laurana.[61] Spannocchi built one of the most magnificent *palazzi* in Siena, Palazzo Spannocchi on the Strada Romana, in the 1470s, which shows an un-Sienese impulse to memorialize his own features. He put a row of worthies along the frontage by the Florentine portrait sculptor Benedetto da Maiano which includes a striking image of himself, had a portrait medal of himself struck and commissioned Sodoma to make a portrait drawing of his son, all actions wildly divergent from Sienese norms.

The impact of the Renaissance in Siena was only welcomed in certain circles. Humanist innovation is primarily connected with people associated with the Monte of the Gentlemen and the Twelve, who had been excluded from active politics. The *monti* in power, conversely, were still inclined to sponsor public art which was in a continuum with the city's icons of good government, and emphasized collective identity, and the ancient contract between the city and the Virgin.

PIENZA

Pius also made an indelible mark on the Sienese countryside by elevating his native village of Corsignano into a small town, Pienza, and raising the status of its church to a cathedral. His poverty-stricken youth left him with an abiding love of the Tuscan countryside, and indeed the country in general. He took the papal court out of Rome when he could: 'on every side about the city there are in summer most delightful greenswards, where to relieve his spirit the pope often went with his cardinals, and sometimes he would sit on some grassy spot under the olives... in these meadows Pius often rested by babbling springs or by shady trees, discussing affairs of state with the Cardinals, or receiving the delegations which followed him wherever he went.'[62] But what he loved above all was the village of Corsignano, and the view from its high ridge, over the Val d'Orcia to Monte Amiata in the blue distance.

Accordingly, he set in motion plans to rebuild Corsignano and in 1459 commissioned the Florentine Bernardo Rossellino to remodel the town so that it would reflect his new status, and would have the necessary facilities for hosting the papal court: whether or not the court shared his love of the Tuscan countryside, he was determined that it would spend the summer there. A village of some 320 crumbling medieval buildings inhabited by sheep farmers, it was not the most promising of sites. However, it did have a healthy climate, cool and pleasant in the summer, which he could use to justify his whim: the foremost architectural theorist of the day, Leon Battista Alberti, had declared in his treatise on *The Art of Building* that 'no device of the mind or exertion of the hand can ever improve climate appreciably... climate depends on the location and formation of the landscape'.[63] Alberti and Rossellino had been in contact for at least a decade before the Pienza project was initiated, and Alberti and Pius were in close contact at the time when the plan was conceived.[64]

Pius took considerable care to get the Siena commune on his side. His first action was to strengthen the fortifications: Corsignano was only nine miles from Montepulciano, a Florentine stronghold. This evidently led them to lend a friendly ear to a series of proposals: he asked them to suspend taxes on Corsignano's annual May market and

The landscape Pius II loved: looking out from Pienza down the Val d'Orcia towards Monte Amiata.

to cancel the debt the town owed to San Quirico, and to reduce or perhaps suspend the tax levied on the sale or transfer of property in Pienza. These measures were charm offensives directed at the people of the town. They were followed up by requests to lessen, or even suspend, the tax levied on the sale or transfer of property in Corsignano, and sharply reduce the debt owed by all persons willing to relocate and invest in the town. These initiatives were clearly aimed at attracting investors.[65]

Having laid the groundwork, the pope negotiated the right to the forced purchase of houses on sites that took his fancy, and began to plan his new town. The first desiderata were a cathedral, since he proposed to make Pienza a bishopric, a great family *palazzo* and a house for the new cathedral's canons. Initially, he used family money, but as the project took shape he began raiding the papal coffers – these three buildings alone absorbed 24,500 ducats from the Vatican treasury. It was fortunate for his grand project that alum was discovered in the Papal States, at Tolfa, bringing a substantial boost to the papacy's financial resources. On his travels, Pius had admired the airy lightness of Northern Gothic churches, so the interior of his new Santa Maria was modelled on an Austrian or Bavarian *Hallenkirch*, with a nave and two side aisles, though it has the first *all'antica* façade of the Renaissance.

The new cathedral at Pienza, designed by the Florentine Bernardo Rossellino and consecrated in 1462. The façade is crowned by Pius II's coat of arms.

Rossellino treated the façade of the cathedral like a Roman triumphal arch. It is distinguished by being the only building in Pienza in white travertine: the other new structures use a yellowish-brown stone quarried locally. The new cathedral was also adorned by treasures: paintings commissioned from the leading Sienese painters of the day, Giovanni di Paolo, Sano di Pietro, Matteo di Giovanni and Vecchietta, the jawbone of St Andrew in an Italo-Byzantine silver-gilt reliquary, and the Pienza cope, a magnificent early fourteenth-century English embroidery, one of the best such to survive, which had been given to Pius by Thomas Palaeologue. The buildings erected by Pius himself were deliberately various. The Palazzo Piccolomini has a classical frontage, the Palazzo Comunale is Tuscan, while the canons' and bishops' palaces are Roman medieval. Whereas the beauty of Siena reflects a desire for uniformity, that of Pienza is based on carefully constructed hierarchies of decoration.[66]

The next phase of the project was a new town hall for Pienza's civic authority and the conversion of the old priors' palace into a residence

for the new bishop. This last was constructed (or, rather, remodelled) under the sponsorship of Cardinal Rodrigo Borgia, later Pope Alexander VI; those who wanted to please the pope were beginning to support his project. Thus the cardinal of Arras Jean Jouffroy, the papal treasurer Gileforte dei Buonconti and the papal intimate Gregorio Loli all built *palazzi* contiguously along the main street, now called the Corso. Cardinal Giacomo Ammanati, who was one of the pope's most loyal supporters, bought four small houses, knocked them down and built a handsome palace with an interior courtyard. The young cardinal of Mantua, Francesco Gonzaga, bought another block of four houses and began to build on the site, although with less enthusiasm.[67]

The townsfolk also started building, and received financial encouragement to do so, but many of the houses were updated and given new façades rather than completely reconstructed. Pius made it clear that the town was his, and not merely by renaming it Pienza. His palace was immediately contiguous to the new cathedral, and both the new square and the main street were dominated by buildings housing clerics of one kind or another, while the lay inhabitants were, literally, sidelined. Visual hindrances, such as projecting balconies, were removed along the Corso, and it is worth noting that the only loggia in the town is that of the Palazzo Comunale. Sixtus IV was advised to eliminate private loggias and porticoes in Rome, so as better to display his control over the city;[68] and it seems that Pius, similarly, was asserting his authority.

The Palazzo Piccolomini was designed with love and care: he wanted it full of light, and comfortable, with a fireplace in every room. It had a loggia on each of the three floors where he could sit and enjoy his beloved view out to Monte Amiata, and there was a kitchen on each floor so that, wherever he was, food would be hot and fresh. His bedroom was east facing, because he liked the early morning sun. Because of his increasingly disabling arthritis, the stairs are easy, and on each floor there are no changes of level. With specifically Sienese practicality, he took great care with the water supply. There was a cistern on the roof, designed to make use of rainwater and snowmelt, which was distributed through iron pipes, and he had a plan for diverting a stream on Monte Amiata so it would feed the Orcia when it ran dry in the heat of the summer.[69]

The bulk of the reconstruction of Pienza occurred between 1459 and 1464. While his grand project at Pienza was the great distraction and pleasure of his last years, Pius was also preoccupied with trying to galvanize the powers of Italy into mounting a crusade against the Turks: quite possibly one reason why he canonized Catherine of Siena was because she had also been an ardent would-be crusader. Unfortunately, the secular authorities were distinctly lukewarm about the idea. In 1464, by now a very sick man, Pius had himself taken to Ancona where a crusading army of mercenaries and adventurers had been assembled, waiting for transport. When a fleet eventually arrived from Venice, Pius was on his deathbed. He was only fifty-nine. The leaderless troops melted away, and the dream was over.

The dream of Pienza, however, had become a reality. Quite a few of the curia were probably cursing at having acquired a Tuscan summer-house which no longer had any political relevance: Francesco Gonzaga, who had offered one excuse after another as to why work on his *palazzo* kept being delayed, thankfully abandoned it with little more than foundations laid out. However, the first two bishops of Pienza were Alessandro and Francesco Maria Piccolomini who took care to protect the new city. Pius's wealthy nephews, Antonio, Andrea and Giacamo Todeschini Piccolomini, had also invested in Pienza, and wished it to flourish. To this day, it remains a wholly personal vision realized in stone.

WOMEN

In the future pope's *Tale of Two Lovers*, when the emperor went to the palace which had been assigned to him in Siena he found four beautiful and well-born women waiting to greet him, one of whom was the heroine, Lucretia. 'Turning to his companions, he said: "Have you ever seen women like these? For my part, I cannot say whether their faces are human or angelic. Surely they are from heaven".' In the real world, as we have seen, the real-life emperor was addressed in Latin by a Sienese lady, Battista Berti. What this shows is that women were taking part in public life, as speakers and not just as decoration, as early as the mid-fifteenth century.

Siena thought of itself as a city of lovely women. A fifteenth-century visitor to Siena, Antonio Cammelli, asserted that 'the beauty of Sienese women is proverbial', and a ceremonial motet, performed for the Feast of the Assumption in 1484, similarly says, 'How shall I be silent about your beautiful women, famous throughout the world?'[70] Sienese paintings suggest that the canon of beauty was strict in the fifteenth century. What was admired was white skin, a mass of curly blonde hair, slanting, wide-set eyes in a rather feline face with a pointed chin, and a long, graceful neck. Francesco di Giorgio Martini, for example, depicts one such noted beauty, Bianca Saracini, floating angelically through the air above the city of Siena, in a frontispiece to a volume of verse in her praise by Benedetto da Cingoli, who was the reader in poetry at the city's university.

Beauty and nobility went hand in hand, because this style of beauty was highly artificial, immensely time-consuming and involved expensive ingredients. Italy is not now, and was not then, a predominantly blonde nation, though the distant Lombard and Frankish strains in the ancestry of the nobility may have given some Sienese the desired hair colour. Aristocratic girls spent hours trying to lighten their hair, as San Bernardino sourly observes, 'bleaching... hair in the sun, washing and drying, washing and drying again'.[71] An Italian Renaissance treatise on cosmetics now in the Walters Art Museum, Baltimore, recommends potash water for hair-lightening, which is caustic, or alternatively, alum. Additionally, sunlight bleaches out the melanin in hair, but damages the texture, as doubtless did the caustic, acid and salt washes used to help the process along, which might explain why the hair of the women depicted by Francesco di Giorgio and his contemporaries is remarkably fluffy: it seems as if colour was more important to them than texture. An intrepid researcher at the Walters Art Museum tried out a couple of these bleaches and found that 'the high mineral content of the decoctions made my hair samples difficult to comb while wet, and "crunchy" in texture after drying'.[72] There would always be a temptation to make the mixtures stronger, to reduce bleaching time, at the risk of a burned scalp.

What made life even more difficult for these Renaissance beauties was that they had to try and keep from getting a tan, while letting the sun get to work on their hair. They perhaps did what later Venetian women did – sit in the sun wearing a big straw hat consisting of a brim only, with the hair combed out over it, thus keeping their faces in the shade. There were also many aids to a pale complexion, from asses' milk to concoctions involving white lead, which were much more dangerous, but more effective, producing a sort of zombie-like pallor.[73]

Many stories suggest that noble Sienese beauties were perceived as part of the city's cultural capital. The stringent sumptuary laws of Siena were completely suspended during the visits of important foreigners whom the city wished to honour with public festivities. Bianca Saracini's mother, Onorata Orsini, was one of the young noblewomen chosen to participate in the 1452 betrothal ceremony for Frederick III and Eleanor of Portugal. Similarly, Bianca herself was trotted out during the visit of Eleanor of Aragon to Siena, en route to Ferrara to marry Ercole d'Este in 1473. The duchess's host was Tommaso Pecci, who set up a stage in front of his house, where 'they danced and celebrated and banqueted, and Bianca and her fellow beauty Branchina danced with the Duchess'.[74] Since the bride-to-be was decidedly plain, she may have enjoyed this only up to a point.

The public role assigned to noble Sienese girls illustrates the ambivalence of the state's attitude towards its aristocracy. Nobles of both sexes, in their best silk and finest jewellery, ornamented the city, and when it was necessary to impress foreigners they were expected to turn out. However, successive Sienese governments stubbornly resisted attempts by several of its noble families at one time or another to make themselves into 'first families' in the style of the Medici, forced them into exile and denied them a direct role in politics, and from day to day they also prevented them from competing with one another in dress and display. When Battista Berti asked the emperor to waive sumptuary legislation, her grievance was of long standing among the noble ladies of Siena: as early as 1291, the ladies of Siena sent a commission to Robert, the count of Arras, who had just arrived in the city as the new Podestà. They begged him to ask the Signoria to lift the restrictions on crowns and garlands of silver and gold set with pearls and precious stones. Robert requested this repeatedly until eventually, on 13 December, the commune used the same strategy as they used on Battista Berti: women were allowed their finery – but only until the first day of January, so at least they could dress up during the Christmas season.[75]

The reason why the commune was so exercised about women's dress is that the clothing of Renaissance beauties was both fantastic and fantastically expensive: to put it in context, a Latin grammar teacher earned about fifty to sixty florins a year around 1540, but enough brocaded velvet for a woman's dress cost 360 florins, and of course it also required trimmings, lining, ornaments and labour, bringing the overall cost up

overleaf The figures in this painting by Liberale da Verona illustrate fifteenth-century standards of beauty, for both sexes. The girl is just about to lose, and the tense expressions suggest there is more at stake than a game.

to about 400 florins. Thus the cost of a single formal gown would have paid a professional man's salary for eight years.[76] Sienese legislators went to great lengths to try and ensure that displaying such garments only occurred at times when it was for the good of the city, and not because noble women, or noble families, were trying to outdo each other. In Francesco di Giorgio's painting of San Bernadino preaching, a group of women on the far left includes a sumptuously dressed and bejewelled golden-haired beauty in red, with ermine-lined sleeves. As Liverpool's Walker Art Gallery, which now owns the picture, observes, we should interpret this figure as a new bride, since women could not appear in public in such garments other than for a brief period immediately after their marriage.[77]

Sienese men as well as women had a passion for fine clothes. The Florentine bookseller Vespasiano da Bisticci has an anecdote illustrating this in his life of Alfonso, king of Naples. The king generally wore plain black, with a gold chain as his only ornament. In fifteenth-century Italy, dress was used to signal social and professional standing, political allegiance and wealth, but anyone as powerful and rich as Alfonso of Naples no longer needed his garments to make a statement.[78] A Sienese envoy, who 'after the way of these people, was very haughty', always appeared before the king in cloth of gold brocade, which would have cost a fortune. The king, who had a grudge against the Sienese at the time, deliberately held audience in an unusually small room, having previously told the other ambassadors to push and hustle the Sienese, till, by the end of the interview, his coat was completely spoiled.[79] From the Sienese point of view, an envoy's magnificent clothes expressed the honour of the city, the honour of the envoy himself and did honour to the king: it was very bad luck for this unfortunate ambassador that Alfonso did not share the same values.

In Lorenzetti's *Allegory of Good Government* in the Palazzo Pubblico, cords lead down from Justice to a figure called 'Concord', who has a huge carpenter's plane on her lap. The plane is a symbol of equality, because it creates a level, smooth surface. It indicates that in the Siena of the Nine, an era when the government were intensely suspicious of the nobles, any citizen who held his head too high would be cut down to size, by taxation or otherwise.[80] The tableau illustrating *Bad Government* also alludes to this: two of the three evil angels who hover over the head of the Tyrant in the *Bad Government* fresco are 'Avarice' and 'Pride', but the third is 'Vainglory', that is, excessive flaunting of wealth and privilege. At the same time, the city was proud of its nobility, and rented their *palazzi*, with their tapestries and expensive furnishings, for the use of high-status visitors. As Luke Syson observes, 'one of the more curious features of the social life of the fifteenth-century city was its emblematic use of the nobles, despite political suspicion of them as a class: they were evidence of a glorious past, and of continuing chivalric values'.[81]

The nobles were officially indulged, with tax breaks granted by the state to enable them to maintain an appropriate lifestyle, because the splendour of their palaces, the aristocratic mien of the men and the glamour of the women were exploited for the adornment of the city as a whole. The 1484 motet already quoted also asks, 'Who can count the splendour of your airy towers?' And, of course, aside from the Torre del Mangia and the bell tower of the Duomo, the towers of Siena were testaments to the pride and ambition of the nobility. Further, the fifteenth-century drive to beautify the city rested to a great extent on the willingness of nobles to erect great *palazzi* with splendid façades, as well as on the commission of public art. Medieval and Renaissance Italy was intensely competitive at all levels of society. Men vied with one another, the *terzi* met regularly for ritual combat, families struggled for precedence, cities measured themselves against their neighbours. Just as in the days of the tall medieval towers, family pride and consequence took visible form as bricks and mortar. In the fifteenth and sixteenth centuries, wealthy and noble families built magnificent town palaces and country villas, which was something of a problem for the authorities; on the one hand, the beautification of the city was highly desirable, and supported its dignity: the construction of buildings with grand façades was positively encouraged, particularly on major thoroughfares such as the Strada Romana. On the other hand, the structures which embodied civic pride also expressed the self-aggrandisement of the aristocracy, which the government was profoundly committed to thwarting.

12

PANDOLFO
THE MAGNIFICENT
AND
HIGH RENAISSANCE
SIENA

PANDOLFO PETRUCCI

Politically, the second half of the fifteenth century in Italy was so hectic that Elizabethan dramatists can be forgiven for imagining that Italians spent their entire time machinating and stabbing one another in the back. For Siena, two key facts are relevant. In the fourteenth century, Siena had grown wealthy on banking and commerce. Five parties, or *monti*, gradually evolved, divided along economic and class lines: the Gentlemen, or noble families; the Nine; bankers and rich merchants; the Twelve, from lower in the social scale; the Reformers and the Populace, lower still. But by the mid-fifteenth century, these were hereditary: you were a Reformer if an ancestor had served in a Reformer government. This was stated explicitly by an edict passed in in February 1494, which established that 'the government of the city of Siena is and will be' composed of members of the five parties and their descendants. Rather than representing different classes, the five *monti* had become the political class of Siena, a single homogeneous elite with an aristocratic social tradition of comfortable – though not necessarily great – wealth, a leisurely way of life, and sustained political importance.

Since the city was no longer a great commercial power, this wealth derived from the land. The historian David Hicks has shown over and over again that an individual who needed cash for an extraordinary expense, such as a daughter's dowry, would rather sell a shop or a house in the city than an inch of land or the oxen which worked it. The fertile Tuscan countryside was the foundation of the city's economy.[1] There was therefore no longer any correlation between what one did and which *monte* one belonged to: Siena's economic decline forced many to abandon businesses which no longer paid and take up other occupations, without regard to the party they might eventually join. A banker could be in any *monte* (Ambrogio Spannocchi, the wealthiest banker in Siena in his day, was a member of the Twelve, not the Nine); and two of the city's most respected and wealthiest men, Pius II's aristocratic nephews, were members of the Populace, theoretically from the lowest level of society to be politically engaged.[2] The chance to hold office was valued by many, but often for the emoluments, the salary and fees that came with it, rather than for the opportunity to participate in government or to exercise power.[3] The fact that office holding was one of the most reliable ways of making money accounts for the way all five *monti* desperately tried to seize control and exclude the other four. Ambrogio Spannocchi, like the slightly later and even wealthier Agostino Chigi, made his money in Rome, as did almost all Sienese of ambition, whether clerical or lay (the alternative place where fortunes could be made was Naples).

Towards the end of the fifteenth century, Siena's staunchly republican tradition was interrupted by Pandolfo Petrucci, who managed, by sheer ability and force of character, to make himself ruler of the city. He did not impose himself as a tyrant, but manipulated the conventions of republican rule to become first citizen. The fifteenth-century world was tending towards monarchy. Throughout Italy, governments were centralizing, and authority increasingly derived from one man or a small number of men, supported by a united body of citizens.[4]

The background to Pandolfo's reign was the turbulent politics of the late fifteenth century. His career was shaped by the generation before him, when leading citizens of the Nine, in particular Pandolfo's father Antonio di Cecco Rosso Petrucci, were willing to risk the independence of Siena in order to win a greater share of power in the city for themselves. In 1456, Antonio attempted a coup in Siena and was exiled to Pisa.[5] The realization as to the full extent of the conspiracy shocked and horrified many Sienese, to an extent that it created support not only for the severe punishment of the conspirators but also for the institution of emergency councils, or Balìe, with extraordinary authority.[6] Pandolfo, who was then head of the Nine, was exiled in 1482, but on 21 July 1487, he and a group of fellow exiles scaled the city walls and seized power, supported by troops of King Ferrante of Naples. The brilliant Sienese artist/engineer Francesco di Giorgio also returned to the city after nearly a decade working for the Dukes of Urbino, probably not coincidentally.

Pandolfo kept a low profile for the first decade of his life in Siena, devoting himself to making money, gaining power and influence and administering the band of mercenaries employed by the Nine. This gave him two useful assets: a small personal fortune and troops who came to owe loyalty not to Siena or the Nine, but to himself.[7] Machiavelli wrote admiringly in his *Discourses on Livy* that 'Pandolfo Petrucci, on his return with the other exiles to Siena, was appointed the command of the public guard, as a mere office of routine which others had declined. Very soon, however, this armed force gave him so much importance that he became the supreme ruler of the State.'[8] He also became head of the Camera del Commune, which put him in charge of the city's arsenal.[9] Charles VIII of France's invasion of Italy in 1494 gave Pandolfo an excuse to gather power into his own hands on the grounds that the security of the city required a dictator, empowered to make quick decisions. The key to his control over Siena was the Balìe. The Magistrato della Balìa had evolved as a council of elder statesmen given extraordinary powers: for instance, to resist the Nine when they tried to take the city in 1456. By the 1490s, it was a combined legislative and executive magistrature which had, for practical purposes, replaced the medieval Signoria and councils as Siena's chief governing body, and ruled continuously. Thus Siena, while apparently maintaining its traditional republican government, which continued to meet, had effectively replaced it with a new political device. Pandolfo set about taking control of the Balìa. He studied diplomacy, with Ludovico 'Il Moro' Sforza, Duke of Milan, as his mentor, learning by practice as a Balìa member, and listening to the Milanese ambassador, who relayed the advice and guidance of Ludovico Sforza.[10]

He tightened his hold on Siena in 1497, when his brother died, enabling him to take over the brother's multiple offices in addition to his own. He married the daughter of another of Siena's powerful men, Niccolò Borghese, and with his father-in-law's backing took over yet more public offices. Siena had finally fallen into the hands of a tyrant, albeit one of a singularly Sienese stamp. By holding several of the principal magistracies which were never intended to be held together, he undermined the city's authority structure from within, though he was always careful to pay lip service to republican institutions. His rule also prospered because it was effective and benign. In particular, he demonstrated to his fellow citizens that he had studied diplomacy to good purpose and steered the city through some major crises. He succeeded in making a peace treaty with Florence in 1498, and established good relations with Charles VIII of France, who had taken Milan by force of arms, and took Siena under his protection. He survived Cesare Borgia's attempt to carve out a new kingdom, supported and abetted by his father, Pope Alexander VI, making a strategic withdrawal into exile for a couple of months in 1503 when Cesare threatened the city, from which he returned with the support of the French and the Florentines. The death of Alexander VI in August that year put an end to Cesare's ambitions, and after that Petrucci's hold on Siena was never seriously challenged.

One respect in which Petrucci was typically Sienese is that he attached a high importance to public art. The main public institutions which employed artists were the Palazzo Pubblico, the Duomo and the Hospital of Santa Maria della Scala. Alberto Aringhieri had been in charge of developing the Duomo since 1480, but in 1505 he fled to Rome because he had every reason to suspect that Pandolfo was planning to assassinate him. He never returned to Siena, and his date of death is unknown. With Aringhieri out of the way, Pandolfo took direct control of all three institutions, so he was able to dictate artistic patronage and urban planning. Like the Nine in the thirteenth century, Petrucci clearly saw art as a way of imposing a particular vision on the city. Contracts for commissions were drawn up in his *palazzo*, and payment was made 'as it shall appear suitable to the Magnificent Pandolfo Petrucci'.[11] What is very noticeable is that, under Pandolfo, Siena became more Renaissance in appearance. Sano di Pietro and his workshop had continued to produce paintings in an essentially fourteenth-century style until his death in 1481: in fifteenth-century republican Siena, his style had seemed a comforting evocation of Sienese tradition.[12]

By contrast, Petrucci, and those associated with him, embraced the innovations in art which we associate with Florence. The Petrucci were looking to become Siena's equivalent of Florence's Medici, so their art patronage reflects their political agenda. In 1506 one of the city's most iconic paintings, Duccio's *Maestà*, was removed from the high altar of the Duomo for being too old-fashioned, and put in a side aisle. It was replaced not with a painting, but with Vecchietta's elaborate bronze ciborium (created 1467/72), which had previously been in the church of the Hospital of Santa Maria della Scala. Pandolfo built himself a palace, known as the Palazzo del Magnifico, around 1504–6, in the Via dei Pellegrini, which was a remodelling of a group of older buildings belonging to the Accarigi family.[13] It was near the baptistery, in a district which was the traditional home of the Petrucci family.[14] A suite of seven rooms in this palace were decorated for the wedding of his heir, Borghese Petrucci, to Vittoria Piccolomini, niece of the recently deceased Pope Pius III, and great-niece of Pius II. The most highly decorated room, the so-called 'Camera Bella', contained eight large classicizing frescoes by fashionable Mannerist painters, Pinturicchio, Luca Signorelli and Girolamo Genga, none of whom were Sienese.[15] It also featured a decorated ceiling, majolica floor tiles set in an elaborate pattern influenced by Islamic tilework and elaborate stucco mouldings.[16]

Other like-minded aristocrats similarly supported new directions in art: Pinturicchio also painted the Piccolomini Library for Francesco Piccolomini, bringing Raphael with him. Luca Signorelli, from Cortona, worked with the Sienese Francesco di Giorgio to decorate the family chapel of Agostino Bichi, one of Petrucci's principal allies.[17] Michelangelo sculpted four niche sculptures for the Piccolomini altarpiece in Siena Cathedral, originally commissioned by Cardinal Francesco Todeschini Piccolomini, later Pope Pius III, which were added to the main structure between 1501 and 1504, representing saints Peter, Augustine (later resculpted as St Pius), Paul and Gregory. Giovanni Bazzi, known as 'Il Sodoma', also came to Siena, possibly at the behest of the Spannocchi banking family. He additionally worked for the Chigi, another family of bankers. One of his early commissions was façade frescoes for Sigismondo Chigi's palace at the Bocca del Casato (1510), painted in chiaroscuro and covered with victories, cupids, exemplary figures, battles and trophies in a sophisticated *all'antica* taste, reflecting the new Renaissance fascination with ancient Rome, the first such work seen in Siena.[18] Façade decorations of this kind were extremely prestigious. Five years later, the Sienese Domenico Beccafumi frescoed the façade of the Palazzo Borghese with classical figures: a reminder that Siena in the past looked very different, and many buildings once had a coat of stucco, since removed. The Palazzo Borghese is located on the Via di Città at Piazza di Postierla, an elite neighbourhood developed by leading families of the new oligarchy, who were giving the gothic buildings a Renaissance update. Of all these artists, only Francesco di Giorgio was both native to, and trained in, Siena. As Luke Syson has argued, Sienese art did adapt and change, producing an elegant synthesis of traditional

overleaf
Pinturicchio painted Penelope pestered by her suitors for the Camera Bella in the Petrucci palazzo: a celebration of marital fidelity. Through the window we see some of Odysseus's adventures.

motifs with new ways of seeing, in the works of new Sienese artists such as Domenico Beccafumi (1484–1551), whose work was much admired, not only in his native city, but by Michelangelo.[19]

The Petrucci era also saw extensive work on the built environment. Pandolfo dreamed of making the Campo more Renaissance in appearance by overhauling the Palazzo Pubblico and the Campo, masking the former with a classicizing façade and circling the Campo with a continuous arcade, a dramatic, and drastic, way of overwriting the republican tradition for which the Palazzo and Campo were the central symbols. The model was probably the Sforza piazza at Vigevano, which turned the piazza into an outdoor antechamber to the ducal residence, especially given that Ludovico Sforza was Petrucci's principal mentor.[20] Actual construction was limited to carving some columns, which were probably eventually recycled for the church of Santa Maria dei Servi, but it is a sobering thought that if Pandolfo's vision had been carried through we might now be writing about Siena as an unspoiled Renaissance gem, and responding to the city in a completely different way.

With his encouragement, the wealthy began to build or remodel great *palazzi*, in a style which introduced Renaissance elements to the traditional gothic architecture of the city. Late fifteenth-century architectural commissions rooted in a modern and essentially Florentine style originate with a small group of patrons originally centred around Pius II and his family, and subsequently adopted by Pandolfo and his associates. The Ufficio dell'Ornato once more declared war on balconies and any structures which overhung or protruded into the street (as we see from Sienese art, these had been quite common in the fourteenth century). Demolishing balconies often led to the replacement of the entire façade, and where possible façades were straightened to improve the street line: a rope was drawn between two points on a street, and any structure, or part of a structure, which invaded the straight line was demolished.[21] The new flat façades had round arches or frames, and classicizing cornices, replacing gothic windows and doors. The aristocracy's desire to aggrandize their families by living in grand *palazzi* was perceived by Petrucci's government as being in the wider interests of the city, because their buildings made it more beautiful. Beautifying the city was thought important enough to offer owners subsidies in order to bring their buildings into line with the new requirements. Thus it was in the fifteenth century that Siena began to take on the form we know; the tall, flat-fronted buildings facing one another along narrow streets.

RENAISSANCE MEN

S iena was forced into developing a tradition of engineering by its geography, because its water supply depended on human ingenuity. Siena's water supply system challenged the engineering skills of its creators, generation by generation, and the city's patronage of scientists and inventors fostered a culture of technological innovation. The men who could produce a painting or a sculpture, cast a cannon and design a windmill or a palace were mostly not humanistically educated, but had attended a different kind of school. As well as the Latin schools which trained humanists, Renaissance Italy had what were called 'abacus schools', which taught practical applications of algebra, arithmetic and geometry to boys between the ages of eleven and sixteen. About twice as many boys went to an abacus school as acquired a humanist education, because this was knowledge which was directly useful. Merchants could apply it to exchanging the florins of Florence for the thalers and guilders of northern Europe, surveyors could use it to work out the height of a wall or to lay out a road, and gunners could use it to calculate the trajectory of a cannonball. The abacus schools taught concrete problem-solving and applied mathematics, not mathematical theory.[22] After an education of this kind, these remarkably versatile 'Renaissance Men' became apprentices in workshops that made and fashioned materials, whether stone, iron and bronze, gold and precious stones, or even paint (an artist's workshop made paint from scratch, and it took a great deal of practical knowledge). They were familiar with manufacturing processes, and acquired a profound understanding of how to work with the materials available. It seems extraordinary now that someone might train as an artist and end up as a military engineer, but there are many examples of such men in fifteenth-century Italy: the Florentine Filippo Brunelleschi, who designed some of his city's greatest buildings, originally trained as a goldsmith, and the painter Duccio was charged with sinking wells in search of the mythical River Diana.

Siena took abacus teachers more seriously than did other Tuscan towns. They were regularly hired and paid from the late fourteenth century, and from the fifteenth there was an abacus master who was entirely sponsored by the commune, and taught for free.[23] Maestro Piero dell'Abaco was teaching practical mathematics for a salary of forty-five florins from 1461, and also acting as a surveyor and technical adviser on the commune's building projects.[24] It was normal for an abacus master to spend part of his time serving the commune in this way, which ensured that their students were being taught by men with direct personal experience of solving practical problems.

The fifteenth century was an age of rapid technological development in Europe. A wide variety of industries used water power, the most efficient source of energy available, and hydraulic engineering was increasingly confident and sophisticated. The arrival of gunpowder together with increasing expertise in large-scale bronze casting brought heavy artillery onto battlefields, and this rapidly forced a complete rethink of defensive fortifications. A third, less obviously dramatic, development, which, like gunpowder, originated in China, was the crank. Cranks and crankshafts convert rotary motion to reciprocating motion, or vice versa; while the concept had been around for centuries, the fifteenth century saw a new appreciation of its potential. For example, a crankshaft can transform the energy produced by wind spinning the sails of a mill, rotary motion, into the back and forth movement of a saw.[25]

In this painting by Giovanni di Paolo, the Holy Family's flight into Egypt takes them through a Tuscan landscape, with one of the Sienese engineer Taccola's ingenious water-powered mills on the river.

One particularly interesting Sienese engineer, Mariano di Jacopo, called Taccola (jackdaw) began his career as a sculptor, since the Duomo records show that he was paid for carving sixteen heads to ornament the choir stalls in 1408.[26] He was also a notary, and a man of quite high social standing, who was entrusted with a variety of jobs on behalf of the city. His notebooks show that by the 1420s he was taking an interest in bridges, river works and water engineering, and he is known to have put some of his ideas into practice. In 1427, he constructed piers for a bridge over the Tiber, did some work on the harbour at Genoa and built a reservoir.[27] He attempted to devise mechanisms for exploiting extant sources of water, as well as to continue looking for new sources of power. In Giovanni di Paolo's 1436 *Flight into Egypt*, in which the Holy Family is travelling via the Tuscan countryside, one of Taccola's watermills is visible on the bank of a river in the middle distance.

Taccola's notebooks show that he was looking as far away as Toledo for models of how hill towns could be supplied with water: the Spanish city was famous for its gardens, which were irrigated by large water-lifting wheels called *norias*.[28] Two of his sketches of water-lifting devices have a city labelled 'Toledo' in the background. A piece of evidence for his contact with the Far East comes in a notebook which illustrates what he calls a 'Tartar Pump'. This name suggests that his knowledge of the device came via the Mongols. It was a chain pump, also for moving water, a mechanism which would eventually revolutionize the mining industry. There were mercantile connections between Siena and the East, since 'Tartar' silks were imported, and even more directly, many Tartar slaves, so Taccola could easily have come across someone able to describe the mechanism. From Taccola's drawing and description, the device came into general European use via the engineers who drew on his work.[29] Taccola was the secretary of the Casa di Sapienza, or 'House of Wisdom', which eventually became the university, and he persuaded it to start offering instruction on technical subjects. It was very unusual in the fifteenth century for a university to offer instruction to non-clerical students, and this broadening of the curriculum helped to establish Siena's reputation as a centre of technical expertise.[30] Brunelleschi visited Siena, and was evidently on friendly terms with Taccola since the latter records a remarkable tirade in which Brunelleschi relieved his feelings about plagiarists and ignorant scoffers, who doubtless were a thorn in the side of all these highly original men.[31] One of Taccola's drawings is of a mercury-driven mill: since mercury was very expensive, this was presumably a small-scale model or a demonstration device used to explain a new engineering concept to a committee.[32]

Taccola was a major influence on Francesco di Giorgio Martini (1439–1501), a singularly versatile Sienese genius famous in his own lifetime throughout Italy, though less well remembered today. He was a personal friend of both Leonardo da Vinci and the architect Donato Bramante. He trained as a painter in the workshop of Lorenzo di Pietro, known as Vecchietta, a painter, sculptor, goldsmith, architect and military engineer, who evidently gave his pupil an all-round education like his own. Francesco di Giorgio's earliest known works are paintings; they include a *Nativity* and *Coronation of the Virgin*, both in Siena, and Vecchietta also taught him to cast bronze, since he was sculpting in bronze as early as 1474. Two bronze angels he created in 1495 adorn the high altar of the Duomo. In 1464, aged twenty-five, he described himself as an artist, but the same time he was evidently learning practical engineering. His master Vecchietta could have instructed him, and probably did, but he clearly also knew Taccola, since the latter let the younger man have access to his notebooks. Francesco copied many devices directly from him. He may well have taken the engineering course Taccola had set up at the Casa di Sapienza.[33]

By the time he was thirty, Francesco di Giorgio was employed by the city of Siena to work on its aqueducts and fountains; he was so successful that he is said to have increased the supply of fresh water to the city by a third. At the age of fifty-two, he was once more called upon to act as the city's senior water engineer, overseeing the supply of drinkable water to the fountains, as well as the drainage of storm water and sewage, and the draining of flooded land. All this was done on the basis of his own practical experience rather than theoretical study: since he had not attended a grammar school, his Latin was weak. By the mid-1480s, he could read the language up to a point, but the architectural historian Joseph Rykwert has shown that although he was acquainted with Vitruvius's treatise on architecture, he completely misunderstood at least one passage.[34] He picked up a considerable amount of academic knowledge as he went along, especially after he went to work for Federico da Montefeltro at Urbino in 1475: at that learned court he had an opportunity to discuss problems in applied mathematics, perhaps with the duke himself, who was interested in the subject, or with some of the mathematicians and humanists who frequented the ducal palace. Such men could consult the famous ducal library, read relevant passages from classical authors with him, translate if necessary, and talk through how classical theory might illuminate his own empirical knowledge.[35]

Ideas and inventions circulated internationally, and good new ideas were rapidly picked up by fellow practitioners. Siena evidently had a whole community of artist/engineers. Both Francesco di Giorgio and Taccola's work circulated among their peers and was extremely influential. Engineering solutions originating with Francesco di Giorgio were reprinted (unacknowledged) in standard engineering textbooks as late as the eighteenth century.[36] One manuscript notebook, now in the British Library, which was created in the 1470s or early 1480s by an unknown Sienese, draws on the work of both men. The first seventy-one pages copy one of Taccola's notebooks, and the 127 that follow draw heavily on Francesco di Giorgio's work. The anonymous creator was not simply copying, but thinking about how to apply his predecessors' discoveries to solving new problems, thinking with pen in hand. Two drawings, for example, show him stumbling towards inventing the parachute. Clearly, he has observed that a large flat surface, such as a banner or a sail, generates air resistance. In the first of the two sketches, a man is jumping, with a sponge between his teeth to ensure that he doesn't damage his jaws on impact, with two long cloth streamers attached to a belt. Eleven pages later, the inventor returns to the problem. This time, the sponge is secured with a strap round the jumper's head, so he won't lose it if he screams, and he is hanging from a conical parachute.[37] This particular invention got no further than the drawing board, but it is an interesting indication of how a Renaissance engineer might work towards realizing a new idea.

Taccola, Francesco di Giorgio and other Sienese engineers were interested in a wide variety of problems. Moving water around was one of them; another was harnessing water power to generate energy or move large objects.

One of Taccola's more speculative inventions indicates that he was familiar with whirligigs. He applied the concept to an automatically propelled paddleboat, which he depicts carrying a man swiftly downstream (though he would have found getting back rather a problem).[38] Taccola and his successors designed all kinds of useful items, such as windmills, builders' cranes, winches, hoists, and pumps. He gave a great deal of thought to devices for civil engineering, which makes good sense in the context of a city that desperately wanted its own port and that was constantly importing building materials. One can infer from his many drawings of salvage and lifting devices, as well as aids to diving, that Taccola thought that recovering building materials and other valuable objects that had dropped into the water while loading and unloading was a problem worth solving. Parachutes and paddleboats may have been entirely theoretical, but many of the inventions we see in these engineers' notebooks were entirely practical, officially tested, and state supported.[39]

One particular problem for the generation active in the 1470s and 1480s was military engineering. The medieval solution to defence had been city walls and towers. Montereggioni, which Siena fortified in the mid-thirteenth century with fourteen tall towers, is one of the best surviving examples: Dante compares the giants which circle the infernal abyss to the spectacular walls and towers of this town. But by the second half of the fifteenth century, defence was no longer a matter of strong walls and a well-chosen site, but of carefully calculated lines of fire. Fortress design thus became the province of the mathematically literate. Gunpowder was known in Europe by the thirteenth century, since the English Franciscan friar and natural philosopher Roger Bacon gives a recipe for it,[40] and guns of a sort started to come into use by the 1350s, but it took a hundred years for the technology to develop to a point where guns became notably more effective than older siege weapons such as the ballista, and militarily decisive. The first major battle to be decided by cannon fire was the fall of Constantinople to the Ottoman Turks in 1453.

An engraving of Francesco di Giorgio (1439–1501), one of the most original and creative architects/ engineers in Renaissance Italy.

A medieval-style tall, but relatively thin, wall could be pierced and brought down by the 300-pound stone balls thrown by the bombards which had come into use in the mid-fifteenth century, and there was precious little the defenders could do about it. Defence adapted rapidly; city walls became shorter and much wider, so that big guns could be moved about on them. They also acquired protective earthworks round the base, reinforced with timber, which could absorb cannon shot without being damaged. By 1500, they had projecting bastions, which in the most advanced forms were arrow-shaped, allowing enfilading fire, and deep, surrounding ditches, which served two purposes: they made it difficult for infantry to approach the city, and they forced miners to dig deep, which was time-consuming. The first person to materially aid an attacking army by mining was Francesco di Giorgio, who in 1495 drove a shaft beneath Naples' Castel Nuovo, packed it with barrels of gunpowder

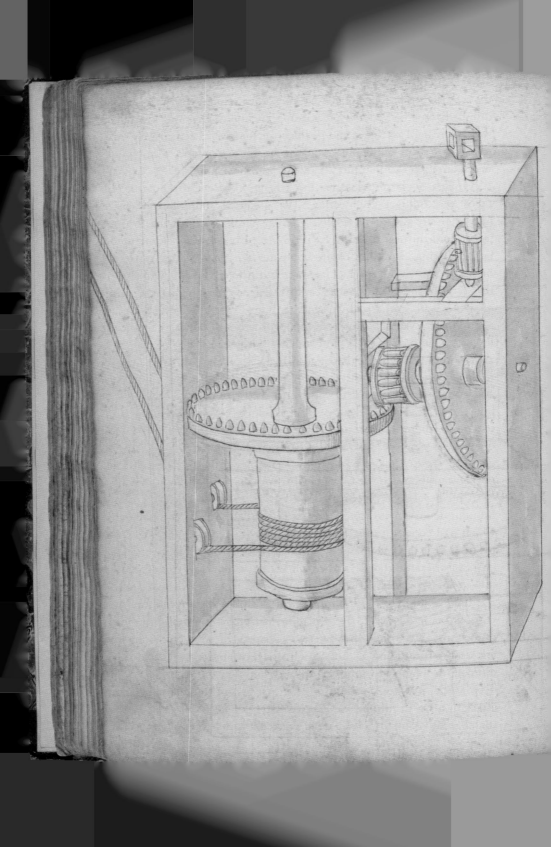

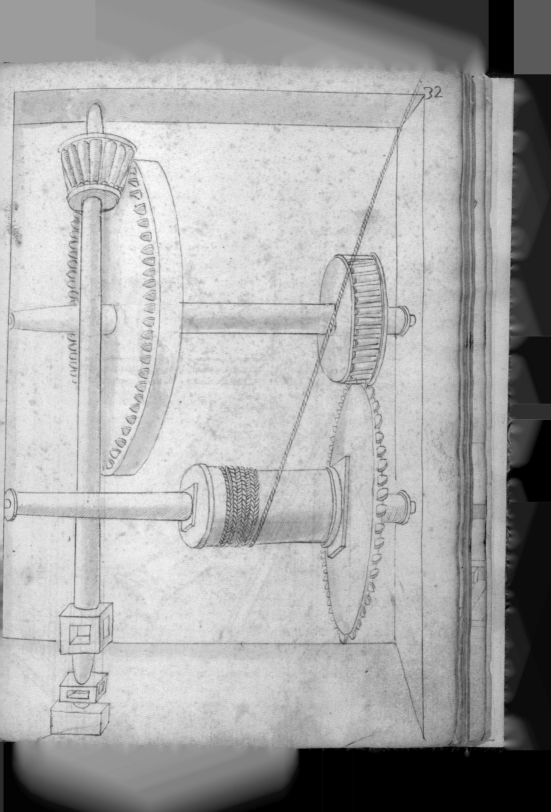

32

and brought down a section of the barbican when it was successfully exploded. From 1500, mining became a basic tactic of siege warfare.[41] Francesco di Giorgio also invented the counter-mine, a system of tunnels stretching out from beneath a fortress, with a room at the end of each as a listening post: sound travels well underground, so when one of the listeners detected that a tunnel was under construction, the nearest room could be filled with gunpowder and blown up. Another refinement he introduced was that his tunnels employed a zigzag construction in order to enhance the explosive effect and reduce blowback.[42]

Francesco di Giorgio was one of the first men to design these new defensive structures. This may be because in the 1470s he worked for Federico da Montefeltro, one of the most successful military commanders of his generation. In 1472, Federico sacked Volterra, having successfully holed its city wall. When he asked Francesco di Giorgio to design defences for him, he presumably shared his practical experience of the structural weakness of standard fortifications. New walls were raised at Volterra, under the supervision, and apparently to the design, of Federico, one of the first professional soldiers to have a keen interest in mathematics. The new structure at Volterra was square in plan with low walls, an escarpment and massive cylindrical towers of the same height at the corners, creating an uninterrupted horizontal plane all around the perimeter which was wide and solid enough for heavy guns to be trundled about on it. The first fortress Francesco di Giorgio designed for Federico, Costacciaro, which guarded his border with Perugia, followed this plan.

In Francesco di Giorgio's treatise on architecture, he introduces his section on fortification with a discussion of bombards and artillery:[43]

previous pages
Two of Francesco di Giorgio's meticulous drawings of crankshaft-driven mechanisms, the basis for drawings in standard engineering textbooks down to the eighteenth century.

opposite
In a notebook now preserved in the British Library, an anonymous Sienese engineer sketches a design for a parachute.

Modern men have recently discovered an instrument of such violence that against it avails neither valour nor arms, neither shield nor the strength of walls, for with that instrument every broad tower must perforce quickly be brought down. By reason of this most powerful machine, called the bombard, all the old devices must certainly be termed useless and obsolete; its impact can only be believed by one who has witnessed it... Hence, not without reason, one may conclude that this instrument may be the foundation of a serious subject, an active principle and a way of proceeding no less. Since at the present time one clearly sees that a number of geometric forms, varying in length and width, correspond to a variety of modes of attack, it seems to me not inappropriate to determine what these forms are.

He is the first military architect to articulate clearly the way that architects needed to respond effectively to the new distance weapons, perceiving that ballistics was a variety of applied mathematics. In 1480, the Turks laid siege to Otranto, in southern Italy, using cannon, and captured it. This was the critical event which led to the world's first massive artillery-oriented defensive system: the city was recaptured by Ferrante of Naples and Matthias Corvinus of Hungary, and refortified by Francesco di Giorgio with the aid of his colleagues and students. It did not, unfortunately, occur to the Sienese at this time that perhaps they should start rethinking their own defences.

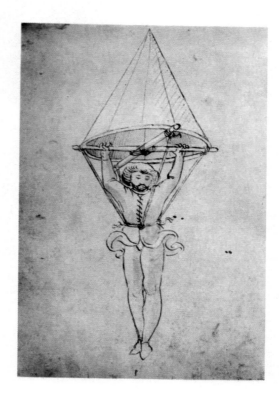

13

SIENESE ART:
THE RENAISSANCE
AND AFTER

S iena lectured its citizenry more insistently about Mutual Goodwill, Justice, and other civic virtues than any other Italian state, perhaps because in practice, the Sienese were so divided among themselves: everyone agreed the desirability of civic harmony, but at the same time, wanted their own particular party to control the city. The message of Lorenzetti's *Allegory of Good and Bad Government* was augmented at the beginning of the fifteenth century by an important civic commission which went to Taddeo di Bartolo, who evidently became the government's favourite painter of that generation. In 1406 he was commissioned to paint a series of frescoes illustrating the life of the Virgin in the chapel of the Palazzo Pubblico, which was to be completed in the remarkably short space of three months, in anticipation of the arrival of Pope Gregory XII in the city. The following year, he painted a huge *St Christopher* in the antechapel, to represent the care of the commune for the weak, and in 1413 was once again commissioned to decorate the antechapel's other walls. The programme was devised by two leading Sienese scholars, Pietro de'Pecci, a doctor of law at the university, and Ser Cristoforo di Andrea, Chancellor of Siena, so it was evidently more of a message than a decoration. This cycle covers the virtues needed for the life of the good citizen, Justice, Fortitude, Magnanimity and Religion, represented by famous men from Roman history held to embody these virtues. They are introduced by Aristotle, who explains, 'as exemplars of the vita civile, I show you these men; if you follow in their sacred footsteps, your fame will grow at home and abroad, and liberty will always preserve your honour'.[1] The theme of Roman virtue was further pursued in the intarsia back panels of a long bench commissioned for the Palazzo Pubblico in 1426 from Matteo di Nanni, depicting heroes of the Roman Republic, Though it was broken

overleaf Taddeo di Bartolo's evocation of life and death in a fifteenth-century hospital, from his suite of frescoes depicting the work of Santa Maria della Scala.

up in 1809, some panels survive, depicting Quintus Curtius, Publius Horatius Cocles, Cato, Manlius Curius Dentatus, Pompey the Great and Scipio Africanus.[2] The iconography may have changed, reflecting the new Renaissance interest in evoking ancient Rome, but once more the Sienese political class was being implored to pursue the Common Good, justice, and unity. Once more, as usual, it turned a deaf ear to the message. The cathedral also patronized Taddeo, and commissioned several frescoes from him which do not survive.

Another major commission of the mid-fifteenth century came from the third of the city's major patrons, Santa Maria della Scala. It was given to Taddeo's nephew, Domenico di Bartolo: a sequence of frescoes decorating the Pellegrinaio depicting the work of the hospital, which he completed in 1444. The name of this enormous fourteenth-century hall suggests that it was originally used to receive pilgrims. Eight scenes survive, in which the sick and wounded are received and cared for, as are abandoned babies and pilgrims, food and clothing are doled out to the poor, children are educated, and eventually adult orphan girls are given dowries and married off. The frescoes, some of which are set in the rooms of the hospitals, allow an extraordinary glimpse into fifteenth-century life, with its strong contrast between the sturdy, well-dressed officials and the skinny, ragged poor. The panel illustrating the care of the sick has all the drama of a hospital casualty unit: one emaciated man seems to be dying, with an attendant bending solicitously over him; the next man, sitting in a chair, has a frightful wound in his thigh and is being washed, while porters are hurrying in from the right carrying a stretcher. In the middle distance, a dog and a cat are squaring up for a fight, and behind them a remarkably stout Dominican is administering the last rites to a patient tucked up in bed. A curious detail is that the walls are covered with fur hangings, presumably for warmth.

Sodoma, a passionate animal-lover, chose to depict himself accompanied by two pet badgers and a chicken in one of the frescoes he painted for the monks of Monte Oliveto.

While Sienese patrons mostly favoured Sienese artists, and the guild of painters actively attempted to limit incursions from foreigners, some did come to the city, though foreign artists were required to pay an entrance fee to the guild of St Luke and post a bond to ensure they would uphold Sienese statutes.[3] Spinello Aretino was commissioned to fresco the Sala dei Priori in the Palazzo Pubblico in 1407 with scenes from the life of Pope Alexander III, a Sienese, who had ruled from

1159 to 1181. He was at odds with the Emperor Frederick Barbarossa for most of his pontificate, which limited his capacity for patronage, and he did not show any favours to his native city. However, he had won his quarrel with Barbarossa, and had been a formidable politician, which is presumably why the commune decided to memorialize him. It is not known why they picked Spinello for the job, rather than Taddeo di Bartolo, who was their favourite painter in the first decade of the new century. Possibly they were nudged in this direction by Pandolfo Petrucci, who brought several foreign artists to work in Siena. Another highly regarded painter, Gentile da Fabriano, who worked in the International Gothic style, came to Siena in 1425 to paint a Madonna for the notaries, now lost.[4]

Sienese art in the Renaissance is far more closely connected with Rome than with Florence. Michelangelo briefly worked in Siena, and the Sienese Baldassare Peruzzi made his career between Siena and Rome.[5]

Gentile da Fabriano seems to have executed his one commission and gone away, but two other strangers who came to the city at the end of the fifteenth century exerted a far greater influence. One was the Perugian Pinturicchio, who decorated the Piccolomini Library and the chapel of St John the Baptist in the Duomo, and also worked for secular clients, notably Pandolfo Petrucci, then the most powerful man in the city. Bernardino Fungai, an important Sienese painter of the late fifteenth century, was influenced by Pinturicchio, though he combined the new naturalism and sophisticated, three-dimensional modelling of forms with the creation of exquisite textile effects created by scratching through paint to an underlying layer of gilding, in a way that is typical of the Sienese tradition.[6]

The other foreigner who painted extensively in early sixteenth-century Siena was Sodoma (Giovanni Antonio Bazzi), a Lombard, who, Vasari says, was brought to Siena by the powerful Spannocchi banking family. Vasari hints that he acquired his nickname as a result of homosexual tendencies. After the death of Pinturicchio, he was the city's leading painter. He seems to have been trained in Milan, since he clearly learned a good deal from Leonardo da Vinci. We know of no major works he undertook for the Spannocchi, perhaps because the family lost their money after the death of Pius III. A beautiful, highly finished black chalk drawing of a long-haired youth is probably a study for a

portrait of Antonio Spannocchi, which, if it was ever made, would have been one of the first formal head and shoulders portraits ever painted in Siena.[7] Sodoma's first major commission was frescoing the refectory of the monastery of Sant'Anna in Camprena, which he completed in 1505. His skill as a portraitist was evidently well known, since the contract required him to represent some of the monks. He went on to fresco the main cloister of Monte Oliveto Maggiore. Subsequently he was invited to fresco the St Catherine chapel in San Domenico with scenes from the life of the saint. One of the quirkier aspects of his art, and life, is his fondness for animals; he kept a menagerie of miscellaneous creatures, including an owl, a monkey and a crow, and frequently tucked little dogs and other beasts into the corners of his compositions. In his self-portrait at Monte Oliveto, he is accompanied by a pair of pet badgers.[8]

Domenico Beccafumi, born in the 1480s, became the most successful Sienese painter of his generation. He was the son of a farm labourer in the Sienese *contado*, and came to the attention of a local landowner, Lorenzo Beccafumi. According to Vasari, little Domenico was standing guard over a flock of sheep and passing the time by sketching in the dust. Impressed by the fluency of the child's drawing, the man took an interest in him and later apprenticed him to a painter in Siena.[9] The future artist took his patron's name as a compliment.

Beccafumi was initially patronized by the Petrucci regime, but after its fall was appropriated by the restored republic to promote their ideals and express a sense of continuity. Beccafumi evidently studied the works of Raphael and Michelangelo, and also those of Sodoma, who was to some degree his rival at the start of his career. His figures are characteristically somewhat elongated and he had a penchant for softly brilliant colour. In the 1510s, he and Sodoma were both frescoing the façades of Sienese palaces with designs after the antique, which must inevitably have become competitive.[10] Both men both worked on the oratory of San Bernardino in Siena, but Beccafumi's work has a fluidity which makes Sodoma's look a little cluttered and academic. Like so many Italian artist-craftsmen, he worked in many media. Apart from painting and fresco, he decorated a bedroom for Francesco Petrucci, sculpted in clay, papier-mâché and bronze, and produced at least one intarsia panel, representing the Conversion of St Paul.[11]

Perhaps his single most spectacular painting is the *Fall of the Rebel Angels*, now in San Niccolò al Carmine, Siena: God the Father, at the top of the composition, wears red robes so brilliant they seem lit from within. This dynamic light illuminates the archangel Michael, who casts down the rebels with a decisive gesture of his sword. The bottom third of the painting, conversely, is lit by a lake of fire which seems to be moving like lava beneath the enormous masonry arches of the angels' prison. Naked angels writhe powerlessly, in a futile attempt to escape.[12] One of his most beautiful, which, conversely, is in quiet earth colours, is now at Chatsworth House in Derbyshire, and depicts the re-dedication of Siena to the Virgin on 15 July 1526, before the Battle of Porta Camollia. The canon of the cathedral, robed in white, stands on the altar steps of the chapel of the Madonna delle Grazie in the vast dimness of the cathedral receiving the keys from the kneeling Prior of the Concistory. A tense, prayerful crowd of leading citizens is watching, only too aware of the army of their enemies massing outside the city. The economy and passion of this painting is almost impressionist.[13] His *Annunciation* is another extraordinary painting, in which the angel and the Virgin are both luminous pink and white figures against a dark archway giving onto open countryside: Gabriel, unusually, is in mid-air, drifting diagonally down towards Mary, who is shrinking away from him.

Between 1529 and 1535, Beccafumi received another major public commission for decorations in the Palazzo Pubblico, a cycle of frescoes in the Sala del Concistoro. As with the commissions from Ambrogio Lorenzetti in the fourteenth century and Taddeo di Bartolo in the fifteenth, the topic of the murals is political, a celebration of republican virtue. Three figures on the ceiling represent Justice, Mutual Goodwill and Love of Country, set in roundels. In the corners are eight famous men, two to a corner, who for one reason or another embody these principles. There is also a frieze containing eight narrative representations of scenes from ancient history. Six out of the eight show either a suicide or an execution: Marcus Manlius is thrown from the Capitoline Hill, his body spiralling through the air. Sons are condemned to death by their own fathers; Publius Mucius sentences his fellow tribunes to be burned. Would-be tyrants are violently and pitilessly punished, while other scenes emphasize heroic virtue and loyalty to republican ideals.[14] The room was used to receive foreign ambassadors and for ceremonial receptions, and the decoration was completed just before the Emperor Charles V paid a visit to Siena. It therefore seems probable that the scheme was carefully weighed and considered, rather than being left to the artist's fancy. For all its brilliance, the cycle represents an uncompromising declaration of loyalty to republican ideals, and the emperor is known to have given it careful consideration.[15]

Beccafumi's other major intervention in the fabric of Siena is the series of pavement inlays he created for the Duomo. More pictorially ambitious than any of his predecessors, he used the marbles to create Michelangelesque tableaux, with subtleties of light and shade never before attempted in the medium. He also executed a fresco of the *Ascension of Christ* in the sanctuary, and made eight bronze candle-holding angels for the chancel. In fact, every major civic commission from 1529 to the fall of the republic went to Beccafumi. Though Beccafumi can be classed as a 'Mannerist', and was profoundly influenced by painters from other traditions, particularly Rome, he has frequent recourse to established Sienese compositional and iconographic types, and 'quotes' from earlier paintings, especially in his altarpieces. For example, his *Stigmatization of St Catherine* (a subject only tackled by Sienese artists), painted in 1514–15, is modelled on Bernardino Fungai's treatment of the same subject (1497). This suggests that in many ways he is the last practitioner of an intact Sienese tradition.[16] The amount of publicly funded work he did in Siena suggests that contemporary Sienese also saw him in this light.

The Sienese painter and architect Baldassare Peruzzi returned to his native city after the Sack of Rome, having spent most of his career in the Eternal City. However, in the anxious years of the 1530s, his service to the city was as a military engineer rather than as a decorative painter. Sodoma and Beccafumi continued to work, dying respectively in 1549 and 1551, but the mid-sixteenth century was a bad time to be an artist in Siena, and those who there were sought work elsewhere. Bartolomeo Neroni, married to Sodoma's daughter Faustina and to some extent Sodoma's stylistic heir, left Siena for Lucca and did not return till a measure of order had been restored after the fall of the republic in 1555. The few art commissions that arose, such as the scenery for Alessandro Piccolomini's play *Hortensio*, mostly went to Neroni.[17] Another painter, Alessandro Casolani, strongly influenced by Beccafumi, made a living producing devotional images.[18] The distinctive Sienese tradition in painting ended as it had begun, with religious art. A family of painters, including Francesco Vanni, his half-brother Ventura Salimbeni and stepfather Arcangelo Salimbeni, influenced, like other Tuscan painters of their day, by Federico Barocci of Urbino, were the principal painters of the seventeenth century. Francesco Vanni emerged as a very successful painter who worked in both Siena and Rome; as did Ventura Salimbeni. The latter's principal contribution to the public art of the city is the four frescoes he painted at the east end of the cathedral, two of which depict the saints of Siena.

14

THE FALL OF
THE REPUBLIC

After the death of Pandolfo in 1512, power passed to his twenty-two-year-old son Borghese, who pursued the same policies as his father, but ineffectively: Pandolfo's rule had been dependent entirely on his personal capacity for leadership, which his son did not share, and the family's grip on the city began to loosen. In 1513, Julius II – the warrior pope – died. While Julius had had little to do with Siena, he had been well disposed towards the city. Pandolfo Petrucci made sure of this by giving him the Villa La Suverana in Casole d'Elsa which he transformed into a splendid Renaissance villa designed by Baldassare Peruzzi and surrounded by beautiful gardens. However, Julius was succeeded by Giovanni de' Medici, who took the name of Leo X, and a Medici pope was not good news for Siena. If anyone had any doubts about this, Leo offered the city a deliberate insult in 1515. On hearing that the pope planned to travel from Rome to Bologna, the Sienese threw themselves into preparations for giving him a magnificent welcome. Cardinals and other members of his entourage came on ahead, and were found appropriate lodgings, firewood, candles and fine wines. Four triumphal arches were prepared, and artists of the calibre of Beccafumi and Sodoma were hired to work on the decorations. At the last minute, after Borghese had ridden to meet him at Bolsena, accompanied by a hundred young nobleman, Leo decided not to come.[1]

Borghese's cousin, Raffaele di Jacomo Petrucci, Bishop of Grosseto, was one of Leo's clients. Having gauged Borghese's capabilities when they met at Bolsena, the pope saw an excellent opportunity to oust him and replace him with a long-term Medici supporter. Only a few months after the pope's deliberate insult, Borghese Petrucci was overthrown in 1516 in a coup organized by Leo, and forced into exile along with his younger brother Fabio. He was replaced at the head of the Sienese government by Raffaele, who was rewarded for his services in 1517 with a cardinal's hat. In the years that followed, the two branches of the family wrestled for control over Siena, and the Sienese, preoccupied by their internal affairs, were rash enough to involve the great powers of the day in the fight. The choice before them was between the papacy and the Habsburg emperors, and, suspicious as they were of the Medici pope, they favoured the emperor. As early as 1520, the government sought to enlist the Holy Roman Emperor, Charles V (nephew of Catherine of Aragon), to help them oust the Petrucci, without perhaps thinking hard enough about the sort of price tag which is attached to help from an emperor. Charles had been fighting François I in Italy since 1521, and in 1525, his commander captured the French king at the Battle of Pavia. Siena was one of the states which had failed to offer any assistance to the imperial army, but when Charles asked them for a subvention they were willing to hand over 15,000 ducats.[2]

In 1524, the Sienese were able to force Fabio Petrucci out of the city, and to return to their old methods of governing. At the

Raphael's portrait of Leo X, the Medici pope, who set in motion the downfall of Siena, with two cardinals, both of them his first cousins. Giulio succeeded him as Clement VII.

end of the fifteenth century, there had been a Government of Ten Priors in place before the Petrucci dynasty wrested power away from them. John Stewart, Duke of Albany, the former regent of Scotland, who was leading François I's troops in Italy, was passing through Siena with a large French force, and helped the Priors' political successors to set up the Government of Nine Priors, a dictatorship of rich merchants.[3] They ruled from 1525 until 1545, and despite the help they had received from the French, were closely tied to Spanish imperial interests.

Fabio and other members of the Nine allied themselves with Leo's successor, Clement VII, who was another Medici (Giulio de' Medici), and returned with a powerful papal and Florentine army to take the city by force. The ensuing battle took place outside the Porta Camollia on 25 July 1526, and was the first time the city had faced heavy artillery. A mere six cannon devastated the northern wall of Siena, which was still a medieval fortification, high and relatively thin. The Sienese had invested in a sizeable extension of the medieval walls in the 1470s, but only a generation later these were effectively obsolete. They were designed for keeping out men, not for withstanding cannon fire. As things were, the papal army could simply knock large holes in the walls which had defended the city for two hundred years. But the Sienese were not to be

cowed. The republican militia, inspired by a rallying speech from their leader, Gianmaria Pini, sallied out of the Porta Fontebranda and Porta della Pescaia, stormed the papal–Florentine position, and captured the guns.[4]

The unexpected victory of the Sienese against papal and Florentine forces at the Battle of Camollia had two important affects, one military, the other political. Having seen the new, more powerful cannon in action for the first time, the Sienese clearly understood that they were going to have to adapt their defences if they hoped to survive.[5] Additionally, in political terms, the Battle of Camollia was a victory for the three smaller parties (the Twelve, Reformers and Populace) against the two upper-class *monti*, the Nine and the Gentlemen. The battle is depicted in a contemporary painting, which illustrates that even after three centuries of trying to keep the *casati* under control, the city was full of noblemen's towers.[6] The dominance of the popular parties created a new and special political situation. Cities which had taken advantage of the city's internal problems and rebelled against Siena were brought back under its control, except Pitigliano in the Maremma, which was being covertly aided by the Nine. The other parties used the occasion to extirpate the remnant of the Nine from Siena. Many of their members were massacred, some were driven from the city, while others fled in fear.

Charles V, painted by Titian. By seeking his help, the Sienese precipitated themselves into his long conflict with the French.

Since they feared further attack from the Petruccis and their allies, and were strongly conscious of their military vulnerability, the Sienese accepted the emperor's protection and began to think about redesigning their walls. The Sienese were well placed to adopt the new technology. In the course of the fifteenth century, their metallurgical expertise allowed them to become a centre for cannon production, and in Francesco di Giorgio Martini, chief military engineer to Federico da Montefeltro of Urbino, they had produced a defensive architect second to none.[7] He had unfortunately died in 1501, but his sketchbooks survived him, and he had successors capable of following up his ideas. This, however, would require both time and money (a great deal of both) and there was plenty to be afraid of. A large and poorly controlled mercenary army, theoretically fighting for Charles V, passed through Sienese territory in 1527, on the way to Rome, where they mutinied, rampaged through the city and sacked it, the greatest disaster in the entire history of sixteenth-century Italy. Just over a year later, what was left of this army was back in Tuscany again, on the way to the siege of Florence (1529–30), which reinstated the Medici as puppets of the emperor.

The answer to Siena's prayers returned to the city in 1527. Baldassare Peruzzi, a Sienese architect and painter, had made his career in Rome, where he designed a grand suburban villa for the fabulously wealthy Sienese banker Agostini Chigi, now known as the Villa Farnesina (built 1508–11), at a cost of more than 23,000 ducats. This established him as one of the city's leading architects;[8] but in 1527, he found himself trapped by the Sack of Rome. Unlike many, he managed to survive both the mercenaries and the plague, typhus and famine which followed on from the devastation wrought in the city. In late June 1527, a Sienese ambassador handed over enough money to ransom him out of the ruins of Clement VII's city and he made his way to Siena. For the next eight years, until 1535, Peruzzi was *Operaio* of the Duomo, and continued to have a private architectural practice, but, above all, he was architect to the republic, with an annual salary of sixty scudi. On 24 October 1527, he was elected to the committee to oversee the walls and defences of the city, and entrusted with making bastions at all the gates, to do work 'at other necessary places', and to make it possible to run round the walls while remaining under cover.[9] What this tells us is that the committee was trying to reach a compromise. Taking down and rebuilding the city walls would be more expensive than they could afford, and take too long. But bastions at the gates would allow defenders to direct fire either at gun emplacements, or parallel to the wall itself if the attackers came too close. Peruzzi and his employers agreed on five bastions, three of which are still standing, at the gates of San Viene, Laterina and Camollia. Peruzzi's structures were up to date, and extremely well thought through. By 1528, both the Florentines and the Milanese were expressing interest in, and curiosity about, his work.[10]

The Battle of Porta Camollia: for the first time, the walls of Siena had to face an onslaught from cannon. The city was still bristling with magnates' towers in 1526.

In late 1529, the Sienese were laying plans for Charles V to make a joyous entry to the city, on his way to Rome to be crowned Holy Roman Emperor. It became clear that the civic budget would not stand the strain of new bastions and decorating the city for the emperor simultaneously, and it is a lesson in Renaissance priorities to learn that the government decided to transfer money intended for defences to the civic decorations.

HOSTEM SENA FUGAT

Tabulam hanc
...arte sua estornas...
...quamvis fortun...
...natui lib...vitate...
...ssel flo...in ded(i)t...
...ALDC...

Peruzzi was redeployed to the creation of triumphal arches, and, from 10 December 1529 to April 1530, work on the fortifications ceased entirely, while the Sienese spared no expense on the palio race and bullfight at which Emperor Charles V was to be present. It proved to be a bad call, since Charles ended up being crowned in Bologna and did not come to Siena until 1536.

The commune embarked on another major art commission at this time, a ceiling for the Sala del Concistoro in the Palazzo Pubblico which depicts Greek and Roman examples of civic virtue, by Domenico Beccafumi, discussed in the previous chapter. The spur to the composition was the imminent arrival of the emperor, so it seems very much more than likely that it was intended not merely to honour him, but to impart a lesson in civics as the Sienese understood it. The design is presided over by Justice, Love of Country and Mutual Goodwill, a trio that suggests that the inspiration is Cicero's *De Officiis*: 'the principle by which society and what we may call its "common bonds" are maintained. Of this... there are two divisions – justice, in which is the crowning glory of the virtues and on the basis of which men are called "good men"; and, close akin to justice, charity, which may also be called kindness or generosity.'[11] The examples are taken from Valerius Maximus's *Memorable Deeds and Sayings*, written around 30 BC. As Pascale Dubus has commented, 'the message proclaimed in the frescoes can be summed up in four words: the Republic or death'.[12] Many of the examples chosen involve a death: the execution of plotters against the republic, or individuals laying down their lives to preserve republican institutions. Work on the frescoes was suspended in May 1530, just when work on the fortifications started again, and resumed in 1535 when it became known that Charles was finally to enter the city, and completed in time for his arrival.[13] All this suggests that Beccafumi's work was seen as being as important to the safety and liberty of the city as that of Baldassare Peruzzi. The Sienese political theorist Francesco Patrizi, the most important humanist authority on government, argued that art was an important means of communicating ideas: the city could use art to create a 'virtuous environment, a symbolic world in which hearing and sight are enlisted in the task of reinforcing disposition to virtue'.[14]

By 1530, the emperor was already becoming a worrying ally. Charles V brought Siena's rival factions together and insisted on a treaty readmitting the exiles. Siena was committed to providing munitions, food and labourers for the siege of Florence, where Charles was determined to bring down the republic and introduce a duke answering to himself, Alessandro de' Medici. Lopez de Soria, imperial envoy in Siena, thought it essential when the army moved on for a garrison of Spanish troops, paid for by the Sienese, to remain behind to secure the reform of the government and ensure that returning exiles felt safe enough to stay.[15] One begins to see why the Sienese might have thought Charles could do with an education in the principles of republican liberty.

A new agreement was reached between Charles and the Sienese in which the emperor evidently called the shots. The exiles were to return, none of the political factions was to be excluded from the government and a garrison of 350 Spanish troops was to guarantee the security of all. Alfonso Piccolomini, Duke of Amalfi, was to be captain general of the republic and the emperor's representative. Since he was descended from one of Pius II's sisters, and was thus Sienese by ancestry, he was a diplomatic choice. On 24 April 1536, Charles V finally staged a triumphal entry into Siena, promising to observe and uphold all the liberties of the city.

Alfonso Piccolomini led the reorganization of the administrative structure of the republic and put the running of the city in Sienese hands. But in 1540 Charles pushed through a reformed constitution intended to share political power between the five *monti*. He also raised taxes and the garrison was enlarged. In 1547, following a number of violent incidents between citizens and troops, who were billeted with the citizens in their houses, the idea of an isolated barracks was mooted, and rapidly overtaken by proposals for a citadel.

This was highly problematic. From an imperial point of view, a citadel was needed to defend Siena from French aggression, and to control lawlessness in city and country. The Sienese, like other Italians, saw immediately that a citadel enabled its builder to oppress the citizens and regarded the move as highly provocative. In Florence, the humanist and historian Bernardo Segni complained of the Fortezza da Basso – a fort inserted in the city's fourteenth-century walls – that the Medici were determined 'to place on the necks of the Florentines a yoke of a kind never experienced before: a citadel, whereby the citizens lost all hope of ever living in freedom again'.[16] A garrison securely based in a fortress had unlimited capacity to intervene in Sienese affairs. It was a physical symbol of dominion, as they well understood: when the Sienese themselves had reconquered Montalcino in 1361, to ensure it stayed subdued, they built a fortress on the edge of the town.[17]

To add insult to injury, the governor expected the Sienese to pay for the structure, raising the money by a special local tax, forced loans and misappropriating money which had been intended to strengthen coastal defences against incursions from Turkish pirates, an intermittent, unpredictable, but serious threat in sixteenth-century Italy. Building material was to be sourced onsite by demolishing the magnates' towers, a symbolic castration of the city. The fortress was designed for the age of artillery, and though it was subsequently destroyed we can learn quite a lot about it from the receipts for labour. The outer wall was constructed like the medieval city walls, two skins of brick or stone, with a layer of dry rubble, or rubble and mortar, between them. But behind it was a massive earthwork, strengthened by faggots and brushwood. A scaffolding frame of timber was constructed and faggots of long twigs bound together laid in layers. Then brushwood and earth were tipped in and rammed well down. Such a structure took a lot of man (and woman) hours, but it was unskilled labour. It utilized whole trees, not just their timber, so it was economical. This type of construction was stable enough to support heavy artillery, and ensured that, though cannon might blow a hole in the wall, the cannonballs would be stopped by the earth and wood behind it.[18]

Piccolomini was replaced as governor of Siena by Don Juan de Luna in 1541, because he was incompetent. Don Juan promptly made himself unpopular by getting involved in Sienese politics, and favouring the Nine at the expense of the other parties. In 1547, he was removed in turn, and replaced by Diego Hurtado de Mendoza, a highly educated man, a writer and diplomat who had earlier served as an imperial envoy to England. Despite his virtues, he was unimaginative, and unsympathetic to the Sienese point of view. At this point, Siena received an enquiring English visitor, Sir Thomas Hoby, who astutely observed: 'The cheefe governance of this citie was in the hands of Don Diego di Mendozza… which manie times cam from Roome to lye there as occasion served him, where at his cumming he was alwaies more honorablie receaved outwardlie then inwardlie beloved.'

Hoby has other interesting things to tell us about Siena in 1547. He greatly appreciated the university, which struck him as excellent value for money: students paid an initial fee of sixty or seventy crowns, and might stay as long as six or seven years. Perhaps in consequence, he found the city full of Englishmen. 'Sir Robert Stafford, Mr. Henry Parkar, Mr. Edward Stradling, Mr. Francis Peto... Besides these I founde in the towne Mr. Peter Whithorn, Mr. William Barkar, Mr. Edward Clere, Mr. Thomas Grynwaye, and Mr. Jhon Ellis.'[19] Siena attracted foreigners, because the university was cheap, the people friendly and their pronunciation was thought particularly attractive. The ideal was to have 'the speech of Florence in a Sienese mouth'.[20]

Hoby found the Sienese hospitable towards strangers, and comments on the unusual public prominence of Sienese ladies, 'most of the women are well learned and write excellentlie well bothe in prose and verse, among whom Laudomia Fortiguerra [Forteguerri] and Virginia Salvi did excell for good wittes'. Sienese noblewomen had taken part in public life since the fifteenth century. In the sixteenth, a number of women were prominent in the intellectual life of the city, participating in 'lively gatherings of witty ladies and wise gentlemen that used to be held in Siena'.[21] They demonstrated this after a local man of letters, Alessandro Piccolomini, visited Petrarch's tomb in 1540 and wrote a poem about the experience. This was answered by Virginia Salvi, and her poem earned a reply from him, a sort of poetical tennis match which was frequently played in contemporary Italy, though not usually between a man and a woman.[22] Other ladies then joined in the game, and the verses were circulated among Piccolomini's literary associates. Five sets of women's verses from this *tenzone* survive.[23]

As well as the university, Siena had an alternative intellectual forum, the Accademia degli Intronati ('the stunned'). A slightly earlier iteration of the Intronati which called itself the Accademia Senese had as its main purpose the advancement of Tuscan Italian, and the Intronati, similarly, concerned themselves with Italian and did not conduct their meetings in Latin, which made them accessible to women. According to its foundation charter, the Academy was founded in 1527, the year of the Sack of Rome. The members were commanded, 'Pray. Study. Rejoice. Trust no one. Believe no one. Care nothing for the world.' In an era in which politics were as difficult and unpleasant as they were in sixteenth-century Siena, one possible intellectual response is to disengage and withdraw into a private world. The declared purpose of the Intronati was to 'promote the study of history, literature and art in the city, the province, and the former State of Siena'. A chapter in the Accademia's statute prohibited the Intronati not only from speaking about politics, but also from participating in them. One form its meetings took was the *veglia*, a social gathering after dinner which women as well as men could attend, which typically involved after-dinner games demanding quick wits and a thorough knowledge of Italian literature. It was presumably in this context that Hoby saw Laudomia Forteguerri and Virginia Salvi distinguishing themselves for their skill at repartee.[24]

One work produced by the Intronati which exercised a major influence on European literature was a play, *Gl'Ingannati* (The Deceived Ones), first performed in 1533, and first published in 1537. The anonymous author identifies himself merely as an Intronato. It went through eight editions, was translated into French several times and performed in Latin, in Cambridge, in 1595. This last performance is particularly significant since the play may well have given Shakespeare the plot for *Twelfth Night*, though there were other comedies which used the 'twins'

Contadina Sanese.   Matrona Sanese.   Artigiana Sanese.

theme first devised by Plautus. However, the plot of *Gl'Ingannati* is particularly close to that of Shakespeare: a merchant of Modena mislays one of his twin children, the boy, at the Sack of Rome. He still has his daughter at home, but she is in love with one Flaminio, who is in love with Isabella. She dresses as a boy, becomes Flaminio's page, and carries his letters to Isabella, who falls in love with her. Eventually her brother reappears and, after a lot of misunderstandings, the male twin marries Isabella, and his sister marries Flaminio.[25]

The Intronati considered themselves a cultural elite free from the restrictions of the universities and the sycophancy of the courts, and therefore able to write as they pleased. One Intronati production which would certainly have displeased any censor is Antonio Vignali's *La Cazzaria*, which means 'the cock-up' ('*cazzo*' being slang for a penis), written around 1525. This is a highly critical political allegory disguised as pornography, and its author was clearly an enthusiastic sodomite, so both disguise and sub-text were equally objectionable.[26] Sodomy in early modern Italy was considered a major sex crime which might bring down divine reprisals, so it attracted punishments such as castration, burning alive and decapitation.[27] In this dialogue, the two principal speakers are Arsiccio and the younger Sodo, who are sexually involved. Siena's five *monti* are represented as genitalia: the Nine, being the most powerful group, are Cocks, and the Gentlemen are Balls, because they are politically dependent on the Nine. In this powerfully male-dominated society, there is a clear sense of phallic hierarchy; and the smaller and weaker *monti* are therefore represented by female organs and anuses. The arrogance of the Cocks leads to counter-plotting by the lesser organs who approach the Balls for support. The Balls betray them to the Cocks, but their treachery is discovered and they are put on trial. Their punishment is that, while the other organs can pair up and have sex, the Balls are forever excluded – a political statement disguised as a sort of pornographic version of one of the *Just So Stories*. Witty, lively and obscene, it was, unsurprisingly, very popular.

Another association which sprang up at this time was the Congrega de Rozzi, or 'association of the uncouth'. This was an association of artisans who knew no Latin, but were determined to use their leisure creatively. Like the Intronati, they wrote plays and poems, many of which

Sienese fashions c.1580: the figure on the left is a countrywoman, the one in the middle is upper class, and the one on the right is an artisan woman from the city.

were about peasants, who were sometimes satirized, but often treated with compassion, making the Rozzi the only group in sixteenth-century Siena to display real sympathy with the people of the countryside; real life 'rude mechanicals' with a point of view.[28] One of their number, Silvestro the Papermaker, wrote nine plays deeply critical of Sienese society, mostly from the point of view of a peasant.[29]

However, while the intellectuals of Siena, both male and female, wrote poems, debated and composed dialogues or scientific treatises, the political situation was worsening. The citizens did not find Don Diego sympathetic. They considered him arbitrary, partisan and unjust. But even if he had charmed them, in any case he was there to implement an imperial policy which they found deeply unpalatable. He also angered them when he confiscated all weaponry, both public and private, in an attempt to control street violence in the city. Meanwhile, banditry in the countryside, especially in the Maremma, reduced the city's income by interfering with cattle raising, and depressing the number of pilgrims using the Via Francigena. This combined with higher taxes to produce widespread impoverishment, with the usual sequel of civic discontent and rioting. But the Sienese interpreted Don Diego's gesture as an indication that he suspected their loyalty to the emperor, and took deep offence.[30]

Part of the problem between Mendoza and the Sienese was that Charles V was not giving his governor enough money to do all that the emperor wished to have done. Thus, Mendoza had to raise funds from the Sienese themselves by taxes and forced loans. His unwanted Spanish soldiers were still billeted on the Sienese, which doubtless caused the usual problems of theft, seduction, rape, drunkenness and general nuisance, and alienated the pro-imperialists. Even so, he did not have enough money to pay his troops, so they also became disaffected, and sold their weapons for cash to the theoretically unarmed Sienese. Many of the Sienese nobles left the city, and retired to their country estates.

Meanwhile, the Sienese lobbied, argued and protested about the citadel. One of the memorials they sent the emperor was signed by a thousand citizens. At the same time, they appealed to their traditional protector, going in procession to the Duomo with the Captain of the People at their head, and presenting the keys of the city to the Virgin, imploring her to protect her city and change the emperor's mind: 'for pity's sake,' he prayed, 'take from him that design, which our good faith does not deserve, and brings with it the destruction of honour, dignity, and our dear liberty…'[31] But for all that, the fortress continued to rise on the hill of San Prospero. Matters came to a head in July 1552. Mendoza was in Rome, trying to raise money, when the Sienese called on French help, and revolted. An army, led by Aeneas Piccolomini delle Papesse, a descendant of Pius II's sister, arrived at the gates of the city and were promptly let in by delighted Sienese. The Spaniards, left in the charge of a young and inexperienced commander, Don Francesco d'Avila, were taken by surprise, bottled up in their incomplete fortress and persuaded to surrender a month later. They were allowed to march out with full honours of war, but their commander left with ominous final words to his Sienese friends, when they met him at the gate to say goodbye; 'you have offended too great a man'. Emperors do not stay in business by allowing proud little cities to defy them.

In the meantime, the mood in the city was euphoric. The French ambassador in Rome, the sieur de Lansach, came to Siena to tell the citizens they were under the protection of the king of France.[32] Joyfully, the citizens started to dismantle the hated fortress – though thriftily, since the outer face was incorporated into the city's defences.[33] The inner walls were taken down and the materials redeployed to complete the outer rampart, thus preserving the defensive function of the structure while making it impossible to use it to control the people of Siena. It had not yet dawned on them that they had not regained their liberty, but made a choice between the Emperor Charles V and the French king, then Henri II. They had also ensured that Charles would counterattack, since by changing masters they had entangled themselves with the power struggle between the Habsburg emperors and the Valois kings for control in Italy. Both thought Siena a desirable prize, with its extensive territory and ports on the Tyrrhenian Sea, and considered it strategically important.

overleaf Euphoric Sienese destroy the hated Spanish citadel; a brief moment of triumph before a series of disasters.

In the winter of 1552, Siena, with her new French allies, prepared to meet the troops of a wrathful emperor. The city was aided by another talented military architect, Giovanbattista Peloro, who built them a group of new fortifications around Camollia, guarding the road to Florence.[34] On New Year's Day 1553, a Spanish force came up from Naples and stopped in the environs of Cortona, where they were joined by a smaller Italian army, and heavy artillery sent by Cosimo de' Medici,

D
INTROITVS ET EXITVS INCEPTVS AÑ · DÑI
A·C·SCRIBA PROANNIS · VI· DIE VLTIMO
NICCOLAO MARTINO, LACTANTIO B
GHEZIO, DE BVRGHESIIS PRIMO, ATQ
PICHOLOMINEO, SIGISMVDO BONINS
SEMESTRE OFFICII EXECVTOR·

M

ORESIO DE FORESIIS EXECVTOR K.TO

RIS CŌPLETIS ANNO ·M·D·L·II·

ORIO, ALEX CVRTO, AGVSTINO

TO OTAVIANO, MARCELLO

ANTO ASIARIO SECVDO

SORIBVS·

Grand Duke of Florence. Duke Cosimo remained technically neutral during the campaign, but in fact supported the imperial troops with food, transport and weapons. The Sienese, meanwhile, beavered away to complete Peloro's new forts, making faggots and hauling baskets of earth for earthwork defences. According to the chronicler Agnolo Bardi, even the Cardinal of Ferrara, Ippolito d'Este, and the Archbishop of Siena came and took a hand with carrying faggots, though not, one suspects, for very long.[35]

One contribution to the defence which attracted a good deal of attention was that of the ladies of Siena. Three women, one from each *terzo* of the city, named by the historian Marco Guazzo, who was writing in 1553, as Laudomia Forteguerri, Fausta Piccolomini and Livia Fausti, formed a battalion of three thousand women and led them to work on the new defences, carrying the banners of the *terzi*.[36] Laudomia Forteguerri can be identified as a strong-minded and unconventional woman poet who was married to a Petrucci. The other names seem to have been garbled.

We have no portrait of any of the female wits of sixteenth-century Siena; however, Sulpizia Petrucci, with her challenging gaze, gives an idea of what they looked like.

Other Sienese women played a part in contemporary political life. Aurelia Petrucci, granddaughter of Pandolfo and daughter of Borghese, wrote an impassioned poem in 1535, calling her fellow citizens to defend themselves against imperial tyranny. It reads, in part,

Where is your valour, beloved Homeland,
That, wretched, you forget the servile yoke,
And in your breast you nourish only discordant thoughts,
Prodigal with what's bad, stingy with what's good for you?...
Draw your scattered limbs into a single body
And let one just will be everybody's law.

This is an absolutely typical piece of Sienese political thinking, upbraiding the citizens for their disunity and advocating, yet again, justice, unity and the common good.[37] The poem was greatly admired, and was the first poem in Ludovico Domenichi's edition of poems by Italian women, published in Lucca in 1559. It also opened the second such collection of women's verse, made by Antonio Bulifon in 1695, by which time it was being read as a lament for the whole of Italy, not just Siena. Aurelia herself survived the fall of Siena, and spent the rest of her life in exile in Rome. Another woman who wrote political verse is the

Virginia Salvi who was admired by Thomas Hoby. The year before he met her, she had been arrested on a charge of sedition, after some of her sonnets critical of the Spanish regime began to circulate anonymously in the city.[38] All of the Sienese ladies who expressed political opinions were passionately pro-French and anti-Spanish, but Virginia displayed unusual personal courage, and was ordered to spend a year rusticating at her father's family estate in Casole d'Elsa.[39] She must have recently returned, clearly undaunted, when Hoby met her.

In 1553, while the men and women of Siena toiled to complete their defences, the imperial army were working on getting the *contado* under control, and, above all, dealing with two towns which were in their way, Monticchiello and Montalcino, both of which were bravely defended. They took Monticchiello only after the defenders had exhausted all their ammunition; Montalcino held out for more than eight weeks. The Montalcinese were saved by an obscure aspect of the overall political

Blaise de Monluc, a ruthless, tough and cynical Gascon, who led the defence of the city.

situation, an alliance between the French and the Ottoman Turks. A fleet of Turkish galleys was sighted in Sienese waters, and Charles's troops were forced to abandon their campaign, because Cosimo was afraid that he might lose his precious cannon.[40] The Sienese naturally put the retreat of their enemies down to the direct intervention of the Virgin Mary, and rejoiced accordingly. 'All the bells of the churches rang out, and the trumpets played from the roof of the Palazzo, in joy for the victory which had been won without a battle. Many old men and women were seen crying from happiness...'[41]

The next phase in the war began when the French king appointed a Florentine exile, Piero Strozzi, as his vicar-general in Siena. First of all, this was a violation of treaty since there was a reciprocal agreement with Florence not to harbour one another's exiles. But also, Strozzi was a sworn enemy of Cosimo de' Medici, who had murdered his father. This gave Duke Cosimo an excuse to enter the conflict directly. The Florentines launched a 'surprise' attack on Siena itself at the end of January 1554. The only thing surprising about it was the precise timing, since the Sienese had been expecting exactly that. Unfortunately, it was not effectively met, since the imperial forces were able to take the new Camollia forts. Both sides then dug in.

Strozzi was convinced that his best chance of saving Siena was to move out of the city and rely on the support of the countryside. He

knew that the imperial troops were already suffering from a shortage of food and money, and when fresh French and Swiss troops arrived in July under the leadership of Blaise de Montluc – a Gascon who may well have been one of Alexandre Dumas's models for D'Artagnan in *The Three Musketeers* – he entrusted the French commander with the defence of the city, and took his cavalry out into the *contado* to meet the imperial troops led by the marquis of Marignano. Unfortunately, his campaign was a disaster. Strozzi was defeated in pitched battle, losing about 12,000 men, and was himself injured, though not killed.

In the early months of 1555, most of the imperial troops in Tuscany were concentrated around Siena. With about 30,000 men, they could blockade effectively, and prevent any food from getting into the city. Siena had market gardens within the walls, but relied on the countryside for most of its food. For a long time, they received provisions via the underground tunnels of their water system, but Marignano burned houses and destroyed vines, olives, orchards and farm animals for four to six miles around the city, and with cover destroyed, was able to control surreptitious movement. The defenders slowly began to starve. All the young men in the city were drafted into a militia, while women, children and the old were set to work improving the fortifications.

The situation within the city was dire. The French cavalry had to leave because there was no fodder for their horses. On 6 August, Monluc, who firmly believed that cruelty was a necessary aspect of war, ordered the 'useless mouths' who could contribute nothing to the war effort to be ejected from the city – that is, the very old, the very young, the blind and the disabled, including 250 orphan children from the hospital.[42] Those, in other words, least able to care for themselves. By the end of the month, any household which had less stored food than could support them for three months was driven out, so the rich thus had a better chance of survival than the poor. In previous sieges, the Florentines had taken care, at least to some extent, of helpless non-combatants exiled from their city, but this time, in order to crush the spirit of the defenders, they left them trapped between the city walls and the enemy lines to starve to death.[43] Monluc wrote,

The list of these useless people I do assure you amounted to 4400 or more…
and these poor wretches were to go through the enemy who beat them back
again towards the city… they drove them up to the very foot of the walls
that they might the sooner consume the little bread we had left, and to see if
the city out of compassion to those miserable creatures would revolt.[44]

Some women saved themselves by prostituting themselves to the
Spaniards, but the Sienese who remained in the city were forced to watch
the rest of the 'useless mouths' beaten and abused, and, ultimately, dying
of hunger. The old men and women who had wept for happiness in
1553 now sobbed in anguish, scrabbling at the city's indifferent walls.
Alessandro Sozzini in his diary of the siege wrote, 'even Nero would
have cried'.[45] Sienese consciences revolted against Monluc, and they
refused to send out any more children, but the hospital was allotted so
little food that bands of small girls went out every day looking for wood
which they could barter for something to eat. This pathetic
spectacle disturbed the Sienese greatly. They suffered
agonies of conscience, as well they might, and became
convinced as their situation became worse and worse that
they were suffering divine retribution for abandoning the
helpless.[46] They had always turned to the Virgin for help;
but would she help people as guilty as they were?

overleaf
An engraving of the
siege of Siena by Philips
Galle, after Jan van
der Straet.

Marignano began to bombard the city into submission in January
1555, without success, but by the end of February the remaining Sienese
were dropping dead in the street from hunger. The Sienese had always
attached great value to the beauty of their women. Alessandro Sozzini in
his diary of the siege wrote of January 1555 that the hardships of the siege
had reduced the lovely noblewomen he had known into unrecognizable
versions of their former selves.[47] The Sienese finally capitulated in
April, and put themselves humbly at the mercy of the emperor, though
a few refused to give up even then. About two thousand Sienese
citizens moved to Montalcino, in a last attempt to resist the Spanish
and Florentine conquest and keep the republic alive through an elected
government, and the use of the official Sienese seal.[48] They were finally
forced to capitulate when the Treaty of Cateau-Cambrésis was signed in
1559, bringing an end to Franco-Spanish conflict in Italy. As a gesture of
goodwill, Cosimo I granted a general amnesty and allowed exiles who
so wished to return peacefully to Siena. All the horrors of the siege had

CAMOLIA

Iohan. Strada-
nus inuentor.

I

Phls Galle fecit

Caroli V. Caesaris, et Cosmi M
ad Camoliam Senarum portam,

florentiæ ducis milites propugnaculum,
inunitum noctu inuadunt, et praesidio nudant.

been endured in vain. It has to be said that the fortifications stood the test of combat, but they could not protect the citizens from starvation.

After the conquest of the city, Charles V gave it to his son, Philip II, then married to Mary Tudor, queen of England, who thus also briefly became queen of Siena. Two years later, Siena suffered a further bitter humiliation when he sold it to Cosimo de' Medici in July 1557. Their fate could have been worse, since Tuscany was subsequently divided into two main administrative districts: the *stato nuovo* (the new state), which consisted of the former Republic of Siena, and the *stato vecchio* (the old state), which was the old Republic of Florence and her dependencies, each governed according to its own laws. The division was maintained because the *stato nuovo* was a Spanish fief and the *stato vecchio* an imperial one, but it had the incidental effect of maintaining Siena's separate identity. However, they had lost the independence they had fought so hard for. Three hundred years after the Battle of Montaperti, they were finally subjects of the Medici, and the Medici arms, together with their grand ducal crown, were added to the façade of the Palazzo Pubblico.[49] Cosimo promptly consolidated his control over the city by rebuilding the hated Spanish fortress between 1561 and 1563. Thereafter Siena was ruled by a governor appointed by the Grand Duke, though the forms and rituals of Sienese government remained, empty of meaning. In a late sixteenth-century painting by Agostino Marcucci, we see the Signoria in their scarlet robes processing solemnly out of the Duomo behind a holy image (probably of the Virgin, and this is probably the Feast of the Assumption), with clerics all in a row, as if everything was as it had always been. But when they were proceeded by standard-bearers, the standards they carried were no longer Siena's black and white *balzana*, but the arms of the Grand Duke.[50]

Ignazio Danti's 1580s frescoes of Siena and Florence emphasise the subordination of Siena to its ancient enemy: its landmarks, the Duomo, the Torre del Mangia, are not shown.

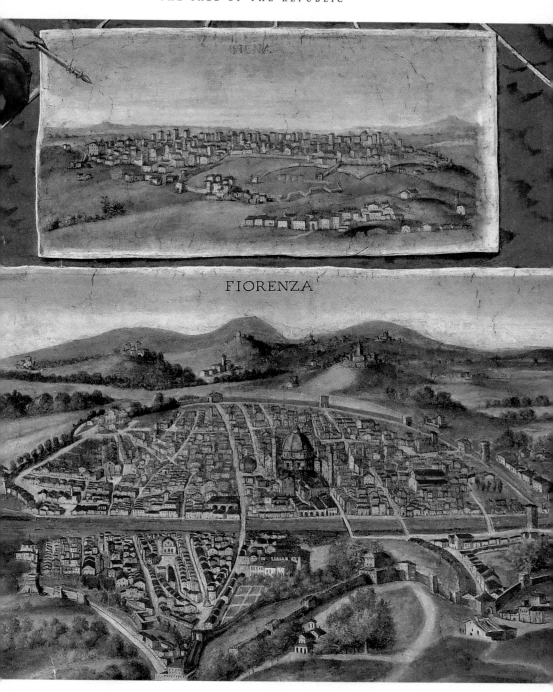

FIORENZA

15

MEDICI
RULE

The Sienese response to their loss of independence was spirited. From immediately after the fall of the republic, Siena began to perceive itself, and to be perceived, in a different way, locating its distinctive characteristics in its art and culture rather than in its political independence.[1] The Dukes were not merciful in victory, and maintained the fiction that they had conquered Siena by force of arms. When Philip Skippon, an English writer and traveller, visited Florence in 1665, he noted that Ferdinando II celebrated the day Cosimo bought Siena from Philip II as if it had been a military victory, with 'a cavalcade of Cavallieri, races, and a few fireworks... the people seeming to rejoice little on this occasion'.[2] As a matter of policy, Siena was maintained in a subaltern role under the Grand Dukes. The main trade and commercial routes through Tuscany bypassed the city.[3] Understandably, resentment towards Florence was fierce.

I once encountered a slightly surreal instance of this when we were in Siena in the summer of 1999 to do some work in the town library, and lunching at the appealingly named Cane e Gatto in Via Pagliarese. We were accosted by a stout lady who was spreading the word of a prophetess in Monterrone, who had seen the following signs and tokens: a red cross in the sky at sunset, two crescent moons appearing together in the sky and Our Lady appearing to her (but not speaking). What she deduced from all this was that the impious city of Florence would be overwhelmed by a great wave on 18 September. It seemed unkind to ask the poor soul how the prophetess thought the Almighty was going to achieve this, but it did, at the very least, suggest that dislike of Florence remained deeply embedded in the culture.

As Judith Hook has observed, the attempt of the Sienese to constitute a republic-in-exile in Montalcino showed an impressive and 'continued belief in the ideals which some Sienese believed to have been at stake during their struggle with Charles V', yet also demonstrated 'little understanding of reality'.[4] In Montalcino, these Sienese exiles engaged in self-deception that bordered on myth-making as they imagined their own sovereignty, even after the fall of their republic. But Lauro Martines has suggested that versions of this play out in other parts of Italy, describing a 'concentration of tremors' that created a crisis in art, religious feeling, and, more generally, the sensibility of the ruling class in sixteenth-century Italy. He depicts writers retreating 'into imagination, seeking ideal models, perfect solutions, alternate worlds, or merely building castles in the air'.[5]

When reality is unbearable, fantasy is sometimes consoling. The reality was that the political lives of Italian states were no longer under their own control, but were at the mercy of the conflict between the Habsburgs and the French kings. Some minor powers, such as the Dukes of Ferrara and Urbino, weathered the storms, but Naples and Milan ceased to be independent states, and Florence and Siena were no longer republics. Italian civic elites struggled to come to terms with the obvious contempt which their new French, Spanish and German masters held them in, so much at odds with their own sense of their value and importance. And economically, Italy was falling behind. Around 1300, Italian cities had accounted for almost a third of Europe's urban population, and had a quarter of the continent's largest cities, 24 out of 103, with populations of at least 20,000. At least three of these, Florence, Venice and Milan, had populations of over 100,000.[6] Italians had once led Europe's economic activity as bankers and traders, but by the second half of the sixteenth century it was the north, the Netherlands above all, which was the economic powerhouse of Europe. While average Dutch incomes increased by 180 per cent between 1500 and 1700, Italy showed no increase at all in economic growth in the same period.[7]

The malaise of seventeenth-century Italy was to a significant extent caused by the luxury trades. For centuries, the wealthy few had bought exotic items from Asia – it was the existence of this trade which brought the plague to Europe – but never, in all that time, had they evolved trade goods which Asia found reciprocally desirable. The result was a continuous flow of gold and silver out of Europe and into Asia, affordable while output from European silver mines remained buoyant, but not afterwards. By the end of the fourteenth century, bullion famine had locked Europe into a state of commercial recession.[8] At the end of the fifteenth century, Europeans began seriously looking for alternatives to trade with the East, turned their backs on the Mediterranean, and began braving the Atlantic. The discovery of the New World gave the Spanish access to the gold and silver of the Americas, and the Portuguese began trading with Africa, which also produced gold. As the perceptive English traveller James Howell observed, the wealth even of mighty Venice 'hath been at a stand, or rather declining, since the Portugal found a Road to the East-Indies'.[9] Italy, without an Atlantic littoral, suddenly found itself at a disadvantage.

The Sienese *contado* had been partly depopulated by the wars of the first half of the century. However, the population overall recovered and increased considerably between 1550 and 1600, though not uniformly so: the Maremma was left to the mosquitoes in the summer, though in winter people still came down from the mountains to overwinter cattle, burn charcoal and perhaps raise a crop of wheat.[10] There was one major easement to the overall situation of the Sienese: because the French and Spanish were no longer fighting one another in Italy and the whole of Tuscany was under one ruler, centuries of endemic warfare finally came to an end. As peace and stability returned, the population rose. Since the Sienese elite was now almost entirely financially dependent on their share of what was produced on their landholdings, they invested in the countryside. Many of them built villas, in order to have a place to entertain, somewhere to retreat from the plague which periodically returned to the city and a place from which to supervise the harvest. It was the Medici era which created the Tuscan ideal landscape, the square farmhouses perched on little hills, with their rows of cypress trees, fields and vineyards.

An interested Englishman, Robert Dallington, visited in 1596 and published a short book, *A Survey of the Great Duke's State of Tuscany*. Two things struck him above all. One was the poverty of ordinary people. In Prato for the Feast of the Assumption, when people would presumably be dressed in their best, he observed that about half of the great crowd in the piazza had straw hats, and a quarter had bare legs. He saw a countryside which was profoundly impoverished: 'that glorie and wealth there is, is in the Cittie, and in the hands of a few.'[11] He describes countryfolk who lived primarily on chestnuts, acorns and foraged plants, and drank water. Dallington estimated that Tuscany produced only a quarter of the grain needed for its population, and noted that very little meat was eaten, even by the better off. His other observation was how relentlessly the people were taxed. There was a tax of 8 per cent on all business transactions, including rents and marriage contracts; the Grand Duke raked in heavy profits on the sales of salt and grain, which were government monopolies; there was a poll tax; and in addition, in every city every egg brought to market and even the smallest purchases taken home by the peasants were taxed. A gentleman from Siena he talked to told him that someone like himself was not allowed to bring the grain from his own farm to the city for his own use, an intrusion of the state into all aspects of life which shocked him.[12] It suggests that, while the Sienese in the days of their liberty had not been slow to impose taxes, they must have found the Grand Duke's exactions burdensome. They had also been considerably kinder to the people of the *contado*, for the excellent reason that they were much more dependent on it than the Florentines.[13]

The doorcase of the Academy of the Intronati, central to the social and intellectual life of Siena, but regarded with suspicion by the Grand Dukes of Tuscany.

Siena itself Dallington thinks of as a strategically desirable possession for the Grand Duke, since it guards the way to Florence from the south. He notices the Duomo, the Fontebranda, and is impressed by the Campo: 'I have not seen a Market-steede, excepting that of *San Marco* in *Venice*, so beautifull.'[14] He was told that the population had considerably declined since it came under Medici rule, and that the upper class lived entirely on rent, and did not trade or involve themselves with banking. Essentially, what he sees is a demoralized city set in a countryside bled white by over-taxation.

One thing that the Sienese had to capitalize on was the beauty of their language: according to many competent judges, it was where the best Tuscan was spoken. As we have seen, the University of Siena was attracting foreign students by the mid-sixteenth century. Henry Wotton, an ambitious young English diplomat, came to Siena in 1592–3 to improve his Italian, and in 1642, James Howell in his *Instructions for Forreine Travell*, advises, 'From thence [Genoa] let him hasten to Toscany, to Siena, where the prime Italian dialect is spoken and not stirre thence till he be master of the Language in some measure'.[15] The first chair of Tuscan language to be established in Italy was founded in Siena. The immediate cause was a group of Germans who had come to the university. They were anxious to improve their Italian, and accordingly they petitioned the Grand Duke of Tuscany, asking him to provide facilities for them to be taught the language. This petition was favourably received, with the result that a '*lettore*', a well-known grammarian, Diomede Borghesi, was appointed in 1688, whose principal duty was to instruct foreign students.[16] Another English traveller, Fynes Moryson, intended to study Italian in Siena, but didn't, because it had become so popular that 'many Dutch and English Gentlemen lived there, which were of my acquaintance', and he was afraid that he would end up talking English most of the time.[17]

In strong contrast to Italy's military and economic decline in the sixteenth century, its culture was vibrant and powerfully influential throughout Europe. Italy's new export was words. Howell, again, writes, 'Italy hath beene alwayes accounted the Nurse of Policy, Learning, Musique, Architecture, and Limning, with other perfections, which she disperseth to the rest of Europe.'[18] Titian became principal painter to the Habsburg emperors, and enjoyed international fame.

POESIS

MISCET VTILE
DVLCI

ˍOETAEˍPRÆSIDIV

MELIORA LATENT

GENERO
THVSCO
INTRONA

COMOEDIA

VITÆ SPECVLV

COMICOR. FAVTOR

MELIORA LATENT

It was still fashionable to learn Italian, but much Italian literature was also translated. Niccolò Machiavelli's political writings were read with fascination and horror, while Castiglione's *The Courtier* set new standards for polite behaviour. The poetry of Giambattista Marino was widely imitated, while Ariosto's fantastical romance, *Orlando Furioso*, published in its final form in 1532, exercised an enormous influence on European literature, and was translated into English at the behest of Queen Elizabeth in 1591 by her godson John Harington. The high status of Italian literature explains why Shakespeare so often turned to Italian sources for his plays, or set them in Italy. New musical forms originating in Italy, the madrigal, and in the next century, opera and oratorio, swept through cultivated Europe.[19]

This defiance of frustrating political developments and turn towards culture as a way of asserting one's status and dignity also characterized the Intronati of Siena. They evolved a new conception of Sienese identity, centred on a new set of values, which no longer revolved around traditional republican ideals but instead focused on a new kind of cultural leadership that claimed to exist separately from the political world. Cosimo de' Medici was highly suspicious of Sienese intellectual life. After his entry into the city in 1561, Sienese printing presses were closed down. Alessandro Piccolomini lobbied successfully for the revival of the Intronati, who had ceased to meet during the last desperate years of the republic, and it was permitted to reopen: he celebrated the reopening of the Academy with his comedy *Ortensio*. This proved to be merely a stay of execution, since Cosimo continued to perceive the academies as possible centres for republican subversion. His suspicions were not without justification. The Academy's entertainments often offered a sly challenge to the political, and religious, order. During the period of Spanish domination, the Intronati's play *Gl'Ingannati* (1532) and the Rozzi's *Travaglio* (1552) both mocked their Spanish masters.[20] Around 1563–4, Girolamo Bargagli's *Dialogue on Games* looked back to wistfully to the palmy days of the 1530s, when Sienese men and women had been able to meet for sophisticated intellectual play: an implicit criticism of the Medici regime.[21]

Other Intronati productions cast a satirical eye on the church, and even on religion. Fausto Sozzini, a heretic and a member of a famously

previous pages
A drawing of the set for the Intronati play, *Ortensio*, with which they hoped to gain the approval of the Grand Duke.

opposite
A Sienese streetscape: though houses in the old town open directly onto the street, lovingly tended plants often offset the mellow ochre of the bricks.

heretical family, was an Intronato. Cosimo called the Inquisition in to investigate. Siena contained many pro-Reformation thinkers; as early as the 1540s, several of the city's religious confraternities had become centres of political intrigue and Protestantism. They invited the noted Sienese preacher Bernardino Ochino to come to the city, fully aware that he was no longer preaching orthodox Catholic belief.[22] Several of the Intronati were also discreetly heterodox.[23] In a dialogue of 1538, the Intronato Marc'Antonio Piccolomini puts a dialogue into the mouths of three of Siena's intellectual women, on whether a perfect woman is perfect by chance or by design. This was not as harmless as it seems: Laudomia Forteguerri, who in fact seems to have been an intellectually audacious woman with scientific interests, argues the case for chance: in effect, arguing for something like Darwinian evolution rather than divine intention, a daring position to adopt in Counter-Reformation Italy.[24]

Papal politics and personal ambition conspired to drive Cosimo towards an increasingly harsh stance on religious dissent. In 1559, the ascension of Gian Angelo de' Medici as Pius IV (though he was from a Milanese branch of the family), strengthened the ties between Florence and the papacy, since cardinals' hats went to two of Cosimo's sons, Giovanni and Ferdinando, in succession. Siena's tradition of freethinking was in jeopardy, since, in a letter of 1560 to the Inquisition, the Duke proclaims himself 'the fiercest persecutor of heretics'.[25] This made Cosimo highly suspicious of the academies. The Intronato Scipione Bargagli wrote to dissuade a friend from visiting because the atmosphere in the city was so oppressive, complaining that 'here, anyone who talks of the Yule log, of parties, of symbols, is accused of heresy; anyone who designs pleasant entertainments for Carnival is accused of plotting against the state'.[26] Parties, discussing folklore and devising symbols were exactly the sort of things the academies enjoyed. They were closed in 1568, and the Intronati did not reopen until 1603. Something worth noticing is that the theatre in which *Ortensio* was staged was constructed in the Sala Grande del Consiglio in the Palazzo Pubblico. While the reason for building it was probably pragmatic, in that it was a large hall not otherwise in use, the Sienese might well have perceived a certain irony that a room which had once been used by the largest number of Sienese who ever took part in the political process was now turned over to fantasy.

The closure of the academies and the press under the Medici did not mean the cessation of intellectual life, though the context for meeting and discussion necessarily became less formal. One family which fared well under Medici rule were the Agostini. They were a political family: at the beginning of the century, Paolo Agostini had been Pandolfo Petrucci's chancellor. After the fall of the republic, his son Marcello was made a marquis by Cosimo I as a reward for his support, and Marcello's son Ippolito was perhaps the leading Sienese intellectual of the second half of the sixteenth century. He was in touch with the leading scientists of Italy, such as Ulisse Aldrovandi, made scientific collections in his home, Palazzo Venturi, accumulated books and bought paintings, sculpture and curiosities. His principal interests were mathematics, natural science, music and drawing. With the academies closed, his palace became an informal meeting place for scholars.

Another witness to Cosimo's religious policy is that he established Jewish ghettos in Florence and Siena, in the latter case over the protests of the Sienese. There had been Jews in Siena for centuries, but this population was now confined to Salicotto, an area near the Campo and the Market, located behind the Palazzo Pubblico, the territory of the Contrada della Torre.[27] The Jews were locked into the ghetto at night until the gates were destroyed by Napoleon's troops in 1801 as a symbol of the community's emancipation.

16

THE PALIO

Thousands flock to Siena every summer for the Palio, one of the most dramatic and peculiar events in the world. After two hours of an extraordinary medieval parade, ten horses race three times round the Campo, which takes less than two minutes. The word Palio, now used for the event, derives from the Latin 'pallium', a rectangular cloth, since the name has been transferred from the prize to the race. Palio banners have always been made of silk. Those of today are hand-painted, employing a different artist each year, but in the past they were much more elaborate and expensive. One of the perennially astonishing things about medieval Italian cities is how much they were prepared to spend on temporary effects. By the fifteenth century, a palio banner was a huge rectangle made from two widths of precious cloth, with a decorative band covering the join, which, for the most prestigious banners, was made of gold and metallic thread and perhaps embroidered with coats of arms. Red and gold were the colours most favoured, and the material might be damask, velvet, or another silk. The banner was lined with miniver, the grey and white winter fur of Russian squirrels, and decorated with braid, cord and tassels, hung on a pole with a crosspiece which had a decorative top, usually a silver lion, or a golden ball. Making the banner was a collaborative effort, involving the craftsmanship of specialist banner-makers, carpenters, furriers, painters, embroiderers and gilders. The banners became ever larger and more expensive over time. The Palio for the Assumption in 1310 cost 50 lire, the one for 1428, 461 lire 12 soldi, and the one for 1515, 800 florins.[1] Only the fall of the republic put an end to the inflation. A palio banner for an important event such as the Feast of the Assumption might be as much as twelve metres tall. The number of squirrel skins used rose with the size of the banner, and by 1400 more than a thousand pelts might be used.[2] Not only was the palio banner an expression of the city's ability to spend lavish sums on valuable fabric, it was also one of pride in the manufacture of local weavers. Sienese banners became larger after the successful establishment of a silk industry in the city.

Palio banners challenge preconceptions of how Renaissance society valued art objects. The cost of making the banner equalled or exceeded payments for panel paintings or frescoes by well-known artists. In 1315 and 1321, Simone Martini was paid a total of 73 lire 8 soldi as payments for painting the *Maestà* fresco in the Palazzo Pubblico in Siena, and subsequent retouching.[3] In 1332, the city spent over 381 lire on the Palio of the Assumption. None of these magnificent objects survive, since once the celebration was over, the banner was worth only the value of its materials, which were therefore recycled or sold. One of the best representations of such a banner is a *cassone* panel by the late fourteenth- and early fifteenth-century artist Giovanni Toscani depicting a palio run in Florence: the gold brocade banner looms over the judges like a giant golden sail, with ermines' tails dangling out of the fur lining.

In the Middle Ages, palio banners provided a moment of civic magnificence at the Feast of the Assumption, which was also a political event affirming Siena's domination over the towns of the *contado*. Communities subject to Siena brought a pound of wax for every hundred lire of their tribute money, three-quarters of it in the form of a large decorated candle to be placed on the high altar, and also brought tribute *palii*. The representatives of the towns and groups within the city processed to the Duomo with their candles from Porta Camollia or Porta Romana, accompanied by the city's own palio banner, always the most magnificent, mounted on a cart, and their own, smaller banners. One of the earliest Sienese town planning ordinances is a statute of 1262 ordering that the two main streets from Porta Romana and Camollia to the Porta di Stalloreggi had to be open to the sky, and any arches or galleries were to be demolished, thus creating a ceremonial way down which the tall banners could process unimpeded.[4] The towns' banners were hung on the piers of the nave from iron rings, replacing the day-to-day black and white marble with a shimmering display of coloured silks.[5] The ceremony of offering was followed by mass in the cathedral, a grand dinner in the Palazzo Pubblico for the dignitaries and a horse race. The route, and length, of the race varied, but it generally started outside the city and ended in a major piazza whenever the winning horse reached the palio banner, which was placed at the finishing point of the race. The goal of a palio race was always the palio itself. Giovanni Toscani's *cassone* panel depicts one such race: the palio banner is in a cart with the judges, and the horses, ridden by jockeys dressed in the colours of their owners, are hurtling towards it. One horse has fallen. In Siena, the Assumption was the city's great gala day. The people who received livery from the city got their new clothes at this time, and for the three days of the celebration women were allowed to wear silk, velvet and jewels in the street.

Horse races accompanied many religious festivals in medieval Italy. In medieval Siena, the most important celebrated the Feast of the Assumption of the Virgin, instituted by 1238 at the latest, the Blessed Ambrogio Sansedoni, from the beginning of the fourteenth century, and San Pietro Alessandrino, instituted in 1414.[6] At the beginning of the sixteenth century, Pandolfo Petrucci added another in honour of his patron saint, Mary Magdalene. Palio races were also sometimes held for a special occasion such as the canonization of Catherine of Siena.

In the seventeenth century, these various celebrations settled down to two races a year, both in honour of the Virgin. One, instituted at the beginning of the seventeenth century, was on 2 July, and celebrated the Madonna of Provenzano. This was a terracotta image of the Virgin mounted on a street corner, allegedly placed by St Catherine, and honoured by Siena's most peculiar local holy man, Brandano.[7] In 1594, a Spanish soldier struck the image with his lance, damaging it. Shortly after, his rifle backfired, killing him, which was considered a miraculous punishment for his disrespect.[8] Work on a new basilica in Provenzano began in 1602, and on 23 October 1611 the image was transferred there. This race was a palio run annually in the Campo (*palio alla tonda*) from 1656 onwards.[9] The second race, which had much more ancient roots in Sienese custom, was run in honour of the Assumption, the city's principal religious festival.

following pages
Giovanni Toscana's depiction of a palio race in the streets of Florence is the best surviving representation of a medieval palio, made of gold brocade and ermine.

The original races in honour of the Assumption were not the Palio we know. They were run on the feast of the Assumption itself, over distance, outside the city at first, and then, after the Nine had straightened and improved the streets sufficiently to make this possible, within the city, probably ending up at the Piazza del Duomo, since the cathedral was the focus for civic celebration. These Palios were prestigious events, as

the magnificent prize banners suggest, and the horses which ran in them were among the best in Italy. The owners of horses entered in the 1461 Palio of the Assumption in Siena included Sigismondo d'Este, Lorenzo de' Strozzi of Ferrara, Count Malatesta of Cesena, and Isotta, the wife of Sigismondo Malatesta. In 1513 and 1514, the owners included Francesco Gonzaga, marquis of Mantua, who was perhaps Italy's premier racehorse breeder at the time, Francesco Maria della Rovere, Duke of Urbino, the Cardinal of Siena, and members of the Sienese banking families of Francesco Petrucci and Augustino Bardi. North African Barbs were favoured, and Palio horses are still referred to as *barberi*.

With the fall of the republic, the significance of the Palio underwent a change. The Feast of the Assumption ceased to be a political event. An annual ceremonial offering *palii* banners and candles was maintained, but it took place in Florence, and was addressed to the Grand Duke on the feast day of John the Baptist. However, when Cosimo de' Medici became ruler of Siena in 1558, he heeded the advice of Machiavelli to 'hold and occupy the people with feasts and spectacles'.[10] He found the *contrade*, the wards into which the city was divided, a convenient instrument for amusing the people with spectacles and games, since their mutual rivalry transformed Sienese patriotism, potentially focused outwards against Florence, into parochial partisanship which took their attention away from their subjection. It was only after the Medici takeover that the *contrade* got involved with palio races.[11] The institution of royal governors in Siena, the first of whom was Caterina, daughter of Ferdinand I and widow of the Duke of Mantua, followed by Prince Matthias, Prince Leopold (brother of Cosimo II), Prince Francesco Maria (son of Ferdinand II) and Duchess Violante of Bavaria, provided a focus for spectacles and public entertainments.[12] Caterina lent her support to the new basilica at Provenzano,[13] Matthias, who was musical, supported both opera and the Palio, and Violante put a permanent stamp on the city by setting the territories and number of the modern *contrade*, and setting the rules for how the Palio was to be run.

The *contrade* are a unique feature of life in Siena. A Sienese born in the city is born into a *contrada*, a unit which has its own church, an administrative centre, a flag, a museum, a symbolic animal, racing colours, and much else besides: the anthropologist Alan Dundes

The Madonna of Provenzano: this unassuming terracotta image became the centre of a major cult in Siena, and a new church was built to house it.

describes it as 'a combination mutual aid society and social club'.[14] The city is divided into *terzi*, and each of these thirds once contained approximately twenty *contrade*. After the plague brought a drastic decline in population, the number of *contrade* shrank to forty-two, and by the eighteenth century amalgamation and attrition had reduced the number to twenty-three. The modern names for the *contrade* are recorded as early as the sixteenth century. In 1679, six of them were abolished by Duchess Violante, with the aim of producing social units of roughly the same size, reducing the total number to seventeen.[15] The *contrade* had ceremonial functions from early in Siena's history, since they are mentioned in a document from the early thirteenth century, a statute establishing the order in which various officials and groups made offerings for the Feast of the Assumption.

Before 1558, the *contrade* mounted popular spectacles on the day after the official Assumption celebrations, focused on the cathedral. These spectacles used the Campo as their stage. The first form of entertainment they offered was a bullfight. These were staged from as early as 1499 and were elaborate affairs. Not all the *contrade* participated every time, since bullfights were expensive. Elaborate costumes were required, as were *macchine*: large and sturdy wooden structures made to look like birds and animals; they were strongly made, and a hard-pressed bullfighter could jump into one as a temporary refuge.[16] Each *contrada* sought to outdo its enemies in the splendour of its costumes and the elaboration of its *macchina*, as well as the dexterity and courage of its fighters. Since these *macchine* often cost a good deal of money, two or more neighbouring *contrade* sometimes combined together to build a particularly magnificent specimen, which may be one of the mechanisms by which *contrade* amalgamated. In a painting from the late sixteenth century, Vincenzo Rustici depicts the procession of the *contrade* before a bullfight. *Contrade* members form a spiral procession winding round the Campo, each competing *contrada* with its *macchina*, which must be human-powered since no horses are visible. Groups of scampering youths in red associate themselves with each of the *macchine*, and are perhaps the bullfighters. Huge banners are waving overhead. Another of Rustici's paintings shows a bullfight in progress. The spectators are standing round the perimeter of the Campo, crowded against a protective barrier, and the *macchine* are parked round the perimeter of the playing space. Each of the participating *contrade* contributed a bull, and these animals were released one at a time.

opposite
The *contrade* parade in the Campo with their banners, preliminary to entertaining the city with a bullfight on the day after the Assumption, depicted by Vicenzo Rustici.

overleaf
Vicenzo Rustici shows members fighting two bulls and a bear, but literary sources suggest that bulls were released one at a time.

The bullfights were banned by order of Grand Duke Ferdinand I in 1590, but the Sienese enthusiasm for brutally dangerous sports continued unabated. The *contrade* substituted buffalo races, in which a buffalo was ridden three times round the Campo, accompanied by a crowd of young men with goads, which they could, and did, use either to stimulate their own animal or to annoy those of their opponents. They also held donkey races, which were in effect punch-ups with added donkeys. Six to ten *contrade* participated, each of which brought thirty men and a donkey to the Campo. They made a circuit, throwing their banners in the air and catching them, after which the valuable banners were tidied away, the officials joined other spectators behind a protective palisade and the donkeys were led to the start. At the signal, the players hurled themselves on the animals, some trying to push the unfortunate donkey forwards while others tried to hold it back, freely trading punches with one another. No man managed to stay on a donkey's back for more than a few seconds before being dragged off. The winner was the first team who managed to get their donkey pushed round two circuits of the Campo.[17]

After the suppression of the bullfights, the *macchine* were no longer required, and the *contrade* substituted processional floats presenting mythological and allegorical tableaux. An engraver called Bernardino Capitelli produced a volume of prints illustrating the six floats which were on display in 1632. His etchings show that these were enormous and fantastical structures, pulled by four horses. He explains the float created by the Contrada delle Torre as follows:

> It was a ship on the ocean waves drawn by two marine horses, on the poop deck was the Tuscan sea, in the middle two Maritime nymphs, in the prow, a Venus with two cupids and outside the ship, Neptune around whom there were a number of Tritons, afterwards followed a buffalo representing a sea monster surrounded by other monsters tended by Proteus the sea shepherd. In the corteggio appeared Galatea with six sirens and the Rivers Ombrone and Arbia, many marine deities, freed slaves and some Turkish and Moorish characters, prisoners in the naval victories of the Grand Duke.[18]

Evidently, the *contrade* were being careful to ensure that their entertainment flattered the Medici and would not be perceived as subversive.

The *contrade* began running horse races in the Campo at some point in the half century after the fall of the republic, since in 1581, one such race, sponsored by the *contrada* of the Onda, attracted a great deal of attention because the jockey for the Drago was a twelve-year-old girl, Virginia Tacci. She finished third, but poems were written in her honour and she was paraded through the city. In 1689, the office of the Biccherna regularized what was becoming the annual running of the Palio of the Contrade in the Campo, to be run with horses on 16 August, the day after the Feast of the Assumption.[19] Thereafter horse races occurred quite frequently, superseding the carnivalesque races with buffalos and donkeys, but were not run with absolute regularity until 1802, when the city took over the responsibility of organization.[20] An English sportsman, Peter Beckford, was in Siena in 1786 and witnessed the celebration of the Assumption.[21] As a keen fox-hunter, he was a good judge of high-risk riding, and he was greatly impressed by the talent and courage of the jockeys, and the formidable challenge offered to both horse and rider by negotiating two ninety-degree turns at full speed. The fifteenth of August was still being celebrated by the commune with a procession, a dinner and a horse race, *alla lunga*, run without riders, for which the prize was a piece of velvet. This was still run by valuable racehorses, since Beckford happens to mention that an animal belonging to the Prince of Naples had been killed on a previous occasion. This race was clearly the continuation of the Renaissance Palio.[22]

overleaf
The float built for the Contrada delle Torre in the mid-seventeenth century. It no longer served defensive purposes, and was simply built for display.

However, he also saw something very like the Palio as we now know it, which was organized by the *contrade* and took place the following day. There are some interesting differences between the spectacle he witnessed and the Palio as it is now. The prize was a silver cup, not a palio banner, which was paid for by three Sienese gentleman, who nominated their successors, an obvious way for the richer Sienese to win influence and gain public credit. The horses were ordinary hired hacks, and the jockeys got them four days before the race, as today. The number of horses was limited to ten, in obedience to an ordinance of Violante of Bavaria, this being an attempt to make the race marginally less dangerous. Trials were run in the morning and evening of the four days, and attracted a large audience: so much so that people watching the Assumption race *alla lunga* would dash off to the Campo the moment the horses swept past them. The trials were even more dangerous than the race itself, because earth was only put down in the Campo on the day of the actual

CARRO DELLA TORRE

Nella sommita sedeua la Fama nauale, appresso alla quale stauano la Verita
è la marauiglia, che conduceuano legate la Mensogna, el'Adulatione. Ap
del carro era Pallade che guidaua i sette Saui della Grecia. Il Re Acritic
Cap.° in habito reale di Sontuosa cõparsa, è Perseo Luogot.° caualcãte l'Hippog

Palio. Beckford saw five horses fall in one day, and noted that if one horse lost its footing, several more might then stumble into, or over, it. Beckford does not mention a procession, though there must have been one, since eight fine new floats were represented in an engraving published that same year. Since these floats were pulled by only two horses, they must have been smaller than the floats of the seventeenth century. The engraving shows that they represented the animal totems of eight of the *contrade*.[23] It thus seems that today's Palio takes over the palio banner from the official Assumption celebrations, while substituting the *contrade* parade with flag-throwing for the parade of city officers performed at the Assumption. Since the Assumption horse race was much less exciting and enjoyable than the *palio alla tonda*, it eventually ceased to be run, some time in the late nineteenth century.[24]

One important change in modern times is that there is much more concern for the welfare of the horses than there used to be. The depth and firmness of the earth is carefully checked, there are padded crash barriers at the two dangerous corners and the horses themselves now have to conform to exacting standards. They are mixed-breed animals, because thoroughbreds are more likely to injure themselves, and particular attention is given to the sturdiness and conformation of their legs.[25] The chosen horses are carefully examined by vets, both when they are chosen and before they run, while the vets remain on standby throughout the race.

While the question of who actually wins the race is enormously important to the Sienese themselves, for visitors the most enjoyable part of the experience is the two-hour pageant rather than the ninety seconds of furious riding. The Feast of the Assumption was always an excuse for dressing up, but the sixteenth-century paintings of Vincenzo Rustici and the engravings of 1630 and 1786 suggest that the festival dress of *contrade* members was much what one would expect for the centuries in question. The early nineteenth-century craze for neoclassicism produced costumes *alla greca* in 1813, replaced in 1839 with costumes *all'spagnuola* and *all'italiana*: Antonio Hercolani's illustration of palio costumes in his *Storia e costumi delle contrade di Siena* (1845) show that these were vaguely medieval belted tunics and tights.[26] The palio clothes were renewed in 1904, with a much more developed grasp of what medieval clothing was actually like, but it was only under the fascists that the palio pageant was visually located in the fifteenth century, where it remains. The Podestà of Siena, Fabio Bargagli Petrucci, convened a committee to restyle the Palio as a coherent medieval event datable to between 1430 and 1480, part of the Mussolini government's highly conscious evocation of a proud Italian past.[27] The Palio was heavily publicized in newsreels, calendars, postcards, and Alessandro Blasetti's film, *Palio di Siena* (1931–2), and thus began to acquire a secondary status as an Italian cultural event rather than being essentially an affair for the Sienese themselves. In more recent times, the Palio has been marketed as a unique experience for tourists, and underwritten by the Banca Monte dei Paschi di Siena, the sponsors of the present costumes.

The history of the Palio is thus one which involves a good deal of change in its continuity. It was, perhaps, cynically encouraged by the Medici as a means of focusing the city on its internal rivalries. But this only succeeded because it became a primary focus of what it meant to be Sienese. The Medici hollowed out the government of the city after they took power, retaining names and to some degree structures without allowing the Sienese to exercise actual power. The Biccherna, which had once consisted of four important administrative offices, became a committee responsible for overseeing some public works and festivals – including the Palio. The Palio therefore became one of the devices whereby the Sienese maintained their dignity in their own eyes, retreating from unpalatable realities into games and fantasy. Additionally, preparations for, machinations around and performance of the Palio became the major function of the *contrade*, a focus for their identity, a stimulus to their formal organization and a cyclical rhythm which fostered their continuity. The *contrade*, as we have seen, were deeply embedded in Sienese social structures, but in the new world of Medicean Siena, the Palio became an instrument of their continued vitality. Once the Palio was established, Palio and *contrade* reinforced one another.[28]

17

THE CITY
AND ARCADIA

Though the Italian economy held together through the sixteenth century, it fell on hard times in the seventeenth.[1] Italy's prosperity depended on exporting goods, especially high-quality woollen and silk textiles, and services, world-wide banking operations and maritime transport.[2] But by the seventeenth century, the new Atlantic powers, the English and Dutch, had ships and financiers of their own. The Thirty Years War in Germany drastically reduced the market for expensive Italian silks, as did the political woes of the Turkish empire, which was embroiled in civil war, reducing the value of trade with the East. Other major Italian luxury exports were mirrors and glass, chiefly Venetian; but the French protected their own silk and mirror industries with import tariffs, and the English, similarly, protected their nascent glass industry.

overleaf
October at a villa in the Sienese countryside, and the condatini are bringing in the grapes. The Sienese nobility spent October in the country, and the master is supervising.

All this weakened the great manufacturing economies such as Venice and Genoa, but in Siena the upper classes were already rentiers, gaining their wealth from the countryside, rather than merchants or bankers, so they were only indirectly affected. Far more damaging was the return of the plague in 1630 and again in 1657. Between these two dates, the greater Italian cities lost about a third of their people. Since agriculture is labour-intensive, this had a direct impact on the prosperity of the city. Philip Skippon noticed in 1665 that although the streets of Siena were lined with grand houses, their windows were not glazed.[3] What kept Tuscany marginally solvent was a massive shift from arable farming to viticulture: the region's reputation as a major producer and exporter of wine dates to the seventeenth century.[4] The Medici Grand Dukes developed Livorno as a free port (meaning that goods traded there were duty-free), which attracted a numerous and cosmopolitan community to the city, and facilitated the export of Tuscan wine.

The *contado* continued to decline. The Maremma was still practically deserted, and the valley of the Chiana abandoned to swamp. Vast stretches of the Tuscan countryside were empty of inhabitants. The poor in both city and country were very poor indeed, but even the upper class were far from wealthy, either by the standards of the past, or by those that prevailed in northern Europe. In 1643, less than 5 per cent of Sienese noble families had an annual income which exceeded 2,000 scudi, and three-quarters of them had 500 scudi or less. By 1692, only 2 per cent had more than 2,000 scudi, and nearly 80 per cent had less than 500.[5] Through the eighteenth century their pleasures were necessarily inexpensive.

One symptom of the straitened circumstances of the upper class, in Siena as elsewhere in Italy, was that they protected their family fortunes by allowing no more than one son, normally the oldest, and perhaps one daughter, to marry. If the heir's marriage did not produce children, then the family might disappear entirely. The number of noble families therefore declined. Subsequent sons were given room, board and pocket money, and allowed to live off their parents, or the fortunate heir.[6] Daughters were sent to convents. Peter Beckford, who spent most of the 1780s in Tuscany, comments, 'at ten years old they are sent to a convent, where they remain till they marry, or as long as their parents think fit.'[7] As he sadly observed, 'marriages are as rare at Siena as at Pisa, and a

multitude of beautiful girls are at this moment in want of husbands'. This pattern was already established in the seventeenth century: though the Chigi were one of the wealthiest families in seventeenth-century Siena, the five sisters of Fabio Chigi, the future Pope Alexander VII, were all sent to convents. Only one of his eleven nieces, the daughters of the only Chigi of the family who married, was found a husband, while the others all became nuns.[8] The Chigi palace at Ariccia, near Rome, contains a room filled with portraits of Chigi nuns, and it is hard to believe that all of them felt a serious call to the religious life.[9] A contemporary Venetian nun, Arcangela Tarabotti, who had been forced into the cloister by her parents, wrote forcefully and bitterly about the way that Italian fathers threw away the lives of their daughters in works such as *Paternal Tyranny*, and *The Hell of Monastic Life*. There is considerable other evidence for seventeenth-century Italian women who felt that they had been condemned to life imprisonment for the crime of being female.[10]

The Room of the Nuns at the Chigi palace of Ariccia: dozens of Chigi daughters cloistered willy-nilly to protect the family patrimony.

In at least some Sienese convents there was a tacit recognition that the inhabitants had no particular vocation to the religious life, and the rules of enclosure were sometimes interpreted rather liberally. In the seventeenth century, Olimpia Chigi Gori Pannilini greatly enjoyed Antonio Cesti's opera *L'Argia*, and wrote to her half-brother in Rome, who was a cardinal, 'I assure you that I was entranced, and I do not think that one can hear more refined or elegant music than this... for that reason, I am thinking of going to all the performances, and yesterday, I took all my girls out of the convent and escorted them to the opera.'[11] But despite these desperate attempts to keep family patrimonies intact, Beckford observes that by the late eighteenth century there were only sixty families in Siena who were rich enough to own a coach.[12] The cultural life of the city began to re-form in the seventeenth century, after the hiatus enforced by Grand Duke Cosimo. The Accademia dei Rozzi reopened in 1601, and the Intronati shortly after. The emphatic distance the academies set between politics and culture had one interesting consequence: it enabled the involvement of women. A notable development of the seventeenth century was that a group of sixteen Sienese ladies who were regular associates of the Intronati decided to create an academy of their own, under the patronage of Vittoria della Rovere, wife of Grand Duke Ferdinando, who visited Siena with her husband on 6 October 1650. Vittoria, who was herself intelligent and well educated, was very interested in women of achievement, and supported, in various ways, the feminist nun Arcangela Tarabotti, women playwrights, women poets in Latin and Italian, and female composers. The Accademia degli Assicurati, or the 'self-assured', was founded in 1654, and the sixteen founder members included two of the nieces of Fabio Chigi. The emblem of the academy was an oak tree, and the oak was the badge of the Della Rovere family, so this was apparently a compliment to Duchess Vittoria. However, the oak was also a Chigi emblem, so it seems highly likely that the choice of an oak tree reflected a double meaning intended to be understood one way in Florence, and another in Siena itself.[13] The academies met for playful debates, Assicuritati inviting male friends, while the Intronati invited ladies, particularly in Carnival season. These encounters were called *gioci di spirito*, flights of fancy, in which each participant displayed his or her wit and elegance. Additionally, people who were known to have particular talents as dancers, singers, or instrumentalists might also be asked to perform.

The people of seventeenth-century Siena were enthusiastic playgoers, and new groups formed to put on comedies. The Scolari, originally university students, and the Sviati, originally artisans from the wool guild, mirrored the earlier Intronati and Rozzi in coming from different social groups, though this distinction was rapidly abandoned and both recruited from the nobility. These might be shoestring productions: a group of young men put on a play by clubbing together, each putting in less than three lire.[14] The city's prestigious Jesuit school, the Collegio Tolemei, which was founded in 1676, regularly produced comedies and tragedies open to the public, which was the custom in Jesuit schools. Additionally, nuns put on sacred dramas in their convents, which were attended by laywomen (though this was officially frowned upon).[15] In a letter of 1 March 1628, when Duchess Caterina was governor of Siena, she wrote to her sister-in-law, Maria Maddalena of Austria, that she was attending performances of sacred comedies, 'which the nuns here [in Siena] do very well'.[16]

These plays were put on at Carnival, and could be quite elaborate affairs: we know nothing of how they were staged, but they often involved music and must have been a welcome diversion from convent routine. Two Sienese convent plays that we know of feature a plot which involves cross-dressing (as monks): in *Eufrosina*, a woman escapes her father's desire that she should marry one Dardano by fleeing to a monastery, where she lives her life as one of the brothers. She is eventually reunited with her father, who visits the monastery in the course of his search for her. She comforts the old man, while still posing as a monk, but falls sick and dies in his arms, revealing at the last minute that she is Eufrosina. The father returns home, decides he still wants Dardano in the family, and produces a previously unmentioned niece, who is in a convent but does not want to become a nun. The play ends with a marriage. One suspects that the archbishop would not have been pleased by the element of wish-fulfilment in this plot.[17]

The re-formed Intronati, who had been given the theatre in the Palazzo Pubblico for their use, no longer regarded playwriting, collectively or individually, as central to their activities. They were concerned with theatre management and rented out their theatre, but their own creative expression was mostly verse. The Rozzi, meanwhile, retreated from social satire, having reformed as an Academy, and turned to more conventional dramatic forms, such as pastoral.[18] Pastoral was immensely popular in seventeenth-century Italy, since elegant make-believe and withdrawal from contemporary reality suited the mood of upper-class Italians.

The fact that very few Sienese had much money to spare meant that they had to find inexpensive ways of entertaining themselves. One was meeting in one another's homes for *conversazione* – informal get-togethers. Each guest contributed a small amount of money so that the host did not stand the entire expense. Sometimes card games were the main feature of the evening, or there might be a dance, or music. The contemporary definition of being a cultivated person included mastering a musical instrument, and ladies with good voices were encouraged to use them: the Sienese had a passion for singing and there was a strong preference for high voices.[19]

Part of the rhythm of the year for the upper class was a retreat into the country. As Beckford observed, 'The first week in October removes all the Nobility and many of the citizens from the town to the country, and during the six weeks the Villeggiatura lasts, Siena is entirely deserted... The extraordinary number of villas in the neighbourhood of Siena furnish constant society.'[20] The Sienese taste for games which required extensive reading and quick wits makes it unsurprising that many of them were skilful performers of improvised dramas, which were considered suitable entertainment during this informal autumn retreat. These impromptu performances were made possible by the stock characters and familiar plots of the *commedia dell'arte*: once every player had adopted a role, the group could rely on a broad consensus of how the characters should relate to one another. Skilled amateurs also performed in informal contexts, such as parties.

On 29 May 1629, Ferdinando de' Medici, who was then Grand Duke, appointed his younger brother Mattias governor of Siena, following the death of their aunt, the then governor, Caterina de' Medici. He arrived in his domain on 27 August and took up residence in the Piazza del Duomo. Since he spent most of his time in Siena, he was immensely popular with the Sienese, not least because of his interest in their pastimes. When in Florence, Mattias, together with his brothers Giovancarlo and Lorenzo, were very closely involved with staging opera in the city, an interest which, in Mattias's case, was developed after he spent the Carnival season in Venice in 1641 and fell in love with the new art form.[21] When he moved to Siena, he naturally took this interest with him. In 1645, he sent to Venice for the plans of his favourite opera house, and commissioned the remodelling of the Intronati's theatre in the Palazzo Pubblico to improve the acoustics. At around the same time, he commissioned a new opera from Pietro Salvetti, set to music by Michele Grasseschi, so that there would be a work to perform when the building work was complete.[22] Salvetti made what was on the face of it the rather curious decision to set his opera, *La Datira*, in tenth-century Scandinavia: in it, the kings of Denmark, Sweden and Norway, together with the Swedish queen mother and a Danish princess, undergo the usual love tangles until the situation is finally resolved with suitable marriages. This Scandinavian setting was almost certainly a compliment to Mattias, since he had been a soldier before he became governor of Siena, and had fought the Swedes in the Thirty Years War. The opera opened on 26 May 1647 and was a great success with the audience, though since it required fifteen soloists and five changes of scenery it was so expensive that Mattias decided not to repeat the experiment. At least three members of the audience were English, the Royalist exiles John and James Bargrave and John Raymond, who thought it 'a noble Italian

Justus Sustermans' portrait of Mattias de' Medici: a younger brother of the Duke, he was extremely popular as a governor of Siena, and a great patron of opera.

Opera'.[23] The three friends had a portrait painted while they were there: it gives an idea of what aesthetic young men looked like in 1647.

The Italian theatre, particularly in Siena, had been playing with comedies of misunderstandings arising from cross-dressed characters from early in the sixteenth century: the Intronati's *Gl'Ingannati*, *Alessandro* and *Ortensio* among them. In these comedies, all the parts were played by men. But in Siena, as elsewhere in early modern Italy, maleness had to be asserted and performed: young men were required to demonstrate their courage and prowess in more or less formal contexts, such as the ritual combats between the men of different *terzi*, or the bullfights and other games which pitted the men of the *contrade* against one another. Femininity was perceived as a default state which men had to work hard to transcend from puberty onwards. Boys and women were perceived as similar, in that they were dependent on, and inferior to, adult males. It was perhaps because maleness was so important, and because it continuously needed to be asserted and defended, that audiences enjoyed seeing sexual identity interrogated within the ludic space of the theatre. Italian opera added intriguing further twists.

In the mid-century, when Mattias staged *La Datira* in Siena, all opera singers were men. Some of them, however, were castrati, i.e. eunuchs. The practice began in church choirs, which did not employ women singers, following St Paul's dictum that women should remain silent in the church. The custom spread out to secular music because of the immense popularity of high voices in baroque Italy, and the special qualities of the castrato sound. From the mid-sixteenth century on, musically talented Italian boys from poor families were castrated (even though the operation was theoretically illegal) to prevent their voices from breaking at puberty. Some at least were willing victims, owing principally to the desperate lack of economic opportunity, since the operation offered a route out of poverty and the chance of fame and fortune for a boy with a good voice.[24] Castration had an effect on other parts of the body besides the larynx and genitalia, as has been demonstrated: the body of a famous eighteenth-century castrato called Gaspare Pacchierotti was exhumed in 2016, and confirmed the evidence of contemporary caricaturists. Because some aspects of bone growth are controlled by sex hormones, castrati developed abnormally long arm and leg bones, and a barrel chest. The pathologists also discovered that Pacchierotti's training had given him hugely developed rib muscles, which would have allowed him to take immensely deep breaths, and produce notes of truly impressive power, volume and length. An unfortunate side effect of his condition was osteoporosis, loss of bone density resulting from lack of male hormones, though he lived to be eighty-one.[25]

It seems strange to us now that martial, larger than life masculine roles in serious opera should be realized by sopranos, but contemporaries did not see this as incongruous. Since castrati were tall and big-chested, they looked the part; and they had enormous, brilliant voices. The most celebrated castrati were major stars, commanding huge salaries. They were also physically admired to an extent which might seem surprising. But Renaissance art and literature consistently celebrate soft-skinned, boyish beauty as attractive to both males and females (Shakespeare's *Venus and Adonis* is an obvious example). Hairy, rugged virility was certainly considered admirable and an indication of superior status, but it was not thought beautiful. According to contemporary thinking about sex difference, castrati were perpetual boys, and many, in their younger days at least, would have been found attractive by their audience. As preachers such as San Bernardino frequently complained, a good few Italian men were attracted to boys. And, as Roger Freitas observes, '[the castrato] inhabited the same intermediate sexual zone as the boy, sharing the erotic mixture of masculine and feminine qualities'.[26] Certainly, a number of castrated opera stars were known to be sexually involved with powerful and important men, while others, perhaps more surprisingly, had affairs with women.[27] We do not know how the roles in *La Datira* were distributed, but two of the singers were certainly castrati, Bartolomeo Melani and Antonio Rivani. Michele Grasseschi, who was cast in the opera but had to drop out because of illness, is known to have been a contralto, and was presumably replaced by one.[28] It is thus highly likely that all five of the leading roles in Siena's first opera, not just Queen Sigrita and Princess Datira, were for high voices.

overleaf
A caricature of two castrati opera stars, unnaturally tall and strangely proportioned. Senesino (Francesco Bernardi), on the left, was from Siena, as his stage name suggests.

ALEXANDER VII

The seventeenth century saw another Sienese on the throne of St Peter. Fabio Chigi (1599–1657) was a member of the illustrious Chigi banking family and a great-nephew of Pope Paul V (1605–21). The

Chigi were a family with two branches, one based in Siena, the other in Rome: Rome was where they made money, but they retained very strong links with their city of origin. Fabio was from the Siena branch, born in Siena and educated there. One of his projects, undertaken just before he was ordained, was to catalogue the works of art to be found in his native city in 1625–6, suggesting both antiquarian tendencies, and an interest in the visual arts. He defended theses in law, philosophy and theology at the university, and subsequently went into the church, where he spent his early career as a clerical diplomat. He was then recalled to Rome in 1651 by Innocent X, to become Secretary of State, and was himself elected pope in 1655. The last Pope Alexander had been Rodrigo Borgia of unhappy memory, but Chigi chose the name not in honour of the Spaniard, but of a previous Sienese pope, Alexander III (ruled 1159–81). As Alexander VII, Chigi is credited with changing the image of Rome through spectacular building projects. His interest in

Cardinal Fabio Chigi, later Pope Alexander VII. Once he became Pope, he transformed the city of Rome, but also intervened substantially in the fabric of Siena.

architecture went back to his early days at the University of Siena, where among other people with scientific interests he encountered Teofilo Gallaccini, a professor of mathematics and philosophy, who was an active member of the Accademia dei Filomati and an architectural theorist.[29] His preferred architect was the sculptor and architect Gianlorenzo Bernini, but he also commissioned work from the painter and architect Pietro da Cortona. He was less generous to Francesco Borromini, perhaps because Borromini could be notoriously difficult.

He took a great interest in his city of origin, and intervened extensively in Siena's cathedral.[30] In 1658 he decided to build a new chapel for the Madonna del Voto. The resulting Cappella del Voto, a riot of gold and lapis lazuli in the right transept of the cathedral, was designed by Benedetto Giovannelli Orlandi and Gianlorenzo Bernini. His music-loving nephew Cardinal Flavio Chigi contributed an organ to the cathedral, which is still in situ. The preparation for this work included the demolition of the old archiepiscopal palace, creating a large space between the cathedral and the new Palazzo di Provincia. It was therefore necessary to put a new outer cladding on the wall of the nave which had up to then been covered by the adjacent palace. A gothic design in pastiche fourteenth-century style was chosen, designed by Alexander's favourite architect, Gianlorenzo Bernini, the master of

Roman baroque. Similarly, when the Palazzo Pubblico was enlarged in 1680, the second floor on both sides was built entirely in the gothic style of the original façade. Thus from as early as the seventeenth century, Siena was deliberately maintaining and enhancing its medieval appearance.[31] Rather than following architectural fashion, the city preferred to maintain its own traditions.

While the Chigi pope's principal contribution to the life of Siena was his work on the urban fabric, the relatives whom he had raised to important and lucrative positions in Rome involved themselves with the city's cultural life. After Duke Mattias died in 1667, the Medici didn't appoint another governor until 1683, Francesco Maria de' Medici. Even then, he was something of an absentee, since he was made cardinal three years later and spent most of his time in Rome or at the Villa de Lappegi outside Florence. From the point of view of the Chigi family, this created a vacuum at the top of Sienese society. Medici indifference to cultural leadership in late seventeenth-century Siena allowed the Chigi to assume a leading role as Siena's first family. They were interested in music, and several of them played musical instruments: Cardinal Flavio Chigi, the pope's nephew, had an organ in his main palace and several harpsichords distributed round his other residences. In 1668, Flavio began to make regular trips back to Siena in the autumn. At the same time, and not coincidentally, the Intronati began fundraising to restore their theatre in the Palazzo Pubblico.[32] The architect chosen for the restoration was a pupil of Bernini's, Carlo Fontana, who would go on to undertake a substantial number of major architectural projects for the Chigi, though his restoration of the theatre may be the first time he worked for them.[33] The Sienese patriciate, and the Chigi, dug deep into their pockets to make the refurbished theatre splendid. Once complete, it was big enough to hold 1,500 spectators. The first work they put on was *L'Argia*, by Antonio Cesti, who seems to have made his musical debut singing in *La Datira* in Siena in 1647, but had gone on to become one of the most popular composers of his day, holding posts at the imperial court in Innsbrück, in Florence and at the papal court in Rome.[34]

In 1672, Carlo Fontana, with some input from Bernini, completed the rebuilding of a ducal palace for Agostino Chigi, outside Rome at Ariccia. Agostino had married Paul V's niece, Virginia Maria Borghese, and taken the titles of Prince of Farnese and Duke of Ariccia. Flavio and Agostino Chigi created an academy with the express purpose of producing operas at Ariccia. The villa had a great hall suitable for theatrical performances, and the family mounted two new operas there, at great expense, in 1672 and 1673.

Fontana also built a villa near Siena for Cardinal Flavio in 1672, the Villa Cetinale. (Of more contemporary interest, in the twentieth century this would become the home of the disgraced Conservative politician Lord Lambton.) Flavio was the most assiduous of the Chigi in visiting his native city, and he equipped his villa with an outdoor theatre where he could host concerts and even an opera: he mounted an unnamed opera at the villa in autumn 1684. He often attended local productions, and sponsored operas at the public theatre, including a restaging of *Adalinda*, which he and his brothers had first put on at Ariccia in 1673. Two-thirds of the operas performed in Siena between 1669 and 1704 show some degree of Chigi involvement, so the family evidently exercised a considerable amount of cultural leadership. A visit to Siena by a member of the Chigi family was the principal motivation for staging an opera through the seventeenth century.

Most of the opera sponsored by the Chigi was pastoral, extolling the virtues of rustic life and the pleasures of the country. One pragmatic reason for this was that pastoral traditionally called for a less elaborate orchestra than tragedy and was cheaper to put on, but, additionally, it fitted with the Sienese mood of the seventeenth century. Under Medici rule, they were politically powerless, so entertainment which harked back to a lost golden age, and suggested that rustic innocence was morally preferable to the grimy and compromised life of the real world, may have had a particular appeal.

SCIENTISTS

The seventeenth-century Italian contribution to the history of science was remarkable. Galileo and his associates in the Accademia dei Lincei are perhaps the most notable, but there was plenty of intellectual life in Siena. Galileo spent a week in Siena in 1633, at the invitation of Archbishop Ascanio Piccolomini, familiarizing the learned men of the city with his new telescope.[35] There is a sceptical, freethinking, critical and scientific streak to Sienese culture, which produced original thinkers of many varieties, from religious dissidents such as the Sozzini to critics, natural philosophers and scientists, and it survived Medicean attempts to suppress it. The seventeenth-century university mathematician Teofilo Gallaccini was a man of the widest intellectual curiosity, whose constellation of interests, which included engineering, architecture and ballistics, made him a worthy successor to Francesco di Giorgio and Baldassare Peruzzi. Sir Kenelm Digby, an Englishman with extensive scientific interests, visited Siena in 1620–21, when he was in his late teens. He was made a member of the Accademia dei Filomati, to whom he presented four papers in Latin on alchemy, cabalism, and the history of cryptography, typical of his wide-ranging interests.[36] He was the dedicatee of a book on gunnery published in Siena while he was staying there, a further indication of his involvement with the intellectual life of the city.

The Jesuit Giovanni Battista Ferrari is one of the most interesting Sienese intellectuals of the seventeenth century. He began his career as an extremely learned professor of Hebrew and Syriac at the Collegio Romano in Rome. He was a considerable scholar of Semitic languages, witnessed by the fact that he was a member of the papal commission charged with translating the Bible into Arabic.[37] But he was also a man of wide interests, and unexpectedly he changed his career path completely in the 1620s to become gardener, designer and horticultural consultant to the Barberini family, shortly after Maffeo Barberini became Urban VIII.[38] There was a tremendous interest in gardening in seventeenth-century Rome, because of the flood of exotic plants from Asia, Africa and the Americas, many of them discovered by the Jesuits themselves, which were being grown in Europe for the first time, including the first really sweet oranges, which the Jesuits discovered in China.[39] The Barberini were laying out magnificent gardens around their *palazzo* on the Quirinal Hill, and it was Ferrari who managed the project. Through his friend and patron Cassiano del Pozzo, he was associated with the Accademia dei Lincei, the most scientifically advanced community in Rome.[40]

Ferrari's lavishly illustrated book *On the Cultivation of Flowers* is the first botanical work to include drawings made from observation under a microscope, which was then a new invention.[41] He was particularly interested in exotics, such as the amaryllis, recently arrived from the Cape, and hibiscus, from China. Lavish in scope and immensely learned, his study also covers garden design and flower arrangements. However, his major contribution to knowledge is *Hesperides*, a response to the Italian passion for citrus fruit, so named because from the second century AD artists had represented the golden apples in the Garden of the Hesperides as citrus. From at least the sixteenth century, no Italian garden of any pretensions was complete without a collection of orange and lemon trees in huge terracotta pots.[42] The book is a lavishly illustrated study of citrus fruit, the first complete description of the limes, lemons and pomegranates, and the first attempt to produce a taxonomy of citrus, an extremely difficult task since they hybridize freely. In fact, there are only three varieties of citrus in nature, mandarins in China, pomelos in the Malay Archipelago and citrons in the lower Himalayas. Human movements brought these populations together, and their natural tendency to interbreed produced hybrids, including lemons, oranges and grapefruit. *Hesperides* was extensively and thoroughly researched: with the help of his friend Cassiano dal Pozzo, Ferrari sent questionnaires to citrus growers throughout Italy, asking for details about the fruit they grew and how they grew it.[43] He came to the conclusion that all citrus fell into one of three categories, lemons, oranges and citrons, which naturally reflects the varieties grown in Italy (he did not know about tropical species). The book also covers all aspects of the history and lore of citrus fruits, including a discussion of citrus as a remedy for scurvy, and what is probably the first recipe for orange marmalade. It is illustrated with engravings designed by some of the greatest artists of baroque Rome.

Ferrari's health was not good, and so, having made his career in Rome, he retired to his beloved Siena in 1650, following the Jesuit custom of returning a sick man to his native place. Another of his books, the *Collocutiones* (1652) is cast in the form of dialogues with friends. One topic of conversation is the games played in various Italian cities, and provides one of the fullest accounts of the Sienese *pugna* and other entertainments.[44] He was a member of the Intronati, and contributed to a volume on Sienese religious figures, dedicated to the Sienese pope, Alexander VII, and probably published in 1659 – perhaps conceived as an antidote to the Intronati's reputation for freethinking and crypto-Protestantism.

Eighteenth-century Sienese also did not lack for intellectual energy. Apart from Ferrari, the city also produced one of the greatest of all botanists, Pier Andrea Mattioli. Santa Maria della Scala had long had a botanical garden, and in the eighteenth century Mattioli's personal collection was added to it.[45] The hospital also acquired a fine anatomy theatre, and was one of the first institutions in Europe to practise widespread vaccination against smallpox.[46]

This interest in plants among Sienese intellectuals was turned to practical use by the distinguished economist Sallustio Bandini and others. Members of the academies worked to raise the productivity of the land which was under cultivation, experimenting with fertilizers, weedkillers and agricultural machinery, and even new crops, including a new species of bean developed in the botanical garden.[47] They also devoted much thought to reclaiming unused land, above all the Maremma. This work urgently needed to be done, since according to one of their number, much of Tuscany consisted of 'vast stretches of country... completely uncultivated, without a tree, without a field, without a farm, without a habitation... populated only by an occasional flock of sheep'.[48] They thus laid the foundations for the expansion and diversification of Tuscan agriculture in the century that followed.

One of the illustrations to *Hesperides*, by Giovanni Ferrari SJ. This book is one of the most advanced botanical studies of its day, an attempt at the taxonomy of citrus fruit.

Politically, the eighteenth century in Siena was a time of stagnation. With the end of the Medici line, the Grand Duchy of Tuscany passed to Francis, Duke of Lorraine, in 1737: born in France, he spent most of his life in Austria and never visited Italy. In 1745, he became Emperor in Austria, and entrusted his Grand Duchy to a regency council. This was particularly bad for Siena, since, under this regime, it thus became merely a territory belonging to a Grand Duchy which was itself peripheral to its duke's concerns. The ambitious and intelligent left the city to make careers in Florence or Rome. The Dukes did not neglect the city entirely. Peter Leopold I of Lorraine reorganized the civic administration of Siena, and attempted, without complete success, to drain the Maremma and the Val di Chiana, aided by a number of Sienese mathematicians and engineers, in particular Leonardo Ximines, who developed a sophisticated system of locks.[49] Another of his progressive interventions in the countryside was to break up his own extensive landholdings and lease sensibly sized units to small farmers at reasonable rates.[50] In 1777, he demilitarized the Medici fortress and made it into a public park, the Lizza, a testimony to the fact that the Sienese no longer needed to be kept down by the Florentines. At the same time, Siena's civic leaders commissioned Carlo Fontana to overhaul the Palazzo Pubblico, and add another storey to the two wings, in the

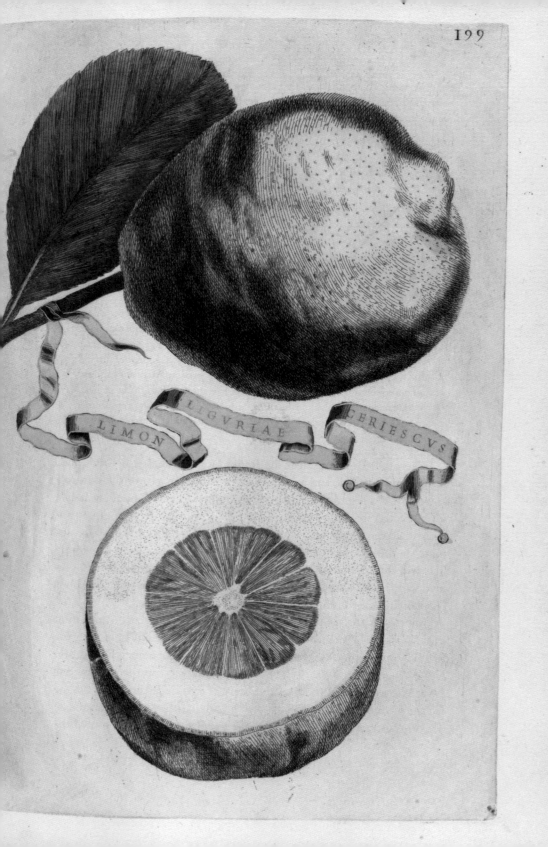

LIMON LIGVRIAE CERIESCVS

same style as the original, and replaced the eight-ton bell in the Mangia tower at great expense. Since the infrastructure was crumbling and the *bottini* were leaking, the city's choice of capital projects is revealing: they considered that nostalgic enhancement of the medieval beauty of the city was more important than maintaining the water supply.[51]

The eighteenth century was the era of the Grand Tour. The first coach route across the Alps was completed in 1771, and went through the Brenner Pass as far as Florence.[52] Siena was not much admired by eighteenth-century tourists, since there was little about the city which appealed to neoclassical taste. However, one Scottish visitor who enjoyed himself enormously was Dr Johnson's future biographer, James Boswell, who arrived in Siena in 1765, aged twenty-five. He wrote to his friend Jean-Jacques Rousseau,

> I had excellent apartments at Siena. I ate well. The wine of the district was very good, and on holidays I regaled myself with delicious Montepulciano… Every morning for two hours I read the divine Ariosto, and you can imagine the effect which that produced on my romantic soul. … the nobility there form a society of the most amiable sort. They have a simplicity, an openness, a gaiety which you cannot imagine without having been there… The Sienese are independent, equal, and content to be so, and when a great prince comes among them, he is politely received, but they do not put themselves out for him.

Like other British visitors, he found Sienese ladies delightful, and, being both romantic and a cad, set about seducing two of them simultaneously. He found Porzia Sansedoni polite, but obdurate: she was a sophisticated woman, who presided over a salon where the most progressive of the Sienese nobility gathered together.[53] Girolama Piccolomini, on the other hand, who was much more naive and also unhappily married, succumbed to the young Scotsman's charm and fell madly in love with him. A disconcerted Boswell beat a swift retreat, and poor Girolama wrote to him at intervals for the next two years.[54]

Effectively, the Tour was brought to an end by the French Revolution in 1789, since the English stopped visiting the Continent until after the fall of Napoleon in 1812. However, in Italy itself the French Revolution had dramatic effects, since the French forces were commanded by one Napoleon Bonaparte. In December 1793, as a young artillery captain, he led the reconquest of Toulon, the key British base in the Mediterranean. Three years later, as sole commander of the Army of Italy, he routed the

Austrian forces at Lodi. Having defeated the Habsburgs and their allies, Napoleon proclaimed himself the liberator of Italy, a view not shared by all Italians. The anti-clericalism of the French Jacobins provoked a savage backlash in Tuscany, a counter-revolution which began in Arezzo and rallied round a statue of the Virgin called the Madonna of Comfort, united under the banner of 'Viva Maria'. Thus, even at the end of the eighteenth century, the Virgin was still strongly associated with leadership in battle. Prominent among the ranks of the insurgents was a woman called Alessandra Cini, a butcher's daughter from Montevarchi. The insurgents stormed Siena, massacred Jacobins and their sympathizers and turned on the city's Jews, who, they believed, had benefited from the French takeover of Italy. In one of the most heinous episodes of Sienese history, nineteen of the city's Jews were burned to death in the Piazza del Campo in the name of the Virgin Mary, in an extraordinary recursion to the most savage aspects of the Middle Ages.[55]

A shock to the city of quite a different kind was the major earthquake of 26 May 1798. It destroyed the Fonte Oliva, the bell tower of the Dominican church and the façade of the venerable church of San Cristoforo, which had been used as the first town hall before the building of the Palazzo Pubblico. Ferdinand III, Grand Duke of Tuscany, set about repairing the city.[56] The earthquake, in fact, was taken as another opportunity to regularize the architecture of Siena, a major episode in the city's long history of creating a particular image of itself. Unstable towers came down, upper floors were demolished, porches pulled apart, windows all made to a similar scale and arches constructed across roads to stabilize leaning buildings: the picturesque arches of the Via della Galluzza, which must be one of the most photographed streets in Siena, date to this renovation. The tower of the Sansedoni household had vied with that of the Mangia till well into the 1750s when it was finally dismantled: the *palazzo* which remains is the seat of the Foundation of the Monte dei Paschi.

18

A VERY GREAT
SIMPLICITY

At the beginning of the nineteenth century, as the result of a deal between Napoleon and the Bourbons, Siena became part of a short-lived kingdom of Etruria with a Bourbon at its head. The evicted Habsburg Duke was given Salzburg as a consolation. In 1807, Napoleon changed his mind, dissolved the kingdom and integrated its territories into France. His sister Elisa was named Grand Duchess. After Napoleon's fall, the Council of Vienna returned Tuscany to the Lorraine-Habsburgs. However, twenty years of French rule had wrought irreversible change in Italy, and, increasingly, Italians began to dream of creating a new, united and independent nation. Italy's regional governments repressed nationalist movements wherever they encountered them, but to no effect: wave upon wave of political exiles left Italy, but continued to agitate in London, Paris and other cities of Europe and America. There was also extensive economic migration, particularly from southern Italy to America from the 1870s onwards, which produced many a 'Little Italy' in the world's great cities.

Meanwhile, Italy was beginning to recover from the abjection of the eighteenth century. One symptom of this was building railways. In 1852, Siena was attached by a branch line to the main Florence–Rome railway, joining it at Chiusi; the engineer, Giuseppe Pianigiani, was subsequently honoured with an elaborate monument in San Domenico which features allegorical figures of Mechanics, Architecture and Physics by the Sienese sculptor Tito Sarrocchi. Italy experienced an industrial revolution, at least in the north, and sustained a new level of economic development, and greater prosperity and increasing confidence brought with them renewed calls for reform. The unification of Italy finally took place in 1860 by the annexation of the various pre-existing Italian states to Piedmont, whose ruler, Vittorio Emanuele II, thus became the first king of Italy. Siena was one of the first cities to sign up to the new regime, which should come as no surprise; far better, from a Sienese point of view, to be a city on a level with all the other cities of Italy, than playing second fiddle to Florence.

Siena had attracted many English visitors from the sixteenth century onwards, drawn by the courtesy of the inhabitants, the general belief that it was a good place to learn Italian, and the pleasantness of the climate in summer. As John Raymond put it in 1648,

> The ayre is very wholsome, much agreeing with the constitution of strangers, the Inhabitants very curteous, a great deale suiting to the humours of forreigners, and besides the purity of the Italian Language, is here profest, and spoken; these and the like conveniences make it much frequented by Travellers, and indeed mov'd us to settle our selves there, for some Moneths.[1]

Apart from the amenities noted by John Raymond, it was possible to live a pleasant life there very cheaply in the nineteenth century, because the Sienese were still so poor and the cost of essential goods and services was correspondingly low. William Hazlitt, visiting in 1825, observed that Tuscany was yet to benefit from the reviving fortunes of the Italian economy:

> life is here reduced to a very great simplicity, absolute necessaries from day to day and from hand to mouth, and nothing is allowed for the chapter of accidents or the irregular intrusion of strangers... We did not meet ten carriages on our journey, a distance of a hundred and ninety-three miles, and which it took us six days to accomplish.[2]

Robert Browning wrote a poem, voiced by 'an Italian person of quality', based on his knowledge of Tuscany, in which the speaker laments that he has to live off his own produce in his villa, bored to tears, because everything that comes into the city has to pay so much tax that he cannot afford to live there.[3]

In 1841, Thomas Cook began to organize group tours of the Continent which were shorter and less expensive than the Grand Tour, prompted by the fast development of railways and encouraged by the discounted train fares offered to parties. Italy's affordability, picturesqueness and outstanding art and antiquities made it a magnet for the new class of tourists, while others were tempted actually to settle in Italy, where their money went so much further than it did at home. In 1854, an adventurous lone traveller, Mrs Westropp, visited a Scottish lady friend who had settled in Siena and observed that 'lodgings are very cheap here; this suite consisting of two excellent sitting-rooms, three bed-rooms, and kitchen, all nicely furnished, lets for about £3 6s. per month'.[4] Foreign visitors and settlers thus brought hard currency into Italy, and played a part in its economic recovery. The English began to venture back to Siena in such numbers that in 1841 there must have been at least twenty-four British families resident, because Lady Olivia Bernard Sparrow persuaded them to club together and pay for regular Anglican services, which were held in Count Venturi's *palazzo* near San Domenico.[5] This community was driven away by the 1848 revolution, which was followed by severe economic depression and a cholera epidemic (in Mrs Westropp's travel notes, the spectre of cholera looms

Allegorical figures for the tomb of the engineer who brought the railway to Siena, by the prolific nineteenth-century sculptor Tito Sarocchi, who also renovated the Fonte Gaia.

over all her adventures), but visitors started returning once things settled down again, especially after Siena acquired its railway.

Tuscany remained very cheap for English and American visitors in the second half of the nineteenth century, which was important to the Browning family, among others. In the summer of 1850, Elizabeth Barrett Browning was recovering from a miscarriage and needed to escape the heat of Florence. The family took a little villa in the country, about a mile and a half from Siena, perched on a hill so that the summer breeze made it pleasantly cool. There was another advantage: the wonderful landscape: 'Magnificent sweeps of view we have from all our windows which all look out different ways – on this side, towards the fantastic profile of the city, seen in silence against the sky... on that side, across the vast Maremma bounded by the Roman mountains.'[6] It was surrounded by vineyards and olive groves, and had a rose garden; exactly what the family needed. By the end of the holiday, Elizabeth was well enough to explore Siena. The Brownings visited the cathedral, where they admired the marble pavement, and the new picture gallery. Medieval Sienese painting did not interest them, though their friend Ruskin was already urging its importance. The paintings which spoke to Elizabeth Browning were the Mannerists, Beccafumi and Sodoma, in which she was very much a child of her time.

The wall of the villa the Brownings took in the Sienese countryside in the summer of 1859, painted by their American friend Hamilton Gibbs Wild.

The preferences of the Brownings echo the judgements in *Murray's Guide to Central Italy* (1843), the Rough Guide of its day. Many English visitors saw Italy through 'Murray's' eyes. Published without an author's name, the guidebook was written by Octavian Blewitt, who was not an art specialist. However, it has a section on Sienese painting, which suggests that the key to early Sienese art is that it expresses deep religious feeling, and identifies Simone Martini as the greatest master. Duccio's *Maestà* and the Lorenzetti frescoes are mentioned, but not admired, or even commented on.[7] In Blewitt's view, Sienese painting lost its way in the mid-fourteenth century, and he reserved his enthusiasm for the Mannerists Sodoma and Beccafumi. Thus the painters whom Blewitt and his readers could actually enjoy were the ones who were very much in dialogue with Roman and Florentine art.

The reason why 'Murray' gave so much space to Sienese art was probably that there had been a recent critical challenge to the Florence-centric view of art history, which is based ultimately on Vasari. It was mounted by the Frenchman Alexis-François Rio. His *De la poésie Chrétienne* (1835) was translated into English in 1854, but was widely read in England before that: since he married an Englishwoman, Rio spent much of his time in England from 1836, and met most of the English people who were genuinely interested in art, whether as critics or collectors.[8] Rio's thesis that it is not formal beauty but truth of religious sentiment that gives value to a work of art led him to present Siena rather than Florence as the cradle of art, and to argue that Duccio's *Maestà* is the greatest of all early Italian paintings. The highly influential popular writer Anna Jameson, who met Rio in the Louvre in 1841, was strongly influenced by his ideas, which inform her own extensive writings on art history.[9]

This rising interest in Sienese art in advanced circles helps to explain why it was increasingly visited by artists and writers. The Brownings

would not visit Siena again for nine years, but when they did they found themselves among friends. The American neoclassical sculptor William Wetmore Story, whom the Brownings had known since 1852, had taken a villa no great distance from theirs, where he was receiving regular visits from the novelist Nathaniel Hawthorne and his family. Another American sculptor and friend of Story's, Hiram Powers, was also in Siena, as was the English poet Walter Savage Landor. Visiting Siena to refresh their interest in Sienese art, the Brownings bumped into Edward Burne-Jones and his friend Val Prinsep, whom they found copying Sienese paintings, 'Ruskin in hand'.[10] These friends would convene in the evenings to talk, generally at the Storys'. Much of the conversation was political, since Italy was moving towards unification, and the Brownings, as liberals, were keenly interested. Meanwhile, their son Pen, now aged ten, was having a wonderful time running wild in idyllic surroundings. The Storys had children he could play with, but he also played with the peasant children, who taught him a game with walnuts called *nocino*, and he was allowed to 'help' with the grape harvest. But his greatest pleasure was riding the Sardinian pony his father had bought for him in a moment of indulgence. Hamilton Gibbs Wild, another American artist friend of the Storys, painted Pen riding in the *contado*, with a view of Siena in the distance.

A street scene in Siena with the Torre del Mangia in the distance, by Susan Isabel Dacre, an artist and suffragette who travelled in Italy and painted several views of the city.

The rediscovery of Sienese art is an important part of the story of the rediscovery of Siena itself. Though Siena created an Accademia di Belle Arti in 1816, the city seldom appeared on art tourists' itineraries until after 1900, which is when Baedeker greatly expanded its section on Sienese art.[11] The extent of the devaluation of early Sienese paintings through the nineteenth century is shown by the lack of respect for their physical integrity. The predellas of medieval altarpieces were more attractive to the English and Americans, most of whom were Protestants, than the central figure of a saint or the Virgin, since they often consisted of lively narrative scenes set in houses and streetscapes, created to illustrate the saint's miracles. Their bright, clear colours, and what could be seen, and marketed, as naive simplicity, gave them a value in Protestant eyes greater than that of a Madonna and Child. Altarpieces were sawn up without compunction so that the individual pictures could be separately sold. Duccio's *Maestà*, once the pride of the cathedral, was taken to pieces. Pandolfo Petrucci had had it taken down from the high altar in 1506, and in 1536 it was recorded on the altar of St Sebastian in the cathedral, but in 1771 it was dismembered in order to fit it into a cupboard. The main surface of the altarpiece was cut into seven vertical strips, the two faces of which were sawn apart and reassembled as separate panels, while the front and rear predellas were separated and cut up into individual scenes.[12] In the nineteenth century, Lord Lindsay observed sadly that 'the two halves [were] hung up facing each other like the dissevered limbs of a martyr, in the northern and southern transepts of the Duomo', and also that they were very dirty. Several of the small scenes from the lives of Christ and the Virgin which had once been part of the reverse were sold: two of them were bought by the London National Gallery in 1883 for a mere £178 the pair.

A few Anglophones started being interested in early Sienese painting in the late eighteenth century. Colin Morison (1734–1809), a Scottish painter and dealer in art and antiquities based in Rome, is known to have made a collection, subsequently seized by Napoleon. Later, James Dennistoun (b.1803), both an Italophile and a very discriminating art collector, bought several, including paintings attributed to Duccio and Lorenzetti. The English collector William Young Ottley, who lived in Italy from 1791 to 1798, bought paintings during his time there, including Duccio's *Crucifixion*.

These collectors were very early into the field. It is telling that William Buchanan's list of the major paintings imported into England from the French Revolution to 1824 lists only two Sienese paintings, one by Sodoma and one by Francesco Vanni, both Mannerists. Clearly, in his view, early Sienese artists were not important.[13] It was perhaps owing to the work of Ruskin and Lindsay, and the influence of his friend Anna Jameson in particular, that Charles Eastlake, the first director of the National Gallery, elected to buy twenty-two early Florentine and Sienese paintings from the dealers Francesco Lombardi and Ugo Baldi in 1856.[14]

John Ruskin, who was also an admirer of Rio, visited Siena in 1840, when he was twenty-one. He admired the town itself and especially the Duomo: 'this town is worth fifty Florences: larger and more massy buildings in general with numbers of the triple venetian window. A noble Square, with a delicately carved fountain in white marble, square walls arabesqued at one side; and a tower running up to an enormous height like that at Vicenza, against purple east cloud, on the other.'[15]

However, the art made no particular impression at the time. In the 1870s, he would lament his missed opportunities, in particular, that he had once had the chance to study Jacopo della Quercia's Fonte Gaia and had not done so,[16] and though he spent little time in the city, he paid Charles Fairfax Murray to copy Sienese paintings for him. Murray made him a copy of Ambrogio Lorenzetti's *Allegory of Good Government*, which he drew on in a lecture on the political conditions necessary to produce great art, which he gave in Manchester in 1857. Lorenzetti's frescoes are also considered at length by Alexander Lindsay, Earl of Crawford, in his *Sketches in the History of Christian Art* (1847), which is probably the first work by a non-Italian to engage seriously with Lorenzetti's work. Lindsay concludes, 'a grander moral lesson was never bequeathed by painter or poet to his countrymen'.[17]

Lindsay, another reader of Rio, follows him in arguing that there was a specifically Christian art tradition. He devoted a chapter of his book to early Sienese art, noting its links with Byzantium and stressing its essentially religious character. He wrote from Siena, on his second visit, 'the Sienese school, I have again and again observed, is quite distinct from the Florentine and to the full as interesting'.[18] He was buying early Italian paintings from the 1840s: the Duccio *Crucifixion* now in the Manchester Art Gallery was once his.[19]

Though clearly there was serious nineteenth-century interest in the subject, it was Bernard Berenson, never slow to take credit, who claimed to have revived interest in Sienese paintings. He avowed in 1902, 'the Sienese country is to me only less fascinating than its art, and its art somehow suits my whim, touches my fancy, is *mine* in a sense that no other is.'[20] However, he and his wife Mary, who, like him, was an art historian, were only two of a number of English and American expatriates who rediscovered Sienese painting around 1900. Another pair of American art historians, Frederick Mason Perkins and his wife Lucy Olcott, settled in Siena in 1900 and made an intensive study of Sienese painting, which they also collected. In 1903, Lucy Olcott Perkins and the Englishman William Heywood, who had also made his home in Siena, collaborated on a guide to the city, Heywood writing the first half, a history, while Olcott Perkins covered the art, focusing principally on the 'primitives', the painters of the thirteenth to fifteenth centuries. Unfortunately, her marriage was disintegrating under the pressure of her husband's mental health issues, and she returned to America to work for the Metropolitan Museum of Art in New York in 1904, where she organized a photo library. In 1909, she returned to Italy as Bernard Berenson's secretary. This was not a success, and after a year she left the Berensons and set up as an art dealer.[21]

Another very important figure in the revival of interest in Sienese art is Robert Langton Douglas (1865–1951). He lived in Italy from 1895 and published a *History of Siena* in 1902. In 1904, he was instrumental in organizing an exhibition of Sienese painting at the Burlington Fine Arts Club in London, for which he wrote the catalogue. The exhibition attracted 4,500 visitors. Meanwhile, Bernard and Mary Berenson were involved with the Mostra d'Antica Arte Senese mounted in the Palazzo Pubblico in 1904, a much bigger affair than the London exhibition, though the latter had a different kind of importance since it introduced Sienese art to the English-speaking world. In 1906, another member of what Douglas called 'the old Siena gang', Robert H. Hobart Cust,

Duccio's Calling of Peter and Andrew, from the reverse of his great Maestà; the sort of picture which evoked a new sympathy with Sienese art. It is now in the National Gallery of Art, Washington DC.

published a study of Sodoma. Thus, Berenson's self-promotion as the unique evangelist of Sienese painting is hardly justifiable: his *Essays in the Study of Sienese Painting* is late into the field, appearing only in 1918. Berenson and Douglas quarrelled venomously; Berenson insisting that Douglas had stolen ideas which he had, in fact, arrived at independently, while Douglas pointed out that Berenson had initially been dismissive of Sienese art. Douglas printed an article on Sassetta, a painter whom the Berensons regarded as their own intellectual property, in the second edition of the *Burlington Magazine* in 1902. Berenson hit back in the next issue, and a feud was on.

It should not be forgotten that there was frequently a commercial aspect to connoisseurship. Both the Perkinses and the Berensons were hunting for pictures, and for rich people to buy them, because they were financially dependent on creating a market by convincing patrons of the value and beauty of the pictures whose sale they were brokering. After the Burlington Club exhibition of Sienese painting, Lucy Olcott Perkins wrote hopefully to Mary Berenson that it ought now to be possible to persuade Americans to buy Sienese paintings. This turned out to be the case: such was the rise of interest in early Sienese paintings, and consequently their value, that by February 1910 the Berensons could

afford to employ Perkins to do the donkey work of buying, mediating, negotiating and exporting.

One serious problem for Berenson and his connections was that many of their finds could not legally be exported. Berenson's quarrel with Douglas was partly about protecting his own status as exclusive authority on Sienese painters, but was also connected with a radical difference of approach. Berenson insisted that connoisseurship alone was necessary: a picture told its own story. Douglas was a believer in archival research. But Berenson's approach may also relate to the fact that it was important for him to be able to waft pictures out of Italy and onto the walls of clients such as Isabella Stewart Gardner in Boston, and the last thing he wanted to emphasize was provenance.

To make a living, the dealers had to buy low and sell high, and thus impoverished Sienese nobles and simple parish priests were persuaded to part with pictures which were subsequently redefined as treasures and sold on to rich American and English clients. In 1896, Charles Fairfax Murray, who as a young man had copied pictures for Ruskin, was buying for Agnew's picture gallery in London. He used to sit in the Caffè Greco in Siena and bang his stick on the table, shouting: 'Bring out your Madonnas! Bring out your Madonnas! Two hundred lire! Two hundred lire!'[22] After 1909, all Italian artworks more than seventy years old required an export licence, and pictures which Berenson himself had talked up as 'important' were unlikely to receive one. One picture which Berenson sold to Isabella Stewart Gardner left Italy at the bottom of a trunk full of dolls.[23] Before 1909, export was more negotiable, but it seems to have been easier to get a licence to send a picture to London than to America. From 1898 to 1905, Mary Berenson, her brother Logan Pearsall Smith and a divorced cousin of theirs called Grace Worthington owned an art and antique shop called Toplady's near St James's Park, run by Mrs Worthington, where, alongside more legitimate business, they disposed of a number of pictures they knew to be fakes, and used 'Miss Toplady' as a cover for sending artworks to Mrs Gardner.[24]

The clandestine aspect of the picture trade brought dealers into shady company. Their search for pictures led the Berensons to Francesco Domenico Torrini, who had an antique shop at 8 Via Cavour. Torrini sold both antique pictures from villages and country places in the Sienese *contado*, and fakes by Icilio Federico Joni, later to become notorious. Joni is best remembered for forging *biccherna* covers, but he also forged other pictures, made 'period' frames and restored damaged originals. The distinction between a heavily restored painting and a completely invented one is not always easy to draw. Where possible, Joni and his confrères used antique panels, which might still carry traces of the original image, even after most of the paint had been scraped off in order to recover valuable gold and pigments.

In the Berenson era, judgements about a painting were based on connoisseurship, and techniques now used such as X-ray and electron microscopy, which get under the surface, were not yet available. Students of Sienese gold-ground paintings have an additional tool, since the artists used small punches to texture areas of gold, and it is now well understood that these are identifiable as belonging to specific studios: this fact has made it possible to identify forgeries.[25] Berenson became aware that Joni existed, and that he had successfully deceived him several times. Mary Berenson's diary for 1899 records, 'we have run our forger to the earth – but a very easy matter it was – for "he" is a rollicking band of young men, cousins and friends, who turn out these works in cooperation, one drawing, one laying in the colour, another putting on the dirt, another making the frames, and some children with a big dog keeping guard over the pictures that were put out in the sunshine to "stagionare" [dry out and season]'. As she justly observes, it was like a Renaissance artists' workshop brought forward in time (apart from the need to bake the paintings in the sun).[26] Joni himself was self-taught, but the men he worked with were drawn from the pool of talent turned out by the Accademia di Belle Arti, which taught the traditional arts of the Middle Ages, and therefore created a battalion of young men capable of restoring – or faking – a medieval painting, such as Umberto Giunti, who eventually acquired the soubriquet of 'the fresco forger'.

overleaf
This 1787 study of Siena is by a Dutch painter, Daniel Dupré, who made a number of careful drawings of Siena and its environs, all suggesting that the city was profoundly underpopulated.

Having unmasked Joni, rather than severing relations with the Torrini, Berenson employed Joni himself, as a maker of frames, a picture finder and as a restorer. Berenson routinely had pictures heavily restored, since collectors in the early twentieth century expected completeness and a high state of finish, making plenty of work for restorers, since five hundred years of wear and tear are bound to cause some degree of damage. Whether Berenson ever consciously passed off a painting he knew to be entirely the work of Joni is a question which cannot be answered. Joni

himself claims that when he and Berenson first met, he brought up the subject of his own painting, *Alberto Aringhieri in Prayer*, which Berenson had bought from Torrini, believing it to be a contemporary image of the Alberto Aringhieri represented by Pinturicchio in Siena Cathedral. This painting was later sold by Berenson at a Christie's sale in London. The relationship continued until 1932, when Joni published *Memoirs of a Painter of Old Masters* (the source of the Aringhieri anecdote), in which he presented Berenson and Perkins as rapacious foreigners profiteering from Italian pictures, which brought the association to an abrupt end.

Sienese 'gold backs' remained collectable up to the Second World War, but the last major collection to feature them strongly is that of Robert Lehman, now displayed at the Met in New York.[27] Sienese painting was a poor fit with modernist orthodoxies and apart from the young John Pope-Hennessy, who had to publish his monographs on Giovanni di Paolo and Sassetta at his own expense (in 1937 and 1939), it attracted little interest in the mid-century. A huge new literature on Sienese art has sprung up since the 1980s, much of which devotedly advocates the continued relevance of the tradition: works such as Hisham Matar's *A Month in Siena*, Patrick Boucheron's *The Power of Images* and Timothy Hyman's *Sienese Painting*, which spring from personal and passionate response to the quality of Sienese art.

Paintings aside, the influx of visitors to the city, 'Murray' in hand, was a spur to the restoration of damaged monuments. When Dickens saw the Campo in 1844, he perceived it as 'a large square, with a great broken-nosed fountain in it'. The Sienese were aware of such responses, and since tourism was beginning to bring in money they accordingly began to invest in restoration.

The Sienese sculptor Antonio Manetti (1805–87) spent two decades, from 1830 to 1850, restoring, or rather replacing, Siena's cathedral sculpture, in particular the sculptures on its façade, many of which were badly weathered. The originals, by Giovanni Pisano and others, had not only suffered from six hundred years of weather, the earthquake of 1768 had actually made them dangerous. When an unfortunate horse was killed by a sculpture plummeting from the façade, the city authorities authorized Manetti to overhaul it. Manetti and his assistants produced copies or, if they were too damaged to copy, interpretations of eroded figures.[28] For most of the nineteenth century, Manetti's workshop was the premier sculpture training ground in Siena; Tito Sarocchi, Enea

Becheroni (1819–85) and, for a short time, the celebrated purist sculptor Giovanni Dupré (1817–82) were trained there.[29] The original sculptures were moved into the Museo dell'Opera del Duomo.

Purism was an important movement in Italian art. Like the Pre-Raphaelites and the Nazarenes, the purists took their inspiration from early Renaissance Italy.[30] In particular, they rejected neoclassicism's drive for aesthetic perfection in favour of developing a more naturalistic style which they considered more appropriate for Christian art. Giuseppe Partini (1842–95) is considered Siena's chief purist architect. He adhered to the principles for architectural restoration established by the French architect Eugène Viollet-le-Duc, which aimed to replace lost or damaged structures with interventions indistinguishable from the original. He taught at the Sienese Accademia di Belle Arti, which suggests that this institution was concerned to produce sculptors capable of restoring or copying medieval sculpture, just as it produced painters capable of reproducing a medieval Sienese painting. He trained a pool of artisans and craftsmen who had a very high level of skill in reproducing forms and decorations from the Middle Ages.

Partini himself acquired a reputation for his ability to re-medievalize existing buildings. He was one of the most successful of many architects who made their careers from reanimating medieval and Renaissance structures in the nineteenth century. He removed baroque additions from the church of San Francesco, and reworked the façades of the three *palazzi* in Piazza Salimbeni to make them consistently gothic.[31] He often worked closely with the sculptor Tito Sarrocchi, notably on the Fonte Gaia.[32] Sarrocchi is also responsible for the sculpture of the economist Sallustio Bandini in the Piazza Salimbeni, and for many of the sculptures in the Misericordia cemetery, outside the walls. Grand Duke Leopold banned burials within churches (and the cloisters of convents) in 1784, leading to the cemetery's creation. The Misericordia came to contain a remarkable collection of nineteenth-century sculpture and painting.

19

SENA VETUS

A t the beginning of the twentieth century the big political question dominating Sienese life was the countryside, as the *mezzadria* system began to break down. The first of many strikes by sharecroppers took place in 1902. Since Italy had won its independence, the countryfolk wanted to see some benefit from their new freedom and developed increasingly left-wing ideas. Relations between landowners and sharecroppers were traditionally hostile, since landowners tended to assume that the peasants would try to cheat them, and were understandably resented. Many landlords were fair and conscientious, and put a substantial amount of their profit back into the land, but, equally, many were not and if they were not, there was nothing that the peasant could do about it. The English-born Iris Origo, who with her noble Italian husband was the most conscientious of landlords and farmed at the confluence of the Val di Chiana and Val d'Orcia, observed that '[*mezzadria's*] strength has lain in an unquestioning conviction on both sides that the system was, on the whole, fair and equitable; it was this conviction that, for six centuries, made it work'. When it evaporated in the course of the 1950s and 1960s, the whole basis of rural life was undermined.[1] Landholding in the countryside was transformed, either into estates where the workers were paid a salary in a conventional manner, or into workers' cooperatives.

The centre of the Origos' estate was the house of La Foce. It was a medium-sized fifteenth-century country villa, with a ground-floor loggia and arches of red brick. Both the house and its territory were very run down, while the farmers lived in abject poverty. The Origos chose this unpromising property because they wanted to make a practical difference to people's lives. As Iris explains, if they had bought a flourishing estate 'we would only have to follow the course of established custom, handing over all the hard work to our fattore, and casting an occasional paternal eye over what was being done, as it had always been done. This was not what we wanted.'[2] Over the next thirty years, they built new roads, including the much-photographed zigzag carriageway lined with cypresses, built new farmhouses, increased the area under cultivation, brought in water, and created schools and clinics. Iris Origo was brought up in the Villa Medici at Fiesole, which was owned by her mother, Sibyl Cutting, and restored for her by an English architect and garden designer, Cecil Pinsent. The Origos turned again to Pinsent to help them with La Foce, and through the 1920s he both remodelled the house and built them a classic Italian garden down the slope of the hill on which the house stands, with travertine terraces, clipped box hedges, citrus in pots, a wisteria pergola and a view out to Monte Amiata in the distance.[3]

One thing which made an enormous difference to the quality of life in Siena itself in the early twentieth century was a great engineering achievement, completed as the First World War was on the point of breaking out: ending the city's dependence on the *bottini* by building an aqueduct to bring water from Vivo, near Monte Amiata, a distance of sixty kilometres. In the nineteenth century, Vivo had had a mill, a tannery, a paper mill and a glass-blowing industry, but all this economic activity ceased when it lost its water; a small community sacrificed to the needs of a larger one.[4] In the war itself, Siena and its *contado* lost six thousand soldiers, and the veterans who did return came home to a difficult political situation. Post-war inflation brought hunger and public health problems, particularly tuberculosis, which spread easily in Siena due to overcrowding and squalid living conditions in parts of the city centre.[5] In post-war elections, the left triumphed through most of the region, prompting a backlash from the landowning elite, and the rise of the fascists.

Once in power, promises to bring back the past glories of Siena won the fascists a good deal of popular support. They undertook a variety of capital projects aimed at bringing in tourists, notably a new railway station and the creation of a civic museum in the Palazzo Pubblico. A fascist-admiring art historian, Maria Sarfatti, even suggested that the city might finally build the giant Duomo proposed in the fourteenth century, a project which had been abandoned because of the Black Death in 1348.[6] One way in which the fascists attempted to stabilize their fragile hold on power was to evoke Italy's glorious past, and many fascist projects evoked ancient Rome, but they also put Italy's Middle Ages and Renaissance to service, as they did in Siena. Displaying the past helped in theory to legitimize Mussolini's claims in the present, but, as so often in intensely local Italy, in Siena grandiloquent initiatives were cannily directed to sensible local ends.

Another reason for these extensive public works was that the shock of the Great Depression was felt in Europe as well as America. By 1930, unemployment in Italy was a serious problem. The fascists' preferred solution was to initiate public projects, providing jobs in construction.[7] Furthermore, the public health official charged with analysing the tuberculosis crisis concluded that 'the fight against tuberculosis in Siena is essentially a problem of housing renovation'.[8] It was not hard for public health officials to demonstrate that there were areas of the city which had become overcrowded slums: the old Jewish ghetto was particularly problematic, since as with ghettoes everywhere, overcrowding was endemic. The region of Salicotto, behind the Palazzo Pubblico, which included the ghetto, was marked for slum clearance and pulled down. The people were relocated to new housing on the urban periphery outside the walls, and the area reconstructed with wider streets and buildings in neo-gothic style. The overall aim of fascist building work in Siena was the reconstruction of an idealized medieval city. One aspect of this was the wholesale removal of any remaining stucco covering from the older brick and stone buildings, though Lorenzetti's *Good Government* frescoes suggest that many houses may have been plastered from as early as the fourteenth century.

overleaf
An anonymous painting of the Palio of 1931: Mussolini's Fascists were keen to promote the Palio as a celebration of aggressive masculine energy.

While the fascists were thus prepared to undertake sweeping interventions in the cityscape, they did not permit private citizens to do so without conforming to their restoring vision for the city, an amalgam of the Siena of the Nine, and that of Pandolfo Petrucci. The Podestà (a title the fascists had revived), Fabio Bargagli Petrucci, enacted a series of laws which required planning permission for any work on a historic building. In a different kind of creative and scholarly dialogue with the past, Count Guido Chigi Saracini founded the Accademia Chigiana, specializing in the revival of what we would now call early music, a personal gesture which contributed to the revitalization of the city. In the countryside, further drainage projects in the Maremma and Val di Chiana finally brought the *contado*'s malarial swamps under control.

Also in the *contado*, two towery hill towns were repaired: San Gimignano underwent a parallel drastic restoration intended to make it appear more medieval;[9] fallen towers at Monteriggioni were reconstructed[10] and the cathedral at Pienza, which had received a baroque makeover despite Pius II's anathemas against interference with his intentions, was more or less rebuilt by Alfredo Barbacci between 1925 and 1933.[11]

Italy entered the Second World War very late, in June 1940, after the fall of France made Germany's victory seem overwhelmingly likely. Iris Origo's account of the war in the Sienese countryside is classic, and based on her diary: she kept her family together and gave birth to her second daughter, but she also made an orphanage for homeless children, covertly aided hundreds of escaped British prisoners of war, partisans and Italian deserters, and after the German occupation, defended her *contadini* from the German authorities. She writes of a community furious about being dragged into war by the fascists, horrified by the Nazis and sympathetic to deserters, refugees, escaped POWs and Jews. The Nazis declared Italian Jews enemy aliens in 1943 and hunted them down, though in Tuscany many were sheltered by neighbours or in convents and remote farms. In Siena itself, Jews hid in the old *bottini*, though fourteen members of the community were captured and sent to concentration camps.[12] Tuscans in both city and country had to cope with being bombed and machine-gunned by the British and Americans: at Siena, the Allies targeted the German railway yards, but luckily the major monuments escaped damage. However, the church of San Francesco was hit, and the outlying Basilica dell'Osservanza was almost totally destroyed. The building which now stands on the site is a fine post-war reconstruction, and forms a distinguished crown to its green hill. Siena's escape from major damage was partly due to Ludwig Heinrich Heydenreich, a German art historian who was made responsible for protecting Tuscan art treasures. He is one of the city's unsung heroes, since he persuaded the German senior command not to defend Siena, but to leave it open once the Allies reached Tuscany.[13] The fascist era ended in 1945, mourned by few, but as far as Siena was concerned its material legacy of urban reconstruction was positive.

While the grievances of the countryfolk were far from satisfied, they were eventually mitigated by the extraordinary economic success of Italy in the 1950s and 1960s. The shabby, poverty-stricken Italy recorded by nineteenth-century visitors was transformed after the Second World War, although for complex social reasons the exteriors of many buildings were left in a condition of apparent dilapidation until late in the twentieth century. The war ended with Italy defeated, in ruins and occupied by foreign armies. After the fall of the fascists, many Italians tended to the left in politics, and the Italian Communist Party was strong. Because the United States was concerned that the country might actually join the communist bloc, they were generous with aid. Italy received one and a half billion dollars through the Marshall Plan between 1948 to 1952.

Italians put the money to good use, investing massively in infrastructure and physical capital and generating what economists call 'Italy's economic miracle'. This had international implications for what had been small and local Italian manufacturers. Nineteenth-century companies such as Barilla and Cirio, which had originally catered to local customers, industrialized on a massive scale and exported huge quantities of dried pasta, tinned tomatoes and cheese. Entrepreneurs in the world's 'Little Italies' opened restaurants and familiarized their host cultures with Italian dishes adapted to local taste. Pasta embedded itself in the cuisines of the world, and Neapolitan pizza became one of the world's most popular foods. It is hard to comprehend how recent the international triumph of Italian food is: in 1746, Alban Butler was absolutely revolted by *pasta in brodo* with grated parmesan: 'Soups made of vermicelli, a sort of paste exactly resembling worms which we could not endure... after Lent was over this vermicelli still formed an ingredient of their soups with the addition of scraped cheese, which formed a disagreeable compound.'[14] Eighty years later, William Hazlitt in Florence was much relieved to find a hotel which offered 'boiled and roast, with English cups and saucers and steamed potatoes'.[15]

Luxury manufactures had been an Italian speciality for centuries, and thus the country had very high levels of craft skills to draw on. Italy's share of world trade almost doubled between 1950 and 1973. Tuscany's contribution to this cornucopia was primarily wine, olive oil and luxury leather goods. Nannini's *panforte da Siena*, with its thirteenth-century-style lettering surrounding a colourful vision of Siena's medieval centre, became a familiar sight in many countries, especially at Christmas. The material standard of living improved vastly for the great majority of the population.

The interclass grievances of countryfolk were mitigated by the end of the *mezzadria* system and the new availability of alternatives: a family who felt exploited by farm work could simply abandon it, perhaps move to the city, or find employment in one of the many artisan industries which sprang up in the countryside. Increasingly, they could also, in one way or another, make money from visitors. By the end of the twentieth century, many picturesque farmhouses, their kitchens adorned with huge, traditional hearths, had been unobtrusively modernized and were giving pleasure to high-spending independent travellers from all over Europe and beyond, for whom the paradisal aspect of the south Tuscan countryside had an ever-increasing appeal, the more so in that it lay completely outside the structures of mass tourism.

Siena itself draws extensively on the products of the surrounding countryside to support its economy. The most economically significant local products are wine, olive oil and truffles, which are sold by outlets in the city, together with local cheese and charcuterie, and distinctive products of the city itself such as *panforte, ricciarelli* and *pici pasta*.

Niki de Saint Phalle's riotously colourful and playful Tarot Garden was created between the 1970s and 1990s, and was her crowning achievement.

The Chianti wine region to the east and north of Siena was enormously successful as an export in the twentieth century, so much so that the traditional bottles nested in straw baskets were a sort of visual shorthand for Tuscany by the 1950s. Mass-market Chianti then became a victim of its own success, though there are now producers working to restore its reputation. The red wines of Montalcino to the south (the last stronghold of the Sienese Republic in 1555) and Montepulciano have replaced Chianti as the most sought-after wines of the area, while the Maremma also now produces fine wines.[16]

The Sienese countryside attracted a variety of artists in the late twentieth century. Niki di Saint-Phalle's Tarot Garden, at Garavicchio in the Maremma, first began to come together in the 1970s and absorbed much of her energy for the following twenty years. It was the work of Antoni Gaudi, especially Park Güell in Barcelona, which first gave her the idea of making a sculpture garden, where she could develop ideas and associations based on the twenty-two major arcana of the Tarot. She wanted to create 'a sort of joyland, where you could have a new kind of life that would just be free', and she wanted to create art on a monumental scale, precisely because women were not expected to.[17] It was chance rather than design which led her to locate her project in Tuscany, since it was an encounter with a friend from her early days as a model, Marella Agnelli, who had since married the president of

Fiat, which produced a site. It was a fourteen-acre estate belonging to Agnelli's brothers, which they gave to her. As the work proceeded, Saint-Phalle co-opted locals to help with the massive task of decorating her enormous creations with mosaic, mirror glass and other ceramics, creating an exuberant, and mostly joyful, scene of brilliantly coloured female monsters.

The French artist Jean-Paul Philippe made a very different kind of sculpture experience at Asciano in 1993. Three stone structures, standing for a window, a chair and a desk, catering to the three basic human positions, standing, sitting and lying down, frame long views out over the Crete Senesi, a house with no walls, roofed by the sky. It is at once permanent and temporary, since the stone structure are in continuous dialogue with the sky and the surroundings. Other sculpture parks are at Settignano, the eclectic collection of the Swiss artist Daniel Spoerri,

which contains 113 installations by fifty-three different artists, at San Giovanni d'Asso, where Il Bosco della Ragnaia is the work of the American Sheppard Craige and his artist wife Frances Lansing, and at Casole d'Elsa, Deva Manfredo's Traumwald, arrangements of stones, and more recently, other found objects, which are sometimes reminiscent of the work of Andy Goldsworthy.

The impulse to create earthly paradises, common to all these projects, is intimately connected with the paradisal quality of the Tuscan countryside itself. Siena has the longest landscape tradition in Western art, going back to the exquisitely mysterious little 'City by the Sea' and Ambrogio Lorenzetti's panoramic view of the *contado* in his fresco of *Good Government*. The European sensibility has long been conditioned to see in the Tuscan landscape itself both a living memory of the sacred landscape inhabited by the saints of Renaissance art and a landscape which is itself one of the most aesthetically valued places in Europe. It is a cherished land, the result of innumerable generations of patient husbandry. As we have seen, the British – and the Americans – fell in love with Italy in the nineteenth century, and their writings have conditioned the eyes and feelings of those who have followed them. Travel to Italy, for people such as the Brownings and Henry James, gave an illusion of travelling back in time to a pre-industrial land populated by unsophisticated people with the manners of the morning of the world, lit by a golden light and set against a backdrop of azure skies, cobalt-blue mountains, and cypress trees.

Italy's crumbling *palazzi* and classical ruins lent themselves particularly well to a different strain of picturesque, romantic or even neo-baroque aesthetics, which embraced urban landscapes as well as the bandit-haunted mountains beloved of Salvator Rosa, especially those of a city like Siena where the grandeur of the past could still be seen amid the decay of the present. Upland Italy was the ideal wild, natural terrain that England lacked in the era after the Enclosure Act; its lowland cornfields, vineyards and wind-silvered olive groves offered both present beauty and a recollection of classical antiquity. In addition to all this, it was also cheap, warm and lit by sunlight which only grew more beautiful at evening.

previous pages
Jean-Paul Philippe's Site Transitoire dominates its hilltop, and evokes a wide variety of moods at different times and seasons.

opposite
Deva Manfredi's Traumwald is created out of found objects, and so in a different way, in dialogue with its landscape.

For generations now the question, 'Do you know the land where the lemon trees blossom?', Goethe's *Kennst du das Land wo die Zitronen blühn*, has resonated with northern Europeans, longing for sunshine and freedom, and release from a rain-scoured, over-organized and inhibited life. More than sixty composers have set Goethe's famous lyrics, a distillation of the charm of Italy, the lemons under blue skies, Palladian villas with statues in the garden, narrow paths through wild mountain scenery, a romantic reconfiguration of the Italian landscapes of Claude and Poussin which had themselves set a standard of beauty for the eighteenth century and beyond. The perfume of citrus flowers and the memory of their glistening leaves and bright fruit are one detail of the Italian countryside which haunts the imagination and aspirations of the north. But Helena Attlee's magnificent study of citrus trees in Italy reminds us that lemons don't just grow; they have to be cultivated with great sophistication, and that the other elements of the fecundity and sheer beauty of the Italian countryside also rest on a foundation of hard work and expert knowledge. Mechanization has made country life a great deal easier, but the landscape is still carefully tended, and even seeming wilderness, and its cherished wild food plants, from chicories to the mushrooms of late summer, often plays an active part in the local economy.

Il Bosco di Ragnaia is another ideal landscape, which in its tranquil beauty, reshapes the long tradition of the Italian garden.

Ruskin's last book *Praeterita* (Things now Past) is a collection of memories of his past life, written between bouts of mental illness. He celebrated the enduring beauty of Siena in the last paragraph of his book:

> Fontebranda I last saw with Charles Norton, under the same arches where Dante saw it. We drank of it together, and walked that evening on the hills above, where the fireflies among the scented thickets shone fitfully in the still undarkened air. How they shone! moving like fine-broken starlight through the purple leaves. How they shone! through the sunset that faded into thunderous night as I entered Siena three days before, the white edges of the mountainous clouds still lighted from the west, and the openly gold sky calm behind the gate of Siena's heart, with its still golden words, 'Cor magis tibi Sena pandit', and the fireflies everywhere in sky and cloud rising and falling, mixed with the lightning, and more intense than the stars.

Ruskin's lovely closing paragraph gathers so much together – passionate English longing for Italy to be the Italy of imagination and not that of nineteenth-century reality, intense and glorious appreciation of fireflies and stars and evening skies, but he has read the inscription wrongly. Siena's story is not straightforward. The impression of medieval survival which it gives is one which has been carefully curated, through a series of campaigns of civic improvement from the fifteenth century to the present day. As early as the seventeenth century, patrons were choosing to employ the local building style rather than bringing new styles to the old streets. Fabio Chigi, as Alexander VII, overhauled Rome and enriched it beyond measure with baroque squares and vistas, but his interventions in Siena, apart from the Cappella del Voto in the cathedral, are in versions of medieval styles, such as the new cladding of the exterior wall of the nave.

While the Sienese have long been renowned for their courtesy towards strangers, the inscription on the Porta Camollia which moved Ruskin, 'Siena opens its heart more to you', was put there by the Florentines to welcome a Medici prince, Ferdinand II, when they rebuilt the gate in 1603. The Sienese were insulted by it at the time, since it could be thought of as the architectural equivalent of a slave collar, and it still annoys them.[18] In fact, it is a most unsuitable motto for the city, since strangers are welcomed only up to a point: they may be met with courtesy and geniality, but the Sienese make a firm distinction between insiders and outsiders. Anyone who is not born a member of a *contrada*, or at least, adopted into one, which most happily can and does happen, will never really be accepted as truly Sienese. Conversely, for someone born in a *contrada*, it will always be home. Hisham Matar tells the tender story of Jordanian refugees settled into the *contrada* of the Torre, who were astonished to find that when they brought their newborn son, a Muslim, home from the hospital, a deputation of *contrada* officials came to ceremonially enrol their child in the Torre. Whatever the family's vicissitudes in the future, their son is growing up belonging somewhere.[19]

Siena has adapted and survived. Two generations after the Black Death, the city was embracing the Renaissance, in its own idiosyncratic fashion. After a devastating siege, total defeat and delivery into the hands of hated Florence, its people found ways to reassert their distinctive cultural identity. The woes of the Monte dei Paschi bank, the second oldest bank in the world, which for decades poured money into the city through its charitable foundation, are the most recent crisis, but doubtless Siena will survive that, too. The city the Nine built might be even more visible today than it was in 1900, thanks to efforts during the past century to 'medievalize' the historic centre. Apart from the fascist interventions discussed above, motorized traffic was banned inside the walls in 1963, except for vehicles belonging to residents with garages, official cars, and delivery trucks; even then, the hours in which they may do so are strictly limited. Other twentieth-century intrusions such as overhead wiring have been removed from sight, while medievalizing reconstructions of numerous sites further emphasize the ineradicable memory of the achievements of the era of the Nine.[20]

The final result of all this care and memory which has been lavished on this city is that it still offers a glimpse into the medieval ideal of the good life as expressed in Lorenzetti's *Allegory of Good Government*. This vision is realized in three dimensions in the streets of the city and in the preservation of the landscape of cypress and olive tree just beyond the ancient gates. It also offers a world-class school of painting displayed in a wide variety of beautiful buildings, with the works of art in many cases still in the rooms for which they were made. Few visitors to the city fail to come away unmoved, few do not feel that, somehow, the ample Piazza del Campo, the enfolding labyrinth of streets, the views of the country beyond, have offered them a glimpse of a great good place, an ideal city persisting on earth. In reality, Siena is neither timeless nor changeless, but over the centuries of its chequered history it has been absolutely, paradoxically, true to a vision of itself.

overleaf
Siena's contado, with its cypresses, vineyards, woods and fields, bathed in the golden light of a summer's evening.

BIBLIOGRAPHY

Acchili, Alessandro et al., 'Mitochondrial DNA Variation of Modern Tuscans Supports the Near Eastern Origin of Etruscans', *American Journal of Human Genetics*, 80 (2007), pp.759–68.

Adams, Nicholas, 'The Life and Times of Pietro dell'Abaco, A Renaissance Estimator from Siena (active 1457–1486)', *Zeitschrift für Kunstgeschichte*, 48 (1985), pp.384–95.
———— 'Knowing Francesco di Giorgio', in Francesco Paolo Fiore (ed.), *Francesco di Giorgio alla corte di Federico da Montefeltro. Atti del Convegno Internazionale di Studi (Urbino, 11–13 ottobre 2001)*, 2 vols (Florence: Leo S. Olschki, 2004), I, pp.305–16.

Addis, Bill, 'Francesco di Giorgio's contribution to the development of building engineering', *Construction History*, 31.2 (2016), pp.39–58.

Alberti, Leon Battista, *On the Art of Building in Ten Books*, trans. Joseph Rykwert, Neil Leach and Robert Tavernor (Cambridge, MA: MIT Press, 1988).

Alexandratos, Rea, '"With the true eye of a lynx": The Paper Museum of Cassiano dal Pozzo', in David Attenborough, Susan Owens, Martin Clayton and Rea Alexandratos, *Amazing Rare Things: The Art of Natural History in the Age of Discovery* (New Haven and London: Yale University Press, 2009).

[Anon.], 'Siena Then and Now', *Burlington Magazine*, 152 (2010), p.213.

[Anon.], 'I Restauri di Monteriggioni', *Il Popolo Senese* (1929), p.3.

Aronow, Gail, 'A Documentary History of the Pavement Decoration in Siena Cathedral, 1362 through 1506', Columbia University PhD, 1985.

Ascheri, Mario, and Bradley R. Franco, *A History of Siena: from its origins to the present day* (Abingdon: Routledge, 2020).

Attlee, Helena, *The Land Where Lemons Grow* (London: Penguin, 2014).

Avery-Quash, Susanna, 'Illuminating the Old Masters and Enlightening the British Public: Anna Jameson and the Contribution of British Women to Empirical Art History in the 1840s', *Interdisciplinary Studies in the Long Nineteenth Century*, 28 (2019), pp.1–32.

Azzolini, Isodoro Ugurgieri, *Le Pompe sanesi, o vero Relazione delli huomini e donne illustri di siena e suo stato*, 2 vols (Pistoia: P. A. Fortunati, 1649).

Bacci, Peleo, *Francesco di Valdambrino emulo del Ghiberti e collaboratore di Jacopo della Quercia* (Siena: Istituto Comunale d'Arte e di Storia, 1936).

Baccinetti, Vilma, 'La Repubblica Senese ritirata a Montalcino (1555–1559)', *Bullettino Senese di Storia Patria*, 47 (1940), pp.1–38, 97–116.

Baggiani, E., 'Il Risanamento Edilizio della Città', *La Balzana*, 4 (1929), p.73.

Baldari, Marco et al., 'Malaria in Maremma, Italy', *The Lancet*, 351 (1998), pp.1246–7.

Balestracci, Duccio and Piccini, Gabriella, *Siena nel Trecento: Assetto Urbano e Strutture Edilizie* (Firenze: CLUSF, 1977).

Balestracci, Duccio, *The Renaissance in the Fields: Family Memoirs of a Fifteenth-Century Tuscan Peasant*, trans. Paolo Squatriti and Betsy Meredith (University Park: Pennsylvania State University Press, 1999).

Banchi, Luciano (ed.), *L'arte della seta in Siena nei secoli XV e XVI: Statuti e documenti* (Siena: Tipografia sordo-muti di L. Lazzeri, 1881).

Baron, J. H., 'The Hospital of Santa Maria Della Scala, Siena, 1090–1990', *British Medical Journal*, 301, no.6766 (22–29 December 1990), pp.1449–51.

Bartalini, Roberto, 'Sodoma, the Chigi and the Vatican Stanze', *Burlington Magazine*, 143 (2001), pp.544–53.

Bartoli, Gianni et al., 'Non Destructive Characterisation of stone columns by Dynamic test: application to the lower colonnade of the Dome of the Siena Cathedral', *Engineering Structures*, 45 (2012), pp.519–35.

Battente, Saverio Luigi, 'The "Gothic Queen": the Myth of Siena in the 19th and 20th Centuries', *A Companion to Late Medieval and Early Modern Siena*, ed. Santa Casciani and Heather Hayton (Leiden and Boston: Brill, 2021), pp.263–87.

Baxandall, Michael, *Painting and Experience in Fifteenth-Century Italy* (Oxford: Oxford University Press, 1972).

Beck, James H., 'The Historical "Taccola" and Emperor Sigismund in Siena', *Art Bulletin*, 50.4 (1968), pp.309–20.

Beckford, Peter, F*amiliar Letters from Italy*, 2 vols (Salisbury: J. Easton, 1805).

Belladonna, Rita, 'Pontanus, Macchiavelli, and a case of religious dissimulation in early sixteenth-century Siena', *Bibliothèque d'Humanisme et Renaissance*, 37.3 (1975), pp.377–85.

Benvoglienti, Bartolomeo, *Trattato de l'origine et accrescimento de la città di Siena* (Rome: Giuseppe de gli Angeli, 1571).

Bianco, W., 'Carciofo (Cynara scolymus L.)', in W. Bianco and F. Pimpini (eds), *Orticoltura* (Bologna: Patron, 1990), pp.209–51.

Birch, Debra J., *Pilgrimage to Rome in the Middle Ages* (Woodbridge: Boydell & Brewer, 1998).

Black, Christopher, *Italian Confraternities in the Sixteenth Century* (Cambridge: Cambridge University Press, 1989).

[Blewitt, Octavian], *Murray's Guide to Central Italy* (London: John Murray, 1843).

Bomford, David et al., *Art in the Making: Italian Painting before 1400* (London: National Gallery Publications, 1990).

Bomford, David, Roy, Ashok and Syson, Luke, 'Gilding and Illusion in the Works of Bernardino Fungai', *National Gallery Technical Bulletin*, 27 (2006), pp.111–20.

Boniface, St, *Letters of St Boniface*, trans Ephraim Emerton (New York: Columbia University Press, 1940).

Boswell, James, *Boswell on the Grand Tour: Italy, Corsica and France 1765–1766*, ed. Frank Brady and Frederick A. Pottle (New York: McGraw-Hill, 1955).

Boucheron, Patrick, *The Power of Images: Siena, 1338*, trans. Andrew Brown (Cambridge: Polity, 2018).

Bowsky, William M., 'The Impact of the Black Death upon Sienese Government and Society', *Speculum*, 39.1 (1964), pp.1–34.
—— 'The Medieval Commune and Internal violence: Police Power and Public Safety in Siena, 1287–1355', *American Historical Review*, 73 (1967), pp.1–17.
—— *The Finance of the Commune of Siena, 1287–1355* (Oxford: Clarendon Press, 1970).
—— (ed. and trans), *The Black Death. A Turning Point in History?* (New York: Holt, Rinehart and Winston, 1971).
—— *A Medieval Italian Commune: Siena under the Nine, 1287–1355* (Berkeley: University of California Press, 1981).

Brandi, Cesare (ed.), *Palazzo Pubblico di Siena: vicende costruttive e decorazione* (Milan: Silvano, 1983).

Braunfels, Wolfgang, *Urban Design in Western Europe: Regime and Architecture, 900–1900* (Chicago: University of Chicago Press, 1988).

Bridgeman, Jane, '"Pagare le Pompe" why Quattrocento sumptuary laws did not work', *Women in Italian Renaissance Culture and Society*, ed. Letizia Panizza (Oxford: Legenda, 2000), pp.209–26.

Brigstocke, Hugh, 'Lord Lindsay: travel in Italy and Northern Europe, 1841–42, for "Sketches of the History of Christian Art"', *The Volume of the Walpole Society*, 65 (2003), pp.161–258.

Brown, Judith M., 'Prosperity or hard times in Renaissance Italy?', *Renaissance Quarterly*, 42 (1980), pp.761–80.

Buchanan, William, *Memoirs of Painting, with a Chronological History of the Importation of Pictures by the Great Masters into England since the French Revolution*, 2 vols (London: Ackermann, 1824).

Buranello, Robert, 'The Hidden Ways and Means of Antonio Vignali's *La Cazzaria*', *Quaderni d'talianistica*, 26.1 (2005), pp.59–76.

Burke, S. Maureen, 'The "Martyrdom of the Franciscans" by Ambrogio Lorenzetti', *Zeitschrift für Kunstgeschichte*, 65.4 (2002), pp.460–92.

Butler, Alban, *Travels through France & Italy, and part of Austrian, French, & Dutch Netherlands: during the years 1745 and 1746* (Edinburgh: Keating, Brown, and Keating, 1803).

Butzek, Monica, *Il Duomo di Siena al tempo di Alessandro VII* (Munich: Bruckmann, 1996).

Caferro, William, *Mercenary Companies and the Decline of Siena* (Baltimore: Johns Hopkins University Press, 1988).
—— 'City and Countryside in Siena in the Second

Half of the Fourteenth Century', *Journal of Economic History*, 54.1 (1994), pp.85–103.

—— 'Mercenaries and Military Expenditure: the Costs of Undeclared Warfare in Fourteenth-Century Siena', *Journal of European Economic History*, 23.2 (1994a), pp.219–47.

—— 'Warfare and Economy in Renaissance Italy', *Journal of Interdisciplinary History*, 39.2 (2008), pp.167–209.

Cagliaritono, Ubaldo, *History of Siena* (Siena: Periccioli Edition, 1983).

Cairolo, Aldo and Carli, Enzo, *Il palazzo pubblico di Siena* (Rome: Editalia, 1963).

Cammarosano, P., 'Le campagne senesi dalla fine del secolo XII agli inizi del Trecento: dinamica interna e forme del dominio cittadino', in *Contadini e proprietari nella Toscana moderna* (Florence: Leo S. Olschki, 1979), pp.153–222.

Campbell, Bruce M., *The Great Transition: Climate, Disease and Society in the Late Medieval World* (Cambridge: Cambridge University Press, 2016).

Cantagalli, Roberto, *La Guerra di Siena (1552–1559)* (Siena: Accademia Senese degli Intronati, 1962).

Capatti, Alberto and Montanari, Massimo, *Italian Cuisine: A Cultural History* (New York: Columbia University Press, 1999).

Capitelli, Bernardino, *I carri delle sei contrade, che comparuero splendidamente in teatro alla luce di ser.o Sole, ue[n]gono hora p[er] lor disauentura oscuramente delineati nell'ombre confuse de miei debili intagli… Siena il dì marzo 1632* (Siena: s.n., 1633).

Carli, Enzo, *The Cathedral of Siena and the Cathedral Museum* (Florence: Edizioni Scala, 1976).

Carus-Wilson, E. M., 'The Woollen Industry', in *Trade and Industry in the Middle Ages*, ed. M. M. Postan and Edward Miller, *The Cambridge Economic History of Europe*, 2nd edn, vol.2 (Cambridge: Cambridge University Press, 1966), pp.613–690.

Casanova, Eugenio, *La donna Senese del quattrocento nella vita privata* (Siena: L. Lazzeri, 1901).

Castelnuovo, Enrico, 'L'infatuazione per i Primitivi intorno al 1900', in *Arti e Storia del Medioevo* (Torino: Einaudi, 2004), IV, pp.785–809.

Castelvetro, Giacomo, *The Fruit, Herbs and Vegetables of Italy*, trans. Gillian Riley (Totnes: Prospect Books, 2012).

Catoni, Giuliano, *A Short History of Siena* (Pisa: Pacini Editore, 2000).

Cecchini, Giovanni and Neri, Dario, *The Palio of Siena* (Siena: Monte di Paschi, 1958).

Chambers, D. S., 'The Housing Problems of Cardinal Francesco Gonzaga', *Journal of the Warburg and Courtauld Institutes*, 39 (1976), pp.21–5.

Christiansen, Keith, Kanter, Laurence B. and Strehlke, Carl Brandon, *Painting in Renaissance Siena* (New York: Abrams, 1988).

Christofani, Mauro, *Siena: le origini, testimonianze e miti archaeologici: catalogo della nostra Siena* (Florence: Olschki, 1979).

Cicero, *De Officiis*, trans. Walter Miller (Cambridge, MA: Harvard University Press, 1913).

Cipolla, Carlo M., 'The Decline of Italy: The Case of a Fully Matured Economy', *Economic History Review*, New Series 5.2 (1952), pp.178–87.

Cochrane, Eric, *Tradition and Enlightenment in the Tuscan Academies, 1690–1800* (Rome: Edizioni di storia e letteratura, 1961).

Coffin, David, *The Villa in the Life of Renaissance Rome* (Princeton: Princeton University Press, 1979).

Cohn, Samuel K., *Death and Property in Siena, 1205–1800: Strategies for the Afterlife* (Baltimore: Johns Hopkins University Press, 1988).

—— *The Cult of Remembrance and the Black Death* (Baltimore: Johns Hopkins University Press, 1997).

—— 'The Black Death: End of a Paradigm', *American Historical Review*, 107.3 (2002), pp.703–38.

—— 'The Historian and the Laboratory: the Black Death Disease', in *The Fifteenth Century XII: Society in an Age of Plague*, ed. Linda Clark, Carole Rawcliffe (Woodbridge: Boydell & Brewer, 2013), pp.195–212.

Collier, Alexandra, 'The Sienese Accademia degli Intronati and its female interlocutors', *The Italianist*, 26.2 (2006), pp.223–46.

Columella, *De Re Rustica*, 3 vols, trans. E. S. Forster and Edward H. Heffner (Cambridge, MA: Harvard University Press, 1953).

Cui, Yujun et al., 'Historical variations in mutation rate in an epidemic pathogen, *Yersinia pestis*', *Proceedings of the National Academy of Sciences of the United States of America*, 110.2 (2013), pp.577–82.

Da Bisticci, Vespasiano, *The Vespasiano Memoirs: Lives of Illustrious Men of the XVth Century*, trans. William George and Emily Waters (London: Routledge, 1926).

Dallington, Richard, *A Survey of the Great Duke's State of Tuscany* (London: Edward Blount, 1605).

Davis, Raymond (trans.), *The Book of Pontiffs* (Liverpool: Liverpool University Press, 1989).

Debby, Nirit Ben-Aryeh, 'War and peace: the description of Ambrogio Lorenzetti's Frescoes in Saint Bernardino's 1425 Siena Sermons', *Renaissance Studies*, 15.3 (2001), pp.272–86.

Dechert, M. S. A., 'City and Fortress in the Works of Francesco di Giorgio: the theory and practice of defensive architecture and town planning', Washington, Catholic University PhD, 1984.

Denley, Peter, 'Academic Rivalry and Interchange: the Universities of Siena and Florence', in *Florence and Italy: Renaissance Studies in Honour of Nicolai Rubinstein*, ed. Caroline Elam and Peter Denley (London: Committee for medieval studies, Westfield college, University of London, 1988), pp.193–208.
———— 'Governments and Schools in Late Medieval Italy', in *City and Countryside in Late Medieval and Renaissance Italy*, ed. Chris Wickham and Trevor Dean (London and Ronceverte: Hambledon Press, 1990), pp.93–107.

Derbes, Anne, 'Siena and the Levant in the Later Dugento', *Gesta*, 28.2 (1989), pp.190–204.

De Wesselow, Thomas, 'The Guidoriccio Fresco: a New Attribution', *Apollo* (1 March 2004), pp.3–12.
———— 'The Form and Imagery of the New Fresco in Siena's Palazzo Pubblico', *Artibus et Historiae*, 30, No. 59 (2009), pp.195–217.

Di Battista, Anthony Paul, 'Building the Bonum Comune', Rutgers University PhD, 1995.

Dini, Giulietta Chelazzi, Angelini, Alessandro and Sani, Bernardina, *Five Centuries of Sienese Painting: From Duccio to the Birth of the Baroque*, trans. Cordelia Warr (London: Thames & Hudson, 1998).

Dubus, Pascale, *Domenico Beccafumi*, trans. Michael Taylor (Paris: Adam Biro, 1999).

Dundes, Alan and Falassi, Alessandro, *La Terra in Piazza: an interpretation of the Palio of Siena* (Berkeley and Los Angeles: University of California Press 1984).

Eisen, Rebecca et al., 'Persistence of *Yersinia pestis* in Soil Under Natural Conditions', *Emerging Infectious Diseases*, 14.6 (2008), pp.941–3.

Eisenbichler, Konrad, '"Un chant à l'honneur de la France": Women's Voices at the End of the Republic of Siena', *Renaissance and Reformation*, NS 27.2 (2003), pp.87–99.
———— *The Sword and the Pen: Women, Politics, and Poetry in Sixteenth-century Siena* (Notre Dame: University of Notre Dame Press, 2012).

Ekholm, Karin J., 'Tartaglia's ragioni: A maestro d'abaco's mixed approach to the bombardier's problem', *British Journal for the History of Science*, 43.2 (2010), pp.181–207.

Ell, Stephen R., 'Some Evidence for Interhuman Transmission of Medieval Plague', *Reviews of Infectious Diseases*, 1.3 (1979), pp.563–6.

English, Edward D., *Enterprise and Liability in Sienese Banking, 1230–1350* (Cambridge, MA: Medieval Academy of America, 1988).

Epstein, Stephan, *Alle origini della fattoria Toscana: L'ospedale della Scala di Siena e le sue terre* (Florence: Salimbeni, 1986).

Fochesato, Mattia, 'Plagues, War, Political Change and Fiscal Capacity: Late Medieval and Renaissance Siena, 1337–1556', *Economic History Review*, 74.4 (2021), pp.1031–61.

Foster, Brett, 'Cecco Angiolieri and Comic-Realistic Sonnets', *Literary Imagination*, 12.3 (2010), pp.266–74.

Franceschi, Franco, 'Big Business for Firms and States: Silk Manufacturing in Renaissance Italy', *Business History Review*, 94.1 (2020), 95–123.

Franco, Bradley R., 'Episcopal Power and the Late Medieval State: Siena's Bishops and the Government of the Nine', *Viator*, 45.2 (2014), pp.255–70.
———— 'The Significance of Montaperti', in *A Companion to Late Medieval and Early Modern Siena*, ed. Santa Casciani and Heather Richardson Hayton (Leiden and Boston: Brill, 2021), pp.31–60.

Freedberg, David, 'From Hebrew and Gardens to Oranges and Lemons, Giovanni Battista Ferrari and Cassiano dal Pozzo', *Cassiano dal Pozzo: atti del seminario internazionale di studi*, ed. Francesco Solinas (Rome: De Luca, 1989), pp.37–72.
———— 'Cassiano, Ferrari and their Drawings of Citrus Fruit', in David Freedberg and Enrico Baldini, *Citrus Fruit* (London: Harvey Miller, 1997).
———— *The Eye of the Lynx: Galileo, his friends, and the beginnings of modern natural history* (Chicago: University of Chicago Press, 2002).

Freitas, Roger, 'The Eroticism of Emasculation: Confronting the Baroque Body of the Castrato', *Journal of Musicology*, 20.2 (2003), pp.196–249.

Freuler, Gaudenz, 'Andrea di Bartolo, Fra Tommaso d'Antonio Caffarini, and Sienese Dominicans in Venice', *The Art Bulletin*, 69.4 (1987), pp.570–86.

Friedman, David, 'Monumental urban form in late medieval Italian commune: loggias and the *mercanzie* of Bologna and Siena', *Renaissance Studies*, 12.3 (1998), pp.325–40.

Frinta, Mojmír S., 'The quest for a Restorer's Shop of Beguiling Invention: Restorations and Forgeries in Italian Panel Painting', *The Art Bulletin*, 60.1 (1978), pp.7–23.

Gardner, Edmund G., *Life of Saint Catherine of Siena* (London: Dent, 1907).

Garrison, E., 'Sienese Historical Writings and the Dates 1260, 1261, and 1262 applied to Sienese Paintings', *Studies in the History of Medieval Italian Painting*, 4.1 (1960–62), pp.23–58.

Ghiberti, Lorenzo, *I Commentari* [1446], ed. Julius von Schlosser, *Leben und Meinungen des Florentinischen Bilders Lorenzo Ghiberti*, 2 vols (Basel: Holbein-Verlag, 1941).

Ghirardo, Diane, *Building New Communities: New Deal America and Fascist Italy* (Princeton: Princeton University Press, 1989).

Gigli, Girolamo, *Diario Sienese*, 2 vols (Siena: F. Landi and N. Allesandri, 1854).

Ginatempo, Maria, *Crisi di un territorio. Il poplolamento della Toscana senese alla fine del Medioevo* (Florence: Leo S. Olschki, 1988).

Giontella, Andrea et al., 'Mitochondrial DNA Survey reveals the lack of accuracy in Maremmano Horse Studbook Records', *Animals*, 10 (2020), pp.1–11.

Gismondi, Angelo et al., 'Dental Calculus Reveals Diet Habits and Medicinal Plant Use in the Early Medieval Italian Population of Colonna', *Journal of Archaeological Science Reports*, 20 (2018), pp.556–64.

Glasfurd, Alec, *Siena and the Hill Towns* (London: Ernest Benn, 1962).

Glendinning, Robert, 'Love, Death and the Art of Compromise: Aeneas Sylvius Piccolomini's *Tale of Two Lovers*', *Fifteenth Century Studies*, 23 (1997), pp.101–20.

Goldthwaite, Richard A., *The Building of Renaissance Florence: An Economic and Social History* (Baltimore and London: Johns Hopkins University Press, 1980).

Gorman, Michael, 'Manuscript books at Monte Amiata in the eleventh century', *Scriptorium*, 56.2 (2002), pp.225–93.

Grand, Stanley Irwin, *Seven Allegorical Engravings from Giovanni Battista Ferrari's De Florum Cultura (Rome, 1633)* (Madison: University of Wisconsin-Madison, 1985).

Green, Monica H., 'The Four Black Deaths', *American Historical Review*, 125 (2020), pp.1601–31.

Grossman, Max, 'A Case of Double Identity: the Public and Private Faces of the Palazzo Tolomei in Siena', *Journal of the Society of Architectural Historians*, 72.1 (2013), pp.48–77.

Guerrini, Roberto and Seidel, Max (eds), *Sotto il duomo di Siena* (Milan: Silvana, 2003).

Hale, J. R., *War and Society in Renaissance Europe* (Stroud: Sutton Publishing, 1998).

Hankins, James, 'The Virtuous Republic of Francesco Patrizi of Siena', in *Renaissance Politics and Culture: Essays in Honour of Robert Black*, ed. Jonathan Davies and John Monfasani (Leiden: Brill, 2021), pp.59–82.

Harris, Anthony, 'Ruskin and Siena', *The Ruskin Lecture* (St Albans: Brentham Press, 1991).

Hazlitt, William, *Notes of a Journey through France and Italy* (London: Hunt and Clarke, 1826).

Hercolani, Antonio. *Storia e costumi delle contrade di Siena* (Florence: A. Hercolani 1845).

Herlihy, David, *The Black Death and the Transformation of the West* (Cambridge, MA: Harvard University Press, 1997).

Herrick, Marvin T., *Italian Comedy in the Renaissance* (Urbana: University of Illinois Press, 1966).

Heywood, William, *Palio and Ponte* (London: Methuen & Co., 1904).

Hicks, David L., 'Sienese Society in the Renaissance', *Comparative Studies in Society and History*, 2.4 (1960), pp.412–20.
———— 'The Education of a Prince: Ludovico il Moro and the rise of Pandolfo Petrucci', *Studies in the Renaissance*, 8 (1961), pp.88–102.
———— 'Sources of Wealth in Renaissance Siena: Businessmen and Landowners', *Bullettino Senese di Storia Patria*, 93 (1986), pp.9–42.

Hoby, Thomas, *The Travaile and Life of Thomas Hoby, Knight*, ed. Edgar Powell (London: for the Royal Historical Society, 1902).

Hook, Judith, *The Sack of Rome* (London: Macmillan, 1972).
———— 'The Fall of Siena', *History Today*, 23.3 (1973), pp.105–15.
———— *Siena: A City and Its History* (London: Hamish Hamilton, 1979).
———— 'Hapsburg Imperialism and Italian Particularism: The case of Charles V and Siena', *European Studies Review*, 9.3 (1979), pp.283–312.

Hourihane, Colum, *The Grove Encyclopedia of Medieval Art and Architecture* (Oxford: Oxford University Press, 2012).

Howell, James, *Epistolae Ho-Elianae* (London: Humphrey Mosley, 1645).
—— *Instructions for Forreine Travell* [1642], ed. Edward Arber (London: English reprints, 1869).

Hub, Berthold, 'Vedete come è belle la cittade quado è ordinate: Politics and the art of city planning in Republican Siena', *Art as Politics in Late Medieval and Renaissance Siena*, ed. Timothy B. Smith and Judith B. Steinhoff (Abingdon: Routledge, 2016), pp.61–82.

Hunt, Edwin S. and Murray, James M., *A History of Business in Medieval Europe, 1200–1550* (Cambridge: Cambridge University Press, 1999).

Hyde, J. K., *Society and Politics in Medieval Italy* (London: Macmillan, 1973).

Hyman, Timothy, S*ienese Painting* (London: Thames & Hudson, 2003).

Hymes, Robert, 'A Hypothesis on the East Asian Beginnings of the Yersinia pestis Polytomy', *The Medieval Globe*, 1, no.1–2 (2014), pp.285–308.

Al-Idrisi, I*l libro di Ruggero*, trans. Umberto Rizzitano (Palermo: Flaccovio, 1966).

Israëls, Machtelt, S*assetta's Madonna della Neve: an image of patronage* (Leiden: Primavera, 2003).
—— 'Altars on the street: the wool guild, the Carmelites and the feast of Corpus Domini in Siena (1356–1456)', *Renaissance Studies*, 20.2 (2006), pp.180–200.
—— 'Sassetta and the Guglielmi Piccolomini altarpiece in Siena', *Burlington Magazine*, 152, No. 1284 (2010), pp.162–71.
—— 'The Berensons "Connosh" and collect Sienese paintings', *The Bernard and Mary Berenson collection of European paintings at I Tatti*, ed. Carl Brandon Strehlke and Machtelt Israëls (Florence: Officina Libraria, 2015), pp.47–69.
—— 'Mrs Berenson, Mrs Gardner and Miss Toplady: Connoisseurship, Collecting and Commerce in London (1898–1905)', *Visual Resources*, 33.1–2 (2017), pp.158–81.

Jackson, Philippa, 'Parading in public: patrician women and sumptuary law in Renaissance Siena', *Urban History*, 37.3 (2010), pp.452–63.

Jameson, Anna, *Memoirs of Early Italian Painters*, 5 vols (Boston: Houghton Mifflin, 1896).

Jenkens, A. Lawrence, 'Pius II's Nephews and the Politics of Architecture at the End of the Fifteenth Century in Siena', *Bullettino Senese di Storia Patria*, 106 (1999), pp.68–114.
—— 'Michelangelo, the Piccolomini, and Cardinal Francesco's Chapel in Siena Cathedral', *Burlington Magazine*, 144, No. 1197 (2002), pp.752–4.

Jenkins, Marianna, 'The Iconography of the Hall of the Consistory in the Palazzo Pubblico, Siena', *The Art Bulletin*, 54.4 (1972), pp.430–51.

John of Salisbury, *Policraticus*, ed. Clement Charles Julian Webb (Oxford: Clarendon Press, 1909).

Johns, Ann, 'Cistercian Gothic in a Civic Setting: The Translation of the Pointed Arch in Sienese Architecture, 1250–1350', *Art as Politics in Late Medieval And Renaissance Siena*, ed. Timothy B. Smith and Judith B. Steinhoff (Abingdon: Routledge, 2012), pp.39–60.

Jones, P. J., 'Communes and Despots: City-states in late medieval Italy', *Transactions of the Royal Historical Society*, 15 (1965), pp.71–96.

Killerby, Catherine Kovesi, *Sumptuary Law in Italy, 1200–1500* (Oxford: Clarendon Press, 2002).

Knecht, R. J., 'The sword and the pen: Blaise de Monluc and his "Commentaires"', *Renaissance Studies*, 9.1 (1995), pp.104–18.

Koenigsberger, H. G., 'Decadence or Shift? Changes in the Civilization of Italy and Europe in the Sixteenth and Seventeenth Centuries', *Transactions of the Royal Historical Society*, 10 (1960), pp.1–18.

Krautheimer, Richard, *The Rome of Alexander VII* (Princeton: Princeton University Press, 1985).
—— *Three Christian Capitals* (Berkeley: University of California Press, 1987).

Kucher, 'Michael, The Use of Water and its Regulation in Medieval Siena', *Journal of Urban History*, 31.4 (2005), pp.504–36.

Kupfer, Marcia, 'The Lost Wheel Map of Ambrogio Lorenzetti', *The Art Bulletin*, 78.2 (1996), pp.286–310.

Lasansky, D. Medina, 'Urban Editing, Historic Preservation, and Political Rhetoric: The Fascist Redesign of San Gimignano', *Journal of the Society of Architectural Historians*, 63.3 (2004), pp.320–53.

Lassels, Richard, *The voyage of Italy, or, A compleat journey through Italy* (Paris: John Starkey, 1670).

Levenson, J. L., 'Romeo and Juliet before Shakespeare', *Studies in Philology*, 81 (1984), pp.325–47.

Levy, Ariel, 'Niki de Saint Phalle's Tarot Garden', *New Yorker*, 18 April 2016.

Lindsay, Alexander, S*ketches of the History of Christian Art*, 3 vols (London: John Murray, 1847).

Lisini, Alessandro (ed.), *Il constituto del commune di Siena volgarizzato nel MCCCIX–MCCCX* (Siena: Lazzeri, 1903).

Luongo, F. Thomas, 'The Historical Reception of Catherine of Siena', *A Companion to Catherine of Siena* (Leiden and Boston: Brill, 2012), pp.23–45.

Lust, Teresa, *A Blissful Feast* (New York: Pegasus Books, 2020).

McClanan, Anne, 'Bulgarini's Assumption with Doubting Thomas: Art, Trade, and Faith in Post-Plague Siena', *A Faithful Sea: The Religious Cultures of the Mediterranean, 1200–1700*, ed. Adnan A. Husain and K. E. Fleming (Oxford: Oneworld, 2007), pp.65–78.

McClure, George, 'Heresy at Play: Academies and the Literary Underground in Counter-Reformation Siena', *Renaissance Quarterly*, 63.4 (2010), pp.1151–1207.
———— *Parlour Games and the Public Life of Women in Renaissance Italy* (Toronto: University of Toronto Press, 2017).

Machiavelli, Niccolò, *Discourses on the First Decade of Titus Livius* (online).
———— *The Prince*, trans. W. K. Marriott (London: J. M. Dent & Sons, 1908).

Mack, Charles R., 'Beyond the Monumental: the Semiotics of Papal Authority in Renaissance Pienza', *Southeastern College Art Conference Review*, 16.2 (2012), pp.124–50.

Maginnis, Hayden B. J., 'The Lost Facade Frescoes from Siena's Ospedale di S. Maria della Scala', *Zeitschrift für Kunstgeschichte*, 51.2 (1988), pp.180–94.
———— *The World of the Early Sienese Painter* (University Park: Pennsylvania State University Press, 2003).

Maltese, Corrado (ed.), *Trattati di Architettura, Ingegneria e Arte Militare (di Francesco di Giorgio Martini)* (Milan: Il polifilo, 1967).

Mamone, Sara, 'Most Serene Brothers-Princes-Impresarios: Theater in Florence under the Management and Protection of Mattias, Giovan Carlo and Leopoldo de' Medici', *Journal of Seventeenth-Century Music*, 9.1 (2003) (online).

Marchetti Valerio, *Gruppi Eretici Senesi del Cinquecento* (Florence: La Nuova Italia, 1975).

Mariani, Riccardo, *Fascismo e 'città nuove'* (Milano: Feltrinelli Editore, 1976).

Marocchi, Mario, *Monaci scrittori: San Salvatore al Monte Amiata tra Impero e Papato (secoli VIII–XIII)* (Florence: Firenze University Press, 2014).

Martines, Lauro, *Power and Imagination: City-States in Renaissance Italy* (London: Peregrine, 1979).

Matar, Hisham, *A Month in Siena* (London: Viking, 2019).

Matassa, Mario, *Tuscany* (London: Phaidon, 2011).

Medicus, Gustav F., 'Domenico Beccafumi and the Sienese Tradition', Indiana University PhD, 1992.

Medioli, Francesca, 'To take or not to take the veil: selected Italian case histories, the Renaissance and after', *Women in Italian Renaissance Culture and Society* (Oxford: Legenda, 2000), pp.122–37.

Milanesi, Gaetano, *Documenti per la storia dell'arte senese*, I (Doornspijk: Davaco, 1969).

Miller, Elisabeth and Graves, Alun, 'Rethinking the Petrucci Pavement', *Renaissance Studies*, 24.1 (2010), pp.94–118.

Misciatelli, Piero, *Studi Senesi* (Siena: La Diana, 1931).

Mitchell, R. J., 'English Student Life in Early Renaissance Italy', *Italian Studies*, 7.1 (1952), pp.62–81.
––, *The Laurels and the Tiara: Pope Pius II, 1458–1464* (London: Harvill Press, 1962).

Monnas, Lisa, *Merchants, Princes and Painters* (New Haven and London: Yale University Press, 2008).

Montanari, Massimo, *L'alimentazione contadina nell'alto Medioevo* (Naples: Liguori, 1985).
———— *Convivio: storia e cultura dei piaceri della tavola: dall'antichità al medioevo* (Rome: Laterza, 1989).
———— *Let the Meatballs Rest and Other Stories About Food and Culture*, trans. Beth Archer Brombert (New York: Columbia University Press, 2012).

Mormando, Franco, *The Preacher's Demons: Bernardino of Siena and the Social Underworld of Early Renaissance Italy* (Chicago and London: University of Chicago Press, 1999).

Moryson, Fynes, *An Itinerary Written by Fynes Moryson* (London: John Beale, 1617).

Muir, Kim and Khandekar, Narayan, 'The technical examination of a painting that passed through the hands of Sienese restorer and forger Icilio Federico Joni', *Journal of the American Institute for Conservation*, 45.1 (2005), pp.31–49.

Muratori, Lodovico (ed.), *Cronache Senesi, Rerum Italicarum Scriptores*, NS 15, pt 4 (Bologna: Nicola Zanichetli, 1939).

Needham, Joseph, *Science and Civilisation in China*, IV.2 (Cambridge: Cambridge University Press, 1965).

Nevola, Fabrizio, 'Lieto e trionphante per la città': experiencing a mid-fifteenth-century imperial triumph along Siena's Strada Romana', *Renaissance Studies*, 17.4 (2003), pp.581–606.

—— *Siena: Constructing the Renaissance City* (New Haven and London: Yale University Press, 2007).

—— '"El papa non verrà": the failed triumphal entry of Leo X into Siena', *Sixteenth Century Journal*, 42.2 (2011), pp.427–46.

—— 'Surveillance and Control of the Street in Renaissance Italy', *I Tatti Studies in the Italian Renaissance*, 16.1–2 (2013), pp.85–106.

—— *Street Life in Renaissance Italy* (New Haven and London: Yale University Press, 2020).

Norman, Diana, *Siena and the Virgin: Art and Politics in a Late Medieval City State* (New Haven; London: Yale University Press, 1999).

Oen, Maria H., 'Ambivalent Images of Authorship', in *Sanctity and Female Authorship: Birgitta of Sweden & Catherine of Siena*, ed. Maria H. Oen and Unn Falkeid (New York: Routledge, 2020), pp.113–37.

Origo, Benedetta, *La Foce: a Garden and Landscape in Tuscany* (Philadelphia: University of Pennsylvania Press, 2001).

Origo, Iris, 'The Domestic Enemy: The Eastern Slaves in Tuscany in the Fourteenth and Fifteenth Centuries', *Speculum*, 30.3 (1955), pp.321–66.

—— *The World of San Bernardino* (London: The Reprint Society, 1964).

—— *Images and Shadows: Part of a Life* (Boston: Nonpareil, 1999).

—— *War in Val d'Orcia* (London: Pushkin Press, 2017).

Palmer, Caroline, 'A fountain of the richest poetry, Anna Jameson, Elizabeth Eastlake and the Rediscovery of Early Christian Art', *Visual Resources*, 33:1–2 (2017), pp.48–73.

Parsons, Gerald, 'O Maria, la tua Siena difendi: the Porta della Riconoscenza of Siena Cathedral', *Zeitschrift für Kunstgeschichte*, 64.2 (2002), pp.153–76.

—— *The Cult of Saint Catherine of Siena* (London: Routledge, 2018).

—— *Siena, Civil Religion and the Sienese* (Abingdon, Routledge, 2021).

Partington, J. R., *A History of Greek Fire and Gunpowder* (Cambridge: Heffer, 1960).

Pasqui, Ubaldo, *Documenti per la Storia della Citta di Arezzo* (Florence, Vieusseux, 1899).

Payne, Alina A., 'Architectural Criticism, Science, and Visual Eloquence: Teofilo Gallaccini in Seventeenth-Century Siena', *Journal of the Society of Architectural Historians*, 58.2 (1999), pp.146–69.

—— *Vision and Its Instruments: Art, Science, and Technology in Early Modern Europe* (University Park: Pennsylvania State University Press, 2015).

Pellegrini, Michele, 'Sancta pastoralis dignitas: poteri, funzioni e prestigio dei vescovi a Siena nell'altomedioevo', in Giampaolo Francesconi (ed.), *Vescovo e città nell'Alto Medioevo: quadri generali e realtà toscane* (Pistoia: Società Pistoiese di storia patria, 2001), pp.257–96.

Pepper, Simon and Adams, Nicholas, *Firearms and Fortifications: Military Architecture and Siege Warfare in Sixteenth-Century Siena* (Chicago: University of Chicago Press, 1986).

Pérès, Henri, *La Poésie Andalouse en Arabe Classique au xie siècle* (Paris: Adrien-maisonneuve, 1937).

Petrioli, Piergiacomo, 'The Brownings and their Sienese Circle', *Studies in Browning and his Circle*, 21 (2001), pp.78–109.

Petrucci, Daniele and Petrucci, Francesco, *The Chigi Palace in Ariccia* (Arricia: Arti Grafiche, 2019).

Phillips, C. P., 'The Crete Senesi: a vanishing landscape?', *Landscape and Urban Planning*, 41 (1998), pp.19–26.

Piccini, Gabriella, 'Economy and Society in Southern Tuscany in the Late Middle Ages: Amiata and the Maremma', in T. W. Blomquist and M. F. Mazzaoui (eds), *The 'Other Tuscany': Essays in the History of Lucca, Pisa, and Siena During the Thirteenth, Fourteenth, and Fifteenth Centuries* (Kalamazoo: Medieval Institute Publications, 1994), pp.215–33.

Piccolomini, Aeneas Sylvius, *Memoirs of a Renaissance Pope: The Commentaries of Pius II*, trans. Florence A. Gragg, ed. Leona C. Gabel (London: Allen & Unwin, 1959).

—— *The Two Lovers: The Goodly History of lady Lucrece and her lover Eurialius*, ed. Emily O'Brien and Kenneth R. Bartlett (Ottowa: Dovehouse Editions, 1999).

Pierini, Marco, 'Giuseppe Partini e Tito Sarrocchi. Restauri e progettazione in trenta anni di collaborazione', *Bullettino Senese di Storia Patria* (1993/1995), pp.496–517.

Pinto, Giuliano, '"Honour" and "Profit": Landed Property and Trade in Medieval Siena', *City and Countryside in Late Medieval and Renaissance Italy*, ed. Trevor Dean and Chris Wickham (London: Hambledon Press, 1990), pp.81–91.

Platzer, David, 'Edward Hutton', *Apollo*, 143, no.409 (March 1996), pp.40–43.

Politol, R. et al., 'Safety aspects and behavior of Siena palio horses', *Journal of Veterinary Behavior*, 6.5 (2011), pp.293–4.

Pope-Hennessy, John, *Learning to Look* (London: Heinemann, 1991).

Prager, Frank D. and Scaglia, Gustina, *Mariano Taccola and His Book 'De ingeneis'* (Cambridge, MA: MIT Press, 1972).

Procacci, Giuliano, *History of the Italian People* (London: Penguin, 1991).

Prudentius, *Opera*, 2 vols, trans. H. J. Thompson (Cambridge, MA: Harvard University Press, 1962–3).

Raymond, John, *An itinerary contayning a voyage, made through Italy, in the yeares 1646, and 1647* (London: Humphrey Moseley, 1648).

Reardon, Colleen, *Holy Concord Within Sacred Walls: Nuns and Music in Siena, 1575–1700* (Oxford: Oxford University Press, 2002).
—— *A Sociable Moment: Opera and Festive Culture in Baroque Siena* (Oxford: Oxford University Press, 2016).

Reis, Jaime, 'Economic Growth, Human Capital Formation and Consumption in Western Europe Before 1800', *Living Standards in the Past: New Perspectives on Well-Being in Asia and Europe*, ed. Robert C. Allen et al. (Oxford: Oxford University Press. 2005), pp.195–225.

Reti, Ladislao, 'Francesco di Giorgio Martini's Treatise on Engineering and Its Plagiarists', *Technology and Culture*, 4.3 (Summer, 1963), pp.287–98.

Reynolds, Robert L., 'Origins of Modern Business Enterprise: Medieval Italy', *Journal of Economic History*, 12.4 (1952), pp.350–65.

Rhodes, Dennis E., 'Sir Kenelm Digby and Siena', *British Museum Quarterly*, 21 (1958), pp.61–3.

Ridolfi, Maria A. Ceppari, Ciampolini, Marco, and Turrini, Patrizia, *L'immagine del Palio: Storia, Cultura, e Rappresentazione del Rito di Siena* (Siena: Monte dei Paschi, 2001).

Romano, Dennis, 'A Depiction of Male Same-Sex Seduction in Ambrogio Lorenzetti's "Effects of Bad Government" fresco', *Journal of the History of Sexuality*, 21.1 (2012), pp.1–15.

Romer, Elisabeth, *The Tuscan Year: Life and Food in an Italian Valley* (London: Weidenfeld & Nicolson, 1984).

Rondoni, Giuseppe, *Tradizioni popolari e leggende di un commune medioevale e del suo contado, Siena e l'antico contado senese* (Bologna: Forni Editore, 1968).

Rosand, Ellen, *Opera in Seventeenth-Century Venice: The Creation of a Genre* (Berkeley: University of California Press 2007).

Rosselli, J. 'The Castrati as a Professional Group and as a Social Phenomenon, 1550–1850', *Acta Musicologica*, 60 (1988), pp.143–79.

Ruggiero, Guido, *The Boundaries of Eros* (New York: Oxford University Press, 1989).

Ruskin, John, *The Diaries of John Ruskin*, I, ed. Joan Evans and J. Howard Whitehouse (Oxford: Clarendon Press, 1956).

Rutigliano, Antonio, 'Lorenzetti's Golden Mean (The Riformatori of Siena, 1368–1385)', New York University PhD, 1989.

Rykwert, Joseph, 'On an (Egyptian?) Misreading of Francesco di Giorgio's', *RES: Anthropology and Aesthetics* (1981), pp.78–83.

Sanchez, Expiración García, 'Agriculture in Muslim Spain', in *The Legacy of Muslim Spain*, ed. Salma Khadra Jayyusi (Leiden: Brill, 1992), pp.987–99.

Sarfatti, Margherita, 'Per la Belleza di Siena: Una Proposta', *La Diana*, 3 (1927).

Scaglia, Giustina, 'The Development of Francesci di Giorgio's Treatises in Siena', *Les Traités d'Architecture de la Renaissance*, ed. Jean Guillaume (Paris: Picard, 1988), pp.91–5.

Scappini, Chiara E., 'History, Preservation and Reconstruction in Siena: the Fonte Gaia from Renaissance to Modern Times', Rutgers University PhD, 2011.

Schevill, Ferdinand, *Siena: The Story of a Medieval Commune* (New York: Charles Scribner's Sons, 1909).

Sella, Domenico, *Italy in the Seventeenth Century* (Harlow: Longmans, 1997).

Shaw, Christine, 'Politics and institutional innovation in Siena, 1480–1489', *Bullettino Senese di Storia Patria*, 103 (1996), pp.9–102.
—— *Popular Government and Oligarchy in Renaissance Italy* (Leiden and Boston: Brill, 2006).
—— and Mallett, Michael, *The Italian Wars* (Abingdon: Routledge, 2019).

Shepherd, Laurie, 'Siena 1531, Genesis of a European Heroine', *Quaderni d'italianistica*, 26.1 (2005), pp.3–19.

Silverman, Sydel, 'On the Uses of History in Anthropology: The "palio" of Siena', *American Ethnologist*, 6.3 (1979), pp.413–36.

Skippon, Philip, *An Account of a Journey Made Thro' Part of the Low-Countries, Germany, Italy and France* (London: Henry Lintot and John Osborn, 1746).

Sliwka, Jennifer, 'Armet se duritia: Domenico Beccafumi and the Politics of Punishment', *Art as Politics in Late Medieval and Renaissance Siena*, ed. Timothy B. Smith and Judith B. Steinhoff (Abingdon: Routledge, 2016), pp.193-4.

Słodczyk, Rozalia, 'Modes of ekphrasis: Simone Martini's Sienese Condottiere through the eyes of Zbigniew Herbert and Gustaw Herling-Grudziński', *Przekładaniec*, special issue, (2018), pp.120-39.

Smith, Christine, *Architecture in the Culture of Early Humanism: Ethics, Aesthetics, and Eloquence, 1400-1470* (Oxford: Oxford University Press, 1992), pp.98-129.

Smith, Timothy B., 'Politics and Antiquity in the Baptist's Chapel Façade', *Art as Politics in Late Medieval and Renaissance Siena*, ed. Timothy B. Smith and Judith B. Steinhoff (Abingdon: Routledge, 2012), pp.141-62.

Southard, Edna Carter, 'Ambrogio Lorenzetti's Frescoes in the Sala della Pace: A Change of Names', *Mitteilungen des Kunsthistorischen Institutes in Florenz*, 24.3 (1980), pp.361-5.

Sox, David, 'The Strange Case of Lucy Olcott Perkins', *Apollo*, 140, no.394 (1 December 1994), pp.43-4.

Sozzini, Alessandro, *Diario delle cose avvenute in Siena: dai 20 Luglio ai 28 Guigno 1555* (Firenze: Gio. Pietro Vieusseux, 1842).

Spufford, Peter, *Money and Its Uses in Medieval Europe* (Cambridge: Cambridge University Press, 1988).

Squatriti, Paolo, *Landscape and Change in Early Medieval Italy: Chestnuts, Economy and Culture* (Cambridge: Cambridge University Press, 2013).

Steinhoff, Judith B., *Sienese Painting after the Black Death, Artistic Pluralism, Politics, and the New Art Market* (Cambridge: Cambridge University Press, 2006).
——— 'Urban Images and Civic Identity in Medieval Sienese Painting', *Art as Politics in Late Medieval And Renaissance Siena*, ed. Timothy B. Smith and Judith B. Steinhoff (Abingdon: Routledge, 2012), pp.15-38.

Steinmann, Linda, 'Shah 'Abbas and the Royal Silk Trade, 1599-1629', *Bulletin of the British Society for Middle Eastern Studies*, 14.1 (1987), pp.68-74.

Stephens, Janet, 'Becoming a Blonde in Renaissance Italy', *Journal of the Walters Art Museum*, 74 (online).

Strehlke, Carl Brandon, 'Art and Culture in Renaissance Siena', in Keith Christiansen, Laurence B. Kanter, and Carl Brandon Strehlke (eds), *Painting in Renaissance Siena* (New York: Abrams, 1988).

Stourton, James, *Great Collectors of Our Time: Art Collecting Since 1945* (London: Scala, 2007).

Syson, Luke, *Renaissance Siena: Art for a City* (London: National Gallery, 2007).

Szymanska, Joanna, 'Transformation of the Urban Fabric in Siena During Fascism: Sventramento and Risanamento of Salicotto, formerly known as The Jewish Ghetto', New Jersey Institute of Technology MA, 2000.

Tacitus, *Histories*, trans. C. H. Moore and J. Jackson (Cambridge, MA: Harvard University Press, 1931).

Tarabotti, Arcangela, *Paternal Tyranny*, ed. and trans. Letizia Panizza (Chicago: University of Chicago Press, 2004).

Thurber, Allison Clark, 'Female urban reclusion in Siena at the time of Catherine of Siena', *A Companion to Catherine of Siena* (Leiden and Boston: Brill, 2012), pp.47-72.

Tilmouth, Michael, 'Music on the travels of an English merchant, Robert Bargrave (1628-61)', *Music and Letters*, 53.2 (1972), pp.142-59.

Tobey, Elizabeth, 'The Palio in Renaissance Art, Thought, and Culture', University of Maryland PhD, 2005.
——— 'The Palio Banner and the Visual Culture of Horse Racing in Renaissance Italy', *International Journal of the History of Sport*, 28:8-9 (2011), pp.1269-82.

Tommasi, Giugurta, *Historia di Siena* (Venice: Giovanni Battista Pulciani, 1625).

Tylus, Jane, 'The Work of Italian Theater', *Renaissance Drama*, NS 40 (2012), pp.171-84.
——— *Siena: City of Secrets* (Chicago: University of Chicago Press, 2015).
——— 'St Catherine and Siena', *A Companion to Late Medieval and Early Modern Siena*, ed. Santa Casciani and Heather Richardson (Leiden: Brill, 2021), pp.69-82.

Valenti, Marco, 'The missed opportunity of a town: Siena, excavations beneath the cathedral', *Il Duomo di Siena*, ed. Gabriele Castiglia (Oxford: Archaeopress, 2014), pp.1-7.

Van der Ploeg, Kees, *Art, Architecture, and Liturgy: Siena Cathedral in the Middle Ages* (Groningen: Egbert Forsten, 1993).

Van Os, Henk, 'Painting in a house of glass: the altarpieces of Pienza', *Simiolus: Netherlands Quarterly for the History of Art*, 17.1 (1987), pp.23-38.

Vignali, Antonio, *La Cazzaria. The Book of the Prick*, ed. and trans. Ian Frederick Moulton (New York: Routledge, 2003).

Voigtländer, Nico and Voth, Hans-Joachim, 'Gifts of Mars: Warfare and Europe's early rise to riches', *Journal of Economic Perspectives*, 27.4 (2013), pp.165-86.

Von Klenze, Camillo, 'The Growth of Interest in Early Italian Masters, from Tischbein to Ruskin', *Modern Philology*, 14.2 (1906), pp.207–74.

Waley, Daniel Philip, *Siena and the Sienese in the Thirteenth Century* (Cambridge: Cambridge University Press, 1991).

Walker, Donald M., 'Human Skeletal Remains from Poggio Imperiale, Poggibonsi (Si)', *Archeologia Medievale*, 23 (1996), pp.715–38.

Ward, Benedicta, *Miracles and the Medieval Mind* (Philadelphia: University of Pennsylvania Press, 1989).

Ward-Perkins, J. B., 'Etruscan Engineering: Road Building, Water Supply, and Drainage', in *Hommages à Albert Grenier, Collection Latomus*, 58, pt 3 (1962), pp.1636–43.

Wegner, Susan E., 'The rise of St Catherine of Siena as an Intercessor for the Sienese', *Renaissance Siena: Art in Context*, ed. A. Lawrence Jenkens (Kirkville: Truman State University Press, 2005), pp.173–95.

Weiss, R., 'The Sienese Philologists of the cinquecento – a bibliographical introduction', *Italian Studies*, 3.1–2 (1946), pp.34–49.

Wenz, Andrea Beth, 'The Discussion and Transmission of Reformed Religious Beliefs in Early Modern Siena', in *A Companion to Late Medieval and Early Modern Siena*, ed. Santa Casciani and Heather Hayton (Leiden and Boston: Brill, 2021), pp.132–53.

Westropp, J. E., *Summer Experience of Rome, Perugia and Siena* (London: William Skeffington, 1861).

White, John, 'Measurement, Design and Carpentry in Duccio's Maestà, Part I', *The Art Bulletin*, 55.3 (1973), pp.334–66.
——— 'Carpentry and Design in Duccio's Workshop: The London and Boston Triptychs', *Journal of the Warburg and Courtauld Institutes*, 36 (1973), pp.92–105.

White, Lynn Jr, 'The Flavor of Early Renaissance Technology', *Developments in the Early Renaissance*, ed. Bernard S. Levy (Albany: State University of New York Press, 1972), pp.36–57.

Wiens, Gavin T., 'Making Siena: Art and State Formation, 1404–1487', Johns Hopkins University PhD, 2019.

Wildman, Stephen and Christian, John, *Edward Burne-Jones, Victorian Artist-Dreamer* (New York: Metropolitan Museum of Art, 1998).

Wilkins, Ernest H., 'On Petrarch's Appreciation of Art', *Speculum*, 36.2 (1961), pp.299–301.

Wollason, George Hyde (ed.), *The Englishman in Italy* (Oxford: Clarendon Press, 1909).

Zambrini, Francesco (ed.), *Il libro della cucina del sec. XIV* (Bologna: Romagnoli, 1863).

Zanatta, Alfredo et al., 'Occupational markers and pathology of the castrato singer Gaspare Pacchierotti (1740–1821)', *Science Report*, 6, 28463 (2016) (online).

Zdekauer, Ludovico, *Il constituto del Comune di Siena dell'anno 1262* (Milan: Ulrico Hoepli, 1897).

Zohary, Daniel and Hopf, Matia, *Domestication of Plants in the Old World*, 3rd edn (Oxford: Oxford University Press, 2000).

Zsoldos, Attila, 'A Sienese Goldsmith as Alispán of Szepes: Italians in the service of the Druget Palatines', *Világ Történet*, 1 (2017), pp.53–74.

NOTES

Preface

1 Matar, p.50.

1 Geography and Prehistory

1 Acchili et al., pp.759–68.
2 Tylus 2015, p.28.
3 Ward-Perkins, pp.636–43.
4 Boucheron, pp.96–8.
5 Valenti, p.4.
6 Benvoglienti, p.20.
7 Cairolo and Carli, p.46.
8 Tacitus, IV.45, pp.84–7.
9 Krautheimer 1987, p.100.
10 Davis, pp.14–26.
11 Pasqui, p.23.
12 Schevill, p.88.
13 Prudentius, II, pp.98–101.
14 Ward, p.124.
15 Birch, p.39.
16 Boniface, pp.38, 140.

2 Early Christian Siena

1 Pellegrini, pp.257–96.
2 Bacci, p.172, Steinhoff 2006, p.140.
3 Baron, pp.1449–51.
4 Steinhoff 2006, p.59.

5 Norman, p.9.
6 Epstein, pp.103–56.
7 Walker, pp.724–5.
8 Romer, p.152.
9 Zambrini, p.10.
10 Montanari, p.299.
11 Gismondi et al., pp.556–64.

3 New Beginnings

1 Pérès, p.216.
2 Campbell, p.81.
3 Martines, pp.22–6.
4 Schevill, p.57.
5 Hyde, p.97.
6 Van der Ploeg, p.16.
7 Hook 1979, p.57
8 Al-Idrisi, p.101.
9 Norman, pp.11–12.
10 De Wesselow, p.199.
11 Waley, pp.72–4.
12 Cammarosano, pp.34–5.
13 English, pp.1–3.

4 Siena, City of the Virgin

1 Muratori, p.202.
2 There is another version of the Montaperti account in Muratori, pp.56–61. For a comparative

analysis of the different versions: their interpolations, their dates of origin and their historical accuracy, see Garrison, pp.23–58.
3 Webb, pp.251–75, Parsons, 2021, pp.1–12.
4 Franco 2021, p.45.
5 Waley, pp.116–17.
6 Hyde, p.129.
7 Grossman, p.53.
8 Waley, p.103.
9 Bowsky, p.64.
10 English, p.41.
11 Derbes, pp.190–204.
12 Printo, pp.81–92.
13 Reynolds, pp.350–65.
14 Johns, pp.40–43.
15 Tylus 2015, p.174.
16 Hook 1979, pp.120–1.
17 Martines, p.37.
18 Ibid., p.41.
19 Waley, p.6.
20 Levenson, pp.325–47.
21 Hook 1979, p.10; Balestracci and Piccini, p.56.
22 Hook 1979, p.11.
23 Waley, p.7.
24 Grossman, pp.50–3.
25 Waley, p.10.

26 Franco 2014, pp.255–70.

27 Checchini and Neri, p.29.

28 Franco 2014, p.258.

29 Franco 2021, pp.31–60.

30 Bowsky 1964, p.13.

31 Denley 1990, pp.93–107.

32 Waley, p.140.

33 Foster, pp.266–74.

34 Martines, p.104.

35 Translator anonymous: https://
blogs.transparent.com/italian/a-
poem-for-january/

5   The Development of the
    Countryside

1 Origo 1999, p.200.

2 Balestracci, p.71.

3 Ibid., p.73.

4 Beckford, II, p.73.

5 Balestracci, pp.29–31.

6 Ibid., p.61.

7 Zohary and Hopf, p.29.

8 Squatriti, p.48.

9 Piccini, pp.215–33.

10 Gorman, pp.225–93.

11 Described by Marocchi.

12 Tylus 2015, p.42.

13 Baldari et al., pp.1246–7.

14 Bowsky 1964, p.10.

15 Caferro 1994, p.96.

16 Bowsky 1981, p 195.

17 Piccini, p.219.

18 Lust, pp.125–7.

19 Giontella et al., p.1.

20 Columella, VI.I.2, II, pp.124–5.

21 Matassa, p.220.

22 Phillips, pp.19–26.

23 Bowsky 1981, p.5.

24 Glasfurd, p.111.

6   The Making of the City

1 Muratori, p.373.

2 Glasfurd, p.56.

3 Bowsky 1967, p.7.

4 Campbell, p.9.

5 Campbell, p.147.

6 Bowsky 1981, p.307.

7 Brandi (ed.), p.415.

8 Muratori, p.258.

9 Milanesi, I, p.181.

10 Johns, pp.39–40.

11 Matar, p.12.

12 Hub, p.67.

13 Braunfels, p.61.

14 Steinhoff 2006, p.31.

15 Scappini, p.50.

16 Ghiberti, I, p.63.

17 Cairolo and Carli, p.49.

18 Di Battista, p.71, Lisini d. v,
r. cdviii (it is divided into six
'distinctions' (d.) and subdivided
into rubrics (r.)).

19 Bowsky 1981, p.15.

20 Waley, pp, 10–11.

21 Di Battista, p.133.

22 Origo 1964, pp.192–3.

23 Denley 1983 pp.193–208.

24 Waley, p.159.

25 Denley 1983, Di Battista, p.233.

26 Di Battista, p.162, Bowsky, 1970,
p.215.

27 Epstein, pp.31–2, 40.

28 Bowsky 1981, p.200.

29 Waley, p.11.

30 Nevola 2007, pp.22–4.

31 Alberti, p.133.

32 Hook 1979, p.27.

33 Kucher, p.514.

34 Carus-Wilson, p.616.

35 Tommasi, pp.171–2, Kucher,
p.520.

36 Schevill, p.123.

37 Bowsky 1981, p.175.

38 Schevill, pp.118–19.

39 Boucheron, p.108.

40 Bowsky 1981, p.201.

41 Ibid., p.174.

42 Prager and Scaglia, pp.10, 34–5.

7   The Duomo

1 Van der Ploeg, p.148, Cecchini
and Neri, p.8.

2 These new discoveries are
described in Guerrini and Seidel.

3 Carli, p.38.

4 Harris, p.3.

5 Carli, pp.39–43.

6 Hook 1979, pp.56–7.

7 Van der Ploeg, p.39 and fig. 7.

8 Ibid., p.46.

9 Parsons 2002, pp.153–76.

10 Bartoli et al., p.521.

11 Carli, p.8.

12 Van der Ploeg, p.51.

13 Ibid., p.38.

14 Moryson, p.162.

15 Hook 1979, p.54.

16 Waley, p.132.

17 Van der Ploeg, p.32, Israëls
2003 describes this unusual
commission.

18 di Battista, p.104.

19 Aronow, p.4.

20 Lassels, p.237.

8 Early Sienese Art

1 Hyman, p.17.

2 Derbes, pp.190–204.

3 Dini, Angelini and Sani, pp.16–17.

4 Hyman, p.23.

5 Dini, Angelini and Sani, p.28, Hyman, p.25.

6 Muratori, p.313.

7 Carli, p.77.

8 White 1973, p.335.

9 Norman, p.69.

10 Ibid., p.87.

11 Syson, p.320.

12 Smith 2012, p.144.

13 Nevola 2013, p.103.

14 Milanesi, p.218.

15 Wilkins, p.301.

16 Jameson, V, pp.31–2.

17 Westropp, pp.261–2.

18 Pope-Hennessy, p.52.

19 Matar, p.7.

20 Ibid., p.80.

21 Słodczyk, p.128.

22 Kupfer, pp.297–301.

23 Debby, p.276.

24 Boucheron, pp.30–2.

25 Southard, pp.361–5.

26 Di Battista, p.71, Lisini d. v, r. cdviii (it is divided into six 'distinctions" (d.) and subdivided into rubrics (r.)).

27 Romano, pp.1–15.

28 Debby, p.279.

29 Hook 1979, pp.104–5.

30 Israëls 2010, pp.166–7.

31 Bomford 1990, pp.50, 51, 89.

32 Maginnis 2003, p.15, Hyman, p.188.

33 White 1973, pp.92–105.

34 Baxandall, pp.20–2.

35 Cohn 1997, pp.265–9, 279.

36 Steinhoff 2006, pp.82–107.

37 Hyman, p.124.

38 McClanan, pp.67–8.

39 Steinhoff 2006, p.67.

40 Ibid., p.58, Maginnis, 1988, pp.180–94.

41 Steinhoff 2006, p.60.

42 Hyman, p.143.

43 Israëls 2006, p.192.

44 Israëls 2010, pp.162, 169.

45 Norman, p.89.

46 Hyman, p.13.

47 Hyman, pp.209–11.

48 Cagliaritono, p.88.

49 Hourihane, p.93.

50 Zsoldos, p.53.

9 The Black Death and After

1 Hook 1979, p.36.

2 Bowsky 1964, pp.7, 9.

3 Eisen et al., pp.941–3, Green, pp.1601–31.

4 Cui et al., p.577.

5 Green, p.1610.

6 Ibid., p.1616.

7 Ibid., p.1618, Hymes, pp.285–308.

8 Green, p.1267.

9 Campbell, p.251.

10 Cohn 2013, p.199.

11 Herlihy, p.26.

12 Cohn 2002, pp.713, 726, 715.

13 Ell, p.564.

14 Cohn 2013, p.197.

15 Translated in Bowsky 1971, p.13.

16 Muratori, p.555.

17 Cohn 1997, p.31.

18 Cohn 1988, p.39.

19 Cohn 2002, p.734.

20 Cohn 1988, p.70.

21 Friedman, p.331.

22 Campbell, p.363.

23 Rutigliano, p.129, Caferro, 1994, p.96.

24 Muratori, p.637.

25 Ibid., pp.653–4, 753.

26 Caferro 1994, pp.90, 97.

27 Fochesato, pp.1031–61.

28 Caferro 1994a. p.230.

29 Caferro 2008 p.182.

30 John of Salisbury, VI.17, p.45. 'quod urbem Senensium… construxerint, non modo fides historiae sed celebris traditio est'.

31 Cagliaritano, p.13.

32 Zdekauer, p.80, Gigli, II, p.223.

33 Beneš, p.90.

34 There are a number of other versions. For a discussion of dating and differences in language see Rondoni, p.15.

10 Sienese Saints and Heretics

1 Burke, p.460.

2 Thurber, pp.47–8.

3 Parsons 2018, p.15.

4 Luongo, p.24.

5 Ibid., p.25.

6 Parsons 2018 , p.11.

7 Oen, pp.113–37.

8 Gardner, pp.50, 56, Parsons, 2018, p.31.

9 Tylus 2021, pp.76–7.

10 Freuler, p.573.

11 Muratori, p.857.

12 Origo 1964, pp.22, 25, 45, 48.

13 Ibid., 1964, p.151.

14 Mormando, p.169.

15 Gardner, p.89.

16 Mormando, p.130.

17 Hook 1972, p.116.

18 Bowsky, 1981 p.76.

19 Belladonna, pp.377–85.

20 Marchetti, pp.51–67; Wenz, pp.132–53.

II Pius II and the Renaissance in Siena

1 Tylus 2015, p.64.

2 Bowsky 1964, p.21.

3 Hicks 1986, pp.9–42.

4 Cohn 1988 p.48.

5 Bowsky 1981, pp.205–6.

6 Hicks 1986, pp.28–32.

7 Pinto, pp.81–91.

8 Goldthwaite, pp.29–30.

9 Hunt and Murray, p.148.

10 Capatti and Montanari, p.36.

11 Bowsky 1981, p.186.

12 Montanari 2012, p.25.

13 Montanari 1989, p.396.

14 Butler, p.180, Capatti and Montanari, p.51.

15 Spufford, pp.245, 247.

16 Brown, pp.761–80.

17 Brown, p.764; Cohn, 2009, pp.110–12.

18 Capatti and Montanari, p.11.

19 Ibid., p.38.

20 Castelvetro, pp.66, 128.

21 Sanchez, p.988.

22 Bianco, pp.209–51.

23 Capatti and Montanari, p.41.

24 Romer, p.106.

25 Matassa, p.184.

26 Capatti and Montanari, p.51–3.

27 Ibid., p.8.

28 Ibid., p.37.

29 Zambrini, pp.73–4, 75.

30 Franceschi, pp.95–123.

31 Steinmann, p.70, Monnas, p.7.

32 'Avuto rispecto quanto l'arte della seta sia cosa honorata, et facci grande comodo et utilità nelle città dov'è moltiplicata (et questo per experientia si vede per quello piccolo principio che infin da ora è fatto nella nostra città) et paia cosa honorevole et utilissima a provvedere che la detta arte della seta quanto si può crescha et augumenti.' Banchi, pp.121–2.

33 Tobey 2011, p.1272.

34 Hicks 1986, p.28.

35 Nevola 2007, pp.8–9.

36 Ibid., pp.36, 38.

37 Nevola 2007, p.7.

38 Syson, p.61.

39 Mitchell 1952, p.74.

40 Mitchell 1962, p.52.

41 Ibid., p.68.

42 Glendinning, pp.101–20.

43 Piccolomini 1999, pp.124–5.

44 Nevola 2020, p.247.

45 Syson, p.216.

46 Origo 2001, p.10.

47 Nevola 2007, p.43.

48 Nevola 2003, p.589.

49 Casanova, p.52.

50 Nevola, 2007, pp.64–5.

51 Piccolomini 1959, pp.102–3.

52 Nevola 2007, p.65.

53 Monnas, p.231.

54 Nevola 2007, p.71.

55 Ibid., p.75.

56 Nevola 2020, p.241.

57 Jenkens 1999, pp.68–114.

58 Wegner, pp.173–95.

59 Mitchell, 1962, p.234.

60 Ascheri and Franco, p.74.

61 Syson, p.24.

62 Mitchell 1962, p.210.

63 Alberti, p.9.

64 Smith, p.100.

65 Mack, p.126.

66 Ibid., p.129.

67 Chambers, pp.28–31.

68 Mack, p.134.

69 Mitchell 1962, p.245.

70 'la bellezza delle donne senesi è proverbiale'. Misciatelli, p.369, Syson, p.11.

71 Christiansen, Kanter and Strehlke, p.296.

72 Stephens (online); Baltimore, The Walters Art Museum, MS W.478, f. 24 r-v, 265.

73 www.sites.eca.ed.ac.uk/ renaissancecosmetics/cosmetics-recipes/skin/

74 Syson, p.206.

75 Killerby, p.121.

76 Bridgeman, pp.216–17.

77 www.liverpoolmuseums.org.uk/ artifact/st-bernardino-preaching

78 Jackson, pp.452–63.

79 Da Biscicci, p.73.

80 Boucheron, p.27.

81 Syson, p.54.

12 Pandolfo the Magnificent and High Renaissance Siena

1 Hicks 1960, pp.415–17.

2 Jenkens 1999, pp.68–114.

3 Shaw 2006, p.7.

4 Jones, pp.71–96.

5 Shaw 1996, pp.9–102.

6 Shaw 2006, p.7.

7 Hicks 1961, p.91.

8 Machiavelli, III.6, p.100.

9 Ascheri and Franco, p.79.

10 Hicks 1961, p.93.

11 Hook 1979, p.69.

12 Syson, p.84.

13 Miller and Graves, p.94.

14 Nevola 2007, p.198.

15 Syson, pp.270–85.

16 Miller and Graves, pp.94–118.

17 Syson, p.57.

18 Bartalini, pp.544–53.

19 Syson, pp.42–59, Strehlke, pp.58, 60.

20 Nevola 2007, pp.203–4.

21 Ibid., pp.18, 101.

22 Ekholm, pp.184–5.

23 Denley 1990, p.105.

24 Adams 1985, pp.384–95.

25 Addis, pp.39–58.

26 Prager and Scaglia, p.5.

27 Beck, p.310.

28 Needham, pp.358–62.

29 Prager and Scaglia, p.52, Origo 1955, pp.321–66. On silk imports, Monnas, pp.13–14.

30 Scaglia, pp.91–5.

31 Prager and Scaglia, pp.11–12.

32 Ibid., p.39.

33 Ibid., p.192.

34 Rykwert, pp.78–83.

35 Adams, 2004, pp.309–11.

36 Reti, pp.287–98.

37 British Library, Add MS 34113, fol. 200v White, 1972, p.53.

38 Prager and Scaglia, p.102.

39 Ibid., p.13.

40 Partington, p.78.

41 Pepper and Adams, p.17.

42 Dechert, p.107.

43 Maltese, pp.417–25.

13 Sienese Art: The Renaissance and After

1 Hook 1979, pp.92–3.

2 Wiens, p.113.

3 Milanesi, I, p.23.

4 Dini, Angelini and Sani, p.202.

5 Jenkens 2002, pp.752–4.

6 Bomford 2006, pp.111–20.

7 Syson, pp.228–9.

8 Catoni, pp.41–2.

9 Dubus, p.19.

10 Syson, pp.320–21.

11 Dubus, pp.32, 38.

12 Ibid., p.138.

13 Syson, pp.303–4.

14 Sliwka, pp.193–194.

15 Hook 1979, p.94.

16 Medicus, pp.2–3.

17 Dini, Angelini and Sani, pp.396–7.

18 Ibid., pp.408–11.

14 The Fall of the Republic

1 Nevola 2011, pp.427–46.

2 Shaw and Mallett, p.176.

3 Glasfurd, p.84.

4 Pepper and Adams, pp.6–7.

5 Ibid., pp.17–27.

6 Steinhoff 2012, p.30.

7 Scaglia, pp.91–8.

8 Coffin, pp.87–97.

9 Pepper and Adams, p.38.

10 Ibid., p.58.

11 Cicero, I.vii.20, pp.20–1, and see Jenkins, p.433.

12 Dubus, p.128.

13 Ibid., p.130.

14 Hankins, p.65.

15 Shaw and Mallett, p.211.

16 Pepper and Adams, p.28.

17 Norman, p.159.

18 Pepper and Adams, pp.72–5.

19 Hoby, p.19.

20 'lengua fiorentina in bocca sanese': see Weiss, p.35.

21 Eisenbichler 2012, p.22, Azzolini, II, p.397.

22 Ibid., pp.26–30.

23 Ibid., pp.32–56.

24 Collier, pp.223–46.

25 Herrick, pp.89–99, and see Shepherd, pp.3–19.

26 Buranello, pp.59–76. For a translation, see Vignali.

27 Ruggiero, pp.111–13.

28 Tylus 2015, p.149.

29 Tylus 2012, p.171.

30 Hook 1979a, p.285.

31 Hook 1973, p.108.

32 Pepper and Adams, p.63.

33 Ibid., p.69.

34 Ibid., pp.79–82.

35 Ibid., p.83.

36 Eisenbichler 2012, pp.154–6.

37 Ibid. p.73.

38 Ibid., p.169.

39 Eisenbichler 2003, pp.87–99.

40 Hook 1979, p.189.

41 Hook 1973, pp.110–11.

42 Knecht, p.108.

43 Cantagalli, pp.333–9.

44 Hale, pp.192–3.

45 Catoni, p.59.

46 Parsons, 2021, p.15.

47 Sozzini, p.344.

48 Baccinetti, pp.1–38, 97–116.

49 Hook 1979, p.80.

50 Ibid., p.201.

15 Medici Rule

1 Battente, p.265.

2 Skippon, p.635.

3 Hook 1979, p.197.

4 Hook 1979a, pp.283–312.

5 Martines, pp.414–15.

6 Campbell p.123.

7 Voigtländer and Voth, p.166, Reis, p.197.

8 Campbell, p.334.

9 Howell, 1645, Letter xxxv, Aug. 1, 1621, p.78.

10 Shaw and Mallett, p.366, Ginatempo, pp.439–88.

11 Dallington, p.29.

12 Ibid., pp.38–9.

13 Caferro 1994, pp.85–103.

14 Dallington, p.26.

15 Howell, 1869, p.41.

16 Weiss, p.36.

17 Moryson, p.155.

18 Howell 1865, p.42.

19 Koenigsberger, pp.1–18.

20 McClure 2010, p.1154.

21 Collier, pp.230–36.

22 Black, p.60.

23 Belladonna, pp.377–85.

24 Eisenbichler 2012, pp.107–10.

25 McClure, 2010, pp.1151–1207.

26 McClure 2017, p.82.

27 Szymanska, p.4.

16 The Palio

1 Tobey 2005, pp.312–13.

2 Tobey 2011, pp.1273–5.

3 Norman, p.50.

4 Checchini and Neri, p.19.

5 Heywood, p.60.

6 Ibid., p.68.

7 Checchini and Neri, p.103, Dundes and Falassi, p.7.

8 Nevola 2013, p.99.

9 Dundes and Falassi, p.8.

10 Macchiavelli 1908. p.182.

11 Checchini and Neri, p.76.

12 Hook 1979, p.198.

13 Checchini and Neri, p.87.

14 Dundes and Falassi, p.20.

15 Checchini and Neri, p.163

16 Tobey, 2005, p.88.

17 Heywood, pp.208–9.

18 Recorded in a book of engravings by Capitelli.

19 Ridolfi et al., p.292.

20 Dundes and Falassi, p.8.

21 Beckford, II, pp.29–36.

22 Ibid., p.33.

23 Checchini and Neri, p.100.

24 Heywood, pp.89–90.

25 Politol, pp.293–4.

26 Illustrations throughout Hercolani.

27 Lasansky, p.346.

28 Silverman, pp.427, 434–5.

17 The City and Arcadia

1 Brown, pp.761–80.

2 Cipolla, pp.178–87.

3 Skippon, p.645.

4 Sella, p.25.

5 Reardon 2016, p.17.

6 Beckford, II, p.4.

7 Ibid., pp.4, 7.

8 Reardon 2016, p.70.

9 Petrucci and Petrucci, p.22.

10 Tarabotti pp.2–32, Medioli, pp.122–37.

11 Reardon 2002, p.127.

12 Beckford, II, p.5.

13 Reardon 2016, pp.39–40.

14 Ibid., p.25.

15 Ibid., p.26.

16 Reardon 2002, p.78.

17 Ibid., p.81.

18 Reardon 2016, p.27.

19 Ibid., p.36.

20 Beckford, II, pp.39, 42.

21 Mamone (online).

22 Reardon 2016, p.11.

23 Tilmouth, p.145.

24 Roselli, p.154.

25 Zanatta (online).

26 Freitas, pp.196–249.

27 Ibid., pp.216, 229–30.

28 Rosand, p.101.

29 Payne 1999, pp.146–69.

30 Butzek, pp.31–8.

31 Van der Ploeg, p.12.

32 Reardon 2016, p.71.

33 Ibid., p.72.

34 Reardon 2016, p.13.

35 Payne, 2015, pp.i–x.

36 Rhodes, pp.61–3.

37 Grand, p.6.

38 Freedberg 2002, p.38.

39 Attlee, p.32.

40 Alexandratos, p.74.

41 Freedberg 2002, p.41.

42 Attlee, pp.5–7.

43 Freedberg 1997, pp.51–4.

44 Freedberg 1989, pp.38–9.

45 Cochrane, p.111.

46 Hook 1979, p.206.

47 Cochrane, p.153.

48 Ibid., p.154.

49 Ibid., p.145.

50 Ibid., p.17.

51 Ascheri and Franco, p.162.

52 Procacci, pp.217–18.

53 Battente, p.271.

54 Boswell, pp.13–14 (Boswell), 134, 137, 216–22, 263–6, 303–16 (Girolama).

55 Procacci, p.261.

56 Tylus 2015, p.18.

18 A Very Great Simplicity

1 Raymond, pp.49–50.

2 Hazlitt, p.270.

3 Robert Browning, 'Up at a Villa – Down in the City', in Wollason, pp.138–42.

4 Westropp, p.248.

5 www.stmarksitaly.com/locations/west-campus

6 Petrioli, p.98.

7 [Blewitt], pp.184, 188.

8 Von Klenze, p.267.

9 Palmer. pp.48–73.

10 Wildman and Christian, p.18.

11 [Anon.] 2021, p.213.

12 White, 1973, p.334.

13 Buchanan, II, pp.21–2.

14 Avery-Quash, p.11.

15 Ruskin 1956, pp.113–14.

16 Harris, p.4.

17 Lindsay, II, pp.66–71.

18 Brigstocke, p.195.

19 Waley, p.208.

20 Israëls 2015, p.47.

21 Sox, pp.43–4.

22 Platzer, p.41.

23 Israëls 2015, p.59.

24 Israëls 2017, pp.158–81.

25 Frinta, pp.7–23.

26 Muir and Khandekar, p.33.

27 Stourton, p.93.

28 Roncucci 2006, p.409.

29 Scappini, pp.177–8.

30 Castelnuvo, pp, 785–809.

31 Hook 1979, p.120.

32 Pierini, pp.496–517.

19 Sena Vetus

1 Origo 1999, p.217.

2 Ibid., p.199.

3 Origo 2001, pp.7–50.

4 Tylus 2015, pp.36–7.

5 Mariani, p.11.

6 Sarfatti, p.211.

7 Ghirardo, p.9.

8 Baggiani, p.73.

9 Lasansky, pp.320–53.

10 [Anon.] 1929, p.3.

11 Van Os, p.27.

12 Tylus 2015, p.107.

13 Origo 2017, p.245.

14 Butler, p.180.

15 Hazlitt, p.250.

16 Livingstone 'Politics of Belonging', p.51.

17 Levy, www.newyorker.com/magazine/2016/04/18/niki-de-saint-phalles-tarot-garden.

18 Tylus 2015, p.4.

19 Matar, pp.72–3.

20 For a deeper discussion of this trend, see van der Ploeg, pp.11–12.

PICTURE CREDITS

433

INDEX

A